IARIA

AA004347

DATA ANALYTICS 2018

The Seventh International Conference on Data Analytics

November 18 - 22, 2018

Athens, Greece

DATA ANALYTICS 2018 Editors

Sandjai Bhulai, Vrije Universiteit Amsterdam, the Netherlands

Dimitris Kardaras, Athens University of Economics and Business, Greece

Ivana Semanjski, University of Zagreb, Croatia/ Ghent University, Belgium

Printed from e-media with permission by:

Curran Associates, Inc.
57 Morehouse Lane
Red Hook, NY 12571

Some format issues inherent in the e-media version may also appear in this print version.

Printed by Curran Associates, Inc. (2019)

International Academy, Research, and Industry Association (IARIA)
412 Derby Way
Wilmington, DE 19810

Phone: (408) 893-6407
Fax: (408) 527-6351

petre@iaria.org

Additional copies of this publication are available from:

Curran Associates, Inc.
57 Morehouse Lane
Red Hook, NY 12571 USA
Phone: 845-758-0400
Fax: 845-758-2633
Email: curran@proceedings.com
Web: www.proceedings.com

Table of Contents

DATA ANALYTICS 2018

Forward

The Seventh International Conference on Data Analytics (DATA ANALYTICS 2018), held between November 18, 2018 and November 22, 2018 in Athens, Greece, continued the series on fundamentals in supporting data analytics, special mechanisms and features of applying principles of data analytics, application-oriented analytics, and target-area analytics.

Processing of terabytes to petabytes of data, or incorporating non-structural data and multi-structured data sources and types require advanced analytics and data science mechanisms for both raw and partially-processed information. Despite considerable advancements on high performance, large storage, and high computation power, there are challenges in identifying, clustering, classifying, and interpreting of a large spectrum of information.

The conference had the following tracks:

- Application-oriented analytics
- Big Data
- Sentiment/opinion analysis
- Data Analytics in Profiling and Service Design
- Fundamentals
- Mechanisms and features
- Predictive Data Analytics
- Transport and Traffic Analytics in Smart Cities

We take here the opportunity to warmly thank all the members of the DATA ANALYTICS 2018 technical program committee, as well as all the reviewers. The creation of such a high quality conference program would not have been possible without their involvement. We also kindly thank all the authors that dedicated much of their time and effort to contribute to DATA ANALYTICS 2018. We truly believe that, thanks to all these efforts, the final conference program consisted of top quality contributions.

We also gratefully thank the members of the DATA ANALYTICS 2018 organizing committee for their help in handling the logistics and for their work that made this professional meeting a success.

We hope that DATA ANALYTICS 2018 was a successful international forum for the exchange of ideas and results between academia and industry and to promote further progress in the field of data analytics. We also hope that Athens, Greece, provided a pleasant environment during the conference and everyone saved some time to enjoy the historic charm of the city.

DATA ANALYTICS 2018 Chairs

DATA ANALYTICS Steering Committee
Sandjai Bhulai, Vrije Universiteit Amsterdam, the Netherlands
Dimitris K. Kardaras, Athens University of Economics and Business, Greece
Ivana Semanjski, Ghent University, Belgium / University of Zagreb, Croatia
Eiko Yoneki, University of Cambridge, UK
Andrew Rau-Chaplin, Dalhousie University, Canada
Rudolf Berrendorf, Bonn-Rhein-Sieg University, Germany
Les Sztandera, Philadelphia University, USA
Kerstin Lemke-Rust, Hochschule Bonn-Rhein-Sieg, Germany
Prabhat Mahanti, University of New Brunswick, Canada

DATA ANALYTICS Industry/Research Advisory Committee
Alain Crolotte, Teradata Corporation - El Segundo, USA
Tiziana Guzzo, National Research Council/Institute of Research on Population and Social Policies - Rome, Italy
Serge Mankovski, CA Technologies, Spain
Yanchang Zhao, CSIRO, Australia
Masahiro Terabe, Mitsubishi Research Institute, Inc., Japan
Thomas Klemas, SimSpace Corporation, USA
George Tambouratzis, Institute for Language and Speech Processing - Athena Research Centre, Greece
Azad Naik, Microsoft, USA

DATA ANALYTICS 2018
Committee

DATA ANALYTICS Steering Committee

Sandjai Bhulai, Vrije Universiteit Amsterdam, the Netherlands
Dimitris K. Kardaras, Athens University of Economics and Business, Greece
Ivana Semanjski, Ghent University, Belgium / University of Zagreb, Croatia
Eiko Yoneki, University of Cambridge, UK
Andrew Rau-Chaplin, Dalhousie University, Canada
Rudolf Berrendorf, Bonn-Rhein-Sieg University, Germany
Les Sztandera, Philadelphia University, USA
Kerstin Lemke-Rust, Hochschule Bonn-Rhein-Sieg, Germany
Prabhat Mahanti, University of New Brunswick, Canada

DATA ANALYTICS Industry/Research Advisory Committee

Alain Crolotte, Teradata Corporation - El Segundo, USA
Tiziana Guzzo, National Research Council/Institute of Research on Population and Social Policies - Rome, Italy
Serge Mankovski, CA Technologies, Spain
Yanchang Zhao, CSIRO, Australia
Masahiro Terabe, Mitsubishi Research Institute, Inc., Japan
Thomas Klemas, SimSpace Corporation, USA
George Tambouratzis, Institute for Language and Speech Processing - Athena Research Centre, Greece
Azad Naik, Microsoft, USA

DATA ANALYTICS 2018 Technical Program Committee

Mohd Helmy Abd Wahab, Universiti Tun Hussein Onn Malaysia, Malaysia
Danial Aghajarian, Georgia State University, USA
Rajeev Agrawal, US Army Engineer Research and Development Center, USA
Cecilia Avila, Universitat de Girona, Spain / Corporación Tecnológica Industrial Colombiana – TEINCO, Colombia
Valerio Bellandi, Università degli Studio di Milano, Italy
Rudolf Berrendorf, Bonn-Rhein-Sieg University, Germany
Nik Bessis, Edge Hill University, UK
Sanjay Bhansali, Google, Mountain View, USA
Jabran Bhatti, Televic Rail NV, Belgium
Sandjai Bhulai, Vrije Universiteit Amsterdam, The Netherlands
Yaxin Bi, Ulster University, UK
Amar Budhiraja, IIIT-Hyderabad, India

Sergio Ilarri, University of Zaragoza, Spain
Olaf Jacob, Neu-Ulm University of Applied Sciences, Germany
Nandish Jayaram, Pivotal Software, USA
Han-You Jeong, Pusan National University, Korea
Giuseppe Jurman, Fondazione Bruno Kessler (FBK), Trento, Italy
Zhao Kang, University of Electronic Science and Technology of China, China
Dimitris K. Kardaras, Athens University of Economics and Business, Greece
Sue Kase, U.S. Army Research Laboratory, USA
Quist-Aphetsi Kester, CRITAC | Ghana Technology University College, Ghana
Navid Tafaghodi Khajavi, Ford Motor Company, USA
Hafiz T.A. Khan, University of West London, UK
Thomas Klemas, SimSpace Corporation, USA
Mohammed Korayem, CareerBuilder, USA
Vitomir Kovanovic, University of South Australia, Australia
Chao Lan, University of Wyoming, USA
Kerstin Lemke-Rust, Hochschule Bonn-Rhein-Sieg, Germany
Shuai Li, Hong Kong Polytechnic University, Hong Kong
Ye Liang, Oklahoma State University, USA
Dimitrios Liparas, Information Technologies Institute (ITI) - Centre for Research & Technology Hellas (CERTH), Greece
Sungsu Lim, KAIST, Korea
Hongfu Liu, Northeastern University, Boston, USA
Honglei Liu, University of California, Santa Barbara, USA
Weimo Liu, GraphSQL Inc., USA
Xiaomo Liu, Thomson Reuters Research, USA
Corrado Loglisci, Università di Bari, Italy
Jose M. Luna Ariza, University of Cordoba, Spain
Prabhat Mahanti, University of New Brunswick, Canada
Arif Mahmood, Qatar University, Doha, Qatar / University of Western Australia, Australia
Sebastian Maneth, University of Bremen, Germany
Serge Mankovski, CA Technologies, Spain
Juan J. Martinez C., "Gran Mariscal deAyacucho" University, Venezuela
Archil Maysuradze, Lomonosov Moscow State University, Russia
Michele Melchiori, Università degli Studi di Brescia, Italy
Letizia Milli, University of Pisa, Italy
Diego Moussallem, University of Leipzig, Germany
Raghava Rao Mukkamala, Copenhagen Business School, Denmark
Wilson Rivera, University of Puerto Rico at Mayaguez (UPRM), Puerto Rico
Azad Naik, Microsoft, USA
Maitreya Natu, Tata Research Development and Design Centre, Pune, India
Richi Nayak, Queensland University of Technology, Brisbane, Australia
Jingchao Ni, Pennsylvania State University, USA
Adrian P. O'Riordan, University College Cork, Ireland
Patrick Obrien, Montana State University, USA

Vincent Oria, New Jersey Institute of Technology, USA
Luca Pappalardo, University of Pisa, Italy
André Petermann, University of Leipzig, Germany
Massimiliano Petri, University of Pisa | University Center 'Logistic Systems', Italy
Gianvito Pio, University of Bari Aldo Moro, Italy
Spyros Polykalas, Technological Educational Institute of Ionian Islands, Greece
Luigi Portinale, Universita' del Piemonte Orientale "A. Avogadro", Italy
Raphael Puget, LIP6 | UPMC, France
Minghui Qiu, Singapore Management University, Singapore
Helena Ramalhinho Lourenço, Universitat Pompeu Fabra, Barcelona, Spain
Zbigniew W. Ras, University of North Carolina, Charlotte, USA / Warsaw University of Technology, Poland / Polish-Japanese Academy of IT, Poland
Andrew Rau-Chaplin, Dalhousie University, Canada
Yenumula B. Reddy, Grambling State University, USA
Manjeet Rege, University of St. Thomas, USA
Alessandro Rozza, Waynaut, Italy
Gunter Saake, Otto-von-Guericke-University Magdeburg, Germany
Anatoliy Sachenko, Ternopil National Economic University, Ukraine
Donatello Santoro, Università della Basilicata, Italy
Anirban Sarkar, National Institute of Technology, Durgapur, India
Burcu Sayin, Izmir Institute of Technology, Turkey
Ivana Semanjski, Ghent University, Belgium / University of Zagreb, Croatia
Salman Ahmed Shaikh, University of Tsukuba, Japan
Piyush Sharma, Army Research Laboratory, USA
Sujala D. Shetty, Birla Institute of Technology & Science, Pilani, India
Rouzbeh A. Shirvani, Howard University, USA
Leon Shyue-Liang Wang, National University of Kaohsiung, Taiwan
Jaya Sil, Indian Institute of Engineering Science and Technology, Shibpur, India
Josep Silva, Universitat Politècnica de València, Spain
Marek Śmieja, Jagiellonian University, Poland
Dora Souliou, National Technical University of Athens, Greece
María Estrella Sousa Vieira, University of Vigo, Spain
Les Sztandera, Philadelphia University, USA
George Tambouratzis, Institute for Language and Speech Processing, Athena, Greece
Mingjie Tang, Hortonworks, USA
Farhan Tauheed, Oracle research labs, Zurich, Switzerland
Marijn ten Thij, Vrije Universiteit Amsterdam, Netherlands
Masahiro Terabe, Mitsubishi Research Institute, Inc., Japan
Juan-Manuel Torres-Moreno, Université d'Avignon et des Pays de Vaucluse, France
Li-Shiang Tsay, North Carolina A&T State University, USA
Chrisa Tsinaraki, EU Joint Research Center - Ispra, Italy
Aditya Tulsyan, Massachusetts Institute of Technology, USA
Murat Osman Unalir, Ege University, Turkey
Roman Vaculin, IBM Research, USA

Genoveva Vargas-Solar, French Council of Scientific Research | LIG-LAFMIA, France
Sebastián Ventura, University of Cordoba, Spain
J. J. Villalobos, Rutgers Discovery Informatics Institute, USA
Stefanos Vrochidis, Information Technologies Institute - Centre for Research and Technology Hellas, Greece
Haibo Wang, Texas A&M International University, USA
Liqiang Wang, University of Central Florida, USA
Wolfram Wöß, Institute for Application Oriented Knowledge Processing | Johannes Kepler University, Linz, Austria
Yubao Wu, Georgia State University, USA
Eiko Yoneki, University of Cambridge, UK
Fouad Zablith, Olayan School of Business | American University of Beirut, Lebanon
Bo Zhang, Watson and Cloud Platform - IBM, USA
Yanchang Zhao, CSIRO, Australia
Yichuan Zhao, Georgia State University, USA
Angen Zheng, University of Pittsburgh, USA
Qiang Zhu, University of Michigan, USA

Copyright Information

For your reference, this is the text governing the copyright release for material published by IARIA.

The copyright release is a transfer of publication rights, which allows IARIA and its partners to drive the dissemination of the published material. This allows IARIA to give articles increased visibility via distribution, inclusion in libraries, and arrangements for submission to indexes.

I, the undersigned, declare that the article is original, and that I represent the authors of this article in the copyright release matters. If this work has been done as work-for-hire, I have obtained all necessary clearances to execute a copyright release. I hereby irrevocably transfer exclusive copyright for this material to IARIA. I give IARIA permission or reproduce the work in any media format such as, but not limited to, print, digital, or electronic. I give IARIA permission to distribute the materials without restriction to any institutions or individuals. I give IARIA permission to submit the work for inclusion in article repositories as IARIA sees fit.

I, the undersigned, declare that to the best of my knowledge, the article is does not contain libelous or otherwise unlawful contents or invading the right of privacy or infringing on a proprietary right.

Following the copyright release, any circulated version of the article must bear the copyright notice and any header and footer information that IARIA applies to the published article.

IARIA grants royalty-free permission to the authors to disseminate the work, under the above provisions, for any academic, commercial, or industrial use. IARIA grants royalty-free permission to any individuals or institutions to make the article available electronically, online, or in print.

IARIA acknowledges that rights to any algorithm, process, procedure, apparatus, or articles of manufacture remain with the authors and their employers.

I, the undersigned, understand that IARIA will not be liable, in contract, tort (including, without limitation, negligence), pre-contract or other representations (other than fraudulent misrepresentations) or otherwise in connection with the publication of my work.

Exception to the above is made for work-for-hire performed while employed by the government. In that case, copyright to the material remains with the said government. The rightful owners (authors and government entity) grant unlimited and unrestricted permission to IARIA, IARIA's contractors, and IARIA's partners to further distribute the work.

Utilizing Data Analytics to Support Process Implementation in Knowledge-intensive Domains

Gregor Grambow
Computer Science Dept.
Aalen University
Aalen, Germany
e-mail: gregor.grambow@hs-aalen.de

Abstract— **In recent times, knowledge-intensive activities and processes have become more and more important in various areas like new product development or scientific projects. Such processes are hard to plan and control because of their high complexity, dynamicity, and human involvement. This imposes numerous threats to successful and timely project execution and completion. In this paper, we propose an approach to support such processes and projects holistically. The basic idea is to utilize various kinds of data analytics on different data sets, reports, and events occurring in a project. This data can be used to fill the gap between the abstract process planning and its dynamic operational enactment. That way, processes can be technically implemented and supported in complicated knowledge-intensive domains and also adapted to changing situations.**

Keywords-data analytics; knowledge-intensive projects; process implementation.

I. Introduction

In the last decades, the number and importance of knowledge-intensive activities has rapidly increased in projects in various domains [1][2]. Recent undertakings involving the inference of knowledge utilizing data science and machine learning approaches also require the involvement of humans interpreting and utilizing the data form such tools. Generally, knowledge-intensive activities imply a certain degree of uncertainty and complexity and rely on various sets of data, information, and knowledge. Furthermore, they mostly depend on tacit knowledge of the humans processing them. Hence, such activities constitute a huge challenge for projects in knowledge-intensive domains, as they are mostly difficult to plan, track and control.

Typical examples for the applications of such activities are business processes in large companies [1], scientific projects [3], and projects developing new products [4]. In each of these cases, responsibles struggle and often fail to implement repeatable processes to reach their specific goals.

In recent times, there has been much research on data storage and processing technologies, machine learning techniques and knowledge management. The latter of these has focused on supporting whole projects by storing and disseminating project knowledge. However, projects still lack a holistic view on their contained knowledge, information and data sets. There exist progressive approaches for storing data and drawing conclusions from it with statistical methods or neural networks. There also exist tools and methods for organizing the processes and activities of the projects. Nevertheless, in most cases, these approaches stay unconnected. Processes are planned, people execute complex tasks with various tools, and sometimes record their knowledge about procedures. However, the links between these building blocks stay obscured far too often.

In this paper, we propose a framework that builds upon existing technologies to execute data analyses and exploit the information from various data sets, tools, and activities of a project to bring different project areas closer together. Thus, the creation, implementation, and enactment of complex processes for projects in knowledge-intensive domains can be supported.

The remainder of this paper is organized as follows: Section II provides background information including an illustrating scenario. Section III distils this information into a concise problem statement. Section IV presents an abstract framework as solution while Section V provides concrete information on the modules of this framework. This is followed by an evaluation in Section VI, related work in Section VII, and the conclusion.

II. Background

In the introduction, we use the three terms data, information and knowledge. All three play an important role in knowledge-intensive projects and have been the focus of research. Recent topics include research on knowledge management and current data science approaches. Utilizing definitions from literature [5], we now delineate these terms in a simplified fashion:

- Data: Unrefined factual information.
- Information: Usable information created by organizing, processing, or analyzing data.
- Knowledge: Information of higher order derived by humans from information.

This taxonomy implies that information can be inferred from data manually or in a (semi-)automated fashion while knowledge can only be created by involving the human mind. Given this, knowledge management and data science are two fields that are complementary. Data science can create complex information out of raw data while knowledge management helps the humans to better organize and utilize the knowledge inferred from that information.

Processes in knowledge-intensive domains have special properties compared to others, like simple production processes [6]. They are mostly complex, hard to automate, repeatable, can be more or less structured and predictable and require lots of creativity. As they are often repeatable, they can profit from process technology enabling automated and repeatable enactment [7].

In the introduction, we mentioned three examples for knowledge-intensive processes: scientific projects, business processes in large companies and new product development. We will now go into detail about the properties of these.

In scientific projects, researchers typically carry out experiments generating data from which they draw knowledge. The amount of processed data in such projects is rapidly growing. To aid these efforts, numerous technologies have been proposed, on the one hand for storage and distributed access to large data sets. On the other hand, many frameworks exist supporting the analysis of such data with approaches like statistical analyses or neuronal networks [8]. There also exist approaches for scientific workflows enabling the structuring of consecutive activities related to processing the data sets [9]. However, the focus of all these approaches is primarily the processing of the scientific data. A holistic view on the entire projects connecting these core activities with all other aspects of the projects is not prevalent. In addition, the direct connection from data science to knowledge management remains challenging.

Business processes in large companies are another example of knowledge-intensive processes. Such processes are often planned on an abstract level and the implementation on the operational level remains difficult due to numerous special properties of the context of the respective situations. Consider a scenario where companies work together in complex supply chains to co-create complex products like in the automotive industry. Such companies have to share different kinds of information. However, this process is rather complicated as the supply chains are often huge with hundreds of participants. A data request from the company at the end of the chain can result in thousands of recursive requests through the chain [10]. For each request, it must be separately determined, which are the right data sets that are needed and can be shared.

A third example are projects developing new products. As example, we focus on software projects because software projects are essentially knowledge-intensive projects [4]. For these, various tools exist from development environments to tools analyzing the state of the source code. In addition to this, usually a specified process is also in place. However, the operational execution relies heavily on individuals that have to analyze various reports and data sources manually to determine the correct course of action in order to create high quality software. This implies frequent process deviations or even the complete separation of the abstract planned process from its operational execution. Furthermore, due to the large amount of available data sets (e.g., specifications, bug reports, static analysis reports) things may be forgotten and incorrect decisions made.

Figure 1 illustrates different problems occurring when trying to implement a software development process on the operational level. In particular, it shows an excerpt of an agile software development process (the Open UP). The process comprises the four phases Inception, Elaboration, Construction, and Transition. Each of these, in turn, comprises an arbitrary number of iterations. Each iteration contains different concrete workflows to support activities like requirements management or software development. As an example, we show the 'Develop Solution Increment' workflow that covers operational software development. It contains concrete activities like 'Implement Solution' where the developer shall technically implement the solution (i.e., a specific feature of a software), which was designed before. However, such activities are still rather abstract and have no connection to tasks the human performs to complete the activity. These tasks are performed with concrete tools, artifacts, and other humans depicted in the blue box of Figure 1. The figure indicates various issues: (1) Such tasks performed with different tools like Integrated Development Environments (IDEs) and static analysis tools are fine-grained and dynamic. Therefore, the workflow cannot prescribe the exact tasks to be performed [11]. Furthermore, the mapping of the numerous real world events to the workflow activities is challenging. (2) In various situations, the developer must derive decisions based on data contained in reports from different tools. One example are specific changes to improve the source code to be applied on account of static analysis reports. Goal conflicts (e.g., high performance vs. good maintainability) may arise resulting in wrong decisions. (3) In various cases, different artifacts (e.g., source code and code specifications) may relate to each other and can be processed simultaneously by different persons, which may result in inconsistencies [12].

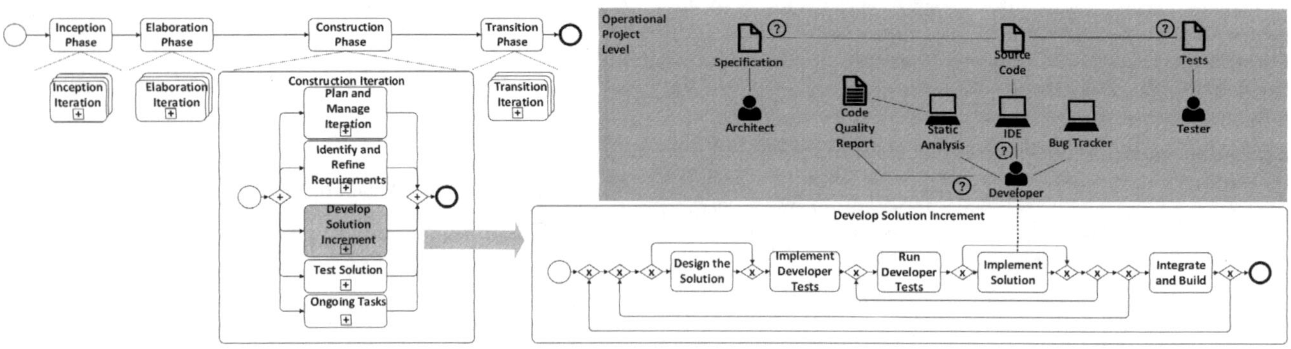

Figure 1. Scenario.

(4) Unexpected situations may lead to exceptions and unanticipated process deviations. (5) The whole process relies on knowledge. Much of this knowledge is tacit and is not captured to be reused by other persons [13]. This often leads to problems.

III. PROBLEM STATEMENT

In Section II, we have defined different kinds of relevant information and shown examples from different domains in which a lacking combination of such information leads to problems with operational process implementation.

In scientific projects, data analysis tools aid humans in discovering information in data. However, the projects mostly neither have support for creating, retaining, and managing knowledge derived from that information, nor do they have process support beyond the data analysis tasks [13][14]. Complex business processes in large companies often suffer from lacking process support because of the high number of specific contextual properties of the respective situations. In new product development, problems often arise due to the inability to establish and control a repeatable process on the operational level. This is caused by the high number of dynamic events, decisions, deviations, and goal conflicts occurring on the operational level.

In summary, it can be stated that process implementation in knowledge-intensive projects is problematic due to the high complexity of the activities and relating data. Processes can be abstractly specified but not exactly prescribed on the operational level. Thus, it remains difficult to track and control the course of such projects which often leads to exceeded budgets and schedules and even failed projects.

IV. FRAMEWORK

In this paper, we tackle these challenges by proposing an approach uniting different kinds of data analytics and their connection to other project areas like knowledge management and process management. That way we achieve a higher degree of automation supporting humans in their knowledge-intensive tasks and facilities to achieve holistic and operational implementation of the projects process.

Because of the high number of different data sets and types and their impact on activities, we think it is not possible to specify a concrete framework suitable for all possible use cases of knowledge-intensive projects of various domains. We rather propose an extensible abstract framework and suggest different modules and their connections based on the different identified data and information types in such projects. The idea of this abstract framework builds on our previous research where we created and implemented concrete frameworks for specific use cases. Hence, we use our experience to extract general properties from these frameworks to achieve a broader applicability.

The basic idea of such a framework is a set of specific modules capable of analyzing different data sets and utilizing this for supporting knowledge-intensive projects in various ways. Each of these modules acts as a wrapper for a specific technology. The framework, in turn, provides the following basic features and infrastructure to foster the collaboration of the modules.

A simple communication mechanism. The framework infrastructure allows each module to communicate with the others to be able to receive their results and provide its results to the others.

Tailoring. The organization in independent modules facilitates the dynamic extension of the framework by adding or removing modules. That way the framework can be tailored to various use cases avoiding technical overhead.

Support for various human activities. The framework shall support humans with as much automation as possible. Activities that need no human intervention shall be executed in the background providing the results in an appropriate way to the humans. In contrast to this, activities that require human involvement shall be supported by the framework. All necessary information shall be presented to the humans helping them to not forget important details of their tasks.

Holistic view on the project. Various technologies for different areas of a project are seamlessly integrated. That way, these areas, like process management, data analysis, or knowledge management can profit from each other.

Process implementation. The framework shall be capable of implementing the process spanning from the abstract planning to the operational execution.

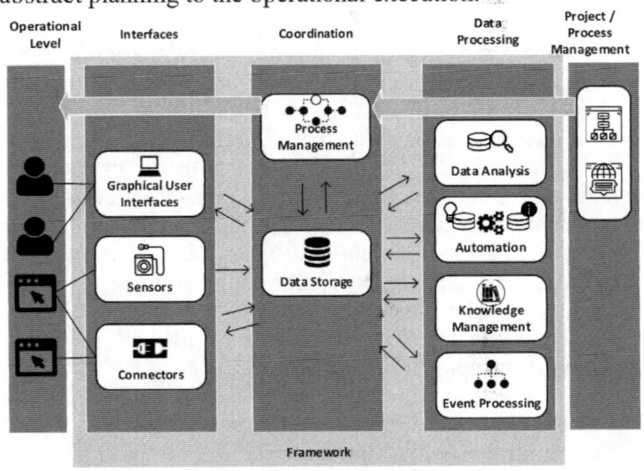

Figure 2. Abstract Framework.

Figure 2 illustrates the framework. We divide the latter into three categories of modules: Interfaces, Coordination, and Data Processing. The coordination category contains the modules responsible for the coordination of data and activities in the framework: The data storage module is the basis for the communication of the other modules by storing and distributing the messages between the other components. The process management module is in charge of implementing and enacting the process. Thus, it contains the technical representation of the processes specified at the project / process management level, which is outside the framework. Utilizing the other modules, these processes can be enacted directly on the operational level where concrete persons interact with concrete tools. This improves repeatability and traceability of the enacted process.

The interface category is comprised of three modules: Graphical user interfaces enable users to communicate with the framework directly, e.g., for controlling the process flow or storing and utilizing knowledge contained in the framework. The sensor module provides an infrastructure for receiving events from sensors that can be integrated into external software tools or from sensors from production machines. That way, the framework has access to real-time event data from its environment. The connector module provides the technical interface to communicate with APIs of external tools to exchange data with the environment.

The data processing category provides the following modules: The event processing module aggregates event information. This can be used, for example, for determining actions conducted in the real world. Therefore, sensor data from the sensor module can be utilized. By aggregating and combining atomic events, new events of higher semantic value can be generated. The data analysis module integrates facilities for statistical data analytics and machine learning. This can be utilized to infer information from raw data, e.g., coming from production machines or samples in scientific projects. The knowledge management component aids humans in managing knowledge derived from it. Both technologies can interact to support scientific workflows. E.g., incoming data can be analyzed and classified and the framework can propose an activity to a human for reviewing the data and record knowledge in a knowledge base.

Finally, the automation component enhances the automation capabilities of the framework. Therefore, various technologies are possible. As a starting point, we propose the following: rules engines for simple specification and execution of rules applying for the data or the project as a whole. One example use case is the automated processing of reports from external tools. Multiple reports can be processed creating a unified report by a rules-based transformation that, in turn, can be processed by other modules. A second important technology for automation are multi-agent systems. They enhance the framework by adding automated support for situations with goal conflicts. Consider situations where deviations from the plan occur and the framework shall determine countermeasures. Software refactoring is one possible use case: When the framework processes reports of static analysis tools indicating quality problems in the source code, software quality measures can help. However, mostly there are too many problems to tackle all and the most suitable must be selected. In such situations, agents perusing different quality goals like maintainability or reliability can autonomically decide on software quality measures that are afterwards integrated into the process in cooperation with the other modules [11].

V. MODULES

This section provides details on the different modules, their capabilities and the utilized technologies.

Data Storage. As depicted in Section IV, the first use case for this module is being the data store for the module communication. Messages are stored here and the modules can register for different topics and are automatically notified if new messages are available for the respective topic. This also provides the basis for the loose-coupling architecture. However, this module is not limited to one database technology but enables the integration of various technologies to fit different use cases. One is the creation of a project ontology using semantic web technology to store and process high-level project and domain knowledge that can be used to support the project actors.

Process Management. This module provides PAIS (Process-Aware Information System) functionality: Processes are not only modelled externally at the project management level as an idea of how the project shall be executed but can be technically implemented. Thus, the enactment of concrete process instances enables the correct sequencing of technical as well as human activities. Humans automatically receive activities at the right time and receive support in executing these. To enable the framework to react on dynamic changes we apply adaptive PAIS technology [15]. That way the framework can automatically adapt running process instances. Consider an example from software development projects: Software quality measures can be inserted into the process automatically when the framework detects problems in the source code by analyzing reports from static analysis tools [11]. This actively supports software developers in achieving better quality source code.

Sensors. This module comprises facilities for receiving events from the frameworks environment. These events can be provided by hardware sensors that are part of production machines. This can also be established on the software side by integrating sensors in the applications used by knowledge workers. That way, information regarding the processed artifacts can be gathered. Examples regarding our scenario from Section II include bug trackers and development tools so the framework has information about bugs in the software and the current tasks developers process.

Graphical User Interfaces. GUIs enable humans to interact with the framework directly. Firstly, this applies to the enactment of processes with the framework. The latter can provide activity information to humans guiding them through the process. In addition, humans can control the process via GUIs indicating activity completion and providing the framework with information on their concrete work. Another use case is storing knowledge in a knowledge store being part of the framework. To enable this, the GUI of a semantic wiki integrated into the framework as knowledge store can be exposed to let humans store the knowledge and annotate it with machine-readable semantics. That way, the framework can provide this knowledge to other humans in an automated fashion. However, GUIs are also used for configuring the framework to avoid hard-coding its behavior matching the respective use case. One example is a GUI letting humans configure the rules executed in the integrated rules engine. Thus, e.g., it can be configured which parts of external reports shall be used for transformation to a unified report the framework will process.

Connectors. This module is applied to enable technical communication with external tools. Depending on the use case, interfaces can be implemented to call APIs of other tools or to be called by these. Consider an example relating to the projects' process: The process is externally modeled utilizing a process modeling tool. This process can be transformed (manually or automatically) to a specification our framework uses for process enactment. In the process enactment phase, the external tool can be automatically updated displaying the current state of execution.

Automation. For this module we proposed two technologies as a starting point: rules engines can be utilized for simple automation tasks. One use case is, as mentioned, automatic transformation of reports from multiple external tools into one unified report. Multi-agent systems are applicable in situations where goals conflicts apply. Consider the example regarding the quality of newly created software: In software projects, often multiple static analysis tools are executed providing metrics regarding the source code quality. Usually, there is not enough time to get rid of all issues discovered. It is often challenging for software engineers to determine the most important software quality measures to be applied. Such projects mostly have defined quality goals as maintainability or reliability of the source code. Quality goals can be conflicting as, e.g., performance and maintainability and different measures support different quality goals. For such situation, agents can be applied: Each goal gets assigned an agent with a different strategy and power. When a quality measure can be applied the agents utilize a competitive procedure for determining the most important quality measure to be applied.

Data Analysis. This module enables the integration of frameworks or libraries for statistical analysis and machine learning approaches like Scikit-learn [8]. The advantage of the integration in the framework infrastructure is option to execute such tools as part of a holistic process. Data that has been acquired by other modules can be processed and the results can also be stored in the frameworks data storage. Furthermore, other modules can be notified so humans can be involved. For example a process can be automatically executed where data is analyzed and the results are presented to humans that, in turn, can derive knowledge from them and directly manage this knowledge with the knowledge management component.

VI. EVALUATION

We now provide two concrete scenarios in which we have created and successfully applied concrete frameworks that implement our idea of this abstract framework. The first one comes from the software engineering domain. For this domain, we have implemented a comprehensive framework including all of the mentioned modules [11][12][14].

This includes the implementation of a key-value store for framework communication on top of an XML database. The latter was also used to store numerous reports from internal and external tools natively. We further applied the AristaFlow BPM suite for process implementation and adaptation and recorded all high level project information in an OWL ontology. Data acquisition was realized by connectors to tools like bug trackers or project management tools and a sensor framework enabling the integration of sensors in tools like Eclipse or Visual Studio. Thus, we recorded events like saving files, which were aggregated via complex event processing to gather information about what humans were working on. Combining this with an integrated rules engine and a multi-agent system, we realized various use cases. One of them was the automatic provision of software quality measures. The framework automatically received reports from static code analysis tools that were transformed into one unified report, which was analyzed by autonomous agents pursuing different quality goals. Via the goal question metric technique they related the problems and quality measures to their goals and chose quality measures to be automatically integrated into developers' workflows. Another use case was activity coordination: with the project ontology we determined relations of different artifacts and could automatically issue follow-up activities for example to adapt a software specification if the interface of a components' source code was changed and vice versa. The integration of a semantic wiki enabled the following: Knowledge was recorded and annotated by humans and thus, the framework could automatically inject this knowledge into the process to support other humans in similar activities. In this project, we applied the framework in two SMEs and successfully evaluated its suitability.

The second scenario involves a business use case in which different companies in a supply chain had to exchange sustainability information regarding their production [10]. The producer of the end product has to comply with many laws and regulations and must collect information from the whole supply chain resulting in thousands of recursive requests. On the operational level, this process is very complex as it is difficult to determine which information is important for sustainability, which one must be externally evaluated to comply, and which information should not be shared as it reveals internals about the production process. To implement such data exchange processes automatically, we applied a more tailored-down version of our framework [16]: The focus were contextual properties that have an influence on the data collection processes. These were modeled in the framework and could be obtained from the frameworks' environment by GUIs and connectors. By analyzing these properties and using the results to adapt processes, we were able to automatically create customized data exchange processes suiting different situations. Due to the size of the supply chain, we combined a content repository for the different documents being exchanged with an in-memory key-value store. In this project, the framework was evaluated by a consortium of 15 companies and was later transferred to one of them to build a commercial tool from it.

These slightly different scenarios demonstrate the advantages of our approach: Its modules can be implemented matching the use case. The framework facilitates the communication between the modules and enables not only data analyses but also automated actions resulting from these supporting process and knowledge management.

VII. RELATED WORK

To the best of our knowledge, there exists no directly comparable approach enabling holistic integration of various data analysis capabilities to support and operationally implement processes in knowledge-intensive domains. However, in different domains, there exist approaches to support projects and processes. One example are scientific workflow management systems [3][9]. Such systems support projects in the processing of large amounts of data. Their focus is the organization and parallelization of data-intensive tasks. Hence, they support the different steps taken to analyze data sets but are not able to support whole projects.

In the software engineering (SE) domain, there have also been numerous efforts to support projects and their processes. Early approaches include the Process-centered Software Engineering Environments (PCSEEs) [17][18]. These environments supported different SE activities and made process enactment possible. However, their handling was complex and configurability was cumbersome what made them obsolete. More recent approaches also exist but these frameworks focused on a specific areas of the projects. Examples are artifact-based support [19] and model-driven approaches [20]. Hence, these frameworks could not provide holistic support for entire projects.

The business domain also features complex knowledge-intensive processes. However, this domain is dominated by tools focusing on the processed data like ERP systems or specialized tools. One concrete example regarding the aforementioned sustainability data use case is BOMcheck [21], a tool that helps companies handling sustainability data. In particular, this tool contains current sustainability information on various materials but is not capable of supporting the process of data handling and exchange.

VIII. Conclusion and Future Work

In this paper, we presented a broadly applicable approach to support process implementation in knowledge-intensive domains. Based on our experience from prior research projects we suggested an extensible set of modules whose collaboration enables holistic support for projects. Furthermore, we proposed technologies, frameworks and paradigms to realize these modules with specific properties.

We have shown problems occurring in projects in different knowledge-intensive domains and provided an illustrative example from the software engineering domain. Such problems are mostly related to operational dynamics, complex data sets, and tacit knowledge. Our framework enables automatic processing of various data sets relating to the activities in such projects to not only support these activities but also their combination to a knowledge-intensive process. Thus, humans can be supported in transforming data to information and information to knowledge.

Finally, as evaluation, we have shown two concrete cases were we have successfully implemented such a framework in different domains. As future work, we plan to extend the set of modules of our framework and to extend the technology options to realize these modules. We also want to specify concrete interfaces of the modules to enable standardized application and easy integration of new technologies. Finally, we plan to specify types of use cases and their mapping to concrete manifestations of our framework.

Acknowledgment

This work is based on prior projects at Aalen and Ulm Universities in cooperation with Roy Oberhauser and Manfred Reichert.

References

[1] M. P. Sallos, E. Yoruk, and A. García-Pérez, "A business process improvement framework for knowledge-intensive entrepreneurial ventures," The J. of Technology Transfer 42(2), pp. 354–373, 2017.

[2] O. Marjanovic and R. Freeze, "Knowledge intensive business processes: theoretical foundations and research challenges," HICSS 2011, pp. 1-10, 2011.

[3] J. Liu, E. Pacitti, P. Valduriez, and M. Mattoso, "A survey of data-intensive scientific workflow management," J. of Grid Computing 13(4), pp. 457-493, 2015.

[4] P. Kess and H. Haapasalo, "Knowledge creation through a project review process in software production," Int'l J. of Production Economics, 80(1), pp. 49-55, 2002.

[5] A. Liew, "Understanding data, information, knowledge and their inter-relationships," J. of Knowl. Manag. Practice 8(2),pp. 1-16, 2007.

[6] O. Isik, W. Mertens, and L. Van den Bergh, "Practices of knowledge intensive process management: Quantitative insights," BPM Journal, 19(3), pp. 515-534, 2013.

[7] F. Leymann and D. Roller, Production workflow: concepts and techniques. Prentice Hall, 2000.

[8] G. Varoquaux et al.: Scikit-learn, "Machine learning without learning the machinery," GetMobile: Mobile Computing and Communications, 19(1), pp. 29-33, 2015.

[9] B. Ludäscher et al., "Scientific workflow management and the Kepler system," Concurrency and Computation: Practice and Experience, 18(10), pp. 1039-1065, 2006.

[10] G. Grambow, N. Mundbrod, J. Kolb, and M. Reichert, "Towards Collecting Sustainability Data in Supply Chains with Flexible Data Collection Processes," SIMPDA 2013, Revised Selected Papers, LNBIP 203, pp. 25-47, 2015.

[11] G. Grambow, R. Oberhauser, and M. Reichert, "Contextual injection of quality measures into software engineering processes," Int'l J. on Advances in Software, 4(1 & 2), pp. 76-99, 2011.

[12] G. Grambow, R. Oberhauser, and M. Reichert, "Enabling automatic process-aware collaboration support in software engineering projects," Selected Papers of ICSOFT'11, CCIS 303, pp. 73-89, 2012.

[13] S. Schaffert, F. Bry, J. Baumeister, and M. Kiesel, "Semantic wikis," IEEE Software, 25(4), pp. 8-11, 2008.

[14] G. Grambow, R. Oberhauser, and M. Reichert, "Knowledge provisioning: a context-sensitive processoriented approach applied to software engineering environments," Proc 7th Int'l Conf. on Software and Data Technologies, pp. 506-515, 2012.

[15] P. Dadam and M. Reichert: The ADEPT Project, "A Decade of Research and Development for Robust and Flexible Process Support - Challenges and Achievements," Computer Science - Research and Development, 23(2), pp. 81-97, 2009.

[16] N. Mundbrod, G.Grambow, J. Kolb, and M. Reichert, "Context-Aware Process Injection: Enhancing Process Flexibility by Late Extension of Process Instances," Proc. CoopIS15, pp. 127-145, 2015.

[17] S. Bandinelli, A. Fuggetta, C. Ghezzi, L. Lavazza, "SPADE: an environment for software process analysis, design, and enactment," Software Process Modelling and Technology. Research Studies Press Ltd., pp. 223-247, 1994.

[18] R. Conradi, C. Liu, and M. Hagaseth, "Planning support for cooperating transactions in EPOS," Information Systems, 20(4), pp. 317-336, 1995.

[19] A. de Lucia, F. Fasano, R. Oliveto, and G. Tortora, "Fine-grained management of software artefacts: the ADAMS system," Software: Practice and Experience, 40(11), pp. 1007-1034, 2010.

[20] F. A. Aleixo, M. A. Freire, W. C. dos Santos, U. Kulesza, "Automating the variability management, customization and deployment of software processes: A model-driven approach," Enterprise Information Systems, pp. 372-387, 2011.

[21] BOMcheck: https://www.bomcheck.net. [retrieved 09, 2018]

Developing Transparent Credit Risk Scorecards More Effectively: An Explainable Artificial Intelligence Approach

Gerald Fahner
Analytic Science
FICO
San Jose, USA
geraldfahner@fico.com

Abstract—**Complex Machine Learning (ML) models can be effective at analyzing large amounts of data and driving business value. However, these models can be nonintuitive, their parameters meaningless, their potential biases difficult to detect and even harder to mitigate, and their predictions and decisions difficult to explain. Lenders, regulators, and customers need explainable models for automating credit decisions. Lack of algorithmic transparency is a broad concern beyond lending, which has led to much interest in "explainable artificial intelligence" [1]. This paper discusses a model family which warrants explainability and transparency by design: the Transparent Generalized Additive Model Tree (TGAMT). Many credit risk models used in the US and internationally belong to this family. Today, these credit scores are developed painstakingly by teams of data scientists and credit risk experts in a tedious interplay of "art and science" in order to simultaneously achieve high predictive performance and intuitive explanations of how the scores are arrived at. The main contribution of this paper is to automate the learning of TGAMT models. We also report benchmark results indicating that TGAMT's achieve strong predictive performance similar to complex ML models while being more explanation-friendly.**

Keywords - explainable artificial intelligence; algorithmic transparency; machine learning; gradient boosting; neural nets; credit risk scoring; scorecard; segmentation; constraining models.

I. INTRODUCTION

Credit scoring has been an early, highly successful and pervasive data mining application. For a comprehensive survey of credit scoring see [2]. Business users in the Financial Services industry frequently rely on the scorecard format to compute scores and to create robust, interpretable and easily deployable scoring solutions for a wide range of applications including marketing targeting, origination, behavior scoring, fraud detection and collections scoring. Scorecards are deployed through automated, rule-based systems to effect impactful, high volume decisions on consumers, such as what product to offer, accept/reject, pricing, limit setting, card authorization and collection treatment, thereby impacting a large part of the economy. Because of the high responsibility shouldered by these systems, model developers and users familiar with the domain seek a high level of transparency and confidence into reasonableness and robustness of the deployed models.

Because no database is perfect, and because future operational conditions tend to differ from past conditions under which data were collected, it has been recognized that incorporation of domain expertise into the data mining process is often essential [3]. It is indeed crucial for scorecard development to strike an appropriate balance between the desire to "let the data talk" and the necessity to engineer the models for deployment. Scorecard technology supports inclusion of domain knowledge into the models, by allowing users to impose constraints, such as monotonicity, on the fitted functional relations.

Modelers who value interpretability nevertheless desire a high degree of flexibility in their scoring algorithms to capture complex behavior patterns and to enable discovery of new, unexpected relationships. This is important in a highly competitive environment characterized by high volumes of automated, high stakes decisions. Being able to capture fainter and more complex predictive patterns that may otherwise escape simplistic models, can make a substantial difference to the bottom line of a business. Segmented scorecards are one response of the scoring industry to these needs. Unlike a single scorecard, which is additive in the predictors, these models can capture interactions between the variables used to define the segments, and the predictors used in the segment-level scorecards. For example, the FICO® Score is constructed as a system of more than a dozen segmented scorecards.

Designing a segmented scorecard system has traditionally been a labor-intensive and rather ad-hoc process during which several segmentation schemes are hypothesized from domain experience and guided by exploratory data analysis. Candidate segmentations are tested and refined to the extent possible given development resources. This process could benefit greatly from more objective and productive approaches.

Independent from these developments in the credit industry and with a different focus, ML ensemble methods, such as stochastic gradient boosting [4] and random forests [5], have been devised in academia. These procedures can automatically learn highly complex relations from data, and despite their flexibility, generalize well to new data if drawn from the same population. These procedures are attractive for ambitious scorecard developers who desire to "leave no stone unturned", because they are automated and scalable, make minimal functional assumptions on consumer behavior, and can generate insights into the learned relationships through various diagnostics aiding variable selection and interaction detection.

But these procedures are not designed to support inclusion of subtle domain knowledge. The resulting models, and how the scores are computed from the inputs for each particular case, can defy simple explanation. While a single shallow classification and regression tree is a transparent model structure which can be understood by direct inspection, this no longer holds true for modern ensemble learners that often yield more accurate predictions by combining hundreds or thousands of trees. Such opacity can render tree ensembles unfit for deployment. In order to engineer successful solutions, businesses need to look beyond off-the-shelf algorithms to customizable scoring procedures. This raises the methodological question of how to design a productive analytic process pipeline that takes full advantage of modern ensemble learning and associated diagnostic procedures, while supporting inclusion of domain expertise into the modeling process.

The reminder of this paper is organized as follows: Section II reviews scorecard technology and discusses examples of imposing domain knowledge into scorecards. Section III describes the TGAMT method to grow segmented scorecard trees guided by a stochastic gradient boosting model, and Section IV reports experiments comparing the US FICO® Score against ML models and TGAMT.

II. SCORECARD TECHNOLOGY

FICO uses its own proprietary scorecard development platform for supervised learning applications including ranking, classification and regression. The platform is designed to facilitate variable transformations (binning), model selection, fitting, incorporation of domain knowledge through functional constraints, validation, reporting and deployment. In the following, we will briefly discuss the main building blocks from a conceptual perspective. Reference [6] provides more details.

The predictive variables in a scorecard are called characteristics. A characteristic is composed of a set of mutually exclusive and exhaustive bins or attributes that comprise the possible values of the underlying predictor. Characteristics can represent continuous predictors after binning them into intervals, discrete or categorical predictors whereby subsets of values can be grouped together into bins, or hybrid predictors, which have interval bins for their continuous value spectrum and categorical bins for their discrete values. Missing values, even different types of missing or special values, are incorporated naturally as additional bins into characteristics. For example, a missing value could be an indicator of risk if a consumer declined to answer a question, in which case it should not be ignored. Or there might be a temporary issue in the historic data which may not replicate itself in the future (an example of nonstationary distributions scorecard development sometimes has to deal with) in which case missingness should be treated differently, for example by imputation or by assigning a neutral score contribution to such a bin, which is part of "score engineering". Before raw variables can be used as scorecard predictors, they need to be binned. Binning of continuous variables allows a scorecard to model nonlinear relationships between inputs and score through flexible stair functions defined over the bins. Categorical variables with thinly populated categories may be binned into coarser categories, and missing and special values may receive their own bins. Various methods exist for binning and improvements to binning have been proposed [7]. Domain expertise frequently enters the binning process.

While methodologies vary between in-house teams, consultants, and software vendors, often the score is computed as a weighted sum over dummy indicator variables associated with the characteristic bins, plus an intercept term.

$$Score = S_0 + \sum_{j=1}^{p} H_j(c_j)$$

$$S_0 = Intercept$$

$$H_j(c_j) = \sum_{i=1}^{q_j} S_{ij} x_{ij}(c_j) = Characteristic\ score\ of\ characteristic\ j \qquad (1)$$

$$S_{1j}, S_{2j}, \ldots, S_{q_j j} = Score\ weights\ associated\ with\ the\ bins\ of\ characteristic\ j$$

$$x_{1j}, x_{2j}, \ldots, x_{q_j j} = Dummy\ indicator\ variables\ for\ the\ bins\ of\ characteristic\ j$$

Each of the p characteristic scores is a stair function defined over the q bins of the characteristic. The stair heights are given by score weights associated with the bins. The model structure is similar to dummy variable regression [8]. However, dummy variable regression has no notion of "characteristics", and variable selection happens on the level of the dummies, which tends to put "holes" into binned variables. In contrast, scorecard development technologies can select on the characteristic level. This can makes the models easier to interpret. In addition, some scorecard development platforms allow to constrain characteristic scores to desired shapes, such as monotonicity, which can be applied globally, or involve ranges or subsets of bins.

A powerful feature of scorecards is their ability to model nonlinear effects through nonparametric stair functions. At the same time, scorecards, and how the scores for each case are calculated, remain easy to explain. A scorecard can be represented in tabular form made up of the characteristics, their bins (or attributes), and their associated score weights, as illustrated by Fig. 1. This scheme shows one variable from each of the five key categories that compose the US FICO® Score and is for illustrative use only. "Points" refer to a scaled version of the score weights in eq. (1). For a given applicant, points are added according to his/her attributes across all characteristics, to compute the total score. The assignment of points to attributes is guaranteed to follow explainable patterns which can be reinforced by the model developer via constraints, for example constraints may be necessary to smooth noise or to mitigate data biases. A typical scorecard may contain between 12 and 20 characteristics. How the variables combine with each other to impact the score is very clear, and explainable. The simplicity of the scorecard format was historically important and still is today, to gain business users' trust in these models, and to facilitate the inclusion of domain expertise into the modeling process.

Category	Characteristics	Attributes	Points
Payment History	Number of months since the most recent serious delinquency	No serious delinquency	75
		0 - 5	10
		6 - 11	15
		12 - 23	25
		24+	55
Outstanding Debt	Overall utilization on revolving trades	No revolving trades	30
		Under 6%	65
		7 - 19%	50
		20 - 49%	45
		50 - 89%	25
		90% or more	15
Credit History Length	Number of months in file	Below 12	12
		12 - 23	35
		24 - 47	60
		48 or more	75
Pursuit of New Credit	Number of inquiries in the last 6 months	0	70
		1	60
		2	45
		3	25
		4+	20
Credit Mix	Number of bankcard trade lines	0	15
		1	25
		2	55
		3	60
		4+	50

Figure 1. Simplified version of a scorecard.

Estimation of score weights in eq. (1) is possible using many approaches. FICO's technology accommodates various objective functions including penalized maximum likelihood for regression, ranking and classification, and penalized maximum divergence (related to discriminant analysis) for classification and ranking. Regression applications include normal, logistic and Poisson regression, whereby the score models the linear predictor as in Generalized Linear Models. In the logistic regression case with a dichotomous dependent variable, the score models log(Odds). The score weights are the decision variables of the ensuing optimization problems. Nonlinear programming techniques can be used to optimize the score weights subject to linear equality and linear inequality constraints. These constraints provide mechanisms to incorporate subtle domain knowledge into the models. For example, inequality constraints between neighboring bins of an ordinal variable can be used to restrict a fitted relationship between the variable and the score to be monotonic. Consider the characteristic score for 'Time On Books (TOB)', assuming for simplicity only 3 TOB bins:

$$H_{TOB} = S_{1,TOB}1\{0 \le TOB < 60\} + S_{2,TOB}1\{60 \le TOB < 120\} + S_{3,TOB}1\{TOB \ge 120\}$$

To enforce a monotonic increasing relation between 'TOB' and the score, specify inequality constraints as follows:

$$S_{1,TOB} \le S_{2,TOB} \le S_{3,TOB}$$

With this, the optimization will solve for the optimal score weights subject to the desired monotonic shape. Monotonicity can be useful for various reasons:

(a) Dependencies between predictors and score can be restricted to intuitive shapes. For example, everything else being equal one might expect equal or higher credit quality associated with longer TOB, or one might expect lower credit quality associated with higher frequency of late payments.
(b) Constraints reduce the hypothesis space and effective degrees of freedom of the model family, hence if constraints are applied sensibly, a constrained model can be less prone to over-fitting [9].
(c) Constraints may be necessary to ensure legal compliance. For example, the US Equal Opportunity Act implies that elderly applicants must not be assigned lower score weights than the younger. An empirical derived, flexible model may not be compliant, in which case a monotonicity constraint can rectify the desired relation.
(d) Imposing constraints may be necessary when adverse decisions, such as credit rejections, need to be justified to customers.

Monotonicity constraints can be imposed over the entire range of an ordinal variable, or they can be imposed over specific intervals, for example to allow for unimodal functional forms, as illustrated by 'Number of bankcard trade lines' in Fig. 1.

The scorecard format comprises a flexible family of functions capable of modeling nonlinear effects of predictors on the score by means of constrainable stair functions. However, eq. (1) specifies an additive function of the predictors which cannot capture interactions between predictors. If the true relationship is characterized by substantial interactions then this model is biased and might under-fit the data. To overcome this limitation, several approaches exist, including:

(a) Creation of derived predictors, such as ratios between the original predictor variables. This is part of data pre-processing or featurization and outside the scorecard model.
(b) Inclusion of cross-characteristics into the models, which generate products of bin indicator variables.
(c) Segmented scorecards, whereby different scorecards apply to different segments of a population.

In the following, we will focus on segmented scorecards, which are most widely used in the financial services, likely because the models are easy to inspect, to interpret and to engineer.

Reference [10] includes an overview of reasons and practices for undertaking model segmentation. The authors report mixed results with a research algorithm for finding good segmentations for credit risk score development data sets. The findings cast doubt over whether segmentations are as useful as they are widely thought to be, when looking at the benefits from a purely predictive standpoint (in terms of improving model fit). There are also other reasons for creating segmented models, such as availability of different variables for different customer types, or a need for subpopulation homogeneity in the segments for managerial reasons. On the other hand, the findings in [11] are more upbeat about the predictive benefits of 2-way segmentations for improving the discriminatory power of the resulting score. According to the omnipresent bias-variance tradeoff, and since a single scorecard is already a flexible model, it stands to reason that segmentation may indeed sometimes do more harm than good, because the larger hypothesis space for the segmented model family makes it easy to over-fit the data, eventually outweighing the benefits of reducing the single-scorecard structural bias. For this reason it is important to carefully navigate the bias-variance tradeoff during segmented scorecard development.

Scorecard segmentations can be represented as binary tree structures. The root node represents the entire population. Starting from the root node, the population is split into child nodes, defined by a first split variable, such as 'TOB' in the example of a simple segmentation given by eq. (2). One of the two child nodes there is further split according to 'Number of accounts' which results in an asymmetric binary tree. Splitting eventually stops and leaf nodes are created. The leaf nodes represent nonoverlapping population segment which together make up the full population. Each leaf node contains a dedicated scorecard denoted by $Scorecard_1$, $Scorecard_2$, and $Scorecard_3$ for the 3 leaf nodes in this example:

$$Score = \begin{cases} Scorecard_1 \; if \; TOB < 24 \\ Scorecard_2 \; if \; TOB \geq 24 \; and \; Number \; of \; accounts < 2 \\ Scorecard_3 \; if \; TOB \geq 24 \; and \; Number \; of \; accounts \geq 2 \end{cases} \quad (2)$$

Another example of a segmented scorecard tree is graphically illustrated by Fig. 2 (bottom left).

In principle, any candidate predictor can define a split. In practice, model developers and domain experts may avoid certain split variables, such as variables that are less trusted, difficult to interpret, or highly volatile. Segment scorecards can be developed independently from each other which is can speed up model development by a team.

To score out a new case, its segment is first identified and then the case is scored out using the associated scorecard, keeping computation light.

The deeper the segmentation tree, the higher the order of interactions the model can capture, and the more degrees of freedom can be devoted to refining the interactions. A single split at the root node (e.g. at 'TOB' = 24) can capture 2-way interactions between 'TOB' and all other characteristics. Further splitting a child node (e.g. 'TOB' >= 24), say, by 'Number of accounts' allows capturing 3-way interactions between 'TOB', 'Number of accounts' and all other predictors, etc. If a segmentation tree is allowed to grow infinitely deep, it can approximate arbitrary orders of interactions, rendering this model family a universal approximator. This is an asymptotic consideration. In practice segmented scorecard trees tend to be rather shallow. One quickly runs out of data, and deeper segmentation trees may underperform shallower ones due to over-fitting. In contrast to traditional classification and regression trees, which can grow deep and become difficult to comprehend, segmented scorecard trees tend to be rather shallow with no more than a few levels. This makes segmented scorecard trees easier to comprehend and to explain than traditional trees. Segmentation variables are typically selected not just with predictive power in mind, but also to make the resulting population segments easy to describe. The US FICO® Score uses more than a dozen segments tuned to distinctly different population segments, such as consumers with:

- Short credit history
- Long credit history without major blemishes
- Long credit history with major blemishes

and other segments that are defined by a segmentation tree of modest depth.

In summary, the family of constrained, segmented scorecards provides a very flexible, yet easy to interpret functional form, capable of representing complex predictive relations characterized by nonlinearities and interactions, whereby subtle domain knowledge can be imposed onto the structure of the segmentation and onto the functional forms of the segment scorecards. Interpretable shallow segmentation schemes with easy to explain scorecards associated with each segment thus form a Transparent Generalized Additive Model Tree (TGAMT). It is state of the art in the credit scoring industry to develop TGAMT's painstakingly by teams of data scientists and credit risk experts in a tedious interplay of "art and science" to simultaneously achieve high predictive performance and intuitive explanations how the scores are computed. The next section introduces a novel algorithmic approach to automatically learn TGAMT's.

III. LEARNING TRANSPARENT GENERLIZED ADDITIVE MODEL TREES

A. *CART-like Greedy Recursive Search*

Given a pre-existing segmentation scheme, developing the associated scorecards is a relatively easy task as long as the segments contain a sufficient number of informative training examples. Finding a good segmentation scheme is however a difficult problem, because the space of possible segmentations is extremely large. Domain knowledge tends to be insufficient to decide on an appropriate segmentation scheme. Due to the large number of possible solutions, it is unlikely that the "best" scheme with "optimal" score performance will ever be found. This is also not likely to be necessary, as there can be many good solutions that are close enough to optimal for all practical purposes. Similar to growing classification and regression trees [12] we apply a greedy recursive search heuristic to grow a TGAMT. Starting with the root node a set of candidate split variables and a finite set of split locations for each split candidate variable (e.g. taken at distribution deciles) are considered to split the current data set tentatively into two parts. It is evaluated whether there is a performance gain by fitting separate scorecards for each subset of the data instead of fitting a single scorecard to the entire current data. If so, the winning split that offers the greatest performance gain is made permanent. This process is performed recursively to grow a TGAMT until there is no more split that provides a performance gain exceeding some threshold, or until the number of training examples in the resulting segments falls below some minimum counts threshold. In the following, we distinguish between two broad approaches to grow the tree: direct and ensemble-guided approaches.

(a) Direct approaches decide on splits based on measures relating to the original dependent variable, characterizing discriminatory power, such as divergence, KS (Kolmogorov-Smirnov statistic) or AUC (Area Under the Curve) for binary dependent variables, or closeness of fit (likelihood statistics) for binary or continuous dependent variables.

(b) Ensemble-guided approaches use a new dependent variable which is the ensemble learner's prediction of the original dependent variable. When the original dependent variable is binary it is sensible to generate the new dependent variable on the log(Odds) scale. A reasonable performance measure for this approach is closeness of fit between the segmented scorecard score and the ensemble prediction in the least squares sense.

Both approaches can employ cross-validation and use out-of-bag estimates to obtain unbiased empirical distributions of gains in the objectives associated with the tentative split. One can thus account for statistical significance when making split decisions. Corrections for multiple comparison testing are also possible. Cross-validation has benefits for smaller data sets (or at nodes in a deeper tree where data become scarce), as it stabilizes split decisions further thus mitigating the risk of over-fitting.

B. Challenges for Direct Approaches

From our experiments, direct approaches face challenges if the dependent variable is very noisy, which is often the case when predicting consumer credit behavior:

(a) As the tree grows, segment volumes decrease rapidly and variances of performance measures increase fast, making split or stopping decisions fraught with uncertainty. This can result in over-fitting and unreliable, unstable segmentation solutions.

(b) Setting minimum counts threshold too low makes it likely to over-fit. Setting the threshold too high makes it likely to under-fit because the tree may not be able to grow deep enough to capture complex interaction effects adequately.

(c) Results are sensitive to choice of the performance gain threshold.

(d) There is no notion of how close or how far away a heuristically derived segmentation solution is from the "optimum".

C. Benefits of Ensemble-Guided Approach

To mitigate these challenges, we developed the hybrid approach, as outlined in Fig. 2 (models shown in the figure are for illustrative use only.) First, the ensemble model is trained involving optimal hyper-parameter search. Various diagnostics for the best ML models are then generated. Data records are scored out by the best ML model and a "Best Score" variable is appended to the data. Next, the TGAMT is grown with the objective to approximate the "Best Score" in the Least Squares sense. Once a segmentation is accepted by domain experts, the segment scorecards can be fine-tuned

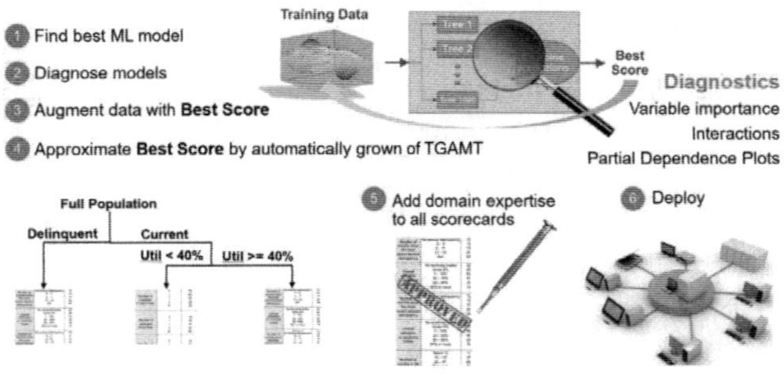

Figure 2. Process flow for learning TGAMT.

based on domain expertise. For example, characteristic selections, binnings, or constraints might be adapted with a view of the specific segment. Finally, the segmented scorecard system is deployed.

In our experience, replacing the original noisy binary dependent variable by a regression-smoothed "Best Score" as new dependent variable, greatly reduces sampling variance in scorecard parameters and uncertainties in split decisions when growing the tree, thus mitigating the risk of overfitting.

To provide motivation and evidence for the effectiveness of the ensemble-guided approach through a simplified experiment, consider the problem of binning the characteristics of a scorecard. If the binnings are too coarse, the relationship between the variables and the score becomes too inflexible to capture the signal accurately; the model is biased. Coarse step function approximations of true relationships, which are often expected to be smooth, may also not be palatable. If however the binnings are too fine, variances of fitted score weights tend to increase and models starts to over-fit. Noisy step function approximations are again not palatable. Typically, scorecard developers may use 5 to 15 bins per characteristic depending on the size of the training sample.

For both the direct and the ensemble-guided approach, we developed 10 scorecards each, all using the same fixed set of predictive variables (mostly ordinal continuous types), but distinguished by the granularity of their binning, ranging from an average of 3.8 bins/characteristic up to 40.9 bins per characteristic, which is a far finer binning than typical. Fig. 3 illustrates the over-fitting problem encountered by the direct approach, as the number of bins is increased. Predictive performance is measured by 5-fold cross-validated AUC. Findings for other common measures of score performance are qualitatively similar. The direct approach was implemented by training the scorecards to maximize divergence, using the original binary dependent variable. Findings for logistic regression are qualitatively similar. The direct approach reaches a performance plateau where it no longer improves beyond 8 bins/characteristic, and starts to over-fit the data beyond 20 bins/characteristic. In contrast, the ensemble-guided approach shows no signs of over-fitting within the tested range. For fine binnings with more than 12 bins/characteristic it is able to improve beyond the best models trained by the direct approach. Our findings indicate

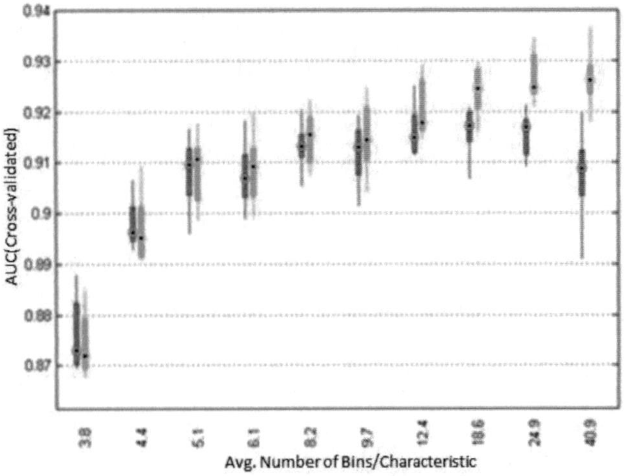

Figure 3. Effect of model degrees of freedom on performance for direct approach (red boxplot) versus ensemble-guided approach (green boxplot).

that the ensemble-guided approach is more resistant to over-fitting than direct approaches and therefore has a potential to train more flexible and more powerful scorecard models. These findings indicate that the ensemble-guided approach to growing TGAMT's will mitigate over-fitting challenges encountered by the direct approach and therefore lead to more stable and improved segmentation solutions.

The ensemble-guided approach has additional practical benefits over the direct approach by informing the learning of TGAMT through diagnostics obtained from ML:

(a) The list of candidate characteristics considered for inclusion into the TGAMT scorecards can be curtailed when it is found that certain variables may be unimportant as predictors in the ML models. Reference [13] proposes a statistic for input variable importance in the context of ensemble learning. Reducing the number of predictor candidates speeds up the learning of TGAMT.

(b) The list of candidate variables for segmentation splits can be informed by interaction diagnostics. Reference [13] proposes a statistic for testing whether any given variable interacts with one or more other variables. Variables with a high value of this statistic may be good split candidates. Variables that do not interact significantly with other variables may be removed from the candidate list of splitters, as no interactions need to be captured involving these variables. This can drastically reduce the search space and further speed up learning of TGAMT.

(c) ML models trained to maximize predictive power provide a "Best Score" upper bound on predictive performance. This bound informs TGAMT developers about the tradeoff they are willing to make between predictive performance and simplicity and transparency of the resulting TGAMT model.

IV. BENCHMARKING THE US FICO® SCORE AGAINST OPAQUE AND EXPLAINABLE MACHINE LEARNING APPROACHES

FICO® Scores are based on characteristics derived from credit bureau reports. The scores are designed to rank order the odds of repayment of credit while being easy to explain, such that higher scores indicate better credit quality. For our case study we chose the latest version of the US FICO® Score which is FICO 9. It is of interest whether ML models that are not restricted to be explainable might outperform FICO 9 by a substantial margin.

A. *Predictive Performance Comparisons*

We created "apples-to-apples" comparisons by developing a Stochastic Gradient Boosting (SGB) model and a multilayer Neural Network (NN) based on the same data set used to develop FICO 9, which consists of millions of credit reports. We allowed the same predictive variables that enter the FICO 9 model to enter the ML models. These comparisons thus provide insights into the potential impact of enforcing explainability constraints on score performance.

We also created "more data" comparisons for which we developed SGB and TGAMT models to investigate the potential performance gains possible for ML when taller and wider data are available for model development. For this we increased the number of candidate variables for the ML models to ca. 10 times as many variables than are input into the FICO 9 model (the additional variables are typically somewhat different versions of the variables used in the "apples-to-apples" comparisons). At the same time we also doubled the number of development records by sampling additional records from the same population from which the FICO 9 development data were sampled.

All important ML hyper-parameters, including learning rates, number of trees, depth of trees, minimum leaf size, number of random features for splitting, and number of hidden neurons, were tuned on a validation sample using multidimensional grid searches in order to warrant best possible performance of these models.

Table 1. compares model performance measures for discriminatory power (AUC, KS) for the various models and comparison scenarios, on bankcard accounts. All models are evaluated on an independent test sample that was not touched for model training and hyper-parameter tuning.

For the "apples-to-apples" comparisons the ML models mildly outperform FICO 9. It has been argued that marginal accuracy improvements observed under "laboratory conditions" may not carry over to the field where they can easily be swamped by other sources of uncertainty, such as

TABLE I. PERFORMANCE COMPARISON

Technology/Comparison	AUC	KS
FICO 9 Segmented scorecards	0.893	61.96
"Apples-to-apples" SGB	0.899	63.07
"Apples-to-apples" NN	0.895	62.48
"More data" SGB	0.902	63.92
"More data" TGAMT	0.894	62.19

changes to the environment and uncertain misclassification costs [14]. Therefore, from a practical perspective, these performance differences are minor. This finding supports that segmented scorecards are a very flexible model class capable of capturing nonlinear and interaction effects similar to complex ML models. Interestingly, explainability constraints on the FICO 9 model impact performance only slightly. This finding is in agreement with an often-made experience by scorecard developers, namely that enforcing explainability constraints, such as monotonicity, on the models often has little or no impact on score performance. This can be explained theoretically by the "Flat Maximum Effect", according to which "often quite large deviations from the optimal set of weights will yield predictive performance not substantially worse than the optimal weights" [14].

For the "more data" comparisons we observe a further mild performance improvement by SGB. The "Best Score" from this SGB model was used to guide the learning of the "more data" TGAMT, as described in Section 3. The resulting TGAMT performs practically on par with the FICO 9 Score. Inspection of its segmentation structure reveals a similar segmentation scheme as implemented by the FICO 9 model. The similarity between the automatically learned TGAMT structure and the laboriously derived FICO 9 segmentation structure is quite remarkable and illustrates the potential of TGAMT learning to increase the effectiveness of credit risk model development.

B. *Opaqueness of Unconstrained Machine Learning*

The opaqueness of ML models can be illustrated by exploring the input-output relationships captured by the models. It is possible to gain insights into the inner workings of ML models by plotting partial dependence functions [15]. These capture the average influences of single predictors, or sets of two or more predictors, on the score. 1-dimensional plots provide a summary of the average contributions of each predictor to the score, as illustrated for two variables in Fig. 4. We chose these variables as representative to illustrate certain problems with explaining opaque SGB models:

(i) Having longer 'Time on Books' intuitively should increase the score (reflecting higher credit quality). This experience is borne out from many score developments. This general directionality is indeed captured by our SGB model, except for many wiggles—presumably capturing noise—that cannot be explained. In our research, partial dependence functions for the more important predictors turned out to be directionally intuitive, except for noisy wiggles.

(ii) The contribution of 'Number of Trade Lines 30 Days Late' is directionally counterintuitive. It is very difficult to explain an increasing score with more trade lines showing late payments. Some of the less important predictors exhibited such counterintuitive behavior in our studies.

There are also two- and higher-dimensional versions of partial dependency plots that summarize joint effects of two or more predictors on the score. In our experience relating to

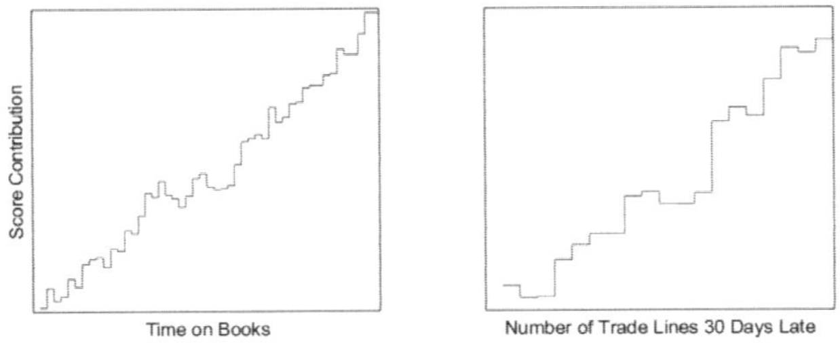

Figure 4. 1-dimensional partial dependence functions derived from the "more data" SGB model, for two predictive variables.

credit scoring, these plots are often difficult to rationalize.

In our experiments these opaqueness phenomena were not artefacts of a specific model, but persisted under variations of hyper-parameter settings for SGB.

V. CONCLUSION

Complex modern ML techniques compete well with state-of-the-art credit scoring systems in terms of predictive power. However, their lack of explainability hampers trust and creates barriers for relegating high-stakes consumer lending decisions to these algorithms. In the artificial intelligence community the notion of an "explainable artificial intelligence" has been popularized whose lines of reasoning and decisions aim to be easily understood by humans, while hopefully not sacrificing substantial performance.

Our contribution is in a similar vein. We demonstrated how performance similar to that of complex and opaque ML models can be achieved within the family of explainable Transparent Generalized Additive Model Trees. The structure of these models was motivated by state-of-the-art credit risk scoring models. We discussed how TGAMT's can be learned automatically and effectively being guided by modern ML techniques. This contrasts with the rather painstaking, high-effort analytic processes, by which many credit risk scoring systems are being developed today. What makes TGAMT's different and more explanation-friendly than complex ML models, is that subtle domain expertise can be easily imposed into the model during its construction. Whereas opaque ML models search for the most predictive model in very large and less structured function spaces, TGAMT searches for the most predictive model in a smaller, more structured subspace of segmented, explainability-constrained scorecard models. We found that TGAMT's sacrifice very little predictive power compared to unconstrained ML models for the credit scoring problem we investigated. Our methods provide an effective approach to develop explainable credit risk scores, by effectively combining the benefits of data-driven ML with diagnostic information and with domain expertise.

This approach might also benefit other application areas where domain knowledge exists, where operational context needs to be taken into account during model construction, and where predictions and decisions need to be accurate, transparent, and easy to explain.

REFERENCES

[1] D. Gunning, "Explainable artificial intelligence research at DARPA," http://sites.nationalacademies.org/cs/groups/pgasite/documents/webpage/pga_184754.pdf [accessed November 2018].

[2] L. C. Thomas, "A survey of credit and behavioural scoring: forecasting financial risk of lending to consumers," International Journal of Forecasting, vol. 16, pp. 149-172, 2000.

[3] A. Feelders, H. Daniels, and M. Holsheimer, "Methodological and practical aspects of data mining," Journal Information and Management vol. 37, issue 5, pp. 271-281, 2000.

[4] J. H. Friedman, "Stochastic gradient boosting," Computational Statistics and Data Analysis, vol. 38, 2000, pp. 367-378, 2000.

[5] L. Breiman, "Random forests," Machine Learning, Volume 45, Issue 1, pp. 5-32, 2001.

[6] FICO White Paper, "Introduction to Model Builder Scorecard," http://www.fico.com/en/latest-thinking/white-papers/introduction-to-model-builder-scorecard [accessed November 2018].

[7] G. Scallan, "Selecting characteristics and attributes in logistic regression," Credit Scoring Conference CRC, pp 1-32, Edinburgh, 2011.

[8] M. A. Hardy "Regression with dummy variables," Sage University Paper Series on Quantitative Applications in the Social Sciences, 07-093. Newbury Park, CA: Sage.

[9] E.E. Altendorf, A. C. Restificar, and T. G. Dietterich, "Learning from sparse data by exploiting monotonicity constraints," in Proceedings of the 21st Conference on Uncertainty in Artificial Intelligence (UAI-05), Edinburgh, pp 18-25, 2005.

[10] K. Bijak and L. Thomas, " Does segmentation always improve model performance in credit scoring?," Expert Systems with Applications, vol. 39, issue 3, pp. 2433-2442, 2012.

[11] D. J. Hand, S. Y. Sohn, and Y. Kim, "Optimal bipartite scorecards." Expert Systems with Applications, vol. 29, issue 3, pp. 684-690, 2005.

[12] L. Breiman, J. H. Friedman, R. A. Olshen, and C. J. Stone, Classification and Regression Trees, Wadsworth, 1984.

[13] J. H. Friedman and B. E. Popescu, "Predictive learning via rule ensembles," Technical report, Department of Statistics, Stanford University, 2005.

[14] D. J. Hand, "Classifier technology and the illusion of progress," Statistical Science, vol. 21, number 1, pp. 1–15, 2006.

[15] J. H. Friedman, "Greedy function approximation: a gradient boosting machine," The Annals of Statistics, vol. 29, number 5, pp. 1189–1232, 2001.

Towards a Scalable Data-Intensive Text Processing Architecture with Python and Cassandra

Gregor-Patrick Heine
and Thomas Woltron

University of Applied Sciences Wiener Neustadt
Institute of Information Technology
Wiener Neustadt, Austria
Email: heine.gregor@gmail.com
Email: thomas.woltron@fhwn.ac.at

Alexander Wöhrer

University of Vienna
Faculty of Computer Science
Vienna, Austria
Email: alexander.woehrer@univie.ac.at

Abstract—**Canonical sentiment analysis implementations hinge on synchronous Hyper Text Transfer Protocol (HTTP) calls. This paper introduces an asynchronous streaming approach. A method for public opinion surveillance is proposed via stream subscriptions. A prototype combining Twitter streams, Python text processing and Cassandra storage methods is introduced elaborating on three major points: 1) Comparison of performance regarding writing methods. 2) Multiprocessing procedures employing data parallelization and asynchronous concurrent database writes. 3) Public opinion surveillance via noun-phrase extraction.**

Keywords–Cassandra; Streaming; Python; Multiprocessing; Twitter; Sentiment Analysis

I. INTRODUCTION

Volume, Velocity and *Variety*, also known as the *3V*, generalize big data problems [1]. A fourth (fifth or sixth) V could be added referring to *Value, Variability* or *Virtual* [2]. Sticking to the more prominent 3V, *volume* naturally stands for a humongous amount of data. *Velocity* refers to the ingress, egress and process speeds. *Variety* is representative of heterogeneous data sets, which may be structured, semi-structured or unstructured. Essentially, the 3V break traditional data processing systems as they fail to scale to at least one of these attributes [3].

Big data has already found its place in business, society administration and scientific research. It is also believed to help enterprises improve their competitive advantage. Managers believe it to be a panacea and take a one-size fits all approach. It is also held in high regard with reference to aiding decision making processes [4].

From a high-level viewpoint, there are seven big data principles [4]: good architecture; variety regarding analytics; many sizes for many needs; perform analyses locally; distributed in memory computations; distributed in memory storage and process data set coordination.

However, without deeper understanding and practical knowledge they remain abstract buzzwords. Putting this into perspective by using an analogy of combustion engines, it becomes clear that it is impossible to repair, let alone build, a V8 (pun intended) by merely knowing the concept of thermodynamics. This paper outlines a practical big data streaming implementation in alignment with the seven principles.

Research Objective: The goal is to develop a scalable data-intensive application for text mining. Theory regarding sentiment analysis and opinion extraction are given in the working hypothesis. A naive architecture is depicted in Figure 1. In order to be able to monitor opinions, the following challenges must be tackled: high frequency real-time HTTP data-streaming; in-memory text mining and persisting results efficiently in a fault tolerant way.

Hypothesis: When following a publisher (or broadcaster) like 'The Hill' it is a matter of time until related public discussions start. The initial post is referred to as headline, which introduces the topic. All consecutive replies are regarded as the discussion's body.

Since topics are defined by nouns, their corresponding noun-phrases can be be listed. It can be argued that noun-frequencies represent a public consensus on what is deemed important in a topic related discussion. Hence a testable hypothesis can be formulated as such:

The more replies a headline receives the higher the number of noun-frequencies. The higher noun-frequencies the more descriptive are associated noun-phrases. When there are highly frequent noun-phrases, a clear public consensus regarding a topic specific headline exists.

We take a novel approach regarding social media sentiment analyses via streaming live data. Canonical approaches hinge on hashtag searches via the Representational State Transfer Application Programming Interface (REST API). Our approach has both, higher data recency and a clearer topic related natural language structure by design.

The rest of the paper is organized as follows. Section II aims at demonstrating how high volumes of data, more specif-

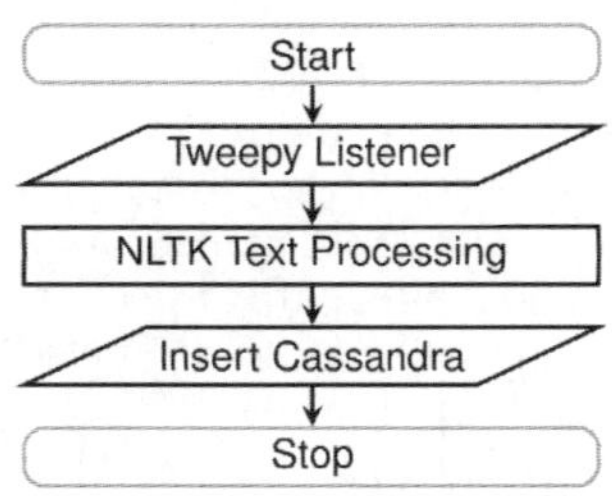

Figure 1. Sequential Python architecture under the Global Interpreter Lock

ically text, can flexibly and efficiently be processed in (near) real-time. Methods for text stream analyses and storage are also illuminated. Our main contribution is described in Section III where we proposes a scalable application architecture and provide a proof of concept implementation and evaluation. We close with our conclusions and future work suggestions in Section IV.

II. Methods & Related Work

Natural Language Processing (NLP): Text mining consists of "a vast field of theoretical approaches and methods with one thing in common: text as input information" [5, p. 1]. An introduction to the traditional field of NLP is quoted to be the "process of language analysis [that is] decomposable into a number of stages, mirroring the theoretical linguistic distinctions drawn between *syntax, semantics* and *pragmatics*" [6, p. 4]. Twitter, with its 140- to 280-character long tweets (or posts) promises to be a rich medium for scientific analysis [7]. Overall, Twitter can be regarded as a platform for political debate [8] and enables measuring the public opinion with regards to politics [9].

Nouns and noun-phrases are likely to converge towards a dominant *thesaurus*. Hinging on frequent nouns and noun-phrases it can be concluded that they are extracted from text. Hence, they are countable and highly frequent noun-phrases can be deemed important. This approach is utilized in the context of online product reviews and is argued to be domain dependent. Essential to this approach is Part-of-Speech (POS) tagging [7].

Mining Tweets: Noun-phrases are indicative of opinions as they use adjectives and adverbs together with nouns. When live-streaming tweets there is no a priori means for clustering them. A topic's context is created retrospectively when reading records from a data store.

News agencies concerned with United States politics are likely to evoke binary reactions. Opinion holders are either in favor or against Democrats or Republicans. Following that train of thought, it can be assumed that neutral political headlines need to be immediately digested and either be supported or opposed.

When tweets are received they cannot be put into context right away. They have to be persisted for later retrieval. While streaming, it is advisable to process text immediately, since it is already held in memory. This allows in memory pointer manipulation, regarding tokenization, Part-of-Speech tagging, chunking and parse-tree creation. All of which are needed for later analysis. When reading from the database, a post's meaning arises through its sequential context. Reading preprocessed noun-lists and iterating them in order to create word frequencies is faster than processing text in bulk after reading.

Parallelization: It appears that computer science has exhausted *Moore's law* as integrated circuits only seem to double every three years. Today, the real performance boost comes from running multiple threads simultaneously. This is also referred to as Thread-Level Parallelism (TLP) [10]. *Amdahl's law* [11] has become more prominent in recent years, it states that program execution time can be improved through running code in parallel [12]. It needs to be noted that this law cannot be exploited *ad infinitum* as it approaches a point of diminishing returns.

Parallelization is a powerful means of increasing processing speed. It needs to be noted that writing parallel code is much harder than writing serial code. However, generally speaking, programmers face a choice between two parallelization paradigms: *data parallelization* has multiple threads performing the same operation on separate items of data while *task parallelization* has separate threads performing different operations on different items of data [13].

Multiple Threads & Processes: When applying data parallelization it is possible to split data sets *symmetrically* (or equally) amongst allocated processes a priori. When employing task parallelization, on the other hand, *asymmetrical* data sets can be *atomized* and put into a queue for dynamic process retrieval. Since we worked with symmetrical data sets, we were able to omit atomization. In our approach, the size of the total data set cannot exceed the size of memory. We split the data set across processor cores of a single machine. Within a distributed computing network (or big data architecture) data records should be split amongst available *worker nodes* [14]. There is a key difference between multiple threads and multiple processes: Processes do not share memory while threads share both state and memory. When performing multithreading, code segments are scheduled by the Operating System (OS). In the presence of only one core (or process) the OS creates the illusion of running multiple threads in parallel when in fact, it switches between the threads quickly, which is referred to as time division multiplexing [10].

Global Interpreter Lock (GIL): Multithreading in Python is managed by the host operating system and uses a mechanism called the Global Interpreter Lock (GIL), which limits the number of running threads to exactly one at a time. The GIL implicitly guards data structures from concurrent and possibly conflicting (write) access to avoid race conditions. Python prefers a serial development approach and takes a trade-off between *easy scripting* and *code performance*. It needs to be noted that the GIL, depending on the Python implementation, is temporarily released for Input Output (I/O) operations or every 100 bytecode instructions. This is the case of CPython implementations, which is the default on most systems. IronPython, PyPy and Jython "do not prevent running multiple threads simultaneous on multiple processor cores"[10, p. 4]. In order to get around CPython's GIL it is necessary to spawn new processes. Hardware specifically speaking, two different multiprocessor architectures exist [15]: 1) Symmetric (equally strong) multi-core chips; 2) Asymmetric multi-core chips with varying processing power.

Python offers a number of packages for spawning processes. However, a particularly useful one is `multiprocessing`. Bundled with it come queues. Only through such package implementations [16] is it possible to take advantage of today's multi-core chip architectures with Python.

III. Implementation & Results

Figure 2 summarizes writing speed results. It becomes clear that a scalable application needs multiprocessing capabilities. It would be best for concurrent insert processes to dispatch dynamically in high load scenarios. High frequency input should be queued, distributed and written as batch operations within intervals.

Single Thread Synchronous Inserts: Inserts into Cassandra take about 1.6 ms on average. In order to compare execution speeds 1,000 and 100,000 records are inserted. Insert operations are executed four times and a simple arithmetic mean of the resulting run times is calculated. In other words, the mean runtime of 1,000 and 100,000 sequential synchronous inserts is 0.9 seconds and 80 seconds, respectively.

Single Thread Concurrent Inserts: Insert speed of large datasets can further be improved via concurrent writes through the Python Cassandra driver. This package exploits Cassandra's Staged Event-Driven Architecture (SEDA) [17]. We went with the recommended setting of core connections multiplied by one hundred `concurrency = 100` [18]. The Cassandra driver invokes a multiprocess instance for concurrently writing while the main program is still under the GIL. Following the same measurements approach, the arithmetic mean of run times equals 0.27 seconds and 29.5 seconds respectively. In essence, this result trisects the synchronous single thread performance.

Multiprocess Concurrent Inserts: Through leveraging Python's multiprocessing module with the Cassandra driver and its SEDA abilities, as introduced in Section II, writing speed can further be accelerated. Following the idea of data parallelization introduced in Section II the workload is distributed onto a number of separate processes as depicted in Figure 3. While all processes run simultaneously, each process is executed on a separate core, the dataset is split equally and distributed accordingly. Execution of 1,000 inserts in parallel yields a meager 0.03 seconds improvement, while 100,000 inserts distributed amongst four processes take 11.2 seconds in total. Each trial's total execution time was determined by the slowest process' runtime.

Cassandra Query Language (CQL): When testing the hypothesis from Section II regarding topic related word convergence tweets need to be retrieved from the database. Cassandra does not support the Structured Query Language (SQL) standard with respect to `GROUP BY, ORDER BY` clauses. Cassandra uses `ORDER BY` implicitly through table declaration via `WITH CLUSTERING` on primary key columns [19]. The order of the composite primary key declaration matters. The partition key decides on which physical node data are eventually stored by mapping rows. The cluster key decides the order of given rows [20]. When dealing with time series data it is advisable to create sectional time intervals. When attempting to retrieve most recent values the clause `WITH CLUSTERING ORDER BY (timestamp DESCENDING)` is needed for table declaration. This overrides the default ascending order [20]. Cassandra does not allow `JOIN` operations. Filtering is supported but may cause malfunctions due to the nature of Sorted String Tables (SSTables) and Log-Structured Merge-Trees (LSM-Trees) [21], [22]. We query for relevant values, allow filtering and iterate returned values via Python lists. The following constitutes a valid example: `SELECT column_a FROM keyspace.table WHERE column_b > 0 ALLOW FILTERING;` [19].

Tombstones are deletion markers [17]. It needs to be pointed out that they also occur when inserting *null values* or *collections*. Time To Live (TTL) data expiration may be an additional cause for Tombstone creations [23]. If a query exceeds the default value of 1,000 tombstones with respect to the `tombstone_warn_threshold` Cassandra issues and logs a warning. When, however, the `tombstone_failure_threshold` exceeds 10,000 tombstones Cassandra aborts the query.

When attempting to isolate tombstone issues it may be worth executing `sstabledump` in the Bourne Again Shell (`BASH`). This produces a JavaScript Object Notation (JSON) file of Cassandra's SSTable, which shows deletion markers as `"d"` next to data entries [23]. However, with Cassandra active, it is recommended to run `flush` first. This *flushes* all in memory data structures (MemTables) of associated tables to disk.

Public Debate Example: An exemplary headline by *The Hill* with `status_id = 974246607607779328` recorded 656 replies. This amount of replies is deemed sufficiently large for demonstrative purposes regarding topic related word convergence. "Senate [Grand Old Party (or Republican Party)] GOP: We will grow our majority in midterms" [24] is the headline of the chosen debate. Preliminary results indicate "that the general opinion, regarding the given headline, appears to be ridicule. Overall, little credence is given [... to] the Trump administration [25]".

Once noun-phrases and their respective user's follower counts have been retrieved from Cassandra and appended to a Python list they need to be traversed. The goal of this operation is to convert the list into a more tractable data structure. Dictionaries, which hold key value pairs, are great for this purpose, as the number of followers can be preserved, which allows more versatile analyses.

In order to get an overview of the public opinion related to the headline, it is recommended to print the six highest ranking

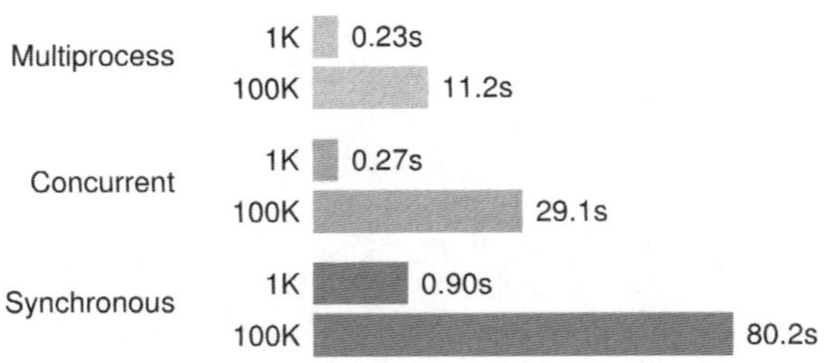

Figure 2. Comparing elapsed seconds inserting records into Cassandra

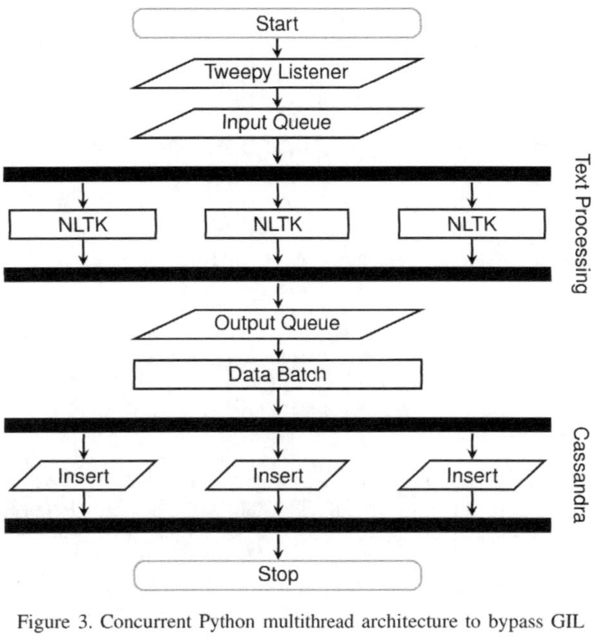

Figure 3. Concurrent Python multithread architecture to bypass GIL

dictionary entries to the Python console. Naturally, the number of followers indicates the *influential weight* of a post whereas overall noun frequencies yield the *public consensus*. Lower case converted stemmed word frequencies best illustrate topic related word convergence. This is due to the fact that the effects of word differences, capitalization, misspellings and affixes are effectively minimized.

IV. Conclusion & Discussion

Elaborating and realizing a scalable data-intensive text processing application relies on several components: 1) suitable data sources, 2) associated use cases, 3) processing power and memory size, 4) data persisting methods. Twitter is one of the biggest social platforms and provides a myriad of data sets. The choice of Cassandra as a highly available database is advocated and its inner workings are illuminated. Overall, a scalable text processing application is developed. The development of a big data application is taken on holistically and finds both innovative and uncommon solutions. Streaming Twitter data in the context of text mining and persisting it with Cassandra has not been discussed as such in literature. Twitter's *discussion* related topics, noun-phrases and word frequency convergences are both reviewed and analyzed in a novel way. This paper specifically contributes to a means of analyzing public debates (or discussions) in (near) real-time. Simultaneously, data is persisted without superimposing topic restrictions via search terms. Introduced methods could also be employed for public surveillance.

The introduced Python prototype still needs better functional `multiprocessing` package integration. Overall, three independent process groups should run concurrently and use queues to communicate as depicted in Figure 3. Our results indicate that inserts into Cassandra can be greatly improved through data parallelization. Future research should focus on accruing records in memory before batch insertion.

Conclusively, it is recommended to keep the real-time streaming focus a priority. Cassandra proves to be an exquisite choice for both data persistance and retrieval. Last but not least, while this paper focused rather on the processing and storage performance of our architecture, further optimization towards an adequate retrieval and re-analysis approach seem promising by combining Cassandra with Apache Hadoop Distributed File System (HDFS) [26] and exploiting Apache Spark [27] on top of an HDFS-based data lake.

Acknowledgment

This work is based on the thesis of G-P. Heine named *'Developing a Scalable Data-Intensive Text Processing Application with Python and Cassandra'*, University of Applied Sciences Wiener Neustadt, April 2018.

References

[1] D. Laney, "3d data management: Controlling data volume, velocity and variety," META Group Research Note, vol. 6, no. 70, 2001.

[2] P. Zikopoulos, C. Eaton, and IBM, Understanding big data: Analytics for enterprise class hadoop and streaming data. McGraw-Hill Osborne Media, 2011.

[3] D. e. a. Jiang, "epic: an extensible and scalable system for processing big data," The VLDB Journal, vol. 25, no. 1, 2016, pp. 3–26.

[4] C. P. Chen and C.-Y. Zhang, "Data-intensive applications, challenges, techniques and technologies: A survey on big data," Information Sciences, vol. 275, 2014, pp. 314–347.

[5] I. Feinerer, D. Meyer, and K. Hornik, "Text mining infrastructure in r," Journal of Statistical Software, vol. 25, no. 5, 2008, pp. 1–54.

[6] R. Dale, "Classical approaches to natural language processing," in Handbook of Natural Language Processing, Second Edition, N. Indurkhya and F. J. Damerau, Eds. Chapman and Hall/CRC, 2010, vol. 2, ch. 1, pp. 3–7.

[7] B. Liu, Sentiment Analysis. Cambridge: Cambridge University Press, 2015. [Online]. Available: ebooks.cambridge.org/ref/id/CBO9781139084789

[8] A. Tumasjan, T. O. Sprenger, P. G. Sandner, and I. M. Welpe, "Predicting elections with twitter: What 140 characters reveal about political sentiment." vol. 10, no. 1, 2010, pp. 178–185.

[9] B. O'Connor, R. Balasubramanyan, B. R. Routledge, and N. A. Smith, "From tweets to polls: Linking text sentiment to public opinion time series." vol. 11, no. 122-129, 2010, pp. 1–2.

[10] N. Singh, L.-M. Browne, and R. Butler, "Parallel astronomical data processing with python: Recipes for multicore machines," Astronomy and Computing, vol. 2, 2013, pp. 1–15.

[11] G. M. Amdahl, "Validity of the single processor approach to achieving large scale computing capabilities," in Proceedings of the April 18-20, 1967, spring joint computer conference. ACM, 1967, pp. 483–485.

[12] S. Binet, P. Calafiura, S. Snyder, W. Wiedenmann, and F. Winklmeier, "Harnessing multicores: Strategies and implementations in atlas," in Journal of Physics: Conference Series, vol. 219, no. 4. IOP Publishing, 2010, pp. 1–7.

[13] D. Gove, Multicore Application Programming: For Windows, Linux, and Oracle Solaris. Addison-Wesley Professional, 2010.

[14] H. Karau, A. Konwinski, P. Wendell, and M. Zaharia, Learning spark: lightning-fast big data analysis. "O'Reilly Media, Inc", 2015.

[15] M. D. Hill and M. R. Marty, "Amdahl's law in the multicore era," Computer, vol. 41, no. 7, 2008, pp. 33–38.

[16] Python Software Foundation, "Python/c api reference manual," *https://docs.python.org/2/c-api/*, 2018, retrieved: 09, 2018.

[17] H. Eben, Cassandra: The definitive Guide. O'Reilly Media, Inc., 2010.

[18] DataStax, "Python cassandra driver," *datastax.github.io/python-driver/index.html*, 2017, retrieved: 02, 2018.

[19] Apache Software Foundation, "Cassandra query language (cql) v3.3.1," *cassandra.apache.org/doc/old/CQL-2.2.html*, 2017, retrieved: 03, 2018.

[20] P. McFadin, "Getting started with cassandra time series data modeling," *patrickmcfadin.com/2014/02/05/getting-started-with-time-series-data-modeling/*, 2014, retrieved: 03, 2018.

[21] G. Graefe, "Modern b-tree techniques," Foundations and Trends in Databases, vol. 3, no. 4, 2011, pp. 203–402.

[22] M. Kleppmann, Designing Data-Intensive Applications: The Big Ideas Behind Reliable, Scalable, and Maintainable Systems. O'Reilly Media, Inc., 2017.

[23] A. Babkina, "Common problems with cassandra tombstones," *opencredo.com/cassandra-tombstones-common-issues/*, 2016, retrieved: 04, 2018.

[24] A. Bolton, "Senate gop: We will grow our majority in midterms," *thehill.com/homenews/senate/378517-senate-gop-we-will-grow-our-majority-in-midterms*, 2018, retrieved: 03, 2018.

[25] G.-P. Heine, "Developing a scalable data-intensive text processing application with python and cassandra," Master's thesis, University of Applied Sciences Wiener Neustadt, 2018.

[26] Apache Software Foundation, "Welcome to Apache Hadoop!" *http://hadoop.apache.org/*, 2014, retrieved: 09, 2018.

[27] Apache Software foundation, "Apache spark unified analytics engine for big data," *http://spark.apache.org/*, 2018, retrieved: 09, 2018.

Big Data Analytics for the Small Social Enterprise
How to Create a Data-Driven Approach to Address Social Challenges?

Soraya Sedkaoui
Dept of Economy University of Khemis Miliana
Algeria
SRY Consulting, Montpellier, France
e-mail: soraya.sedkaoui@gmail.com

Salim Moualdi
Dept of Economy University of Khemis Miliana
Algeria
e-mail: moualdis@yahoo.com

Abstract— **Big data and the use of data analytics are being adopted more frequently, especially in companies that are looking for new methods to develop smarter capabilities and tackle challenges in the dynamic processes. This study pays a particular attention to the role of big data analytics as an immense potential for addressing societal challenges. It focuses on how to conduct a data-driven approach to better address social concerns and challenges that social enterprises, especially the small ones, are dealing with. The purpose of this paper is to explore and show how social enterprises can harness the potential of big data and how the analytics power can help them find creative solutions to the various societal concerns.**

Keywords: big data; social innovation; SSEs; Analytics; data-driven.

I. Introduction

In the context of social advancement, the availability of big data enables every individual in a developing community to engage in economic activities, such as social entrepreneurship [1]. Exploiting big data can also be used to help make decisions to reduce large-scale social problems and address societal challenges. Many experiences, over the world, show how big data analytics can generate value for social good.

Glow, for example, developed an app using big data to empower women to gain better insights into their reproductive systems. Or, IBM's Canadian Smarter Health study aggregates millions of data elements from monitors in ICUs to identify early warning signs of potential newborn infections, pinpointing issues that even the most experienced doctor would not have caught using traditional practices [2]. Also, social listening data helped AT&T to identify the growing sensitivity to texting while driving as a relevant cause and communications platform.

At this stage, one must wonder 'how do they do it?' Somehow, the answer lies in the fact that these enterprises have seen the potential in using analytics not only to differentiate their business models but also to innovate. The power of big data has evolved to become a primary tool in creating patterns, modeling, and recognizing predictive patterns, which, in effect, offers valuable insights for social entrepreneurship to create life-changing opportunities [2].

Despite its importance for Social Innovation (SI), we have noticed that few studies have analyzed the power of big data in enhancing Small Social Enterprise (SSEs). SSEs are concerned as well with the big data phenomenon, which is also changing the social impact and needs

A SSE is a form of enterprise that places the general interest above profit, which aims to meet social and environmental challenges while remaining economically viable. The fields of application of big data analytics in social context are numerous, such as: occupational integration, disability, diet, environment, etc. From health to agriculture and transport, from energy to climate change and security, many business models recognize the opportunities offered by the enormous amounts of data created in real-time. These models can be provided as a roadmap for this category of enterprise that seeks to become more successful social actors by leveraging big data analytics to guide their social engagements.

But, they must understand the evidence of new opportunities for finding appropriate solutions to societal problems through big data analytics, which has opened new doors and unleashed data's potential. Furthermore, the paper creates a roadmap to help them to deal with social issues when working with big data.

Therefore, in this study the following research question will be answered: *How can social enterprises drive an analytical approach to get more value out of the data and optimize their business model in order to better conduct their project?* Through this question, we recall the context of big data, its importance in conducting decision-making, its challenges and the role it plays as a complement to create new opportunities for SSE in order to address the societal issues.

This study will cover and discuss the basic concepts that lie behind the big data analytics in order to highlight its importance in the SI ecosystem. It does not focus on the technical aspect of big data, such as how to store and process large amounts of data, rather, it explores why and how SSEs might engage operationally with data analytics to better operate in their ecosystem and derive solutions that allow them to improve SI.

The rest of this paper is organized as follows. Section II describes a short overview of big data analytics. Section III describes the challenges and the relevant questions when working with data. Section IV gives key elements to undertake in big data analytics for SI. Section V discusses the development of a data-driven approach for the SSE. The conclusions close the study.

II. Background: Understand Before Undertake

Before talking about how the social sector can use big data for SI, this section will discuss the basic concepts of big data analytics in order to understand the potential of working with data.

A. Data Analytics Power

Many companies have realized that knowledge is power, and to get this power they have to gather its source, which is data, and make sense of it [3]. This was illustrated by the famous "knowledge pyramid" (see [4]), described as a "knowledge discovery".

According to the Oxford dictionary, data are defined as: "*the quantities, characters, or symbols on which operations are performed by a computer, which may be stored and transmitted in the form of electrical signals and recorded on magnetic, optical, or mechanical recording media*".

The potential of data analytics algorithms is deeply related to the potential of data because data are the material that Information Technology (IT) tools will harness. Data are, therefore, a form of wealth, and exploiting it results in an essential competitive advantage for an ever-tougher context. In big data age, enterprises will come across many different types of data (structured, semi-structured and unstructured), and each of them requires different tools and techniques.

The power of data analytics and their applications, in the big data age, is no longer to prove. All sectors are warming up to the benefits of big data analytics. Big data has radically changed the way data are collected and analyzed since it introduces new issues concerning volume (how much?), velocity (at what speed?) and the variety (how diverse?) of the data available today.

Understanding big data means dealing with data volumes that are significantly higher than those previously analyzed, at an incomparable speed (velocity), all while integrating a widely richer data variety. It is no more about the word 'big' now, but it is more about how to handle this 'big' amount of structured, semi-structured and unstructured data, that cannot be managed with traditional tools, and deal with its high diversity and velocity to generate value [5].

The added value of big data is the ability to identify useful data and turn it into usable information by identifying patterns, exploiting new algorithms, tools and new project solutions. The idea behind the term 'big data' is the one that justifies that we talk about revolution and not a simple development of data analysis. What big data brings is the ability to process and analyze all types of data, in their original form, by integrating new methods and new ways of working.

The case of many companies' experiences illustrates that data can deliver value in almost any area of business. Turning data into information and then turning that information into knowledge remains a key factor for business success. So, data in itself is not a power; it is its use that gives power, and more one gives an exchange of data and information, more one receives [6].

Big data then is about collecting, analyzing and using data efficiently and quickly with new tools to gain a competitive advantage by turning data into knowledge and generate value.

B. How to Generate Value and Extract Useful Knowledge

Overall, the approach seems to be simple: (i) we need data; (ii) we need to know what we want to do with it and (iii) how to do it. This idea can be formalized using the following definition [7]:

"Analytics is the process of developing actionable insight through discovery, modeling and analysis, and interpretation of data".

While:

- The idea of *actionable insight* is applied to convey that the objective of analytics is to generate results that directly increase the understanding of those involved in the decision-making process [8].
- *Discovery* refers to the problem definition and exploratory element of analytics; the identification, collection, and management of relevant data for subsequent and/or concurrent analysis. This discovery stage integrates in [8] emphasis on a problem definition, with what [9] conceptualizes as data management, which includes:
  - Problem definition: identify what data to collect, and begin acquiring it. But, the volume of data manipulated by some companies has increased considerably and is now in the order of Petabytes, Exabytes, and even Zettabytes. Chen et al. [10] highlight the multitude of techniques that allow organizations to tap into text, Web, social networks, and sensors, all of which enable the acquisition and monitoring of real-time metrics, feedback, and progress.
  - Data collection: The collection and combination of semi-structured and unstructured data require specific technologies, which also have to account for data volume and complexity.
  - Data management: Data management involves the storage, cleaning, and processing of the data.
- *Modeling and analysis* are concerned with applying statistical models or other forms of analysis against real-world or simulated data. The middle stage of this categorization involves making sense of the acquired data, to uncover patterns, and to evaluate the resulting conclusions [11].
- *Interpretation* involves making sense of the analysis results of, and subsequently conveying that information in the most comprehensible form onward to the relevant parties. In another words, making sense of different types of data and generate value from it, results in some form of finding.

The most important asset of big data has to do with the fact that they make it possible to apply knowledge and create considerable value. But, before one attempts to extract useful knowledge, it is important to understand the overall approach that leads to finding new knowledge. The process defines a sequence of steps (with eventual feedback) that should be followed to discover knowledge in data. To complete each step successfully, effective data collection, description, analysis, and interpretation must be applied [5][12].

Each step is usually realized with the help of available software tools. Data mining is a particular step in this process – application of specific algorithms for extracting models. The additional steps in the process, such as data preparation, data selection, data cleaning, incorporation of appropriate prior knowledge, and proper interpretation of the results of mining ensure that useful knowledge is derived.

III. Enhance Innovation with Big Data

This section is interested in investigating the challenges that SSEs are dealing with in order to map out an efficient plan to improve solutions for social issues.

A. Challenges that Social Enterprises are Dealing with

Recently, many studies have employed big data and analytics for SI [13][14]. The potential for innovation through data uses and analyzes exists, but, it should be noticed that there are some obstacles to overcome. The challenges that social enterprises are dealing with are in many ways very complex compared to those of enterprises in business or science sector, which can make the use of big data that much more difficult. In this context, greater attention must be paid to the data security and privacy.

So, being a social enterprise is a challenge itself and small enterprises must recognize the importance of investing in big data analytics, given its important role as a value generator. In order to harvest value from big data, social enterprises have to address some challenges, such as:

- *Big data dimension:* Each dimension presents both challenges for data management and opportunities to advance decision-making. The 3 V's provide a challenge associated with working with big data. The volume emphasizes the storage, memory and computing capacity of a computing system and requires access to a computing cloud. The velocity stresses the rate at which data can be absorbed and meaningful answers produced. The variety makes it difficult to develop algorithms and tools that can address that large variety of input data [15].
- *Technological context:* One of the main issues is the incompatible IT infrastructures and data architectures. IT systems and software should be able to store, analyze, and derive useful information from available data [16]. The most successful companies understand the limitations of the technology behind their big data operation and recognize the importance of combining analysis with a sound understanding of the context, a good intuition for the industry, and a critical attitude towards insights derived from data.
- *Managerial context:* The keystone of big data exploitation is to leverage the existing datasets to create new information, enriching the business value chain [15]. The major challenge to overcome is the management's lack of understanding of the potential value big data can bring to companies [16]. The goal was to manage the increasing amount of data, information and to ensure its usage and flow across the organization. Data are required to be managed in different steps and most of all analyzed [17], for organizations to gain knowledge and value.

A large part of this challenge, for SSEs, lays in the complexity of data collection, data analysis, data security, and how to turn that data into usable information by identifying patterns, exploiting new algorithms, tools, and new solutions to address social concerns. They are required to deal with these several issues to be able to seize the full potential of big data.

B. Making Plans: Beginning by Understanding

The biggest confusion of the importance of big data (*why?*), as with every major innovation, lies in the exact scope (*what?*), and its implementation (*how?*). In this context, SSEs must pay attention to the data's boundless opportunities, if they want to generate solutions to address social challenges. They must adopt a 'data-driven approach'. To better conduct this approach, one needs to have a clear objective. In other words, the clearer the objectives, the more focused and rewarding the analytical approach will be.

Of course, there are multiple ways a social enterprise can become more data-driven. For example, by using big data technologies, exploring new methods able to detect correlations between the quantities of available data, developing algorithms and tools that can address that large variety of input data, by optimizing the Business Intelligence process, and more.

SSEs must, therefore, seek the information where it is not, and the most popular way is probably to ask a lot of questions and see what sticks. SSEs must seek for the innovative idea by asking relevant questions [5]. Two essential components are needed to question whether data analytics can or cannot add value to a SSE:

- *Data:* What should be done here is exploring all possible paths to recover the data in order to identify all the variables that affect, directly or indirectly, the phenomenon that interests the social project. An important procedure is to understand the data that will be collected and then analyzed. The idea is that the more we have a good understanding of our data, the better we will be able to use them wisely. This aims to precisely determine where we should look for the data, which data to be analyzed and identify the quality of the data available but also link the data and their meaning from a business perspective.
- *Definition of problem statement:* Everything in big data analytics begins with a clear problem statement. Determining what type of problem a social enterprise is facing with, will allow the enterprise to correctly choose the technique that can be used. The success of an analytics approach cannot be possible without the clarification of what

we want to achieve and what is need to be changed to embrace the advancement that big data entails. This is not just valid in big data context but in all areas.

Big data is opening up a number of new areas for social enterprise. Just as Facebook has made it easier to share photos, new analytics products will make it far easier not just to run analysis but also to share the results with others and learn from such collaborations [18].

Public institutions, such as the US government, the World Bank, etc., have understood the power of data analytics. They made their data available (open data) to be exploited and analyzed. This perspective allows many enterprises and businesses to create innovative applications able to address societal concerns.

Asking interesting questions develop their inherent curiosity about data that they are working on. The key is thinking broadly about how to transform data into a form which would help to find valuable tendencies and interrelationships. The following types of questions seem particularly interesting to better guide a social project:

- What things can SSEs learn from the data?
- How can they ever understand something they cannot see (making sense)?
- What techniques, methods, and technology do they need to improve their project strategy?
- How to avoid mistakes and get the best models?
- How can they learn lessons by analyzing available data, and what they can do with it?
- How to use the results (models) efficiently?
- What impacts do they expect on the choices to be made? Etc.

This kind of questions allow them to better conduct their project based on data and analytics, that means think about the 'meaningful' of data, so its 'practice' [5].

IV. Big Data Analytics and Social Enterprise

This section discusses the key elements that can help the enterprise to conduct a data-driven-approach for SI.

A. *Big Data for Social Sector: Challenges and Opportunities*

The generalization of the cloud, intelligent devices, big data and Artificial Intelligence (AI) coupled with new human-machine interfaces have revolutionized the business world and upset the entire economic landscape. With the emergence of smart devices, the Internet of things (IoT) and big data age, more and more social enterprises rely on the use of technology.

According to [2], the concept of smart data is considered as an exponential part of creating a prosocial brand. In her research, she discussed the opposite characteristics of doing social good and big data because both recognize the important aspects of contemporary markets. The SSE seeks to create a sustainable business strategy that will encourage the formation of social values while big data encompasses growth expectations attributed to private markets [1].

Social enterprises can also promote the achievement of SI through the utilization of big data analytics. It is the case of many examples that highlight the potential of big data for SI. The idea is to combine the passion for social change with the data analytics field.

In Bhopal India, for example, the Panna Tiger Reserve is using drones (unmanned aerial vehicles) to safeguard against tiger poachers. The data collected has allowed them to improve the efficacy of their efforts and to prove the impact of their activities, thus encouraging greater support and funding for their initiatives [2].

Also, the 'Ushahidi' application, designed to map violence after the Kenyan elections in 2008, collects and disseminates data about urban violence, allowing users to avoid it and public authorities to prevent it. As for the 'I Wheel Share' application, it facilitates the collection and dissemination of urban data likely to be useful for people with disabilities [5].

Or even 'Deuxio' the portable sensor developed by 'Plume Labs', which measures local air pollution in real-time and communicates results and data with users. The 'Victor & Charles' provides service that allows hotel managers to access the digital social profile of their customers in order to adjust at best their services.

The Social Innovation Program of Qatar Computing Research Institute (QCRI), in partnership with several humanitarian organizations, applies big data analytics to improve humanitarian response.

Also, the Daniel Project, another successful example of using big data analytics for social impact, Intel's collaboration with Not Impossible Labs to 3D-print prosthetic arms for a 14-year old war victim. Intel's data competencies contributed significantly to the technological solution [2]. The video of this initiative, shared on social media, captured the hearts and imaginations of consumers across the world and earned Intel more than a half-billion online impressions, an impressive quantification of the intrinsic value of social branding [2].

These examples and many others show the potential of data-driven approach and its actual impact in helping solve social problems. Big data is considered a new form of capital in today's marketplace [19][20], many firms fail to exploit its benefits [21]. For SSEs, it is known that they are unlikely to analyze data on the same scale as large companies (Google, Facebook, Amazon, IBM, etc), due to their limited sources, skills and IT tools.

It is possible that they are engaging with the free big data tools provided by companies like Google, without forgetting the increase in the prominence of social networks and the fact that engaging with social media, which can help generates exposure and traffic for SSEs at a much lower cost than traditional marketing approaches [22].

But, it is to highlight that they are unlikely to have capacities and sophisticated tools to capture, prepare, analyze and manage generated data. In another word, they are not prepared to fully use the unprecedented amounts of data that they are able to collect for their unique target populations or the social issues they address.

Also, there are several social challenges that social enterprises are aiming to address, be it environmental, education, and/or health problems, the innovations that can be drawn from data are limitless [23]. As for the concept of smart data, for example, integrating the approach towards social entrepreneurship brings out an initiative in reinforcing social values while using information as its core component [1].

The literature suggests that entrepreneurial orientation is a useful lens through which to consider the use of big data analytics in small enterprises. The two dimensions of entrepreneurial orientation, which point to the link between small enterprise and big data capabilities, are [16]:

- *Innovativeness:* Achieving social mission through innovativeness refers to the ability to solve social problems or in effect to create social value. This supports a contention that it will be a key indicator of whether social entrepreneurs will adopt big data analytics.
- *Proactiveness:* Proactive enterprises can make use of big data analytics to improve their understanding of their customer and their sector, with the condition that they have access to the right sources of information. It is, therefore, an important element to consider when looking at big data adoption in SSEs. For example, through retaining the environment, this reflects the tangible and intangible results of breaking patterns, changes in the system, and new discoveries towards process improvement.

So, SSEs have to examine how to exploit successfully the diverse and voluminous data and how to use the analytical techniques in order to accomplish their mission and support sustainable change.

B. Develop a Data-Driven Approach for SSEs

In order to succeed in an analytical approach and boost a big data project, it is necessary for social enterprises to prepare it in advance. To do this, three essential questions must be asked:

- *Why:* The first question to ask is "why? ". In most cases, this question will inevitably occur during the initial briefing with a consultant or client. Many big data projects are launched only because the term big data is in vogue. Many executives board the wagon and begin to approve massive investments of time and money to develop a data platform. Most of the time, this strategy is based entirely on the motive that *"everyone is doing it"*. An in-depth analysis of the goal that a social enterprise wants to achieve, by analyzing the data, as well as an assessment of the investments and expertise that the project needs, are required but too often overlooked in the context of the deployment of a big data strategy.
- *What:* In all sectors, companies are now considering turning the corner on big data and analytics. They recognize in the data a largely untapped source of value creation and an exclusive factor of differentiation. But, many don't know which approach to tackling. What social enterprise is trying to do? Does the project objective creating an innovative market, or find a new channel that requires information on client interest and future profitability?
- *How:* While companies do see the great potential that big data analytics can bring to improve their business performance, the reality is that many are struggling to generate value from available data. Gartner [24] study shows that many big data projects remain blocked and that only 15% have been deployed in production. Examining such failures, it appears that the main factor is in fact not related to the technical dimension, but rather to the processes and human aspects that prove to be as important. Conduct a data-driven project means also to be able, in particular, to answer questions, such as: How can we be sure that big data could help us to create social impact? Who should be involved and when? What are the key steps that need to be attentive? Is the project on the right track to succeed? Etc. It is therefore essential, for data-driven orientation, to ensure:
  - For the data: quality, security, structure ...;
  - For the process: well-defined organization, a data-driven culture, its direction ...;
  - For tools: IT infrastructure, storage, data visualization capability, performance monitoring.

In order to extract value from big data, it must be processed and analyzed in a timely manner, and the results need to be available in such a way as to be able to effect positive change or influence business decisions. It is also important to ensure that the social project is progressing towards the intended result (as depicted in Fig. 1).

Small enterprise in the age of big data, must rely on varied analytical approaches to thought and action to create and implement solutions that are socially, environmentally, and economically sustainable. Being a data-driven in business, social or science sector means being at the heart of data valuing and intervene at all stages of the data value chain: problem definition, data collection, preparation, modeling and solution creation.

New analytics approach in big data age combines predictive and prescriptive analytics to predict what will happen and how to make it happen. Analytics uses and applications improve the efficiency of the decision-making process and generate value.

SSEs have to expand their efforts to move their small business from using only traditional business intelligence (BI) that addresses descriptive analysis (what happened) to advanced analytics, which complements by answering the "why", "what" and "how" questions.

Ultimately, 'data science' and the algorithm of machine learning are inevitable as they can help extract various kinds of knowledge from data, which can be referred to the social solutions.

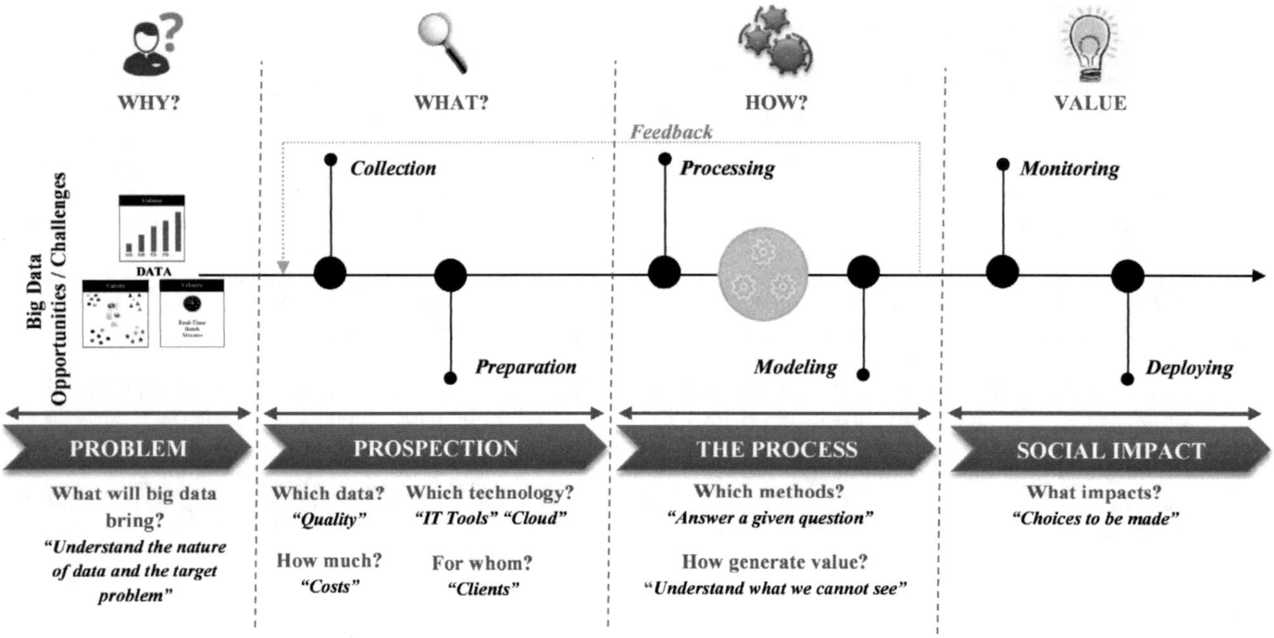

Figure 1. Data-driven approach for SSEs (create value from data)

SI is based on the power of data and analytics, which leads to the need for the exploitation of the data potential. The principle is that by analyzing, in real-time, the data collected by GPS, satellites, smartphones, social media ... around the world, it is possible to identify trends, make connections and predictions. SSEs are leveraging the opportunities of big data universe and must create their own approach based on data analytics to better derive social impact [25][26].

V. Discussion

Analytics widens SSEs scope as an entity, giving them the ability to do things they never thought were possible. For example, it offers timely insights, to allow them making better decisions, about SI opportunities; it also helps them to ask the right questions and supports them to extract the right answers as well.

Clearly, the use of big data analytics will provide numerous opportunities to build social approach based on data that will effectively and efficiently cater to the needs of the various entities. In this context, the United Nations Global Pulse has been created to harness digital data using analytics tools in order to understand changes in people well-being.

To improve decision-making processes in the choice of infrastructure, geolocation data are useful. In Senegal for example, a GSMA project has identified the most relevant trajectories for the construction of a road, in line with the data of journeys operated by mobile phone users. The data are also used to define maps of illiteracy rates. The same goes for Ebola, where the mobility of citizens is analyzed to anticipate population movements.

Also, in partnership with WHO (World Health Organization), the GSMA has addressed tuberculosis risks by using anonymous mapping data to measure disease peaks and predict people at higher risk [27]. The association is also tracking the resistant forms of malaria using anonymous data to identify the source and routes of transmission of this disease.

The 'Give Directly NGO' that provides direct donations to poor people in Africa, is now equipped with a poor village recognition algorithm based on an automatic analysis of Google Earth satellite imagery [5][28].

Also, 'Simpa Networks', an Indian social enterprise that rents out-of-use solar panels to households without access to electricity and donates them after a rental amount, has obtained a predictive model to identify, among its new customers, most likely to go through the rental process [29].

Many examples have shown that data-driven solutions have transformative impacts on SI. These examples have taken the importance of data from the power of its use and purpose rather than its volume. These enterprises have understood that it is the analytics process that can bring innovative and social benefits.

So, it is the data analysis that will extract all the value and especially allows developing a more detailed understanding of the uses. Powerful analytics tools can then be used to process the information gathered in large sets of structured, semistructured, and unstructured data.

Data analytics algorithms can provide teams with a deeper level of evidence so that they can better differentiate which activities have the greatest social impact and redesign their services accordingly.

Be able to act effectively on diverse aspects of data analysis techniques and IT tools give SSEs the power to better adapt big data analytics to social needs.

Join the arena of data-driven to SI provides alight on several points, in this context, some initiatives should be stepped:

- Map out the demand in the social sector to identify the nature of issues and the solutions needs.
- Explore the social impact of big data, and identify mechanisms through which SI is achieved [30].
- Identify the existing social project in this field in order to have a clear vision about the opportunities and challenges and identify gaps to better draw their program.
- Preparing a solid IT infrastructure to meet the challenge and be more competitive in the SI context.
- Founding a strategy-based approach, which must be tailored to analytics practices and techniques in order to address issues and face social challenges, including practices in which they implement their own concepts for their entrepreneurial orientations.

The placement of these initiatives should be coordinated with the launch of the social entrepreneurial creative spaces and the pilot projects (where they could be employed). In this term, the SI ecosystem must be redesigned and updated through the integration of the factors and the needs to better draw the roadmap for SSEs to enable them to use big data and advanced analytics for social good towards the achievement of social change.

Therefore, the efforts should concentrate on creating a roadmap for success that covers several stages:

- Set up the entrepreneur's social issues direction (identifying its mission, vision and strategic and operational objectives).
- Establish policies, principles, resources and expertise guidelines to control ICT and big data usage.
- Evaluate and analyze the current situations and the necessary changes and additions to reach the desired result.
- Identify priorities and use them to determine the most important components and techniques that would offer the greatest social effects with the smallest investment.
- Realize new SI opportunities for further development by monitoring current analytics developments and their effects and the arising issues and new requirements.

SI often has a positive connotation associated with notions of openness, collaboration or inclusion, unlike other commercial innovations. Whether it takes the form of new practices, new measures, new programs or new policies, big data analytics will facilitate the appropriation and adaptation of social innovations, alleviating those apprehensions and will benefit the greatest number of people.

This innovation is placed at the intersection of three areas: innovation, social problems and digital technologies that increase the quantities of data. To launch a big data project, SSEs have to master the way it works (see Fig. 1). In this context, we propose two approaches [31]:

- *Bottom-Up Approach*: This approach goes from the bottom (the technique) to the top (the organization). With this approach, social enterprises will first validate the technical choices through a PoC and a case of use that they consider relevant. Once the project has been validated, they can continue with other experiments on ancillary domains (data analysis, visualization, etc.) or quickly realize a use case and bring value immediately. This organization is highly iterative both technically and functionally. This is obviously the method that brings the fastest results and can support enterprises' strategies; in contrast, its visibility is limited.
- *Top-Down Approach:* This approach will first impact the organization of the social enterprises to enable them to launch big data projects. They must define a big data strategy for their entire social objective, a schedule of implementation of the concrete objectives that often result in new offers for the company or the improvement of existing offers. With this approach, the concrete results are longer to obtain. In contrast, objectives, responsibilities, and sponsors are clearly identified.

From the several examples mentioned in this paper we can notice that big data analytics can meaningfully support social innovation across health, housing, education, employment, etc. But, it should be noticed that the exploration of the data alone will not solve major social problems. Financial and technological resources are also needed. Therefore, it is necessary to include enough resources and finance to support the analytics' uses by entrepreneurs for social good. This investment is essential to reap the full benefits of big data and realize all the envisioned features and capabilities.

The ability of social enterprises to adopt big data analytics may be understood by looking at their role in the determination of the data-driven culture and how they are deploying their resources to engage with and make use of analytics tools and methods in their field.

VI. Conclusion and Future Work

To promote the SI process based on data analytics, specific attention will be paid to the SSEs that want engaging in this field. This is important because, it helps to understand their roles, their needs, the challenges they are dealing with, the social value they can generate, and their position in the SI ecosystem. Thus, it is needed to address the existing need for theoretical and methodological frameworks, which build on the different elements that iterate in the social construction of SI and account for its complexity and contextual dimensions [32].

This paper addresses the importance of big data for small SSEs, without covering all the areas where data analytics may benefit the social innovation. It allows an understanding of the importance of big data for social sector and how these tools can revolutionize and help the SSEs to evaluate the efficiency of the social project in order to enhance their future directions.

This paper contributes to SI literature by creating a data-driven approach that can help the social enterprise to grow in unprecedented ways by harnessing the available data and understand the social needs and issues. This work paves the ground for developing a more mature data-driven approach, where real case studies are involved to test the efficiency of this approach in meeting various social impacts through a flexible data analytics process.

Future research should focus on data-driven SI, as this relates to the results and outcomes of data use, from generating innovative social solutions (products or service) to improving business and social efficiency. To better analyze the social impact of big data, more empirical studies are needed to understand more reasons for which social enterprises must integrate big data analytics in the SI ecosystem.

REFERENCES

[1] M. T. Matriano and F. R. Khan, "Technological platforms for social entrepreneurship and community engagement", International Journal of Management, Innovation & Entrepreneurial Research, vol. 3 n°1, pp. 40-47, 2017.

[2] L. Pascaud, Smart data at the heart of Prosocial Brands, Kantar Added Value, [retrieved: February, 2018] http://added-value.com/2015/01/23/smart-data-at-the-heart-of-pro-social-brands/

[3] S. Sedkaoui, "Statistical and Computational Needs for Big Data Challenges", In A. Al Mazari (Ed.), "Big Data Analytics in HIV/AIDS Research", (pp. 21-53). Hershey, PA: IGI Global, 2018, doi:10.4018/978-1-5225-3203-3.ch002

[4] R. L. Ackoff, "From data to wisdom", Journal of Applied Systems Analysis, vol. 15, pp. 3-9, 1989

[5] S. Sedkaoui, Data analytics and big data, London: ISTE-Wiley, 2018.

[6] B. Martinet and Y. M. Marti, Economic Intelligence: How to Give Competitive Value to Information , Paris, Editions d'Organisation, 2001.

[7] A. Van Barneveld, K. E. Arnold, and J. P. Campbell, "Analytics in higher education: Establishing a common language", EDUCAUSE learning initiative, vol. 1 n°1, pp. l-ll, 2012

[8] A. Cooper, "What is analytics? Definition and essential characteristics", CETIS Analytics Series, vol. 1 n°5, pp. 1-10, 2012.

[9] A. Labrinidis and H. V. Jagadish, "Challenges and opportunities with big data", Proceedings of the VLDB Endowment, vol. 5 n° 12, pp. 2032-2033, 2012.

[10] H. Chen, R. H. L. Chiang, and V. C. Storey, "Business intelligence and analytics: From big data to big impact", MIS Quarterly, vol. 36 n°4, pp. 1165-1188, 2012.

[11] G. S. Tomar, N. S. Chaudhari, R. S. Bhadoria, and G. C. Deka, The Human Element of Big Data: Issues, Analytics, and Performance, CRC Press, 2016.

[12] W. W. Piegorsch, Statistical Data Analytics, New York: Wiley, 2015.

[13] R. Dubey, et al, Can big data and predictive analytics improve social and environmental sustainability?, Technological Forecasting and Social Change, in press, 2017.

[14] C. Njuguna and P. McSharry, "Constructing spatiotemporal poverty indices from big data", Journal of Business Research, vol. 70, pp. 318-327, 2017.

[15] S. Sedkaoui, "The Internet, Data Analytics and Big Data", Chapter 8. In Gottinger, H.W (Eds), "Internet Economics: Models, Mechanisms and Management" (pp. 144-166), eBook Bentham Science Publishers, Sharjah, UAE, 2017.

[16] S. Sedkaoui, "How data analytics is changing entrepreneurial opportunities?", International Journal of Innovation Science, Vol. 10 n° 2, pp.274-294, 2018. https://doi.org/10.1108/IJIS-09-2017-0092

[17] S. Kudyba, "Information Creation through Analytics", In S. Kudyba (Ed.), "Big Data, Mining, and Analytics. Components of Strategic Decision Making", (pp. 17-48). Boca Raton: CRC Press Taylor and Francis Group, 2014.

[18] D. Feinleib, Big Data Bootcamp: What Managers Need to Know to Profit from the Big Data revolution, Apress, 2014.

[19] V. Mayer-Schonberger and K. Cukier, Big Data: A Revolution That Will Transform How We Live, Work and Think, Boston, Ma: Houghton Mifflin Harcourt, 2013.

[20] G. Satell, Five things managers should know about the big data economy. Forbes, 2014.

[21] S. Mithas, M. R. Lee, S. Earley, and S. Murugesan, "Leveraging big data and business analytics", IT Professional, vol. 15 n° 6, pp. 18–20, 2013.

[22] L. C. Schaupp and F. Bélanger, "The value of social Media for small businesses", Journal of Information Systems, vol. 28 n° 1, pp. 187-207, 2014.

[23] A. Peredo and M. McLean, "Social entrepreneurship: A critical review of the concept", Journal of World Business, vol. 41 n°1, pp. 56-65, 2006.

[24] Gartner, (2016), "Investment in big data is up but fewer organizations plan to invest", [retrieved: November, 2017] https://www.gartner.com/newsroom/id/3466117

[25] D. Archibugi, "The social imagination needed for an innovation-led recovery", Research Policy, vol. 46 no.3, pp.554-556, 2017.

[26] W. Bijker, "Constructing Worlds: Reflections on Science, Technology and Democracy (and a Plea for Bold Modesty)", Engaging Science, Technology, and Society, vol. 3, pp.315-331.

[27] GSMA Press Office, (2018), "GSMA expands big data for social good initiative, announces successful first wave of trials", [retrieved: September, 2018] https://www.gsma.com/newsroom/press-release/gsma-expands-big-data-social-good-initiative-announces-successful-first-wave-of-trials/

[28] Z. Guo, et al," Identification of Village Building via Google Earth Images and Supervised Machine Learning Methods", Remote Sens, MDPI, vol. 8n° 271, pp. 1-15, 2016.

[29] GSMA, (2017), "Mobile for Development Utilities Lessons from the use of mobile in utility pay-as-you-go models", [retrieved: September, 2018] https://www.gsma.com/mobilefordevelopment/wp-content/uploads/2017/01/Lessons-from-the-use-of-mobile-in-utility-pay-as-you-go-models.pdf

[30] I. Pappas, M. L. Jaccheri, P. Mikalef, and M. Giannakos, "Social innovation and social entrepreneurship through big data: developing a research agenda", proceeding of the 11th Mediterranean Conference on Information Systems (MCIS), Genoa, Italy, 2017. 12, pp. 1-14.

[31] S. Sedkaoui, Big Data Analytics for Entrepreneurial Success, New York: IGI Global, 2018.

[32] G. Cajaiba-Santana, "Social innovation: Moving the field forward. A conceptual framework", Technological Forecasting and Social Change, vol. 82, pp. 42-51, 2014.

Dynamic Scenario-based Selection of Data Aggregation Techniques

Oladotun Omosebi*, Nik Bessis*, Yannis Korkontzelos*,
Evangelos Pournaras†, Quanbin Sun* and Stelios Sotiriadis‡

* Department of Computer Science, Edge Hill University, Ormskirk, United Kingdom
Email: {Oladotun.Omosebi, Nik.Bessis, Yannis.Korkontzelos, Quanbin.Sun}@edgehill.ac.uk

† Professorship of Computational Social Science, ETH Zurich, Zurich, Switzerland
Email: epournaras@ethz.ch

‡ Department of Computer Science and Information Systems, Birkbeck, University of London
Email: s.sotiriadis@dcs.bbk.ac.uk

Abstract—**The Internet of Things introduces a new paradigm where small scale sensor devices can be used to capture data on physical phenomena. The potential scale of data that will be captured by such devices stands to transcend the capabilities of today's client-server architectures. The necessity to reduce the data volume has been reflected in enormous research interests dedicated towards developing new data aggregation techniques for sensor networks. However, the application-specific nature of data aggregation techniques has resulted in the development of a large volume of options, thereby introducing new problems of appropriate selection. This paper introduces a unique method to deal with this problem by proposing a classification approach for data aggregation techniques in wireless sensor networks. It presents the theoretical background for the selection of a set of high-level dimensions that can be used for this purpose, while a use case is presented to support the arguments. It also discusses how the dimensions dictate data collection procedures and presents how this framework can be used to develop an adaptive model for the dynamic selection of data aggregation techniques based on the characteristics of a sensing application use case.**

Keywords–Internet of Things; Wireless Sensor Networks; Big Data; Data Aggregation; Adaptive Model.

I. Introduction

Sensor devices consist of physical devices that have sensor capabilities to capture data on selected phenomena. Examples of such phenomena include weather conditions and city pollution. They host a limited source of power, networking and memory. A combination of such devices forms a Wireless Sensor Network (WSN), which can be deployed into various environments to sense and track various forms of phenomena [1]. WSNs are especially applicable to scenarios where the environment is not conducive for human habitation, such as in earthquake, tsunami or tornado events, or in continuous monitoring situations such as city carbon monoxide pollution or for weather monitoring. Due to the characteristics of such scenarios, implying that they may never be repaired or maintained, they need to manage their processing in order to extend their internal power supplies [2], [3], [4]. In order to ensure this, the generated data needs to be accumulated and reduced in size before transmission to a base, a process referred to as data aggregation. Data aggregation becomes possible because most sensor deployments keep sensors in close proximity for communication purposes. This leads to sensors capturing similar data, which become duplicates when transmitted. Thus, the goal of a data aggregation technique is to reduce the data duplication and perform further data compression, before transmission [5], [6]. This task has also drawn much attention due to the emerging Internet of Things (IoT), where a multitude of physical objects will be equipped with sensors and networking capabilities [7], [8], [9], [10].

Data aggregation techniques need to be application-specific to manage power consumption efficiently [3], [7], [11]. This has led to the proposal of a large number of techniques for various application scenarios, thus leading to a large pool of options. Selecting the right technique for the right scenario becomes a challenge, especially for researchers [12]. This challenge becomes amplified in the IoT, where sensors would be expected to have some form of self-organization.

This paper presents a proposal for a unique classification method for data aggregation techniques used within WSNs. It identifies a set of dimensions that can be used to classify the different operational stages of a data aggregation technique. The term Dimensions in the context of this study is used to represent a high level identifiable feature of a WSN technique. It serves as an encompassing term for several low granularity characteristics. Under these dimensions, the WSN characteristics that are important for a technique, such as node homogeneity, node count and location awareness, are associated with the technique and referred to as its attributes. Several selected techniques are matched with their attributes to compile a database of associations. These data will be used to build a model to utilise the correlation to dynamically classify techniques based on application characteristics and thus, provide a recommendation in the form of one or more techniques [13], [14].

The remaining of the paper is organized as follows: Section II presents the background to our study. Section III presents a use case scenario that will serve as a reference point for our discussions. Section IV discusses our proposed method. Section V presents our evaluation plan and Section VI provides a conclusion and discusses our next steps.

II. Background

A. Wireless Sensor Networks and Data Aggregation

Distributed data aggregation involves the decentralized computation of significant properties within a network that can be utilized by applications . Examples include the average workload distribution across the network or the number of nodes active on the network. Such a task is especially applicable within a WSN, where the aggregation or compression of data is based on the several network-based parameters such as node location, distribution and resource distribution

TABLE I. LIST OF VARIOUS CLASSIFICATION APPROACHES

Article & Author	Dimensions used for classification
A Survey of Distributed Data Aggregation Algorithms [6]	Data aggregation function types (e.g. duplicate sensitive and duplicate insensitive); Communication requirements; Routing protocol; Network Type (e.g. structured-hierarchical, unstructured-flooding/broadcast, etc.)
Data Aggregation in Wireless Sensor Networks: Previous Research, Current Status and Future Directions [12]	Topology type; Objective
Practical data compression in wireless sensor networks: A survey [16]	Energy efficiency
A Taxonomy of Wireless Micro-Sensor Network Models [17]	Communication function; Data delivery model; Network dynamics with respect to power demand
Issues of Data Aggregation Methods in Wireless Sensor Network: A Survey [18]	Strategy; Delay; Redundancy; Accuracy; Energy consumption; Traffic load
Data-aggregation techniques in sensor networks: A survey [19]	Network lifetime; Latency; Data accuracy; Security
A survey on sensor networks [20]	Protocol layer

[6], [15]. Researchers have in the last decade, proposed numerous techniques for data aggregation dedicated to unique WSN scenarios. The volume of options has grown to such unmanageable proportions and presented a new challenge of selecting right technique for the right application. This has motivated other researchers to propose classification methods for the various options.

B. *Classification Approaches*

While most technique classification approaches are based on surveys, they have selected a set of WSN characteristics to guide their classification method. Some approaches identified in literature are listed in Table I.

Table I presents the classification approaches taken by several researchers. The right column shows the various WSN characteristics used as yardsticks in the classification process, which provide a reliable means of evaluating the techniques. The following observations can be made: a group of WSN techniques, which have optimised certain characteristics to achieve efficient data aggregation, have been compared by the authors based on those characteristics; based on the approach taken by the authors, minimal effort has been applied to establishment of correlations between two or more techniques. In contrast to these, this paper proposes a uniquely different approach. We identify dimensions to enable us classify WSN characteristics within the scope of data aggregation. The dimensions will allow us to develop correlations between techniques and their attributes. For example, the Low-Energy Adaptive Clustering Hierarchy (LEACH) protocol [21] utilises an algorithm, random cluster head rotation, in order to evenly distribute energy consumption accross all nodes. This algorithm would be categorized under a dimension, referred to as *Algorithms*, and associated with the LEACH technique as an attribute. The association of attributes to techniques will help us to compare and contrast them with similar techniques, as well as to relevant application scenarios. This strategy also enables us to explore opportunities for new approaches to data aggregation [22]. The next section discusses the theoretical background of the identified dimensions.

C. *Dimensions*

The top goals of a data aggregation technique as used in a WSN include the minimization of energy consumption, latency, bandwidth, and the extension of network lifetime. In order to achieve these goals, a data aggregation technique needs to closely match the target application scenario. To develop a model that will enable this functionality, there is need to develop a classification method to identify appropriate techniques based on the use case. This approach involves the definition of a set of dimensions into which WSN characteristics can be classified. Afterwards, the characteristics can be associated with techniques. In summary, we identified seven dimensions namely: *Assumptions*, *Objectives*, *Specifications*, *Algorithms*, *Applications*, *Performance Metrics*, and *Evaluation*. While the dimensions are expected to follow an order as presented, a subject that is expatiated further in a later section, the theoretical background for their identification is presented in the following paragraphs.

Most WSN applications have inherent constraints that are determined by their topology, network structure and acceptable communication channels. For example, a wildfire event demands that sensors are deployed after the event has started, and that sensors are well protected and have similar characteristics in order to obtain reliable data. Within literature, such constraints are stated as assumptions. For instance, in [23] assumptions are made about sensor nodes having a single sensor, while the network consists of a single cluster. In [24], the authors highlight the need for nodes to have prior knowledge of the network-wide data correlation structure. In [2], the authors specify that all nodes use a fixed compression factor. We selected the term *Assumptions* as one of our dimensions based on further literature review. Within our context, we therefore define *Assumptions* as the set of pre-conditions under which a technique must operate. Thus, the variables representing assumptions are considered immutable during the operation of the technique.

After a realization of the constraints of the application context, identified as assumptions of the technique, the objectives of the technique can be stated. In [24], the authors define the application context in which their objective of "solving the Slepian Wolf coding problem" can be realized. In [25], the authors state their objective as "Efficient Cluster Head Selection Scheme", while also defining the context in which the objective will be realised. In [26], the authors state their objective, based of group communications in multiple target scenarios, thereby implying the constraints. This essentially motivated us to select *Objective* as a high-level dimension to use in our classification process.

On identifying the constraints and objectives of the technique, a set of parameters are selected. Such variables are considered mutable and used to optimize the technique. In this paper we refer to such variables as *Specifications*. Such variables have been used extensively in literature on data aggregation. For instance, [23] emphasise the need to specify appropriate number of nodes in their technique to apply the K-means algorithm. [26] proposed an algorithm, the Two-Tier Aggregation for Multi-target Apps (TTAMA), which is expected to be aware of the communication settings of nodes in order to effectively perform aggregation. [27] use node count in the network to adjust the response of their technique based on the objective to develop a low-cost topology construction algorithm. In conclusion, we define a technique's *Specifications* as the parameters that can be modified during the operation of the technique, and thus, are applicable for optimization.

With the combination of the assumptions, objectives and specifications, the technique requires a set of algorithms to perform its functions. Essentially, a data aggregation technique achieves its objective based on selected algorithms. For instance, the Shortest Path Tree [28], Minimum Spanning Path [29], and use of Euclidean Distance [30]. In [28], the authors combined the sleep and awake algorithm, with a threshold-based control system to apply adaptability to their technique. [31] proposed a structure-free protocol to aggregate redundant data in intermediate nodes to dynamically compute the data transmission delay for nodes based on their position. In [32], a framework to enable decentralized data aggregation was developed by using a routing algorithm based on a gossip protocol. In [33], the authors developed a gossip-based decentralised algorithm for data aggregation that relies on crowd-sourced data and computational resources. In this paper, we have thus, selected *Algorithms* as a dimension.

After the last four dimensions, a simulation is essential to generate data that can be used to validate that the technique has met its objectives. This strategy is demonstrated by many proposals from literature [26], [28], [34]. We identify this step as a dimension called *Application*, since it represents the running of the technique in a given use case.

After the simulation, the technique can be evaluated based on generated data. In our classification approach, we have identified two more dimensions to cater for this: *Performance Metrics*, and *Evaluation*. We define the *Performance Metrics* as the selected attributes of a technique that can be used to evaluate its performance. These are expected to relate directly to the set of objectives and specifications as discussed earlier [12]. For instance, authors in [35] selected metrics such as energy dissipation over time, data received over time, and node lifetime over time, in order to compare the LEACH and LEACH-C techniques. In [28], in order to evaluate the Adaptive Energy Aware Data Aggregation Tree (AEDT) technique, which targets extending network lifetime, the authors selected metrics such as average end-to-end delay, average packet delivery ratio, energy consumption and network lifetime. Similarly, in evaluating the TTAMA technique [26], the authors selected number of communication rounds and node energy level after each round.

The dimension termed *Evaluation* has been chosen to represent the values that can be used to compare techniques based on their performance. Thus, *Evaluation* holds the results of *Simulations* and *Measurements* with respect to the *Performance Metrics*. It is hoped that a generalized reference point can be developed to be utilized in the comparison of techniques using the values under this dimension.

III. Contribution

Our contribution in this paper includes the proposal of a unique classification approach for data aggregation techniques as used in WSNs. These dimensions will enable the classification of techniques based on selected WSN characteristics. The dimensions will be used to develop an adaptive model that will enable the dynamic selection of techniques based on the context. From an academic perspective, such a model would enable researchers to identify relevant and related characteristics of different techniques and their applicable scenarios. It also enables a researcher to strategically select a technique based on a set of characteristics representing a target application scenario.

IV. Use Case Description

We present a use case in this section to serve as an illustration for further discussions. Wildfires are a frequent occurrence in summer weather, where high temperature levels remain persistent in the midst of low humidity [36]. They present a situation where several uncontrolled events lead to tremendous damage if left unabated. In order to monitor the wildfire event, the value of a few context-based parameters need to be known. For example, in order to detect the movement or direction of the fire, it is necessary to observe the temperature distribution in the region in real-time. This will require frequent sensing of temperature levels as the fire moves across the region. In order to ensure that the nodes can continue to provide this data, they could be made homogenous, implying that they have similar computing, sensing or power capabilities. This reduces the inherent complexity of calculating approximate temperatures since only an average need be obtained across all nodes on a frequent basis. This demonstrates the necessity for the right data aggregation technique to be chosen for a given scenario. The selected technique must be able to obtain accurate values for the network-wide resource distribution and application context parameters such as the need for real-time frequent sensing.

The above scenario represents one out of numerous use case scenarios. While a huge number of techniques have been proposed in the past, there remains the possibility that one or more use cases have not been catered for. The IoT in conjunction with new 5G services is especially expected to provide new use cases that have not been considered yet. This underscores our proposal for the need to develop an adaptive and dynamic model for data aggregation techniques. Such a model can be used to assess current and new application contexts, to select the right data aggregation techniques and procedures, as well as establish new approaches for new scenarios.

V. Proposed Method

A. Framework Development

Based on the foregoing discussions, Figure 1 presents the workflow across the mentioned dimensions. We discuss the diagram with respect to the numbering of the paths. A data aggregation technique is developed for a particular set of *Objectives*. However, before these objectives can be realised, the application context constraints must be identified. This relationship is identified by line 1. Once the objectives are stated, they should be validated when the technique is applied to a use case. This is possible by selecting appropriate parameters that can be used to represent the objective. For instance, a technique targeting energy reduction needs to select energy consumed, etc., as an evaluation metric. In order to effectively use this parameter for evaluation, its value needs to be adjustable in order to compare different states of the technique's operation. The set of parameters that will enable this adjustment fall into the *Specifications* dimension of the technique. These relationships are represented on paths 2 and 7. On selecting the specification parameters and stated

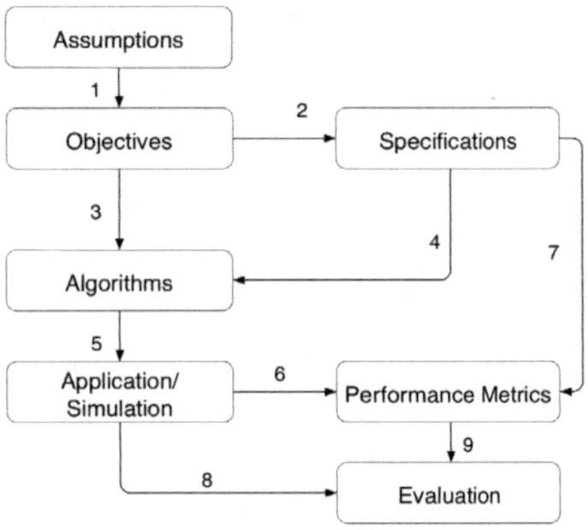

Figure 1. Links/workflow between the various high-level dimensions

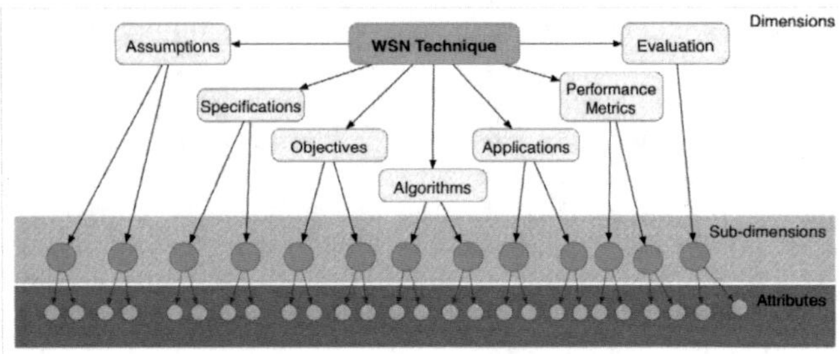

Figure 2. Representation of hierarchical dimensions that enable the categorization of technique characteristics

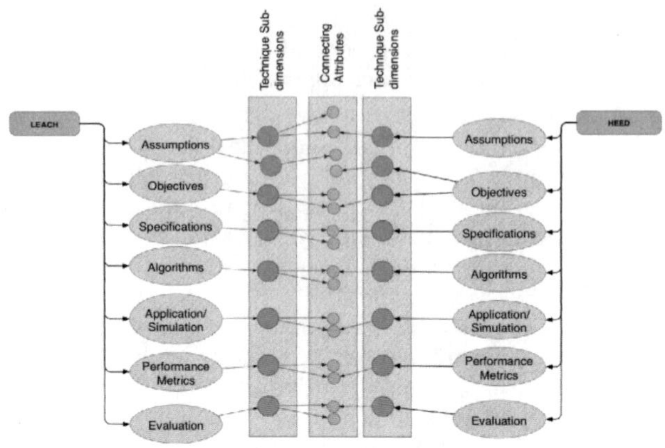

Figure 3. Illustrating how high-level dimensions enable identification of correlations between two data aggregation techniques

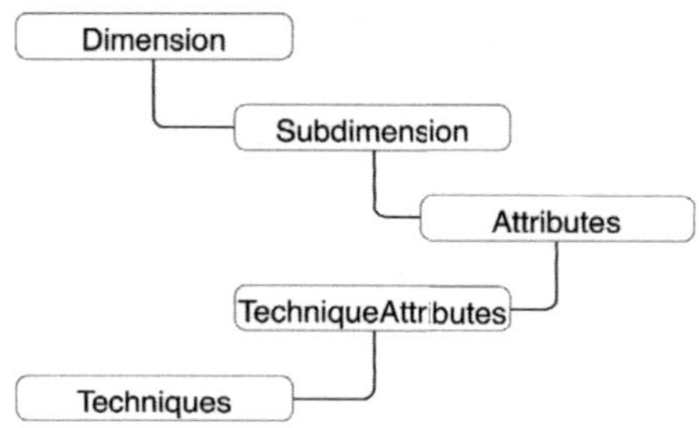

Figure 4. Database structure for storage of technique attributes

objectives, a group of *Algorithms* (paths 3 and 4) are applied to implement the technique. Parameters under the foregoing dimensions can then be used to develop a simulation of the technique for a specific application, represented as path 5. The application (simulation) will generate data that can be used to validate the objectives by applying the *Performance Metrics* (path 6). The results obtained from applying the metrics to the application would provide the *Evaluation* results (path 8 and 9).

Figure 2 represents the full illustration of a WSN technique based on our proposed framework. It shows a hierarchy with three levels, specifying levels on which a technique can be defined. The top level is referred to as *Dimensions*. The second level, named *Subdimensions* provides a categorization function for the set of characteristics. The third level, called *Attributes*, represents the WSN characteristics.

A further illustration of how this framework can be used to identify the relationship between two techniques is shown in Figure 3. In this case, the techniques LEACH [21] and HEED (Hybrid Energy-Efficient Distributed) [3] are chosen as sample techniques. Their associated attributes are used to build an association between the two enable a process of matching the techniques. In Figure 3, the middle column with blue circles represents the commonly shared attributes between the two techniques. For instance, both techniques, i.e. LEACH and HEED, share the attribute *homogeneous network*, a characteristic that falls under the *Assumptions* dimension. This creates an association between the two techniques.

B. Data Collection

Based on the defined framework, data needed to be gathered from sources that could provide primary descriptions for new data aggregation techniques. Based on this, the primary source of data were academic articles on data aggregation techniques, supported by books that discussed data aggregation in WSNs. The framework was used as a guide to select values for the attributes, and to build the subdimensions. Figure 4 shows the database structure that was used to store the data. The boxes represent the tables in the database, while the lines between them indicate that they share foreign key relationships.

Presently, the number of techniques stored is 125, while 7 dimensions, 132 subdimensions, and 385 attributes have been identified. An example of a technique "signature" based on the content of the database is shown in Table II represented in JSON format.

VI. Model Design and Evaluation

Some analysis of the data already stored within the database is shown in Figure 5. It represents the currently identified correlations between techniques and their attributes. The x axis holds a number for each attribute, while the y axis shows the total number of techniques that have the same attribute. Figure 5 presents a high level visualisation of the correlation between techniques and attributes.

Figures 6 and 7 depict the preliminary plan for the architecture of the model, indicating the expected input and

TABLE II. JAVASCRIPT OBJECT NOTATION (JSON) REPRESENTATION OF A TECHNIQUE BASED ON THE DEFINED FRAMEWORK

LEACH {
assumptions: ["homogenous initial energy"],
objectives: ["Extend Network Lifetime"],
specifications: ["2-Stage Operation", "Centralised Control", "Periodic Sensing"],
algorithms: ["stochastic election", "TDMA Timing", "Code Division Multiple Access", "Uniform Initial Energy", "Cluster Formation by Associates"],
performance_metrics: ["network lifetime"],
application: ["base in proximity", "packet size", "network size", "node count", "radio propagation power"],
evaluation: [] }

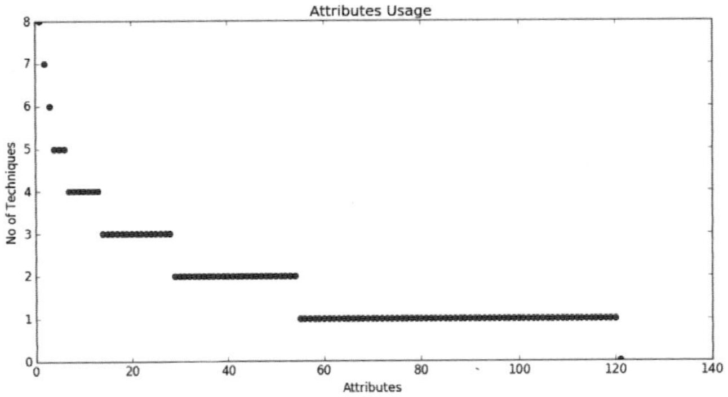

Figure 5. Technique-Attributes correlations graph based on the data stored within the database

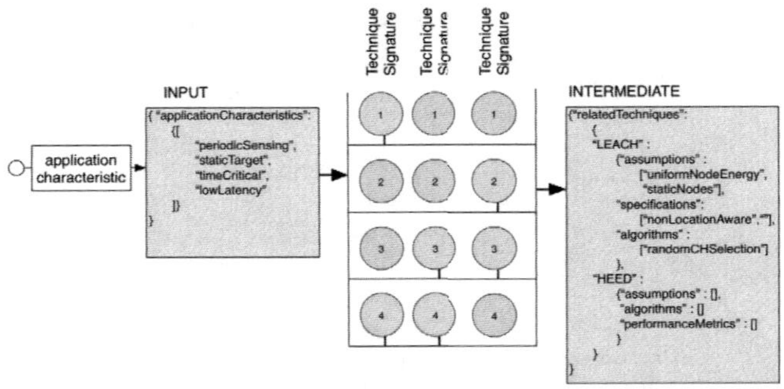

Figure 6. Preliminary plan for an advanced stage of the model — first part

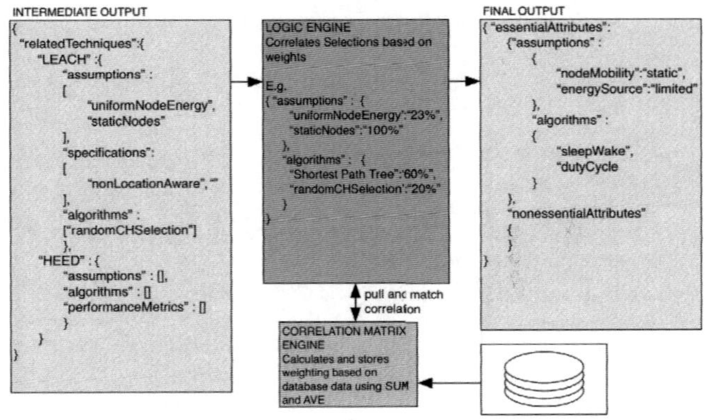

Figure 7. Preliminary plan for an advanced stage of the model — second part

output formats. The figures present a single use case scenario where application characteristics serve as the input data. The term "technique signature" is used in Figure 6 to indicate that a set of attributes can be used to uniquely distinguish a technique from another, otherwise referred to as its signature. Figure 6 indicates that the input is expected to be in JSON and should describe the request based on a format that will need to be determined. Each circle represents a single attribute, such as location awareness. Thus, a combination of circles arranged vertically represent a single technique's set of attributes and is referred to as a "Technique Signature". A technique signature is expected to uniquely distinguish a technique. The group of 3 shown in Figure 6 represents a larger collection of techniques that are used at this stage to compare and match input requirements with stored or learned correlations between techniques and attributes. Thus, this stage could be implemented as an Artificial Neural Network. The input will consist of a specification describing the application scenario and set of requirements. The output will consist of a recommendation of a technique or a combination of techniques applicable to the given scenario. Figure 7 represents the stage that receives the output from Figure 6, where the output is validated based on prior learning. The output from this next stage provides the expected output from the model. The design will be improved upon as we progress.

VII. Conclusion

In this paper, we have presented a design of our proposal for an adaptive model that is able to dynamically select data aggregation techniques based on application context metadata. This capability finds utilization in the emerging Internet of Things where the number of active sensors, and subsequently the generated data, is expected to grow exponentially. We intend to improve on the output shown in Figure 5 by obtaining more data, while ensuring that the data is consistently cleansed to make it suitable for its purpose. We will then apply machine learning to the final data in order to develop the adaptive model. A set of use cases will be developed to test the model to ensure its effectiveness.

References

[1] S. Boubiche, D. E. Boubiche, A. Bilami, and H. Toral-Cruz, "Big data challenges and data aggregation strategies in wireless sensor networks," IEEE Access, vol. 6, 2018, pp. 20 558–20 571.

[2] A. Avokh and G. Mirjalily, "Dynamic balanced spanning tree (dbst) for data aggregation in wireless sensor networks," 2010 5th International Symposium on Telecommunications, 2010, pp. 391–396.

[3] S. Chand, S. Singh, and B. Kumar, "Heterogeneous heed protocol for wireless sensor networks," Wireless Personal Communications, vol. 77, no. 3, 2014, pp. 2117–2139.

[4] M. Trovati, N. Bessis, A. Huber, A. Zelenkauskaite, and E. Asimakopoulou, "Extraction, identification, and ranking of network structures from data sets," in 2014 Eighth International Conference on Complex, Intelligent and Software Intensive Systems. IEEE, 2014, pp. 331–337.

[5] T. Du, S. Qu, K. Liu, J. Xu, and Y. Cao, "An efficient data aggregation algorithm for wsns based on dynamic message list," Procedia Computer Science, vol. 83, 2016, pp. 98 – 106, the 7th International Conference on Ambient Systems, Networks and Technologies (ANT 2016) / The 6th International Conference on Sustainable Energy Information Technology (SEIT-2016) / Affiliated Workshops.

[6] P. Jesus, C. Baquero, and P. S. Almeida, "A survey of distributed data aggregation algorithms," IEEE Communications Surveys & Tutorials, vol. 17, 2015, pp. 381–404.

[7] Y. Shen, T. Zhang, Y. Wang, H. Wang, and X. Jiang, "Microthings: A generic iot architecture for flexible data aggregation and scalable service cooperation," IEEE Communications Magazine, vol. 55, no. 9, 2017, pp. 86–93.

[8] C. W. Tsai, C. F. Lai, M. C. Chiang, and L. T. Yang, "Data mining for internet of things: A survey," IEEE Communications Surveys Tutorials, vol. 16, no. 1, 2014, pp. 77–97.

[9] S. Yang, "Iot stream processing and analytics in the fog," IEEE Communications Magazine, vol. 55, no. 8, 2017, pp. 21–27.

[10] E. Pournaras, J. Nikolic, P. Velásquez, M. Trovati, N. Bessis, and D. Helbing, "Self-regulatory information sharing in participatory social sensing," EPJ Data Science, vol. 5, no. 1, 2016, p. 14.

[11] L. Krishnamachari, D. Estrin, and S. Wicker, "The impact of data aggregation in wireless sensor networks," in Proceedings 22nd International Conference on Distributed Computing Systems Workshops, 2002, pp. 575–578.

[12] S. Randhawa and S. Jain, "Data aggregation in wireless sensor networks: Previous research, current status and future directions," Wireless Personal Communications, vol. 97, no. 3, 2017, pp. 3355–3425.

[13] F. Xhafa, E. Asimakopoulou, N. Bessis, L. Barolli, and M. Takizawa, "An event-based approach to supporting team coordination and decision making in disaster management scenarios," in Third International Conference on Intelligent Networking and Collaborative Systems (INCoS). IEEE, 2011, pp. 741–745.

[14] D. J. McCloskey, M. Trovati, and C. S. Zimmet, "Using a dynamically-generated content-level newsworthiness rating to provide content recommendations," 2013, international Business Machines Corp. US Patent 8,386,457.

[15] V. Daiya, T. S. S. Krishnan, J. Ebenezer, K. Madhusoodanan, S. A. V. SatyaMurty, and B. Rao, "Dynamic architecture for wireless sensor network-implementation analysis," in 2016 International Conference on Wireless Communications, Signal Processing and Networking (WiSPNET), 2016, pp. 1206–1211.

[16] T. Srisooksai, K. Keamarungsi, P. Lamsrichan, and K. Araki, "Practical data compression in wireless sensor networks: A survey," Journal of Network and Computer Applications, vol. 35, no. 1, 2012, pp. 37–59, Collaborative Computing and Applications.

[17] S. Tilak, N. B. Abu-Ghazaleh, and W. Heinzelman, "A taxonomy of wireless micro-sensor network models," SIGMOBILE Mob. Comput. Commun. Rev., vol. 6, no. 2, 2002, pp. 28–36.

[18] S. Sirsikar and S. Anavatti, "Issues of data aggregation methods in wireless sensor network: A survey," Procedia Computer Science, vol. 49, 2015, pp. 194–201, proceedings of 4th International Conference on Advances in Computing, Communication and Control (ICAC3'15).

[19] R. Rajagopalan and P. K. Varshney, "Data-aggregation techniques in sensor networks: A survey," IEEE Communications Surveys Tutorials, vol. 8, no. 4, 2006, pp. 48–63.

[20] I. F. Akyildiz, W. Su, Y. Sankarasubramaniam, and E. Cayirci, "A survey on sensor networks," IEEE Communications Magazine, vol. 40, no. 8, 2002, pp. 102–114.

[21] M. J. Handy, M. Haase, and D. Timmermann, "Low energy adaptive clustering hierarchy with deterministic cluster-head selection," in 4th International Workshop on Mobile and Wireless Communications Network, 2002, pp. 368–372.

[22] V. K. K. S. Ghai, "Data aggregation to improve energy efficiency in wireless sensor networks," International Journal of Innovative Research in Information Security, vol. 3, 2016, pp. 9 – 12.

[23] H. Harb, A. Makhoul, D. Laiymani, A. Jaber, and R. Tawil, "K-means based clustering approach for data aggregation in periodic sensor networks," in 2014 IEEE 10th International Conference on Wireless and Mobile Computing, Networking and Communications (WiMob), 2014, pp. 434–441.

[24] Z. Huang and J. Zheng, "A slepian-wolf coding based energy-efficient clustering algorithm for data aggregation in wireless sensor networks," in 2012 IEEE International Conference on Communications (ICC), 2012, pp. 198–202.

[25] M. Arshad, M. Alsalem, F. A. Siddqui, N. Kamel, and N. M. Saad, "Efficient cluster head selection scheme in mobile data collector based routing protocol," in 2012 4th International Conference on Intelligent and Advanced Systems (ICIAS2012), vol. 1, 2012, pp. 280–284.

[26] A. Riker, E. Cerqueira, M. Curado, and E. Monteiro, "A two-tier adaptive data aggregation approach for m2m group-communication," IEEE Sensors Journal, vol. 16, no. 3, 2016, pp. 823–835.

[27] K. Beydoun, V. Felea, and H. Guyennet, "Wireless sensor network infrastructure: Construction and evaluation," in 2009 Fifth International Conference on Wireless and Mobile Communications, 2009, pp. 279–284.

[28] D. Virmani, T. Sharma, and R. Sharma, "Adaptive energy aware data aggregation tree for wireless sensor networks," Computing Research Repository (CoRR), vol. abs/1302.0965, 2013.

[29] W. Wang, B. Wang, Z. Liu, L. Guo, and W. Xiong, "A cluster-based and tree-based power efficient data collection and aggregation protocol for wireless sensor networks," Information Technology Journal, vol. 10, 2011, pp. 557–564.

[30] D. Mantri, N. R. Prasad, and R. Prasad, "Grouping of clusters for efficient data aggregation (gceda) in wireless sensor network," in 2013 3rd IEEE International Advance Computing Conference (IACC), 2013, pp. 132–137.

[31] P. Mohanty and M. R. Kabat, "Energy efficient structure-free data aggregation and delivery in wsn," Egyptian Informatics Journal, vol. 17, no. 3, 2016, pp. 273–284.

[32] M. Jelasity, S. Voulgaris, R. Guerraoui, A.-M. Kermarrec, and M. van Steen, "Gossip-based peer sampling," ACM Transactions on Computer Systems (TOCS), vol. 25, no. 3, 2007.

[33] E. Pournaras, J. Nikolic, A. Omerzel, and D. Helbing, "Engineering democratization in internet of things data analytics," in 31st IEEE International Conference on Advanced Information Networking and Applications, AINA 2017, Taipei, Taiwan, March 2017, pp. 994–1003.

[34] P. Nie and B. Li, "A cluster-based data aggregation architecture in wsn for structural health monitoring," in 2011 7th International Wireless Communications and Mobile Computing Conference, 2011, pp. 546–552.

[35] H. Rahman, N. Ahmed, and I. Hussain, "Comparison of data aggregation techniques in internet of things (iot)," in 2016 International Conference on Wireless Communications, Signal Processing and Networking (WiSPNET), 2016, pp. 1296–1300.

[36] National Georgraphic, "Learn more about wildfires," www.nationalgeographic.com/environment/natural-disasters/wildfires/, online; accessed 25 July 2018.

Analysis of Twitter Communication During the 2017 German Federal Election

Marek Opuszko, Laura Bode, Stephan Ulbricht
Friedrich-Schiller-University Jena
Department of Business Informatics, Jena, Germany
Email: marek.opuszko@uni-jena.de, laura.bode@uni-jena.de, stephan.ulbricht@uni-jena.de

Abstract—**Even before 2016 elected US president Donald Trump made the microblogging service Twitter a tool for political campaigning and broadcasting, the online service with millions of users gained attention in public events, scandals or sport events. The question still remains open to what extent the analysis of Twitter communication reveals insights into to political discurse during elections. This study uses the context of the 2017 German federal election to investigate the political communication within the Twitter network during 10 weeks leading to the election in September 2017. Almost 1,500,000 million tweets are analyzed using three different lexica: SentiWS, Linguistic Inquiry Word Count (LIWC) and German Political Sentiment Dictionary (GPSD). In order to gain deeper insights, the users producing the tweets are investigated. The results show that users strongly differ in their activity on the network and perform statistical tests to evaluate differences among the user groups.**

Keywords–Social Media; Twitter; Sentiment; Elections

I. Introduction

Political communication via social media and especially microblogging services, such as Twitter have intensified in recent years. Digital platforms are used by numerous actors to inform themselves politically and to exchange thoughts and ideas [1]. In many countries, social media are used by politicians and political parties more frequently as a medium for election campaigns and political marketing [2]. Especially negative political statements can often attract people's attention and gain high efficacy and attention [3].

As the popularity of social media increases, so does the likelihood that people will find ways to abuse them for their own purposes. One type of abuse in the political online debate is the so-called Astroturf, in which politically motivated individuals and organizations use several remote controlled accounts to give the appearance of broad and spontaneous support for a candidate or opinion [4]. Symptoms include various types of unlawful use, such as spam infiltrating social networks [5]. In addition, in recent years, political actors around the world have begun to use the digital power of automated programs called social bots [6]. They purposefully mimic human behavior, actively engage in the opinion-forming process and have the potential to distort discussions in social networks and manipulate public opinion [7], [8].

Twitter, in particular, has become an ideal destination for exploiting automated programs through its growing popularity and open nature [9]. Automated accounts are often characterized in Twitter by high activity in terms of large tweets, which are generated in connection with political events during very short timespans.

From the growing need to identify highly active, opinion-forming actors in the digital political discourse, the task of this work is to quantify the message traffic in the context of the 2017 German federal election on Twitter and to quantify the influence of highly active users on the general mood in the election campaign debate. Important questions include the contribution of highly active users to political communication for the 2017 federal elections and their potential influence on other users. In addition, it should be determined whether the generated mood of highly active users, in polarity or strength, agrees with or differs from the majority tonality of the users. The question is whether highly active users differ significantly in their behavior from other users. This is especially interesting due to the fact that a new party, called the "Alterantive für Deutschland (AfD)", entered the stage of German politics and vies for attention.

The paper is organized as follows. In Section II we will provide the research background on election analysis in twitter and the special features to this subject. Section III we will lay out the research method and details of the data collection. Furthermore, the different lexica used in this work are introduced. Another aspect is the meassurement of user activity, which is also addressed in this section. The results of the analyses are presented in Section IV. The result presentation is divided into a descriptive analysis, results from investigating the different user groups and the sentiment investigations. The work concludes with a summary and interpretation of the results and gives indications of future investigations.

II. Research Background

In our study, we use 1,475,838 tweets published in the months leading up to the federal election of the national parliament in Germany in 2017. The election took place on September 24th 2017. The elections in 2017 are entering a new chapter in the history of the Federal Republic of Germany, as in this election for the first time a new party, the *AfD*, by many considered a "right-wing" or populist party enters the stage [10], [11]. The German party landscape consists of 7 relevant parties, Social Democratic Party *SPD*, Christian Democratic Union *CDU*, Christian Social Union in Bavaria *CSU*, Alternative for Germany *AfD*, Free Democratic Party *FDP*, The Left *LINKE* or *DIE LINKE* and Alliance 90/The Greens *GRÜNE*, where CDU and CSU form a federal union called *CDU/CSU* or short *Union*. The strongest group in the new Bundestag, with a share of 32.9%, was the CDU / CSU parliamentary group. The SPD reached 20.5%. The AfD made its first entry into the Bundestag with 12.6%. The FDP managed with 10.7% to return to parliament. The Left achieved 9.2% and The Greens 8.9% of the votes [12].

Not only since the 2016 elected US president Donald Trump uses the online service Twitter to process political statements, microblogging services are in the focus of science [13]–[15]. Many researchers investigate the effects on the political landscape or the reflections of real world events in online social networks like Twitter [16]. It remains unclear whether networks like Twitter either mirror or shape political discurs and if so, to what degree [17]. Despite this uncertainty, there is an ongoing discussion about the influence of possible bots or agents from other countries on local political events, such as the Brexit [17], [18] or the 2016 US elections [19], [20].

Despite the unique properties of tweets compared to other textiles, they have proven to be a reliable source for sentiment analysis. One of the earliest works in which Twitter data was used for sentiment analysis is by Go et al. [21]. They used tweets with emoticons to train a machine learning algorithm and were able to predict the mood in tweets with high accuracy (about 83%). Bermingham and Smeaton also announced in 2010 that classifying short microblogging entries is much easier than classifying longer blog entries [22]. Barbosa and Feng showed that the performance of sentiment analysis in Twitter can be improved by incorporating social relationships and connections, for example a user's followers [23] on Twitter. Further work has been done to introduce new automated methods of sentiment analysis and to optimize existing approaches to increase the classification accuracy of Twitter texts in a variety of contexts. This emphasizes the ability of Twitter sentiment analysis as a scientific tool to investigate human communication, hence, political communication. Tumasjan et al. found out that political sentiment towards parties and politicians can be linked to real events and political demands of the actors using sentiment analysis of the 2009 general election [16]. The results showed both, a lively discussion and conversations among the users. The study was further able to attribute the election result to the proportion of tweets which mentioned a specific party. Furthermore, research has shown, that Twitter usage varies significantly among its users [24].

In the political context regarding Twitter sentiment, negative moods are frequently identified. For example, news coverage of the 2008 US presidential election revealed negative sentiment rather than positive sentiment in response to specific political events, such as television debates [25]. Another work showed that the general mood of the Twitter debate on the 2008 US presidential election was also rather negative [26].

III. METHOD

The data used in this work was collected in a 10 week period leading to the federal elections in Germany on 24th September 2017 using the official Twitter API [27], [28]. During this period, all tweets containing at least one hashtag reference to one of the top parties *SPD, CDU, CSU, AfD, FDP, LINKE, GRÜNE* were collected. The resulting raw dataset comprised 1,475,838 tweets. Since only German tweets are evaluated, the tweets were extracted from the multilingual tweets for further use. Language recognition was performed using the N-gram based text classification of Cavnar and Tenkle [29]. The described speech recognition process classified 1,255,666 tweets as German. The dataset also included 225,371 entries with hashtags of the two chancelor canididates *Merkel* und *Schulz* which have been removed in this work, since we concentrate on party related content. The resulting dataset then comprised 1,030,295 entries. All relevant hashtags are listed in Table I. They are already subdivided into hash tag groups with subsequent hashtags.

In a further step, additional special characters and HTML elements, such as "&" were removed from the text corpus.

TABLE I. NUMBER OF HASHTAG ENTRIES BY HASHTAG

Party hashtag	Number of entries	Asigned hashtags
AFD	515,615	#AFD, #AfD, #afd, #TrauDichDeutschland, #traudichdeutschland, # noAfd, #NoAfD, #AfDwaehlen, #NeinZuAFD, #afdstoppen, #fckafd, #FCKAfD, #AberKeineAFD, #afdverhindern
SPD	154,397	#SPD, #Spd, #spd, #spdde, #EsistZeit, #esistzeit, #EsIstZeit
CDU	149,980	#CDU, #Cdu, #cdu, #fedidwgugl
FDP	71,570	#FDP, #Fdp, #fdp
LINKE	31,206	#LINKE, #Linke, #linke, #DIELINKE, #dielinke, #DieLinke, #Linken, #NURDIELINKE
GRÜNE	46,794	#GRÜNE, #Grüne, #Gruene, #Grünen, #Gruenen, #DieGruenen, #DarumGrün, #GrueneVersenken
CSU	54,649	#CSU, #Csu, #csu

To determine the mood of a text by means of lexicon-based sentiment analysis, different dictionaries can be used. In the past, several such directories have been developed. Each with different strengths and weaknesses [30]. Due to the focus on a German text corpus, the use of dictionaries is limited to German lexica. In this work, three word-based sentiment lexica will be used: SentimentWS [31], Linguistic Inquiry Word Count [32] and German Political Sentiment Dictionary [33].

SentiWS is a publicly available, German-language dictionary provided by the University of Leipzig and is suitable for sentiment analysis based on the German language [31], [34]. The words are weighted in the interval -1 to 1, depending on the level of expressiveness. SentiWS includes 1,818 positive and 1,650 negative words, or 16,406 positive and 16,328 negative word forms, and includes nouns and verbs in addition to sentiment-bearing adjectives and adverbs. SentiWS is based, among other enhancements, on the General Inquirer, a popular English language sentiment dictionary whose words have been systematically translated into German and then manually reworked [31].

The *LIWC* is a text analysis software with an integrated dictionary [32]. It was published in 2001 by Pennebacker et al. [35] and has been developed for the automatic analysis of texts in the one-word-procedure and provided by Dr. med. phil. Markus Wolf from the University of Zurich. With the aid of the stored dictionary, words are assigned to one or more predefined language categories. The language categories cover grammatical-linguistic characteristics of the text as well as thematic-content-related aspects, such as positive and negative emotions or the presence of social and cognitive speech content. The program also tracks how many words in a text could be assigned to categories and considers this in relation to the length of the text. The precission rate of the German LIWC dictionary was cited with 63% in the past while the English dictionary is cited with 73% [32]. In the context of the general election in 2009, the LIWC software was used in 2010 by Tumasjan et al. [16] for political sentiment analysis in Twitter.

The *GPSD* is a German lexicon by Haselmayer and Jenny [33] especially developed for the analysis of political communication. The words contained are weighted along a 5-step negativity scale from 0 (not negative) to 4 (very strong negative). Assuming swarm intelligence, Haselmayer and Jenny used the crowd-coding method and had texts reviewed by a large number of anonymous non-experts. They achieved reliable results through crowd-coding and advocated the use of custom dictionaries.

To address the questions of user activity differences it is necessary to determine a users' activity in the Twitter network. According to Bruns and Stieglitz, a user's activity can be described in the simplest way by the number of tweets generated by a user for a certain hashtag [36]. If this activity is determined for all users, the relative contribution of users or user groups to the overall communication for a hashtag can be determined. User activity in communicative situations on Twitter and other platforms is likely to be described by a long-tail distribution: a comparatively small group of highly active users generate most of the content, while a much larger number of less-active users only account for a small amount of Tweets [37]. According to Bruns and Stieglitz, it is often meaningful to group the users into groups based on this law. They work with a 90/9/1 distribution established by Tedjamulia et al. [38], which allows users of social networks to be divided into the following three groups:

- The most active 1% of users
- The other, still very active 9% of users
- The remaining, less active 90% of users

In this way, it can be examined how dominant the most active 1% of users are within the entire hashtag conversation on Twitter and whether there are obvious differences between the activity patterns of these groups [39].

IV. RESULTS

A. Descriptive Analysis

As highlighted in Table I, the number of hashtag entries strongly differs by party (hashtag) and does not reflect the election outcomes. In particular, the hashtag group *#AFD* shows an extremely frequent occurrence with over 500,000 cases, which corresponds to a share of almost 50% of all entries, yet having an election result of 12.6% of the votes. On the other hand, the strongest group in the elections, the CDU/CSU union with 32.9% of the votes only accounted for 14.64% of the entries of party hashtags. As a short conclusion, the users mentioning the *AFD* hashtag are either very active or there is a big controversy around that hastag within the Twitter community. This is further highlighted in Figure 1 where the percentage of each hashtag of the 7 party hashtag groups is stacked upon reflecting the percentage of entries per day. The *AFD* hashtag dominates the whole timespan having numerous days when the percentage reaches values higher than 50%.

To assess possible activity differences, all users producing tweets where grouped in three activity groups. The classification of users based on their activity was based on the 90/9/1 distribution presented in Section III. The division of the data set into the three activity groups was realized by quantile division. For quantile formation, users were sorted by their tweet frequency (activity) in descending order, and then the 100%, 99%, and the 90% quantiles were determined to create the 1%, 9%, and 90% user groups. Each of the three subgroups of the activity groups created included the proportion of tweets generated by the Twitter users of each group.

Figure 2 shows the number of tweets by each user group. The results clearly show that 1% of the Twitter users in the

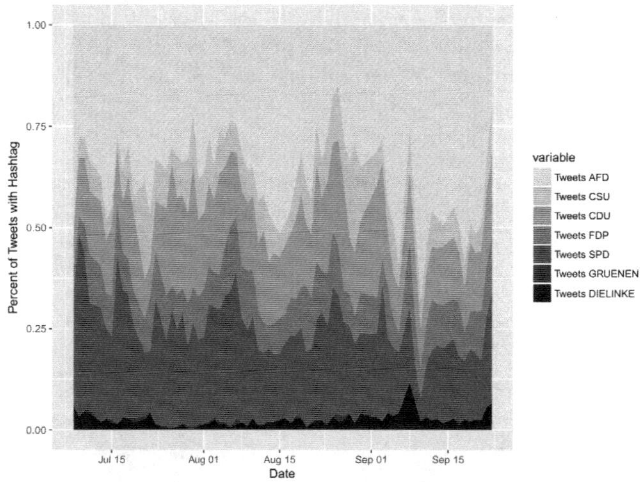

Figure 1. Hashtag share in tweets per day in percent

dataset account for the majority of all tweets in the dataset. The 1% group even accounts for more tweets than the lower 90% of the users. This confirms the presumption of the existence of a long tail in the user activity.

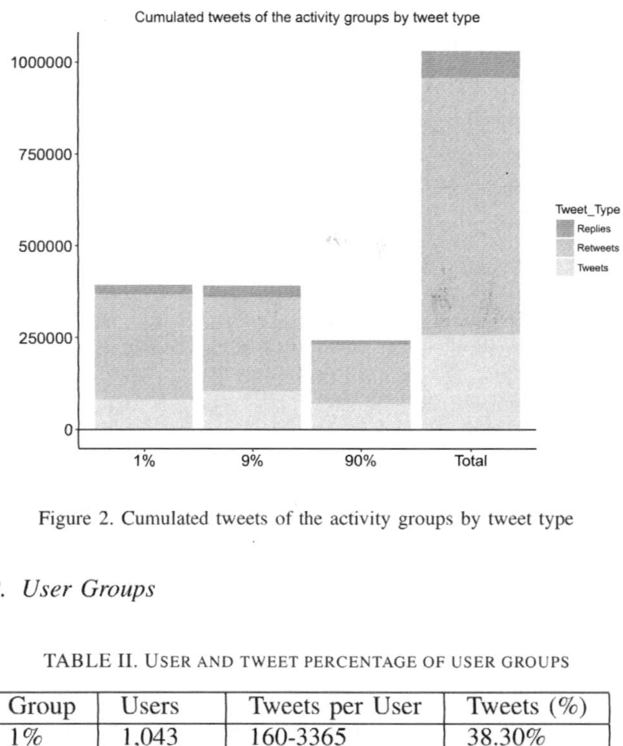

Figure 2. Cumulated tweets of the activity groups by tweet type

B. User Groups

TABLE II. USER AND TWEET PERCENTAGE OF USER GROUPS

Group	Users	Tweets per User	Tweets (%)
1%	1,043	160-3365	38.30%
9%	8,851	16-159	38.07%
90%	93,816	1-15	23.63%
Total	103,701	1-3365	100%

Table II lists the number of user per group and the percentage each group accounts for. To answer the question wheter one user group shows a higher "reach" in terms of "Twitter reach", the reach *R* has to be determined. The potential reach R of an activity group was defined as the sum of the possible reach indicators of the Twitter API (number of followers, number of retweets and number of favorites) across all tweets of an activity group. Followers are the number of users subscribed to the twitter user posting a tweet. Figure 3 shows the mean potential reach of all user groups in terms of followers and retweets. The first group (1%) showes the highest numbers of average followers per tweet with 5097.46. Also the number of retweets is the highest in this group with a value of 0.83 retweets per tweet on average.

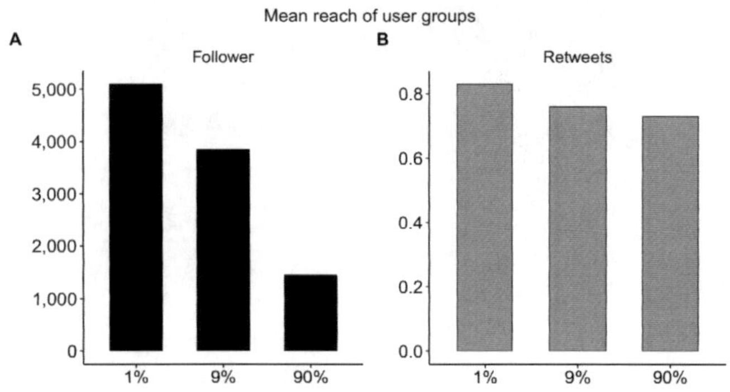

Figure 3. Mean reach of user groups

C. Sentiment of Election Tweets

As highlighted in Table III, the mean sentiment values of the activity groups SentiWS [-0.099; -0.073] and GPSD [-2.721; -2.591] were mainly in the negative and LIWC [1.302; 2.404] exclusively in positive territory. The difference between the activity groups was particular large in LIWC. The standard deviation (SD) was very high for all three procedures and for all activity groups. This was especially true for the lexica SentiWS and LIWC. It is noticeable that despite different scales of measurement, all three lexica displayed the same trend: the average sentiment value was highest in the 90% group of users, lower in the 9% group and lowest in the 1% group. This observation was significant at a level of $p < 0.001$ for all dictionaries.

TABLE III. MEAN SENTIMENT VALUES OF DICTIONARIES

Group	SentiWS	LIWC	GPSD)
1%	-0.099 (SD 0.331)	1.302 (SD 9.242)	-2.721 SD(1.528)
9%	-0.089 (SD 0.328)	1.723 (SD 9.143)	-2.669 SD(1.504)
90%	-0.073 (SD 0.325)	2.404 (SD 9.283)	-2.591 SD(1.449)

D. Sentiment in Hashtag Groups

In this section, a sentiment comparison of the hashtag groups introduced in Table I was performed. Figure 4 visualizes the proportionate (A) and mean (B) sentiments of the hashtag groups. The generated sentiment of the hashtag conversations were very different. The highest sentiment was generated by the AfD (41.20%), followed by BTW17 (20.62%), SPD (12.31%) and CDU (11.33%) and again with a considerable distance FDP (4.89%), CSU (4.10%), GRÜENE (3.67%) and LINKE (1.90%). The proportionate sentiment of the hashtag conversations were related to their tweet proportions. For example, the AFD with 41.2% had the highest sentiment shares and was with 39.98% the most sentiment-bearing Hashtag. The average sentiment per tweet slightly varied from -2.59 (LINKE) to -2.75 (AfD). The standard deviation was very high for all hashtag conversations.

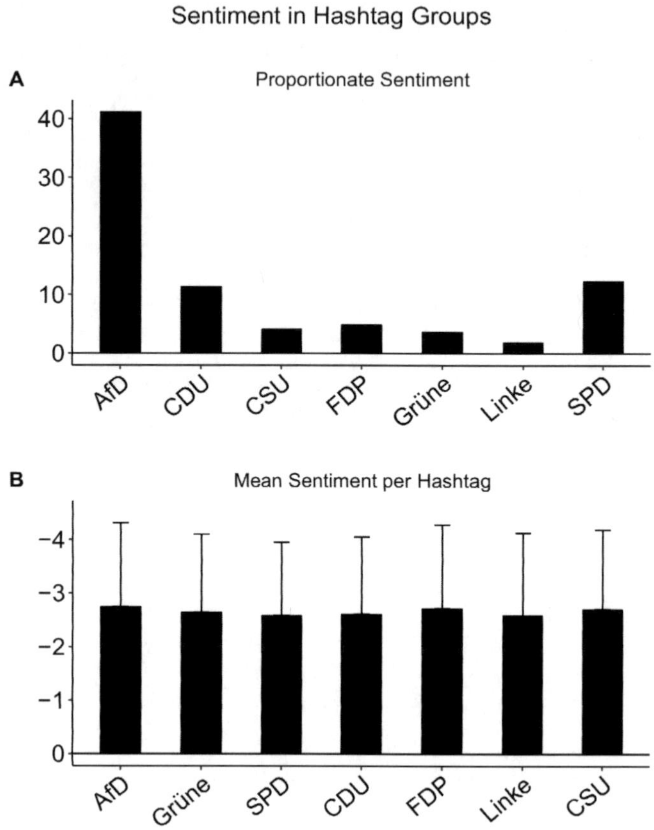

Figure 4. Sentiment per Hashtag Group

To investigate significant differences among the hashtag groups and the user groups in terms of sentiment, a Dunn test was performed [40] to compare group differences. Prior to the Dunn Test a Kruskal-Wallis test was performed to prove an existing effect of the actitivity and hastag groups on the sentiment. Table IV contains the associated p-values of the multiple mean comparisons.

TABLE IV. P-VALUES OF THE MULTIPLE MEAN COMPARISONS WITH THE DUNN TEST

Hashtag Group	1:9	1:90	9:90
AfD	0.349	0.047*	0.029*
CDU	0.018*	0.000***	0.000***
CSU	0.091	0.001**	0.017*
SPD	0.005**	0.000***	0.000***
LINKE	0.446	0.010*	0.002**
GRÜENE	0.188	0.225	0.329
FDP	0.000***	0.000***	0.180

$*p < 0.05$, $**p < 0.01$, $***p < 0.001$

For CDU and SPD, there were significant differences in moods between all activity groups (see Table IV). The sentiment becomes increasingly negative from the 90% group through the 9% group to the 1% group). For AfD, CSU and LEFT, the 90% group differed significantly from the other activity groups. Conversely, the pairwise comparisons of 1% and 9% showed no significant differences. For FDP, the 1% group differed significantly from the other two groups and for GRÜENE there were no significant differences between the activity groups.

E. Interpretation

The 10% of the most active users (1% and 9% together) generate more than three quarters of the content, while the remaining 90% together make up just under a quarter of the tweets. Reach via followers and retweets increases with user activity: the mood of highly active users (1% group) reaches on average more followers and their tweets are retweeted more often than those of the other activity groups. Tweets from the 9% group are most often favored. Around 68% of the total tweets produced are retweets, just under 25% are tweets and about 7% are answers. The sentiment polarity for the 2017 general election is positive after evaluation of the LIWC software and negative according to the results from SentiWS and GPSD. The sentiment between the activity groups shows significant differences and becomes more negative as users become more active. This trend is evident in all dictionaries. Especially the hashtag groups on CDU and SPD follows this observation, while other hashtags do not always show significant results. Although the sentiment differences are highly significant, the overall effect is rather low.

V. Conclusion and Future Work

We analyzed over one million tweets during the pre-election phase of the German federal elections in 2017. The overall results show that twitter is indeed an online platform for political discussion.

First, it will be discussed which spectrum of activity, expressed in terms of tweet share and reach, of highly active users on the political discussion on the 2017 German federal election on Twitter. The participation of highly active to active (1% - and 9% - group) and less active users (90% - group) is in the ratio 3: 1 (see Table II). 75% of the content is thus generated by a small, very active group. A similar trend was also observed in other political debates on Twitter: For example, in the Twitter debate on the 2009 general election, more than 40% of the news was produced by only 4% of the users [16]. This effect has been shown multiple times in past. News tweets comprising the standard political hashtag for political discussions #auspol in Australia, more than half were generated by the 1% most active users, while the majority of users remained inactive [36]. Howard and Kollanyi's (2017) Brexit referendum investigations also found that less than 1% of accounts accounted for almost one third of all content [17]. This strong imbalance in users' communication shares, which seems to emerge in political discussions on Twitter, can also be seen during the communication to the 2017 general election. The participation of the users in this dataset most likely seems to follow the rule that Bruns and Stieglitz refer to: A small minority of Twitter users dominate the discussion with their content.

However, the user groups not only generate different numbers of tweets, their contents are also differentially visible to the Twitter community: the average reach in terms of followers and retweets increases with the activity of the groups and peaks in the highly active user group. This suggests that highly active users may pass the generated mood to more users than the less active users due to the higher number of followers. Their content is also retweeted more frequently, reaching more potential readers. The level of influence of highly active users on the Twitter community about their increased reach therefore seems to be higher than that of less active accounts.

The SentiWS and GPSD lexicons produced negative averages for mood in the dataset, while the LIWC software was positive. It can be assumed that negative tweets and thus negative moods dominate the data set and the general communication surrounding the election. As described in Section II, there seems to be a trend towards negative overall attitudes in political debates on Twitter. This trend was largely confirmed in the present work. Negative sentiment during the election campaign could be attributed to the fact that negative campaigns against parties, and in this case against their party-specific hashtags, seem to have proven effective considering Twitter reach.

In contrast to Tumasjan et al. [16], this study could not directly link the amount of tweets posted to election results. Nevertheless, the study shows that Twitter can serve as a tool to study the political debate during an electoral phase. Since the hashtags in all hashtag groups contain both, positive and negative sentiment, the sole number of hashtag per group is a limited predictor for election outcome. The study has, however, several limitations. The integration of other linguistic methods, which take into account sentence structure, part of speech and word location (part of speech tagging, negation, reinforcing words) would be another step to increase the classification accuracy.

In addition, sentiment values could be calculated on the basis of fixed expressions and phrases instead of words. It might also be useful to introduce special adjustments to informal texts and the Twitter-specific language by, for example, incorporating common typos, urban speech, speller and Twitter-specific vocabulary into the algorithm. Samples from the data set in this context gave the impression that only few spelling and grammatical errors were made. This could be related to the seriousness of the issue: Actors in the political discussion want to preserve their reputation and credibility through clear and correct language.

Furthermore, emoticons could be investigated, since they have already been successfully embedded in the sentiment analysis of Twitter data in other works [21]. In the tweet texts, however, no significant amount of emoticons could be identified, which may be related to the fact that the political discussion is a more serious topic in which emotional expressions about emoticons are rather avoided. In order to increase the accuracy of classification, the calculation of the sentiment values at the sentence level could also be varied by calculating not the sum of all values, but the mean value. This standardization could more accurately capture the polarity of the text. At the same time, however, the information about the intensity of the mood would be lost.

References

[1] C. Thimm, J. Einspänner, and M. Dang-Anh, "Twitter als wahlkampfmedium [Twitter as a campaign medium]," Publizistik, vol. 57, no. 3, 2012, pp. 293–313.

[2] M. Meckel, C. Hoffmann, A. Suphan, and R. Poëll, "Politiker im netz: Treiber und hürden der social media-nutzung unter bundes-und landtagsabgeordneten. [Politicians online: Drivers and barriers of social media use among members of federal states parliaments and national parliaments]," vol. 24, 2013 (accessed September 3, 2018), pp. 1–71. [Online]. Available: http://www.isprat.net

[3] H. D. Wu and N. S. Dahmen, "Web sponsorship and campaign effects: Assessing the difference between positive and negative web sites," Journal of Political Marketing, vol. 9, no. 4, 2010, pp. 314–329.

[4] J. Ratkiewicz, M. D. Conover, M. Meiss, B. Goncalves, A. Flammini, and F. Menczer, "Detecting and tracking political abuse in social media," Proceedings of the 5th AAAI International Conference on Weblogs and Social Media (ICWSM'11), 2011, pp. 297–304.

[5] A. H. Wang, "Don't follow me: Spam detection in twitter," International Conference on Security and Cryptography (SECRYPT), 2010, pp. 142–151.

[6] S. Hegelich and D. Janetzko, "Are social bots on twitter political actors? empirical evidence from a ukrainian social botnet," ICWSM, 2016, pp. 579–582.

[7] C. Freitas, F. Benevenuto, S. Ghosh, and A. Veloso, "Reverse engineering socialbot infiltration strategies in twitter," in Proceedings of the 2015 IEEE/ACM International Conference on Advances in Social Networks Analysis and Mining 2015 - ASONAM '15, J. Pei, F. Silvestri, and J. Tang, Eds. New York, New York, USA: ACM Press, 2015, pp. 25–32.

[8] S. C. Woolley and P. N. Howard, "Political communication, computational propaganda, and autonomous agents - introduction," International Journal Of Communication, vol. 10, no. 9, 2016, pp. 4882–4890.

[9] Z. Chu, S. Gianvecchio, H. Wang, and S. Jajodia, "Who is tweeting on twitter: Human, bot, or cyborg?" in Proceedings of the 26th Annual Computer Security Applications Conference on - ACSAC '10, C. Gates, M. Franz, and J. McDermott, Eds. New York, New York, USA: ACM Press, 2010, pp. 21–30.

[10] F. Decker, "The alternative for germany: factors behind its emergence and profile of a new right-wing populist party," German Politics and Society, vol. 34, no. 2, 2016, pp. 1–16.

[11] N. Berbuir, M. Lewandowsky, and J. Siri, "The afd and its sympathisers: finally a right-wing populist movement in germany?" German Politics, vol. 24, no. 2, 2015, pp. 154–178.

[12] Büro des Bundeswahlleiters, "Bundestagswahl 2017: Endgültiges ergebnis [Federal election 2017: Final results of the federal returning officer]," 12.10.2017 (accessed September 3, 2018). [Online]. Available: https://www.bundeswahlleiter.de/info/presse/mitteilungen/bundestagswahl-2017/34_17_endgueltiges_ergebnis.html

[13] B. L. Ott, "The age of twitter: Donald j. trump and the politics of debasement," Critical Studies in Media Communication, vol. 34, no. 1, 2017, pp. 59–68.

[14] A. Ceron and G. d'Adda, "E-campaigning on twitter: The effectiveness of distributive promises and negative campaign in the 2013 italian election," New Media & Society, vol. 18, no. 9, 2016, pp. 1935–1955.

[15] S. Wattal, D. Schuff, M. Mandviwalla, and C. B. Williams, "Web 2.0 and politics: The 2008 u.s. presidential election and an e-politics research agenda," MIS Quarterly, vol. 34, no. 4, 2010, pp. 669–688.

[16] A. Tumasjan, T. O. Sprenger, P. G. Sandner, and I. M. Welpe, "Predicting elections with twitter: What 140 characters reveal about political sentiment," Proceedings of the Fourth International AAAI Conference on Weblogs and Social Media, 2010, pp. 178–185.

[17] P. N. Howard and B. Kollanyi, "Bots, #strongerin, and #brexit: Computational propaganda during the UK-EU referendum," CoRR, vol. abs/1606.06356, 2016, pp. 1–6. [Online]. Available: http://arxiv.org/abs/1606.06356

[18] A. Bakliwal, J. Foster, J. van der Puil, R. O'Brien, L. Tounsi, and M. Hughes, "Sentiment analysis of political tweets: Towards an accurate classifier," Proceedings of the Workshop on Language in Social Media (LASM 2013), 2013, pp. 49–58.

[19] A. Bessi and E. Ferrara, "Social bots distort the 2016 u.s. presidential election online discussion," First Monday, vol. 21, 11 2016, p. 1.

[20] N. Persily, "The 2016 us election: Can democracy survive the internet?" Journal of democracy, vol. 28, no. 2, 2017, pp. 63–76.

[21] A. Go, R. Bhayani, and L. Huang, "Twitter sentiment classification using distant supervision," Processing, no. 150, 2009, pp. 1–6.

[22] A. Bermingham and A. F. Smeaton, "Classifying sentiment in microblogs," in Proceedings of the 19th ACM international conference on Information and knowledge management - CIKM '10, J. Huang, N. Koudas, G. Jones, X. Wu, K. Collins-Thompson, and A. An, Eds. New York, New York, USA: ACM Press, 2010, pp. 1833–1837.

[23] L. Barbosa and J. Feng, "Robust sentiment detection on twitter from biased and noisy data," Coling 2010 - 23rd International Conference on Computational Linguistics, Proceedings of the Conference, 2010, pp. 36–44.

[24] C. Honey and S. C. Herring, "Beyond microblogging: Conversation and collaboration via twitter," in System Sciences, 2009. HICSS'09. 42nd Hawaii International Conference on. Ieee, 2009, pp. 1–10.

[25] F. Wanner, C. Rohdantz, F. Mansmann, D. Oelke, and D. A. Keim, "Visual sentiment analysis of rss news feeds featuring the us presidential election in 2008," Visual Interfaces to the Social and the Semantic Web (VISSW 2009), Sanibel Island, Florida, 8th February 2009, 2009, pp. 1–8.

[26] N. A. Diakopoulos and D. A. Shamma, "Characterizing debate performance via aggregated twitter sentiment," in Proceedings of the 28th international conference on Human factors in computing systems - CHI '10, E. Mynatt, D. Schoner, G. Fitzpatrick, S. Hudson, K. Edwards, and T. Rodden, Eds. New York, New York, USA: ACM Press, 2010, pp. 1195–1198.

[27] I. Twitter, "Instant historical access to tweets," 2018 (accessed September 3, 2018). [Online]. Available: https://developer.twitter.com/en/products/tweets

[28] ——, "Tweet data dictionary," 2018 (accessed September 3, 2018). [Online]. Available: https://developer.twitter.com/en/docs/tweets/data-dictionary/overview/tweet-object

[29] W. B. Cavnar and J. M. Trenkle, "N-gram-based text categorization," Proceedings of SDAIR-94, 3rd Annual Symposium on Document Analysis and Information Retrieval, 1994, pp. 161–175.

[30] M. Taboada, J. Brooke, M. Tofiloski, K. Voll, and M. Stede, "Lexicon-based methods for sentiment analysis," Computational linguistics, vol. 37, no. 2, 2011, pp. 267–307.

[31] R. Remus, U. Quasthoff, and G. Heyer, "Sentiws - a publicly available german-language resource for sentiment analysis," Proceedings of the 7th International Language Ressources and Evaluation (LREC'10), 2010, pp. 1168–1171.

[32] M. Wolf, A. B. Horn, M. R. Mehl, S. Haug, J. W. Pennebaker, and H. Kordy, "Computergestützte quantitative textanalyse," Diagnostica, vol. 54, no. 2, 2008, pp. 85–98.

[33] M. Haselmayer and M. Jenny, "Sentiment analysis of political communication: Combining a dictionary approach with crowdcoding," Quality & quantity, vol. 51, no. 6, 2017, pp. 2623–2646.

[34] Universität Leipzig, "Sentiws," 2018 (accessed September 3, 2018). [Online]. Available: http://wortschatz.uni-leipzig.de/de/download

[35] J. W. Pennebaker, M. E. Francis, and R. J. Booth, Linguistic Inquiry and Word Count – LIWC2001. Mahwah, N.J: Erlbaum, 2001.

[36] A. Bruns and S. Stieglitz, "Towards more systematic twitter analysis: Metrics for tweeting activities," International Journal of Social Research Methodology, vol. 16, no. 2, 2013, pp. 91–108.

[37] K. Weller, A. Bruns, J. Burgess, and M. Mahrt, Eds., Twitter and society, ser. Digital formations. New York, NY: Lang, 2014, vol. 89. [Online]. Available: https://www.peterlang.com/view/product/30225

[38] S. J. Tedjamulia, D. L. Dean, D. R. Olsen, and C. C. Albrecht, "Motivating content contributions to online communities: Toward a more comprehensive theory," in System Sciences, 2005. HICSS'05. Proceedings of the 38th Annual Hawaii International Conference on. IEEE, 2005, pp. 193b–193b.

[39] A. Bruns and S. Stieglitz, "Quantitative approaches to comparing communication patterns on twitter," Journal of Technology in Human Services, vol. 30, no. 3-4, 2012, pp. 160–185.

[40] O. J. Dunn, "Multiple comparisons among means," Journal of the American Statistical Association, vol. 56, no. 293, 1961, pp. 52–64.

Social Media and Google Trends in Support of Audience Analytics: Methodology and Architecture

Nikos Kalatzis, Ioanna Roussaki, Christos Matsoukas, Marios Paraskevopoulos, Symeon Papavassiliou
Institute of Communications and Computer Systems
Athens, Greece
e-mails: {nikosk@cn, ioanna.roussaki@cn, cmatsoukas@cn, mariosp@cn, papavass@mail}.ntua.gr

Simona Tonoli
European & Funded Projects Department
Mediaset
Milan, Italy
e-mail: Simona.Tonoli@mediaset.it

Abstract — **In recent years, there have been various research efforts aiming to investigate how social media are used to express or influence TV audiences and if possible to estimate TV ratings through the analysis of user interactions via social media. Given that these efforts are still in their infancy, there is a lack of an established methodology for designing such frameworks or services. This paper reviews the most dominant existing approaches and identifies the fundamental design principles aiming to generate best practices and guidelines for such systems. It then proposes a methodology and a reference architecture that can be employed by those that aim to exploit social media data to support audience analytics and extract TV ratings. Finally, this paper introduces and evaluates the utilisation of Google Trends service as an additional information source in support of audience analytics.**

Keywords-social media data; audience analytics; methodology; reference architecture; Twitter; Facebook; Google Trends.

I. INTRODUCTION

TV ratings have been crucial for the society due to the fact that they influence the popular culture, but also for the media industry as they are the basis for billions of dollars' worth of advertising transactions every year between marketers and media companies [1]. For more than 50 years, TV ratings are estimated by sampling the audience with specific installed hardware on TV devices. In the meantime, there is an increasing trend of people watching TV programs that on the same time are also interacting via social media services posting messages or other content mediating their opinions. In addition, new services are drastically changing the media consumption patterns as for example it is now possible to watch TV programs on YouTube regardless of location or time.

This proliferation of social media utilisation by large population portions along with recent advances in data collection, storage and management, makes available massive amounts of data to research organisations and data scientists. Exploiting the wealth of information originating from huge repositories generated for example by Twitter and Facebook has become of strategic importance for various industries. However, the availability of massive volumes of data doesn't automatically guarantee the extraction of useful results, while it becomes evident that robust research methodologies are more important than ever.

There are already various research efforts aiming to exploit data originating from social media sources in support of audience analytics. Until today, these efforts are mainly offered to complement the traditional TV ratings and do not aim to substitute them. However, as stated in [2], traditional approaches are demonstrating various limitations due to the fact that they are necessarily sample based with a relatively small number of installed metering devices due to the high cost of them. In addition, traditional approaches can hardly take into account new viewing behaviours such as the mobility of audience members and nonlinear viewing.

This paper aims to review the most dominant research efforts for social media analytics focusing on the extraction of additional insights about TV audiences. Based on this review and on authors' own evaluations, this paper proposes a five stage methodology and introduces a reference architecture that can be used as a starting point for any research work studying the usefulness of social media data for audience analytics purposes.

The rest of this paper is structured as follows. Section II reviews the main research initiatives that aim to extract audience analytics metrics by monitoring any related keyword-specific traffic across selected social media. Section III proposes a methodology for building a social-media based audience analytics framework and maps the most dominant related research initiatives to specific decisions made across the five steps of this methodology. Section IV introduces a reference architecture suitable for the implementation of such a framework. Section V presents experimental findings that support the extension of social media data sources with Google Trends data aiming to optimise the performance of the proposed audience analytics framework. Finally, conclusions are drawn and future plans are exposed.

II. RELATED WORK

In recent years, there is an increasing trend on analysing social media and Internet search engines utilisation for studying and examining behaviour of people with regards to various societal activities. The proper analysis of these services goes beyond the standard surveys or focus groups and has the potential to be a valuable information source leveraging internet users as the largest panel of users in the world. Researchers and analysts from a wide area of fields are able to reveal current and historic interests for communities of people and to extract valuable information about future trends, behaviours and preferences. Some of the fields where social media analytics have been employed for such purposes include: *economy* (stock market analysis [3] and private consumption prediction [4]), *politics* (opinion polls [5] and predictions of political elections [6]), *public health* (estimate spread of influenza [7] and malaria [8]), *sports* (predict football game results [9]), *tourism* (places to be visited by observing the most frequently attended places in a given location [10]), *demographics* (identifying gender and age of selected user groups [11]) and *infotainment* elaborated upon hereafter.

There are numerous research initiatives that apply social media analytics to estimate potential popularity of multimedia content. For example, authors in [12] propose a mechanism for predicting online content's popularity by analysing the activity of self-organized groups of users in social networks. Authors in [13] attempt to predict IMDB movie ratings using Google search frequencies for movie related information. Similarly, authors in [14] are applying social media analytics for predicting potential box office revenues for Bollywood movies based on related content shared over social networks. In the work presented in [15], social media and search engines utilisation are analysed during the pre-production phase of documentaries in order to identify appealing topics and potential audiences.

Based on the findings of the aforementioned initiatives, social media data demonstrate a relevant and flexible predictive power. The underlying relations among social media data and predictive variables not known a priori. The extraction of these variables and the utilisation of the appropriate algorithms can lead to quantitative statistical predictive models of several social targets of interest. A research field that gains significant attention with huge economical potential is the application of social media analytics in support of audience estimation for TV shows. Some of the existing efforts are presented here after.

One of the first approaches towards this scope is presented in [16]. Authors introduced concepts such as "Textual relevance", "Spatial Relevance", and "Temporal Relevance" along with the respective formulas for measuring the relevance of a Tweet with a targeted TV show. These metrics were utilized along with the total volumes of tweets and users for calculating the popularity of TV shows. However, cross-validation of this approach with ground truth data is missing.

The research presented in [17] mainly focuses on TV drama series that airs once a week. Authors attempt to estimate future audience volumes of TV shows through a predictor which is based on three layer back-propagation neural network. The predictor is fed with input from Facebook (e.g., number of related posts comments, likes, and shares) along with the ratings of the first show of the season and the rating of the previous show. According to the authors, the prediction accuracy of this approach based on Mean Absolute Percentage Error (MAPE) was from 6% to 24%.

The work presented in [18] is one of the first attempts for creating a statistical model with the goal of predicting the audience of a TV show from Twitter activity. Authors collected a large number of Tweets containing at least one of the official hash-tags of the targeted political talk shows. After analysing the data, a significant correlation was discovered between Twitter contributors per minute during airtime and the audience of the show's episode. Based on these results, a multiple regression model was trained with part of the dataset and utilized as a predictor for the remaining observations to evaluate its performance.

In [19], interactions between television audiences and social networks have been studied, focusing mainly on Twitter data. Authors collected about 2.5 million tweets in relation with 14 TV series in a nine-week period aired in USA. Initially, tweets were categorised according to their sentiment (positive, negative, neutral) based on the use of a decision trees classifier. Further analysis included the clustering of tweets based on the average audience characteristics for each individual series, while a linear regression model indicated the existence of a strong link between actual audience size and volume of tweets.

Authors in [20] defined a set of metrics based on Twitter data analysis in order to predict the audience of scheduled television programmes. Authors mainly focus on Italian TV reality shows, such as X Factor and Pechino Express where audiences are actively engaged. According to the authors, the most appropriate metrics are related to the volume of tweets, the distribution of linguistic elements, the volume of distinct users involved in tweeting, and the sentiment analysis of tweets. Based on these metrics, audience population prediction algorithms were developed that have been validated based on real audience ratings.

Similarly, research efforts presented in [2] and [21] are utilising Twitter data in an attempt to improve TV ratings, but these approaches lack extensive validation.

III. METHODOLOGY FOR BUILDING A SOCIAL-MEDIA BASED AUDIENCE ANALYTICS FRAMEWORK

In the last years, the vast use of social media gave us the ability to accurately predict or discover various events exploiting data freely available online. The most suitable methodology that enables researchers to build an efficient audience analytics mechanism based on social-media data has been studied by several initiatives [22]-[24]. Building on these and based on the main big-data mining principles [25]-[27], as well as on the online social network data collection and analytics trends and approaches [28]-[30], we propose a five-stage methodology that is depicted in Figure 1 and is briefly described in this section.

The five main steps that compose the proposed methodology for social media data exploitation in support of audience analytics are the following:

1. SM Data Identification

- Identify the most appropriate social media sources to be used such as popular SM networks (e.g., Twitter, Facebook, Google+, YouTube, LinkedIn, Pinterest, Instagram, Tumblr, Reddit, Tumblr, Snapchat, etc.) or more focused sources (e.g., web fora, blogs, message boards, news sites, podcasts, Wikis, etc.).

- Identify the type of data (e.g., comments, tweets, posts, likes, shares, links, connections, user account details, etc.) to be collected.
- Specify the criteria to be used for data collection (e.g., keywords, hashtags, timeframe, geographic area, language, user account properties, etc.)

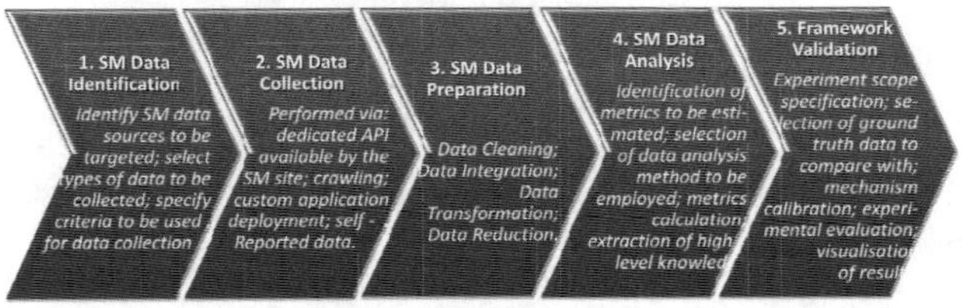

Figure 1. Social media data mining methodology in support of audience analytics.

2. SM Data Collection

- Most often, the SM sites provide an Application Programming Interface (API) that can be used by the developers to collect data based on the type and criteria specified in previous Phase. In this case, initially the necessary libraries need to be installed, the authorization needs to be obtained and finally a decision needs to be made regarding the platform/language to be used for writing the data collection software.
- In case no such API is made available by the SM site, crawling can alternatively be used with an automated script that explores the social media website and collects data using HTTP requests and responses.
- Another method that enables collection of SM data is the implementation and deployment of a custom application based on an SM site that monitors its usage.
- If the methods above cannot be employed, self-reported data can be used instead, which requires for directly asking the users about their interests, opinion, experience, etc., mainly via online questionnaires or in-situ surveys.

  Various shortcomings and limitations need to be carefully addressed during the "Data Collection" phase. For example, the standard version of Twitter API enforces "Rate Limits" allowing a certain number of calls on 15 minute intervals. In addition, the standard Twitter API allows the retrieval of Tweets for a period of the last 7 days. In a similar manner, Facebook enforces strict privacy protection policies which are limiting the amount of information that can be retrieved. These policies are subject to frequent updates which services consuming the APIs should follow.

3. SM Data Preparation

- Data cleaning (or cleansing) aims to fill in missing values, smooth out noisy data, identify and remove outliers, minimise duplication and computed biases, and correct inconsistencies within the data collected in the previous phase. Given that data are collected based on criteria such as the inclusion of a keyword or a hashtag it is highly possible that the actual Tweet or Facebook post to be irrelevant with the targeted show. In a similar manner, during this phase data generated by automated software scripts – known as bots – should also be identified and filtered out.
- Data integration combines data from multiple social media sources into a coherent store, while it aims to detect and resolve any data value conflicts or data redundancies that may arise in this process.
- Data transformation converts the raw social media data into the specified format, model or structure. Methods used for this purpose include: normalization (where numerical data is converted into the specified range, i.e., between 0 and one so that scaling of data can be performed), aggregation/ summarisation (to combine features into one), generalization or attribute/feature construction (where lower level attributes are converted to a higher standard or new attributes are constructed from the given ones in general) and discretization (where raw values of a numeric attribute are replaced by interval labels).
- Data reduction aims to obtain a reduced representation of the social media data set collected that is much smaller in volume but yet produces the same (or almost the same) analytical results. Methods employed for this purpose include: data compression, data sampling, and dimensionality reduction (e.g., removing unimportant attributes) and multiplicity reduction (to reduce data volume by choosing alternative, smaller/more compact forms of data representation).

4. SM Data Analysis

- At this stage the pre-processed SM data collected need to be analysed in order to extract results linked with the popularity of the broadcasted TV program. Specific metrics are defined indicating audience statistics aspects, such as: number of messages referring to the targeted show (e.g., tweets, posts), number of interactions associated with a post (e.g., liked, favorited, retweeted, shared, etc.), number of unique users participated in the overall interactions. In some cases, researches are setting their own objective functions and define their own scores for evaluating the generated Social Media buzz.
- Aiming to identify correlations between the Social media data and the actual audience's interest, the following statistical approaches are often utilised by the research community: Logistic Regression (LR), Density Based Algorithm (DBA), Hierarchical Clustering (HC), AdaBoost, Linear-Regression(Lin-R), Markov, Maximum Entropy (ME), Genetic Algorithms (GA), Fuzzy, Apriori, Wrapper, etc.
- Inference of higher level information based on the analysis of raw collected data aiming to extract additional characteristics of the audience. Processing raw data through sophisticated algorithms allows the extraction of information that are not provided by directly by SM APIs, such as the classification of a post/tweet with regards the sentiment (positive,

negative, neutral) and the profile of the SM user (e.g., gender, age, political views, hobbies, other preferences). Towards this scope, there are numerous data analytics techniques that have been applied by researchers [31], each suitable for specific problems and domains. These tasks are usually handled as a classification/ categorization problem.

5. Framework Validation

- Validation of the outcomes generated by the Data Analysis step allows drawing the respective conclusions whether and in which extent the overall approach achieved the desired outcomes. Within the scope of estimating audience volumes interested or watched a TV show through the analysis of SM data, often the Data Analysis results are cross-validated with published audience rates metrics.
- These metrics also contain audience profile information (e.g., age, gender, location, occupation) hence advanced analysis methods can also be cross validated. However, these metrics are not always publicly available or the published measurements are generic and not include details about the profile of audiences.
- So far, realisation of such techniques has revealed various shortcomings mainly related to the over or/and under representation of certain societal groups within SM services. Statistical approaches for validation include but are not limited to: Root Mean Square Error, Mean Absolute Error, Pearson correlation coefficient, Akaike Information Criterion, etc.

The proposed methodology described herewith has been used by the authors in several situations in the domain of social media data exploitation for audience analytics or prediction purposes. In all occasions, it has proven to be very effective, when proper elements and configuration are employed at each stage.

As already stated, the five-step methodology is the outcome of a thorough review of the most dominant state of the art approaches in the area of social-media data processing in support of TV show audience analytics. To this end, Table 1 presents a summary of this analysis, where the various steps employed by the most popular approaches presented in the state of the art review in Section II are mapped to the main elements of the methodology proposed herewith, while the specific mechanisms employed are identified.

TABLE I. MAPPING THE MOST DOMINANT STATE OF THE ART WORK TO THE PROPOSED METHODOLOGY STEPS

Reference	Step#	Step Elements
[2]	**Step 1**	Japan geo-tagged tweets containing hashtags related with the show and the TV channel. Targeted genres of shows are: News, documentary, talk show, life style
	Step 2	Native Twitter API
	Step 3	Algorithm for calculating score reflecting the relevance of tweets with targeted show
	Step 4	Identification of overall popularity of the show based on the volume of "relevant" tweets and the absolute number of users
	Step 5	No cross-validation with ground truth data
[20]	**Step 1**	Tweets containing hashtag related to Reality shows in Italy
	Step 2	Collection of Tweets based on "Twitter Vigilance" multiuser tool developed for research purposes
	Step 3	Sentiment Analysis based on a score for positive, negative, and neutral mood
	Step 4	Predict audience of scheduled TV programmes based on volumes of (re)tweets, of unique users "tweeting", sentiment analysis scores for each textual element in the tweets. Statistical approaches utilised are: Principal Component Analysis, Multi-linear Regression & Ridge Models
	Step 5	RMSE-Root Mean Square Error, MAE - Mean Absolute Error
[19]	**Step 1**	Tweets containing the official hashtag of selected popular USA TV series, possible hashtag derivatives, official account of the television program.
	Step 2	Python script, interacting with Twitter Streaming API that allows for real-time downloading of tweets containing certain keywords.
	Step 3	Sentiment categorization based on Knime Decision Trees algorithm. Manual classification for an initial set of 14,000 tweets.
	Step 4	Audience prediction estimation based on the calculation of volumes of positive, neutral and negative tweets considering different time frame windows: (i) within 3 hours after episode start, (ii) within 24 hours after episode start Statistical approaches utilised are: Linear Regression Models
	Step 5	p-value and t-test significant test
[17]	**Step 1**	Data from Facebook "fan pages" regarding the TV shows: #page posts, #fans posts, #page posts comments, #fans posts likes, #fans posts shares, #fans posts comments, #page posts likes. Taiwan: TV drama series aired once a week.
	Step 2	Facebook API for collecting data from the official page of the show
	Step 3	Repeated respondents in the same article were filtered out to avoid large amount of increased responses due to special events (such as quizzes or Facebook Meeting Rooms, etc.)
	Step 4	Accumulation of the broadcasted TV programs' word-of mouth on Facebook and apply the Backpropagation Neural Network to predict the latest program audience rating.
	Step 5	Mean Absolute Error, Mean Absolute Percentage Errors
[21]	**Step 1**	Tweets containing only the most commonly used TV shows hashtags Netherlands: Country's top-25 TV shows with high number of tweets. #tweets #hashtags (tweets posted half an hour before broadcast, during broadcast and half an hour after the end on the shows)
	Step 2	Native Twitter API
	Step 3	None
	Step 4	Correlation of tweets volumes with audience measurements with the utilisation of Linear Regression Models.
	Step 5	Pearson correlation coefficient
[32]	**Step 1**	Official Facebook page of TV show. USA: Reality, Drama and Sports series. Average engagement per post, Fans on Facebook, Posts in Total, Links in Total, Photos in Total, Videos in Total, Included question post in Total, Unique engaged audiences on Facebook
	Step 2	Facebook API
	Step 3	Not specified
	Step 4	Data Visualization of Correlations, PCA for Dimension Reduction, Multiple Regression Analysis
	Step 5	Akaike Information Criterion, Bayesian Information Criterion, ANOVA, Word Cloud Analysis

IV. PROPOSED ARCHITECTURE FOR SOCIAL MEDIA-BASED AUDIENCE ANALYTICS

Based on the proposed methodology and building on the architectures proposed by the most popular state of the art related initiatives, this section proposes a reference architecture suitable for social media based audience analytics. Among the design principles of this architecture is the ability of the service to query various Social Media

Services (e.g., Twitter and Facebook) through pluggable connectors for each service. The respective high level functional view is presented in Figure 2 and its core modules are described hereafter.

RestAPI: It exposes the backend's functionality v a REST endpoint. The API specifies a set of SM data mining functions where the service consumer provides as input various criteria such as data sources, data types, keywords, topics, geographical regions, time periods, etc.

SM Data Query Management: This component orchestrates the overall execution of the queries and the processing of the replies. Given the input from the user (e.g., targeted keywords, targeted location, time frame) several properly formulated queries are generated that are forwarded to the respective connectors/wrappers to dispatch the requests to several existing Social Media services available online. The SM Data Query Management enforces querying policies tailored to each service in order to optimize the utilization of the services and to avoid potential bans.

Social Media Connectors: A set of software modules that support the connection and the execution of queries to external services through the provided available APIs or via tailored crawlers. Connectors are embedding all the necessary security related credentials to the calls and automate the initiation of a session with the external services. Thus, the connectors automate and ease the actual formulation and execution of the queries issued by the SM Data Query Management component. Some example APIs that are utilized by the connectors are: Twitter API, YouTube Data API v3, Facebook API.

SM Data Collection Engine: Given that each external service will reply in different time frames (e.g., a call to Google Trends discovery replies within a few seconds while Twitter stream analysis might take longer time periods) the overall process is performed in an asynchronous manner, coordinated by the Data Collection Engine,

SM Data Pre-processor: This module performs the necessary data cleaning aiming to improve the quality of the collected data and to prepare them for the actual data analysis through data transformation mechanisms that models raw data into a uniform model.

SM Data Analytics Engine: This module maintains a repository of statistical and data mining methods that can be applied on data sets previously prepared by the SM Data Pre-processor module.

Analysis Results Database Management: The outcome from various data analysis tasks are maintained to a local database. The Database Management module supports the creation, retrieval, update and deletion of data objects. Hence, it is feasible for the user to compare analysis tasks reports performed in the past with more recent ones and have an intuitive view of the evolution of trend reports in time.

Front End: The Front-End visualizes the results providing the following output: (i) various graphs presenting the absolute volume of retrieved messages (e.g., number of tweets, number of Facebook posts), (ii) calculated scores indicating audience interest for different shows, per location (country), time period, (iii) higher level information e.g., audience's sentiment or gender.

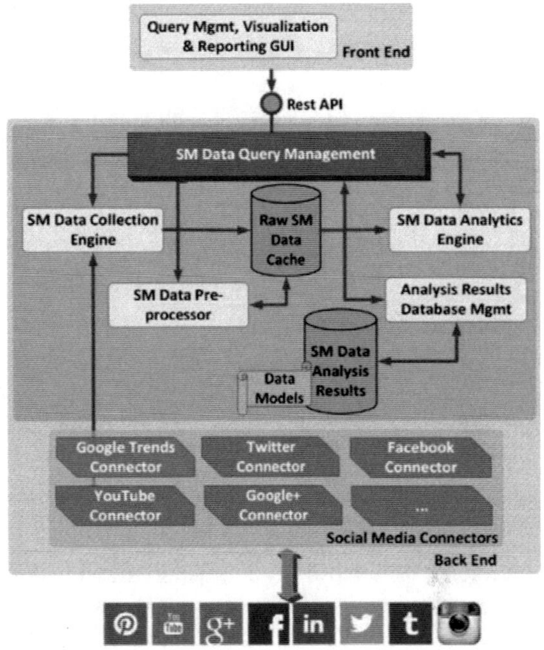

Figure 2. Reference Architecture for using social media data to support audience analytics.

A proof of concept of the described architecture has been implemented in Python 3 programming language. For the SM Data Analytics Engine the scikit-learn [33] python package has been integrated, while results are stored in a MySQL relational database. Currently connectors for Twitter, Facebook and Google Trends have been integrated.

V. WHAT ABOUT GOOGLE TRENDS?

Based on the state of the art review, the research work conducted so far by various initiatives on the domain of Social Media data usage to extract information related to audience analytics focuses on Twitter and Facebook. In certain occasions, the obtained results are not of adequate quality and reliability. In an attempt to treat this, the authors are currently experimenting with using additional information obtained via Google Trends [34]. Google Trends is a public web facility of Google Inc. that presents how often a specific search-term is entered on Google Search relative to the total search-volume across various regions of the world, and in various languages. The idea is to couple this information with data extracted by Twitter for example in the framework of a TV show or program in order to enhance the quality of the respective audience statistics extracted.

In an initial attempt to evaluate this approach, we focused on the Italian talent show "Amici di Maria de Filippi" that broadcasts for the last 17 years and lies among the most popular shows in Italy. The show airs annually from October until June, thus being appropriate for yearly examination of the data. In this study, data of the year 2017 have been used, split in two semesters as elaborated upon subsequently.

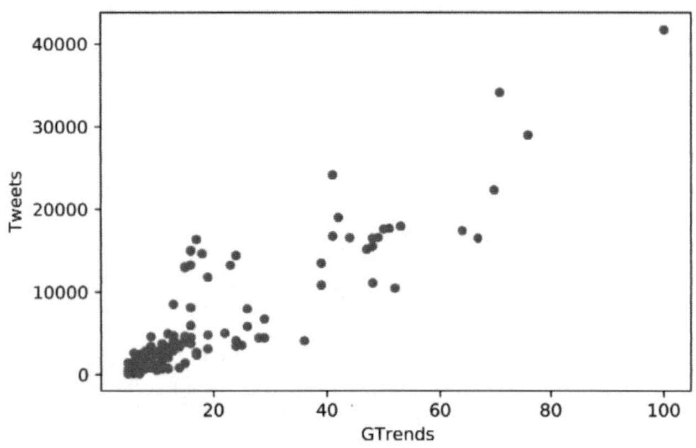

Figure 3. Correlation of Google Trends and Twitter data for the term '#amici16' targeting the first semester of 2017

Google Trends (GTrends) provides a variety of chronological and geographical metrics that show the search activity for the term in question. The one used in this study is a time series of the relative search figures -search volume for the term divided by the total volume of the day- normalized between 0 and 100. One limitation of the platform is that one can only get daily figures for a maximum range of 270 days, which of course is less than a year. To overcome this obstacle, the year has been split in two semesters, which also allows us not to mix results, since the TV season starts during the second semester of the year. Data from GTrends require no further processing, since they are provided in the format required for this experiment.

On the other hand, the data obtained via Twitter have been extracted on a monthly basis and have been grouped based on date in order to acquire the daily volume. Tweets retrieval was based on the hashtags '#amiciXX' where XX corresponds to the number of the consequent season that the show is aired. During the period January -June 2017 and based on the hashtag '#amici16' there where 882024 tweets collected while during the period July to December 2017 and based on the hashtag '#amici17' there where 135288 tweets collected.

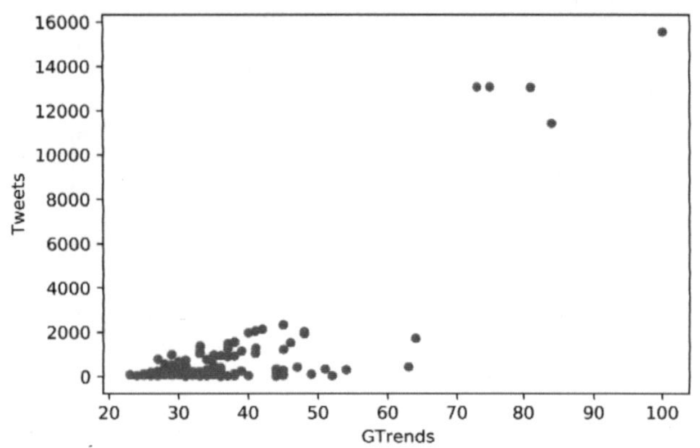

Figure 4. Correlation of Google Trends and Twitter data for the term '#amici17' targeting the second semester of 2017.

In order to verify the correlation between data originating from Google Trends and those originating from Twitter, the Pearson correlation coefficient was utilised. The obtained results for the first semester of 2017 are illustrated in Figure 3 and lead to coefficient of 0.893 and to significance of approximately 10-32. This indicates that the two datasets are strongly correlated, since we secured that the figures of each set are matched 1-1 and the low significance ensures that this result cannot be produced randomly. The respective outcomes for the second semester of 2017 are presented in Figure 4 and lead to correlation coefficient of 0.816 and to significance of about 10-30. The slightly lower correlation demonstrated can be fully justified by the fact that the show does not broadcast during the summer and thus there is lower activity both on Twitter, as well as on Google, resulting in lower correlation results. Nevertheless, the findings indicate a strong relation between Twitter and Google Trends data. The aforementioned results confirm what the authors originally expected: Data obtained from Google Trends and Twitter at the same period and subject are strongly (linearly) correlated and this of course can be further exploited in a variety of research purposes.

VI. CONCLUSIONS & FUTURE PLANS

This paper presents a review of existing research initiatives that exploit online user activity data across social media to extract information linked to audience statistics and TV ratings. Among the core findings of this analysis is that existing mechanisms can mainly act as a complement approach to the traditional TV ratings, but are not able yet to fully substitute them. However, there is an imperative need to further investigate such mechanisms, as traditional audience metering approaches are demonstrating various limitations, especially due to the change of viewing behaviours such as audience's mobility and nonlinear viewing.

Most of the investigated approaches employ common data analysis steps that have been studied herewith, along with the prevailing statistical and data mining methods utilised. Building on these and considering the online social network data collection and analytics trends and approaches, this paper proposed a five-stage methodology that enables any interested party to build an efficient audience analytics mechanism based on social-media data. Based on the defined methodology and building on the architectures proposed by the most effective state of the art related initiatives, a reference architecture in support of social-media based audience analytics extraction is introduced and elaborated upon. Finally, this paper identifies Google Trends as a valuable source of information that, to the best of the authors' knowledge, has so far not been investigated by any of the existing approaches on this topic. Future plans include further evaluation of the proposed methodology and architecture by extracting qualitative and quantitative audiences' characteristics and metrics in various settings, and cross validating these with ground truth data collected with the traditional audience rating measurement approaches. Moreover, the authors have already kicked off an extended evaluation of the usability of Google Trends in the application domain of TV show audience analytics based on several shows and couple the respective data with other SM data to improve the quality and accuracy of the estimated and predicted TV ratings.

ACKNOWLEDGMENT

This work has been supported by the European Commission, Horizon 2020 Framework Program for research and innovation under grant agreement no. 65020601.

REFERENCES

[1] S. Sereday and J. Cui, "Using machine learning to predict future tv ratings", Data Science, Nielsen, Vol. 1, No. 3, pp. 3-12, Feb. 2017.

[2] S. Wakamiya, R. Lee, and K. Sumiya, "Towards better TV viewing rates: exploiting crowd's media life logs over twitter for TV rating", 5th ACM Int. Conf. on ubiquitous information management and communication, pp. 412-421, Feb. 2011.

[3] F. Ahmed, R. Asif, S. Hina, and M. Muzammil, "Financial Market Prediction using Google Trends", Int. Journal of Advanced Computer Science and Applications, Vol. 8, No.7, pp. 388-391, July 2017.

[4] N. Askitas and K.F. Zimmermann, "Google econometrics and unemployment forecasting", Applied Economics Quarterly, Vol. 55, No. 2, pp. 107-120, Apr. 2009.

[5] B. O'Connor, R. Balasubramanyan, B.R. Routledge, and N.A. Smith, "From tweets to polls: linking text sentiment to public opinion time series", 4th AAAI Int. Conf. on Weblogs and Social Media (ICWSM 2010), pp. 122–129, May 2010.

[6] A. Tumasjan, T. Sprenger, P.G. Sandner, and I.M. Welpe, "Predicting elections with twitter: what 140 characters reveal about political sentiment", 4th AAAI Int. Conf. on Weblogs and Social Media (ICWSM 2010), pp. 178–185, May 2010.

[7] A. J. Ocampo, R. Chunara, and J. S. Brownstein, "Using search queries for malaria surveillance, Thailand", Malaria Journal, Vol. 12, pp. 390-396, Nov. 2013.

[8] S. Yang, et al., "Using electronic health records and Internet search information for accurate influenza forecasting", BMC Infectious Diseases (BMC series), Vol. 17, pp. 332-341, May 2017.

[9] S. Sinha, C. Dyer, K. Gimpel, and N.A. Smith, "Predicting the NFL Using Twitter", Machine Learning and Data Mining for Sports Analytics Workshop (ECML/PKDD 2013), pp. 137-147, Sep. 2013.

[10] A. Chauhan, K. Kummamuru, and D. Toshniwal, "Prediction of places of visit using tweets", Knowledge and Information Systems Journal, Vol. 50, No. 1, pp. 145-166 , Jan. 2017.

[11] O. Giannakopoulos, N. Kalatzis, I. Roussaki, and S. Papavassiliou, "Gender Recognition Based on Social Networks for Multimedia Production", 13th IEEE Image, Video, and Multidimensional Signal Processing Workshop (IVMSP 2018), IEEE Press, Jun. 2018, pp. 1-5, doi: 10.1109/IVMSPW.2018.8448788

[12] M.X. Hoang , X. Dang , X. Wu , Z. Yan, and A.K. Singh, "GPOP: Scalable Group-level Popularity Prediction for Online Content in Social Networks", 26th Int. Conf. on World Wide Web, pp. 725-733, Apr. 2017.

[13] A. Oghina, M. Breuss, M. Tsagkias, and M. de Rijke, "Predicting IMDB movie ratings using social media", 34th European Conf. on Advances in Information Retrieval (ECIR 2012), pp. 503-507, Apr. 2012.

[14] B. Bhattacharjee, A. Sridhar, and A. Dutta, "Identifying the causal relationship between social media content of a Bollywood movie and its box-office success-a text mining approach", Int. Journal of Business Information Systems, Vol. 24, No. 3, pp. 344-368, 2017.

[15] G. Mitsis, N. Kalatzis, I. Roussaki, E. Tsiropoulou, S. Papavassiliou, and S. Tonoli, "Social Media Analytics in Support of Documentary Production", 10th International Conference on Creative Content Technologies (CONTENT 2018) IARIA, Feb. 2018, pp. 7-13, ISSN: 2308-4162, ISBN: 978-1-61208-611-8

[16] S. Wakamiya, R. Lee, and K. Sumiya, "Crowd-Powered TV Viewing Rates: Measuring Relevancy between Tweets and TV Programs", Int. Conf. on Database Systems for Advanced Applications (DASFAA 2011), pp. 390-401, Apr. 2011.

[17] W. Hsieh, Y. Cheng, S.T. Chou, and C. Wu, "Predicting tv audience rating with social media", Workshop on Natural Language Processing for Social Media (SocialNLP) under 6th Int. Joint Conf. on Natural Language Processing (IJCNLP 2013), pp. 1–5, Oct. 2013.

[18] F. Giglietto, "Exploring correlations between TV viewership and twitter conversations in Italian political talk shows", Aug. 2013, doi: 10.2139/ssrn.2306512.

[19] L. Molteni and J. Ponce De Leon, "Forecasting with twitter data: an application to Usa Tv series audience", Int. Journal of Design & Nature and Ecodynamics, Vol. 11, No. 3, pp. 220–229, Jul. 2016.

[20] A. Crisci, et. al, "Predicting TV programme audience by using twitter based metrics", Multimedia Tools and Applications Journal, Vol. 77, No. 10, pp. 12203–12232, May 2018.

[21] B. Sommerdijk, E. Sanders, and A. van den Bosch, "Can Tweets Predict TV Ratings?", 10th Int. Conf. on Language Resources and Evaluation (LREC 2016), pp. 2965-1970, May 2016.

[22] C. Oh, S. Sasser, and S. Almahmoud, "Social Media Analytics Framework: The Case of Twitter and Super Bowl Ads", Journal of Information Technology Management, Journal of Information Technology Management, Vol. 26, No. 1, pp. 1-18, Jan. 2015.

[23] M.H. Cheng, Y.C. Wu, and M.C. Chen, "Television Meets Facebook: The Correlation between TV Ratings and Social Media", American Journal of Industrial and Business Management, Vol. 6, No. 3, pp. 282-290, Mar. 2016.

[24] W. Fan and M. Gordon, "The Power of Social Media Analytics", Communications of the ACM, Vol. 57, No.6, pp.74-81, June 2014.

[25] A. Gandomi and M. Haider, "Beyond the hype: Big data concepts, methods, and analytics", Int. Journal of Information Management, Vol. 35, No. 2, pp. 137-144, Apr. 2015.

[26] X. Wu, X. Zhu, G.Q. Wu, and W. Ding, "Data Mining with Big Data", IEEE Transactions on Knowledge and Data Engineering, Vol. 26, No. 1, pp. 97-107, Jan. 2014.

[27] K. Kambatla, G. Kollias, V. Kumar, and A. Grama, "Trends in big data analytics", Journal of Parallel and Distributed Computing, Vol. 74, No. 7, pp. 2561-2573, July 2014.

[28] A. Gandomi and M. Haider, "Beyond the hype: Big data concepts, methods, and analytics", Int. Journal of Information Management, Vol. 35, No. 2, pp. 137-144, Apr. 2015.

[29] X. Wu, X. Zhu, G.Q. Wu, and W. Ding, "Data Mining with Big Data", IEEE Transactions on Knowledge and Data Engineering, Vol. 26, No. 1, pp. 97-107, Jan. 2014.

[30] K. Kambatla, G. Kollias, V. Kumar, and A. Grama, "Trends in big data analytics", Journal of Parallel and Distributed Computing, Vol. 74, No. 7, pp. 2561-2573, July 2014.

[31] M.N. Injadat, F. Salo, and A.B. Nassif, "Data mining techniques in social media: A survey", Neurocomputing, Vol. 214, pp. 654–670, Nov. 2016.

[32] J. Min, Q. Zang, and Y. Liu, "The influence of social media engagement on TV program ratings", 2015 Systems & Information Engineering Design Symposium, pp. 283-288, Apr. 2015.

[33] http://scikit-learn.org/ [accessed July 2018]

[34] https://trends.google.com/ [accessed July 2018]

Stance Classification Using Political Parties in Tokyo Metropolitan Assembly Minutes

Yasutomo Kimura

Otaru University of Commerce
Department of Information and Management Science
Hokkaido, Japan
Email: kimura@res.otaru-uc.ac.jp

Minoru Sasaki

Ibaraki University
Ibaraki, Japan
Department of Computer and Information Sciences
Email: minoru.sasaki.01@vc.ibaraki.ac.jp

***Abstract*—Stance classification is an important component of argument mining. We focus on politicians' utterances in assembly minutes to classify political parties affiliation. This paper describes a novel stance classification task that classifies each politician's utterance for the politician's stance. Our task is to classify politicians into 20 political parties using their utterances in the Metropolitan Assembly minutes. Japanese assembly members are divided into many political parties in the local assembly. Our proposal is to apply several baseline methods to our novel dataset, which includes political parties in the Metropolitan Assembly minutes. In this paper, we define a political stance for a political party in Japan. We assess the difficulty of our dataset to evaluate several baseline methods, such as Support Vector machines (SVM), decision tree, random forest, and Naive Bayes.**

Keywords–Stance classification; Political party; Local assembly minutes.

I. Introduction

Automatic classification is abundant in social science research, such as political science and economics [1], and stance classification is a core component of argument mining [2][3]. We address the problem of classifying politicians' stances in terms of political parties. Previous research has defined a stance classification as a binary classification [4][5], and the datasets are usually generated by tweets or debates.

In this paper, we propose a novel stance classification approach to political parties using both assembly minutes and political parties. We define a political stance for a political party in Japan. The Japanese governmental structure of local governing bodies is called a dualistic representative structure. Assembly members interrogate a governor to confirm whether the governor's master plans should be carried out. These questions and answers are recorded in the assembly minutes, which are transcripts instead of summarized texts in Japan.

Furthermore, our goal is to classify each assembly member's political stance using the Tokyo Metropolitan Assembly minutes. Politicians' stances occasionally change over time, and each politician's stance depends on the individual political issue. Thus, there should be a large spectrum of political stances.

We focus on political parties in the Tokyo Metropolitan Assembly minutes in Japan. The number of political parties in the assembly minutes is usually higher than the number of national parties; there were 20 Tokyo Metropolitan parties between 2011 and 2015.

The main interest of this research is that political stance is primarily a question of classification using domestic political parties. In Japan, assembly members occasionally change political parties through their policies. Previous classification tasks have not used the content of the utterances to classify political stances that reflect political beliefs.

Our contributions can be summarized as follows:

1) Novel dataset for stance classification: We created a corpus for stance classification using political parties exceptional to Japan.
2) New approach to stance classification: Our task was to classify each assembly member into multiple political parties.
3) Evaluation of task difficulty: We applied the previous methods to the dataset.

The rest of this paper is organized as follows. Section II briefly reviews related work on the stance classification. Section III describes the classification of the political party. Section IV describes the experiment. Finally, we conclude this paper in Section V.

II. Related Work

Stance classification is the challenge faced when classifying the attitude taken by an author in a text.

In the International Workshop on Semantic Evaluation, SemEval-2016 Task-6 focused on detecting political stance in tweets [3]. The task is a shared task for detecting stance in tweets; given a tweet and a target entity, such as "Hillary Clinton" and "Legalization of Abortion". A system must determine whether the tweet is in favor of the given target, against the given target, or neither. For articles that mention the claim, the data is divided into the following three stances: "for", "against" and "observing." They classified articles into three stances.

This paper described public debate functions as forums for both expressing and forming opinions, which is an important aspect of public life [4]. It attempted to classify posts in online debates based on the position or stance that a speaker takes on an issue, such as favoring or obstructing the issue.

Information about a political party was used for stance classification [6]; however, the political party was only used as a feature of classification. They annotated six contexts as features, such as political party, profile, and tweet.

III. Classification of Political Party

A. Task Definition

This task is a classification for determining the political party from an assembly member's utterances. We focused on the Tokyo Metropolitan Assembly minutes as a political dataset. Previous research has created a corpus of the local assembly minutes of 47 prefectures from April 2011 to March 2015 [7]. We provided the political party information to the Tokyo Metropolitan Assembly minutes. The dataset comprised 36,046 lines.

B. Dataset

Figure 1 presents an image of the dataset, which includes a speaker's name, utterance, and political party in the Tokyo Metropolitan Assembly. We used a party identification number (ID) as the political party information. Each utterance included a specific topic, such as the new Tokyo bank, the Tokyo Olympics or a care insurance system. We divided the dataset into portions of the Metropolitan Assembly minutes. In addition, we divided the utterances into a training dataset and a test dataset with the percentage ratio 8:2; the first portion was the training data, which constituted 80% (421 utterances) of the dataset, and the second portion was the test data, which constituted 20% (106 utterances) of the dataset. There were 527 assembly members in total and 174 distinct members.

The dataset contained the minutes of the Tokyo Metropolitan Assembly from April 2011 to March 2015. Japan is divided into 47 prefectures, including Tokyo, Kyoto and Osaka. The corpus contained the local assembly minutes of the 47 prefectures from April 2011 to March 2015 [7], a four-year period that coincides with the term of office for assembly members in most autonomy. In this study, we focused on the Tokyo Metropolitan Assembly minutes in Japan, and used a dataset comprising politicians' utterances and political parties in the assembly minutes. This classification model was used to build a classifier for political party by each politician's utterance. We attempted to classify political parties affiliation in the Tokyo Metropolitan Assembly. Table I contains 20 political parties that are in the Tokyo Metropolitan Assembly.

TABLE I. NAME OF 20 POLITICAL PARTIES IN THE TOKYO METROPOLITAN ASSEMBLY. THESE POLITICAL PARTIES ARE THE POLITICAL STANCES.

ID	Abbreviation	Name of political party
0	DP	Democratic Party
1	TMK	Tokyo Metropolitan Komeito
2	TMLDP	Tokyo Metropolitan Liberal Democratic Party
3	CN	Consumer Network
4	JCPTMA	Japan Communist in Party Tokyo Metropolitan Assembly
5	AC	Autonomous Citizen
6	JCPTMG	Japan Communist Party in Tokyo Metropolitan Government
7	I	Independent
8	I(R)	Independent (Restoration)
9	TRP	Tokyo Restoration Party
10	I(FALDP)	Independent (Fresh Air Liberal Democratic Party)
11	JRP	Japan Restoration Party
12	TMAEP	Tokyo Metropolitan Assembly Everyone's Party
13	EP	Everyone's Party
14	EPT	Everyone's Party Tokyo
15	TMCR	Tokyo Metropolitan Combination and Restoration
16	I(DBT)	Independent (Deep Breathable Tokyo)
17	BT	Bright Tokyo
18	TMRP	Tokyo Metropolitan Restoration Party
19	I(TEI)	Independent (Tokyo Everyone's Innovation)

IV. Experiment

The purpose of this study was to evaluate the difficulty of the dataset. Our task was to classify politicians into 20 political parties using their utterances in the Tokyo Metropolitan Assembly minutes.

A. Method

We assessed the difficulty of our dataset to evaluate several classification methods, such as SVM, Naive Bayes, k-nearest neighbor, random forest and decision trees. We constructed word vectors from segmented words. Experimental data were segmented into words using the Japanese morphological analysis tool MeCab [8] with the Japanese dictionary IPADIC.

B. Results

Table III shows the results of comparative experiment and the parameters. The correct answer rate is calculated as follows:

$$\frac{Number \quad of \quad correct \quad political \quad parties \quad ID}{Number \quad of \quad test \quad data}$$

We confirmed that the highest correct answer rate was 0.5377, given by the Naive Bayes.

C. Discussion

In this comparative experiment, the highest accuracy was 0.5377, determined by Naive Bayes. The difficulty and cause for the low accuracy rate for this corpus are explained. We consider the dataset to be unbalanced, since the number of members depends on political party. The number of members in the test dataset that belonged to party ID2 was 52. Figures 2 and 3 show the confusion matrix for the test dataset and show that their methods nearly predicted three parties: ID0, ID1, and ID2. There were 80 members in the top three political parties. However, SVM and Naive Bayes predicted 105 and 106 members, respectively, in the top three parties, which included ID0, ID1, and ID2. Thus, we should consider the number of assembly members in each party.

V. Conclusion

In this paper, we described a new approach to stance classification and created a new data set. The dataset comprised 168 members, 20 political parties and 527 utterances. We conducted performance evaluation experiments with multiple machine learning methods to evaluate the difficulty of the datasets. The accuracy rate of Naive Bayes had the highest performance, 54%. We evaluated the difficulty of the dataset for stance classification and determined that future work shuld consider the number of members in each party.

Speaker	Utterances in Tokyo Metropolitan assembly minutes	Political party ID	
A	(snip) 次に、株式会社新銀行東京に関する特別委員会の継続調査について、反対する立場から意見を述べます。 Next, I will express my opinion on the continuing investigation by the special committee concerning the new bank corporation Tokyo from the standpoint to oppose. (snip) オリンピック・パラリンピックを、多くの人々に夢と希望を与え、日本を再生させていくシンボルとして位置づけていくことが非常に重要と考えます。 I think that it is very important to give Olympic and Paralympic Games dreams and hopes to many people and to position them as a symbol that makes Japan revitalize.	1	Training data
B	(snip) 次に、介護保険制度について申し上げます。 Next, I will tell you about the long-term care insurance system. (snip) 最後に、オリンピック・パラリンピック招致について申し上げます。スポーツに関する施策の推進を図るべきと考えます。 Finally, I would like to mention about the Olympic and Paralympic Games bid. I think that we should promote measures related to sports.	2	Training data
C	(snip) よって、二〇二〇年にオリンピックを再び招致することには賛成できません。 Therefore, I can not agree to invite the Olympics again in 2020. (snip)	5	Training data
D	(snip) 次に、オリンピック・パラリンピックについてお伺いします。 同時に、東日本大震災から日本が再生するための極めて大きな牽引力となるものです。 Next, I will ask about the Olympic and Paralympic Games. At the same time, it will be an extremely big driving force for Japan to regenerate from the Great East Japan Earthquake.	— (Select an ID among 20 political parties.)	Test data

Figure 1. Overview of dataset.

TABLE II. EXPERIMENTAL DATASET DIVIDED INTO TWO DATASETS OF 80% AND 20%: TRAINING DATA AND TEST DATA. COLUMNS INCLUDE NUMBER OF MEMBERS, NUMBER OF WORDS, AVERAGE WORDS, MEDIAN, MAXIMUM AND MINIMUM.

ID	Party	Training data (Separation by utterance unit)						Test data (Separation by utterance unit)					
		Member	Word	Ave	Med	Max	Min	Member	Word	Ave	Med	Max	Min
0	DP	132	156,191	1,183	1,036	6,823	14	13	15,939	1,226	1,022	3,164	414
1	TMK	64	100,016	1,563	1,151	4,723	94	15	21,046	1,403	1,089	4,783	371
2	TMLDP	132	179,856	1,363	1,155	6,391	2	52	54,299	1,044	1,106	6,763	14
3	CN	19	14,330	754	754	1,336	203	4	3,476	869	797	1,301	582
4	JCPTMA	30	51,324	1,711	1,170	4,649	28	11	16,650	1,514	1,242	5,046	27
5	AC	2	2,915	1,458	1,476	1,484	1,431	0	0	0	0	0	0
6	JCPTMG	7	8,059	1,151	943	3,406	331	0	0	0	0	0	0
7	I	3	10,264	3,421	2,512	6,247	1,505	0	0	0	0	0	0
8	I(R)	1	1,272	1,272	1,272	1,272	1,272	0	0	0	0	0	0
9	TRP	6	3,272	545	464	1,062	253	0	0	0	0	0	0
10	I(FALDP)	4	3,002	750	851	1,280	19	1	1,329	1,329	1,329	1,329	1,329
11	JRP	2	1,051	526	526	570	481	0	0	0	0	0	0
12	TMAEP	4	3,199	800	904	998	393	0	0	0	0	0	0
13	EP	4	3,471	868	868	1,262	474	0	0	0	0	0	0
14	EPT	3	2,833	944	712	1,576	545	2	2,075	1,038	1,038	1,229	846
15	TMCR	5	4,370	874	741	1,494	418	2	2,608	1,304	1,304	1,849	759
16	I(DBT)	1	1,353	1,353	1,353	1,353	1,353	1	1,289	1,289	1,289	1,289	1,289
17	BT	2	2,172	1,086	1,086	1,272	900	0	0	0	0	0	0
18	TMRP	0	0	0	0	0	0	4	4,016	1,004	1,069	1,528	350
19	I(TEI)	0	0	0	0	0	0	1	754	754	754	754	754
Total	-	421	-	-	-	-	-	106	-	-	-	-	-

TABLE III. RESULTS OF COMPARATIVE EXPERIMENT. TEST SET INCLUDES 106 UTTERANCES.

Method	Parameter	Correct answer rate
SVM	kernel=rbf	0.3962
Decision tree	depth=3	0.3113
k-NN	k=3	0.4334
Random Forest	depth=5 tree=10	0.3490
Naive Bayes		0.5377

ACKNOWLEDGMENTS

This work was supported by JSPS KAKENHI Grant Number JP16H02912 . The research funded for / supported by the open collaborative research program at the National Institute of Informatics (NII) Japan is (FY2018).

REFERENCES

[1] J. Grimmer and B. M. Stewart, "Text as data: The promise and pitfalls of automatic content analysis methods for political texts," *Political Analysis*, vol. 21, pp. 267–297, 2013, awarded Political Analysis Editor's Choice Award for an article providing an especially significant contribution to political methodology. Replication Data: here.

[2] F. Boltuzic and J. Šnajder, "Toward stance classification based on claim microstructures," in *Proceedings of the 8th Workshop on Computational Approaches to Subjectivity, Sentiment and Social Media Analysis*. Association for Computational Linguistics, 2017, pp. 74–80. [Online]. Available: http://aclweb.org/anthology/W17-5210

		Prediction											
	ID	0	1	2	3	4	10	14	15	16	18	19	
Correct party ID	0	7	0	6	0	0	0	0	0	0	0	0	13
	1	1	5	9	0	0	0	0	0	0	0	0	15
	2	23	0	29	0	0	0	0	0	0	0	0	52
	3	3	0	1	0	0	0	0	0	0	0	0	4
	4	10	0	0	0	1	0	0	0	0	0	0	11
	11	0	0	1	0	0	0	0	0	0	0	0	1
	14	2	0	0	0	0	0	0	0	0	0	0	2
	15	1	0	1	0	0	0	0	0	0	0	0	2
	16	0	0	1	0	0	0	0	0	0	0	0	1
	18	3	0	1	0	0	0	0	0	0	0	0	4
	19	1	0	0	0	0	0	0	0	0	0	0	1
Total		51	5	49	0	1	0	0	0	0	0	0	106

Figure 2. Results of prediction by SVM. This prediction unit is a speech unit.

		Prediction											
	ID	0	1	2	3	4	10	14	15	16	18	19	
Correct party ID	0	9	1	3	0	0	0	0	0	0	0	0	13
	1	3	6	6	0	0	0	0	0	0	0	0	15
	2	8	2	42	0	0	0	0	0	0	0	0	52
	3	4	0	0	0	0	0	0	0	0	0	0	4
	4	7	0	4	0	0	0	0	0	0	0	0	11
	11	0	0	1	0	0	0	0	0	0	0	0	1
	14	2	0	0	0	0	0	0	0	0	0	0	2
	15	2	0	0	0	0	0	0	0	0	0	0	2
	16	0	0	1	0	0	0	0	0	0	0	0	1
	18	0	0	4	0	0	0	0	0	0	0	0	4
	19	0	1	0	0	0	0	0	0	0	0	0	1
Total		35	10	61	0	0	0	0	0	0	0	0	106

Figure 3. This figure shows the result of the prediction by the Naive Bayes. This prediction unit is a speech unit.

[3] S. Mohammad, S. Kiritchenko, P. Sobhani, X. Zhu, and C. Cherry, "Semeval-2016 task 6: Detecting stance in tweets," in *Proceedings of the 10th International Workshop on Semantic Evaluation (SemEval-2016)*. San Diego, California: Association for Computational Linguistics, June 2016, pp. 31–41. [Online]. Available: http://www.aclweb.org/anthology/S16-1003

[4] M. A. Walker, P. Anand, R. Abbott, and R. Grant, "Stance classification using dialogic properties of persuasion," in *Proceedings of the 2012 Conference of the North American Chapter of the Association for Computational Linguistics: Human Language Technologies*, ser. NAACL HLT '12. Stroudsburg, PA, USA: Association for Computational Linguistics, 2012, pp. 592–596. [Online]. Available: http://dl.acm.org/citation.cfm?id=2382029.2382124

[5] D. Sridhar, L. Getoor, and M. Walker, "Collective stance classification of posts in online debate forums," in *Proceedings of the Joint Workshop on Social Dynamics and Personal Attributes in Social Media*. Baltimore, Maryland: Association for Computational Linguistics, June 2014, pp. 109–117. [Online]. Available: http://www.aclweb.org/anthology/W14-2715

[6] K. Joseph, L. Friedland, W. Hobbs, D. Lazer, and O. Tsur, "Constance: Modeling annotation contexts to improve stance classification," in *Proceedings of the 2017 Conference on Empirical Methods in Natural Language Processing*. Copenhagen, Denmark: Association for Computational Linguistics, September 2017, pp. 1115–1124. [Online]. Available: https://www.aclweb.org/anthology/D17-1116

[7] Y. Kimura, K. Takamaru, T. Tanaka, A. Kobayashi, H. Sakaji, Y. Uchida, H. Ototake, and S. Masuyama, "Creating japanese political corpus from local assembly minutes of 47 prefectures," in *Proceedings of the 12th Workshop on Asian Language Resources (ALR12)*. The COLING 2016 Organizing Committee, 2016, pp. 78–85. [Online]. Available: http://www.aclweb.org/anthology/W16-5410

[8] T. Kudo, K. Yamamoto, and Y. Matsumoto, "Applying conditional random fields to japanese morphological analysis," in *In Proc. of EMNLP*, 2004, pp. 230–237.

The Impact of Social Media on User's Travel Purchase Intention

Stavros D. Kaperonis
Communication, Media and Culture
Panteion University
Athens, Greece
email: skap@panteion.gr

***Abstract*—Social media influences the tourist industry. This conceptual model research investigates the impact of Social Media (SM) on user's travel purchase intention and attitude. Data were collected from SM users in order to measure if there is a relationship between specific factors of SM and user attitude on travel purchase intention through Structural Equation Modeling (SEM). The main purpose of the research is to find out if there is a positive relationship among the following SM factors and travel purchase intention. That is, source credibility and user attitude, information reliability and user attitude, user enjoyment while searching for travel information, perceived value in travel services information and user attitude. This study presents a theoretical conceptual model based on the theory of credibility, information, enjoyment, and perceived value in SM and the potential connection of those factors to the customer attitude and purchase intention in travel services.**

Keywords-Social media; costumer attidude; purchase intention; credibility; enjoyment; information; perceived value; SEM.

I. INTRODUCTION

SM users outran 2 billion in 2016, globally. Facebook was the most popular social network with 1.86 billion/month active users for 2016. Daily Internet users spend 135 minutes on SM. In the fourth quarter of 2016, 1.149 million users of Facebook accessed SM via mobile devices every month [1].

Today Information Technology (IT) has enhanced SM and the words "connecting" and "exchanging" have been replaced by the words "searching" and "selling" through the web [2]–[4]. Tourist industry and hospitality had also become an essential tool for accessing different sources of tourism [5][6]. The Internet has conquered the travel industry. Younger generations, especially Gen Y, are much more active in planning trips; they send and receive information via a variety of sources, including mobile devices (e.g., videos, SM). They make online reservations and think about potential destinations to visit. Users seek to be part of a wide range of traveling experiences and they are more responsive to online advertising. SM and mobile devices support these new ways of expression.

The paper is structured as follows: Section II presents the research background. Section III presents the research methodology and hypotheses. Section IV contains the conclusion of our empirical study and the next steps to be followed.

II. RESEARCH BACKGROUND

Today SM networks, like Facebook and Instagram, allow people from different locations to interact and develop relationships or share travel experiences (e.g., posting photos and videos, sharing context) [7]. This information can be very useful to potential travelers and can be personalized [8]. There are installed SM apps in every smart device and they are used as a tool for finding more travel information, with search engines providing direct access [9]. Researchers, [10] found that purchase intention is one dimension of customer behavior. Behavior is assessed through purchase intention and consumers' behavioral patterns are examined [11]. Behavior is correlated to purchase intention [11][12] and this relationship has been empirically tested on tourist industry [13][14] and it has been found that customers' information reliability and satisfaction becomes an important factor of e-behavioral intentions. Website design and information quality is essential for user satisfaction. There are many theories about value, such as consumption value, service value, consumer value, and perceived value [15]–[18]. When we talk about perceived value [15][19], we refer to consumer's perception, price and quality of a product, evaluating cost and benefit factors. In order to proceed with SEM, we assume our conceptual research model, presented in Figure 1, which is measured by the following four variables: source credibility, enjoyment, information reliability and perceived value, in connection with customers' attitude and purchase intention in travelling. In order to confirm our Conceptual Research Model, we will use SEM, which incorporates the confirmatory approach, needed to justify our hypotheses. SEM uses confirmatory analysis rather than exploratory analysis for data. We can assess the measurement model validity with Confirmatory Factor Analysis (CFA), which compares the theoretical measurement with actual model. SEM provides clear estimates of the errors in our parameters. Indeed, alternative methods (such as those using the regression or the general linear model) assume that errors all through the independent variables are eliminated. However, ignoring mistakes, could possibly lead us to serious inaccuracies, especially if mistakes are significant. Such methods are avoided by using the SEM. SEM can incorporate both measurable and obscure variables. SEM method is preferred because it estimates the multiple and interrelated dependence in a single analysis.

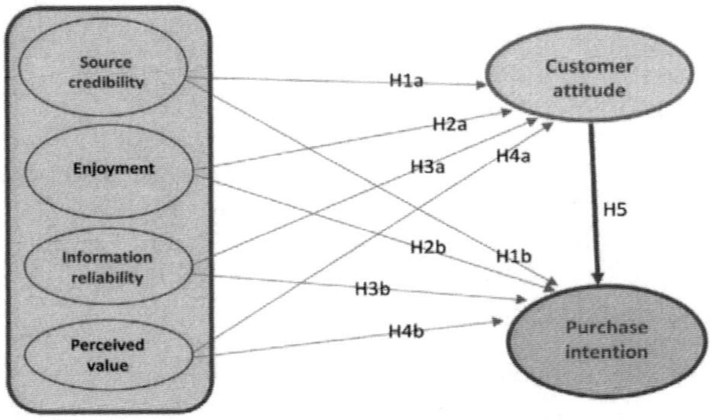

Figure 1. The Conceptual research model

III. Research Methodology and Hypotheses

Our study examines which factors and in which way travel information searches in SM networks, affect travelers' purchase intention [20]–[22] and decision making. In mental accounting theory, travel information is examined, more in the context of SM use, rather from a user's tech perspective [15][16]. Based on the perceived value and the usage of SM in the tourism sector, we developed our research model, Figure 1. In this context, perceptual value is defined in terms of quality and price performance or cost-benefit. Variables are categorized as source credibility, information reliability, enjoyment and perceived value. In addition, perceived value leads to the usage of SM in order to search for travel information as a consequence of value perception.

Based on previous section theory, we design the presented research model in Figure1. We select travelers' purchase intention as the main theory of the SM usage developed in our research model. Framing this, travelers' purchase intention is defined in terms of credibility, enjoyment, information reliability and perceived value as a trade-off between costs and benefits [15][16][23]. The confirmation of this model, Figure1, will give us a clear view of how the user decide to book a travel. In this way we are expanding previous researches on the use of SM by travelers in order to enhance our understanding of how travelers choose travel destinations in SM and in which way these four important variables affect traveler purchase intention and interact with customer attitude.

A. Source credibility

Source credibility is defined as the factor upon which information is perceived as believable and trustworthy by users [24]. Source credibility works as a main factor in decision-making procedures and become aware by high levels of risk [25]. Thus, source credibility is relevant within the context and the information through computer and user interaction [24]. Researches have shown that source credibility influence user attitude as a peripheral factor because it affects human judgment [26]. Source credibility influences persuasion when evidence is fuzzy. In this case, hands-on processing can partially become cognitive processing [27]. For example, celebrities are one type of exogenous factor, which may enhance source credibility by influencing users' judgement [26].

H1a. Source credibility has a positive influence on customer attitude

H1b. Source credibility has a positive influence on purchase intention

B. Enjoyment

Enjoyment has a significant effect on technology admittance that enforces the meaning of usefulness [28] and internal motivation that transforms user feeling to use a computer because it is enjoyable. In this case, authors referred to enjoyment as the "extent to which the activity of using the computer is perceived to be enjoyable in its own right". When people use technology and feel pleased or joyful, they perceive technology as a contributory value and they are willing to use it again and again [29][23] said that the meaning of perceived value incorporates two different values (utilitarian and hedonic). Hedonic value explained the entertainment and emotional worth of shopping. Researchers have shown that enjoyment positively affects perceived value [15][17] and the intention of using hedonic information [30]. Enjoyable feelings created by using SM apps encourage travelers not only to search information for travel destinations but also to interact with others. Travelers interact with each other by sharing photos or videos [6]. We therefore assume the following:

H2a. Enjoyment has a positive influence on customer attitude

H2b. Enjoyment has a positive influence on purchase intention

C. Information reliability

Studies in marketing have shown that consumer preferences are driven by value. Consumers are essence persons who seek to maximize usage [23]. The Internet provides travelers with many choices to choose, from many destinations to visit. This is the reason why they aim information reliability through a strenuous information search [31]. Direct access to alternative sources of information through SM builds a trust between words-of-mouth (eWOM) users and expertise travel agents. The combination of easy search and information reliability help travelers to search, and evaluate a destination, and read new experiences related to a trip. Reliability of information is considered as a major factor for the traveler in order to perceive value when using SM [6].

Travelers searching for reliable and credible information provided by the interaction between users of social media rather than by obtaining the information through travel websites [6]. Travelers use SM networks like Facebook or Instagram, which are connected to User Creative Contents (UCC) travel destinations, to share their experiences (e.g., photos, videos). By that, some travelers evaluate this reliable and credible information for a trip, reflecting their desire to engage online. The structure of information reliability is akin to the source information concept of information quality [32], which is the output characteristics of the accuracy, timeliness, and completeness offered by the source information. Quality of information of a traveler destination has become a driving force on user decision making [33] assuming that reliability of information influences purchase intention, hypothesizing the following:

H3a. Information reliability has a positive influence on customer attitude

H3b. Information reliability has a positive influence on purchase intention

D. Perceived value

Perceived value theory has also been adopted in travel destinations and shows high levels of influence in the future intention of travelers to discover the new or the same destinations [34][35] shows that in cruise travel services emotional factors are important in the perceived value. In cruise vacationer's behavioral intention is influenced by hedonics or pleasure of the perceived value. Travelers evaluate the travel information in SM based on their perceptions of what they are willing to achieve and what to sacrifice. Perceived value involves a balance between costs and benefits and an interaction between customer and service [36][28] analyze in the cost-benefit theory that the discrimination of perceived ease of use and perceived usefulness is similar between product performance and the effort of using the product. In high levels of perceived value in SM, travelers are likely to use a travel information search and in the low levels of the perceived value, travelers show greater resistance toward travel information searches in SM [33]. When travelers search for information its more likely to select or reject it based on the perceived benefits and the associated sacrifices of use, according to [28].

H4a. Perceived value in travel services information from SM has a positive influence on customer attitude

H4b. Perceived value in travel services information from SM has a positive influence on purchase intention

E. Data collection

The data for this study has been collected through a convenient sample e-survey from SM users. The e-survey was sent with a Facebook link in over of 500 users' profile. The number of responders was over of 400 users. The age range of the responders was between 18 and over 54.

The e-survey is separated in three sections. The first section outline users' habits on social networks and derive which are the most important criteria for purchasing products or services for them. The second section outline the factors that influences user purchase travel decision. In order to complete the survey, the third section is collecting data for classification and statistical processing.

F. Data analysis

This research study adopted Structural Equation Modeling (SEM) to test the hypotheses. By using SEM we want to evaluate our proposed model, analyze and explain the collected data [37]. All variables can be directly observed and thus qualify as manifest variables, called path analysis. In SEM terms, y enclose the endogenous variables and χ enclose the exogenous variables [38]. Variables that are influenced by other variables in a model are called endogenous variables. Variables that are not influenced by another other variables in a model are called exogenous variables. Covariances, such as the one between χ_1, χ_2, χ_3 and χ_4 are represented by two-way arrows, Figure 2. Paths acting as a cause are represented by one-way arrows. Each individual effect of source credibility, enjoyment, information reliability and the perceived value can be separated and is said to be related to customer attitude and purchase intention. The structural equations for this model are:

$$y_1=\gamma_{11}\chi_1+\gamma_{12}\chi_2+\gamma_{13}\chi_3+\gamma_{14}\chi_4+e_1 \quad (1)$$

$$y_2=\gamma_{21}\chi_1+\gamma_{22}\chi_2+\gamma_{23}\chi_3+\gamma_{24}\chi_4+e_2 \quad (2)$$

$$y_2=\psi_{21}y_1+e_3 \quad (3)$$

In our proposed research we can see a model with two y variables and four χ variables. For the reason of the multiple dependent variables, the covariances and the variances of the exogenous factors x's are given and are estimated by the values of the sample. As a result of this, is very difficult to contribute to the falsification of the model. Freedom degrees of our model counts the elements in the Φ matrix containing four values of γ, and one of ψ.

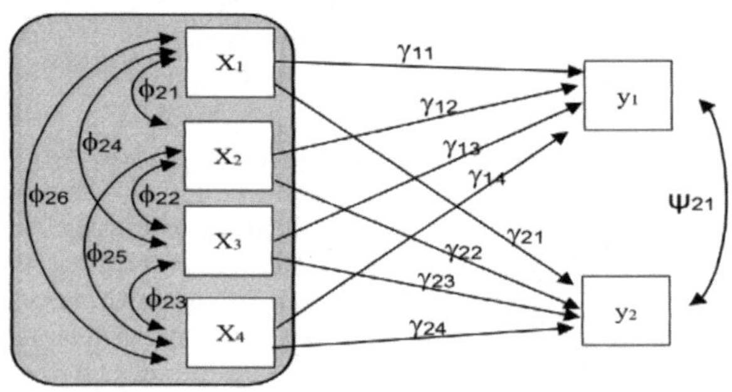

Figure 2. Proposed research model

Thus, the are exactly as many free parameters as there are the data points. Transformations of the data are created by the parameters. Σ matrix does not impose any restrictions to our model, meaning that it has 0 freedom degrees. In our SEM analysis we are going to include all individual items that load onto the observation variables, their relationships, variances, disturbance or errors.

In this study, the measurements were taken from other studies focused in the four manifest variables known as source credibility, information reliability, enjoyment, and perceived value. To measure the manifest variable of credibility, we adapted four items studied by [39], for the manifest variable of enjoyment four items from a study performed by [40] were adapted, for the manifest variable of information reliability four items from a study performed by [33] were adapted and for the manifest variable of perceived value items four items from [15][16] were adapted. For every single item we use multi-measurement items to overcome the limitations. For the reason that every single item has a high rate of measurement error we usually aim to capture all the attributes of a structure. All of these 16 items were measured on 5-point Likert scales ranging from strongly disagree (1) to strongly agree (5).

In this research, the Amos 24.0 SEM analysis package will be used to test and estimate our conceptual model. Two different approaches are going to be used for testing our research hypotheses. The first approach is with confirmatory factor analysis (CFA) and the second with analysis of variance regression (ANOVA). After the validation of our measures, SEM will be used to test the validity of the proposed model and hypotheses. For the validity of our model is needed to test the goodness-of-fit, [41], assisted by the, goodness of-fit index (GFI) [42], adjusted goodness-of-fit index (AGFI) [41], comparative fit index (CFI) [43], and root mean square error of approximation RMSEA [44]. GFI, AGFI and CFI must have values between 0.9 and 1.0 to indicate a good fitting model. RMSEA with a value below 0.80 is recommended [45][46].

In order to evaluate our structural model in a predictive manner, we need to calculate the R^2s for the manifest variables, source credibility, enjoyment, information reliability and perceived value and discover the relationship with travel purchase intention. According to multiple regression results, R^2 indicates the amount of variance explained by the exogenous variables [47].

IV. CONCLUSION

The aim of this article is to create a model by which we will be able to interpret the effect of specific SM factors on user purchase intention as far as a travel service is concerned. The theoretical background and the research gap that led us to the study of the specific case, are elaborated in the article. The results will show us whether there is a correlation or relationship among the following factors and the travel service purchase intention and user attitude. The factors are: source credibility, information reliability, enjoyment, and perceived value. As a next step to this research, we will analyze the data collected from the e-survey and test the validity of our research model by detecting the factors that influence the user purchase intention when traveling, through SM browsing. With SEM we going to check our assumptions and confirming our model. The data analysis by use of the SEM will determine the critical factors concerning the customer attitude towards travel purchase services. Furthermore, by use of the SEM method we will be able to look into other variables which can influence purchase intention, such as age and income, and also the how way they interact with reliability, enjoyment and perceptual value.

REFERENCES

[1] "Global time spent on social media daily 2017 | Statista." [Online]. https://www.statista.com/statistics/433871/daily-social-media-usage-worldwide/. [Accessed: 03-Oct-2018].

[2] S. Choi, "An empirical study of social network service (SNS) continuance: incorporating the customer value-satisfaction-loyalty model into the IS continuance model," *Asia Pacific J. Inf. Syst.*, vol. 23, no. 4, pp. 1–28, 2013.

[3] N. Chung, H. J. Han, and C. Koo, "Mediating roles of attachment for information sharing in social media: social capital theory perspective," *Asia Pacific J. Inf. Syst.*, vol. 22, no. 4, pp. 101–123, 2012.

[4] C. Koo, Y. Wati, and J. J. Jung, "Examination of how social aspects moderate the relationship between task characteristics and usage of social communication technologies (SCTs) in organizations," *Int. J. Inf. Manage.*, vol. 31, no. 5, pp. 445–459, 2011.

[5] R. Law, R. Leung, and D. Buhalis, "Information technology applications in hospitality and tourism: a review of publications from 2005 to 2007," *J. Travel Tour. Mark.*, vol. 26, no. 5–6, pp. 599–623, 2009.

[6] M. Sigala, E. Christou, and U. Gretzel, "Social Media in Travel," *Tour. Hosp. Theory, Pract. Cases*, 2012.

[7] E. Parra-López, J. Bulchand-Gidumal, D. Gutiérrez-Taño, and R. Díaz-Armas, "Intentions to use social media in organizing and taking vacation trips," *Comput. Human Behav.*, vol. 27, no. 2, pp. 640–654, 2011.

[8] D. K. Kardaras, S. Kaperonis, S. Barbounaki, I. Petrounias, and K. Bithas, "An Approach to Modelling User Interests Using TF-IDF and Fuzzy Sets Qualitative Comparative Analysis," in *IFIP International Conference on Artificial Intelligence Applications and Innovations*, 2018, pp. 606–615.

[9] Z. Xiang and U. Gretzel, "Role of social media in online travel information search," *Tour. Manag.*, vol. 31, no. 2, pp. 179–188, 2010.

[10] V. A. Zeithaml, L. L. Berry, and A. Parasuraman, "The behavioral consequences of service quality," *J. Mark.*, pp. 31–46, 1996.

[11] I. Ajzen and M. Fishbein, "Understanding attitudes and predicting social behaviour," 1980.

[12] R. L. Oliver and W. O. Bearden, "Disconfirmation processes and consumer evaluations in product usage," *J. Bus. Res.*, vol. 13, no. 3, pp. 235–246, 1985.

[13] F. Buttle and B. Bok, "Hotel marketing strategy and the theory of reasoned action," *Int. J. Contemp. Hosp. Manag.*, vol. 8, no. 3, pp. 5–10, 1996.

[14] I. Ajzen and B. L. Driver, "Application of the theory of planned behavior to leisure choice," *J. Leis. Res.*, vol. 24, no. 3, pp. 207–224, 1992.

[15] H.-W. Kim, H. C. Chan, and S. Gupta, "Value-based adoption of mobile internet: an empirical investigation," *Decis. Support Syst.*, vol. 43, no. 1, pp. 111–126, 2007.

[16] H.-W. Kim, Y. Xu, and S. Gupta, "Which is more important in Internet shopping, perceived price or trust?," *Electron. Commer. Res. Appl.*,

vol. 11, no. 3, pp. 241–252, 2012.

[17] S. Gupta and H. Kim, "Value-driven Internet shopping: The mental accounting theory perspective," *Psychol. Mark.*, vol. 27, no. 1, pp. 13–35, 2010.

[18] S. Kim, S. Holland, and H. Han, "A structural model for examining how destination image, perceived value, and service quality affect destination loyalty: A case study of Orlando," *Int. J. Tour. Res.*, vol. 15, no. 4, pp. 313–328, 2013.

[19] V. A. Zeithaml, "Consumer perceptions of price, quality, and value: a means-end model and synthesis of evidence," *J. Mark.*, pp. 2–22, 1988.

[20] R. H. Thaler, "Mental accounting and consumer choice," *Mark. Sci.*, vol. 27, no. 1, pp. 15–25, 2008.

[21] R. Thaler, "Mental accounting and consumer choice," *Mark. Sci.*, vol. 4, no. 3, pp. 199–214, 1985.

[22] R. Thaler, "Toward a positive theory of consumer choice," *J. Econ. Behav. Organ.*, vol. 1, no. 1, pp. 39–60, 1980.

[23] R. Sánchez-Fernández and M. Á. Iniesta-Bonillo, "The concept of perceived value: a systematic review of the research," *Mark. theory*, vol. 7, no. 4, pp. 427–451, 2007.

[24] S. W. Sussman and W. S. Siegal, "Informational influence in organizations: An integrated approach to knowledge adoption," *Inf. Syst. Res.*, vol. 14, no. 1, pp. 47–65, 2003.

[25] B. Mak and K. Lyytinen, "A model to assess the behavioral impacts of consultative knowledge based systems," *Inf. Process. Manag.*, vol. 33, no. 4, pp. 539–550, 1997.

[26] A. Bhattacherjee and C. Sanford, "Influence processes for information technology acceptance: An elaboration likelihood model," *MIS Q.*, pp. 805–825, 2006.

[27] S. Chaiken and D. Maheswaran, "Heuristic processing can bias systematic processing: effects of source credibility, argument ambiguity, and task importance on attitude judgment.," *J. Pers. Soc. Psychol.*, vol. 66, no. 3, p. 460, 1994.

[28] F. D. Davis, "Perceived usefulness, perceived ease of use, and user acceptance of information technology," *MIS Q.*, pp. 319–340, 1989.

[29] F. D. Davis, R. P. Bagozzi, and P. R. Warshaw, "Extrinsic and intrinsic motivation to use computers in the workplace 1," *J. Appl. Soc. Psychol.*, vol. 22, no. 14, pp. 1111–1132, 1992.

[30] H. Van der Heijden, "User acceptance of hedonic information systems," *MIS Q.*, pp. 695–704, 2004.

[31] Y.-H. Hwang and D. R. Fesenmaier, "Unplanned tourist attraction visits by travellers," *Tour. Geogr.*, vol. 13, no. 3, pp. 398–416, 2011.

[32] W. H. DeLone and E. R. McLean, "Information systems success: The quest for the dependent variable," *Inf. Syst. Res.*, vol. 3, no. 1, pp. 60–95, 1992.

[33] N. Chung and C. Koo, "The use of social media in travel information search," *Telemat. Informatics*, vol. 32, no. 2, pp. 215–229, 2015.

[34] A. S. Lo and C. Y. S. Lee, "Motivations and perceived value of volunteer tourists from Hong Kong," *Tour. Manag.*, vol. 32, no. 2, pp. 326–334, 2011.

[35] T. Duman and A. S. Mattila, "The role of affective factors on perceived cruise vacation value," *Tour. Manag.*, vol. 26, no. 3, pp. 311–323, 2005.

[36] A. Payne and S. Holt, "Diagnosing customer value: integrating the value process and relationship marketing," *Br. J. Manag.*, vol. 12, no. 2, pp. 159–182, 2001.

[37] J. F. Hair, W. C. Black, B. J. Babin, R. E. Anderson, and R. L. Tatham, "Multivariate data analysis (Vol. 6)." Upper Saddle River, NJ: Pearson Prentice Hall, 2006.

[38] R. B. Kline, "Promise and pitfalls of structural equation modeling in gifted research.," 2010.

[39] S. Ha and J. Ahn, "Why are you sharing others' tweets?: The impact of argument quality and source credibility on information sharing behavior," 2011.

[40] J.-J. Wu and Y.-S. Chang, "Towards understanding members' interactivity, trust, and flow in online travel community," *Ind. Manag. Data Syst.*, vol. 105, no. 7, pp. 937–954, 2005.

[41] K. G. Jöreskog and D. Sörbom, *LISREL 8: Structural equation modeling with the SIMPLIS command language*. Scientific Software International, 1993.

[42] L.-T. Hu, P. M. Bentler, and R. H. Hoyle, "Structural equation modeling: Concepts, issues, and applications," *Eval. Model fit*, pp. 76–99, 1995.

[43] P. M. Bentler and D. G. Bonett, "Significance tests and goodness of fit in the analysis of covariance structures.," *Psychol. Bull.*, vol. 88, no. 3, p. 588, 1980.

[44] J. H. Steiger, A. Shapiro, and M. W. Browne, "On the multivariate asymptotic distribution of sequential chi-square statistics," *Psychometrika*, vol. 50, no. 3, pp. 253–263, 1985.

[45] A. Diamantopoulos and J. A. Siguaw, "Introducing LISREL: A guide for the uninitiated," *London ua*, 2000.

[46] B. M. Byrne, "Structural equation modeling with LISREL," *Prelis, and Simplis*, pp. 196–199, 1998.

[47] D. Barclay, C. Higgins, and R. Thompson, *The Partial Least Squares (pls) Approach to Casual Modeling: Personal Computer Adoption Ans Use as an Illustration*. 1995.

Profiling using Fuzzy Set QCA for Medical Diagnosis

The Case of Anemia

Stavroula Barbounaki
Merchant Marine Academy of Aspropyrgos
Athens, Greece
e-mail: sbarbounaki@yahoo.gr

Nikos G. Dimitrioglou
National Technical University of Athens
Athens, Greece
e-mail: nikosdimitri@mail.ntua

Dimitris K. Kardaras
Athens University of Economics and Business
Athens, Greece
e-mail: Kardaras@aueb.gr; dkkardaras@yahoo.co.uk

Ilias Petrounias
The University of Manchester
Manchester, UK
e-mail: ilias.petrounias@manchester.ac.uk

***Abstract*— Despite the fact that anemia is a common disease, its diagnosis can be elusive. The signs and symptoms of anemia are generally unreliable in predicting the degree of anemia. Its diagnosis is mainly based on information of patient history and results of diagnostic tests that measuring indicators correlated to the disease. This paper suggests an approach to anemia diagnosis for adults by utilizing the fuzzy set Qualitative Comparative Analysis (FsQCA), which is not been used previously in medical diagnosis. The FsQCA, as an extension of QCA, is using fuzzy sets and entails the analysis of necessary and sufficient conditions to produce the some outcome, such as morbidity and severity. This paper aims to produce a set of causal configurations that can be used to assess and diagnose a medical case. The data set is collected from medical data sources. The factors to be considered are physiological indicators, such as hemoglobin, ferritin, mean corpuscular volume and hemoglobin, as well as age, gender and comorbidity. The anemia diagnosis is the outcome set used in this study. The proposed approach is tested for its accuracy and validity.**

Keywords-medical diagnosis; intelligent systems; fuzzy logic; QCA; healthcare.

I. INTRODUCTION

Fuzzy sets were introduced by Zadeh [1] as a formalism that can represent and manipulate problems that are ill-structured due to the uncertainty that characterizes them. It was specifically designed to mathematically represent uncertainty and vagueness and to provide formalized tools for dealing with the imprecision intrinsic to many problems.

Fuzzy logic attempts, to 'simulate' the human mind in order to improve the cognitive modeling of a problem [2]. The notion of an infinite-valued logic was introduced in [1] seminal work "Fuzzy Sets" where he described the mathematics of fuzzy set theory. This theory proposes that membership functions [3] represent linguistic variables, i.e., fuzzy sets, by assigning a number over the range of real numbers [0,1]. If an element does not belong to the fuzzy set with certainty, it is then assigned with 0, which represents the false and if an element certainly belongs to the fuzzy set, it is then assigned to 1, which represents the true. Every element, which is a member of a fuzzy set, has some grade of membership. The function that associates a number to each element (x) of fuzzy set (A) of the universe (X)is called membership function $\mu(x)\_A$, $x \in X$. Fuzzy logic expands to a great number of applications from power utilities and glass processing to washing machines and videos to medical, financial, supply chain management, decision support systems in various business areas [2].

In the field of medicine, computerized diagnostic systems have been proposed to assist physicians. Due to the probabilistic nature of choosing a diagnosis, it is possible that a physician will select the most likely diagnosis instead of the correct one [4]. To overcome uncertainty, many computerized diagnostic systems have been developed for miscellaneous diseases, such as diabetes [5], cancer [6], and cardiovascular diseases [7]. The accuracy of some systems matches actually the diagnostic abilities of physicians [8]. In particular, fuzzy logic and hybrid systems can be used to assist physicians in this decision process [9]. This approach uses fuzzy logic, to represent uncertainty better in order to improve diagnosis accuracy in a clinical context. For instance, a neuro-fuzzy network has been proposed to determine anemia level of a child [10]. The results indicate that the predicted anemia level values are very close to the measured values. Furthermore, an adaptive neuro-fuzzy inference system was developed to diagnose the iron deficiency anemia [11].

This paper suggests an approach to anemia diagnosis for adults by utilizing the fuzzy set Qualitative Comparative Analysis (FsQCA), which is not been used previously in medical diagnosis. Anemia is a common blood disorder in which Red Blood Cell (RBC) mass is reduced or the concentration of hemoglobin in blood is very low, resulting in a decrease in the oxygen-carrying capacity of it. The definition is population-based and varies by gender and race [12]. Despite the fact that anemia is a common disease, its diagnosis can be elusive. The signs and symptoms of anemia are generally unreliable in predicting the degree of anemia. Its diagnosis is mainly based on information of patient history and results of diagnostic tests that measuring indicators correlated to the disease. The most common diagnostic tests are Complete Blood Count (CBC) and Peripheral Blood Smear (PBS) assessment. However, the exact range of normal values for a given anemia factor is not well-defined among the medical community. Hence, values found that are near the upper or lower normal limits can be misinterpreted, possibly leading to false diagnosis. FsQCA, as an extension of QCA, is using fuzzy sets and entails the analysis of necessary and sufficient conditions to produce the some outcome, such as morbidity and severity.

II. METHODOLOGY

This paper proposes an approach to analyze patient medical data and diagnose a case of anemia as well as to determine the type of anemia. The proposed approach has been used and tested with a sample medical data set of 20 patient health records. This paper utilizes the FsQCA in order to produce causal combinations that best lead to reliable diagnosis. The FsQCA is particularly important for investigating intertwined relationships between multiple factors that affect a dependent variable. The dependent variable in this paper, i.e., the outcome set is the diagnosis regarding the existence of anemia [13]. The FsQCA analyses the sets of relationships among causes. In FsQCA variables are modelled as sets. FsQCA may produce alternative multiple paths, i.e., alternative causal combinations that can produce high consistency and coverage outcomes [14][15]. This analysis is performed separately for men and women due to different ranges of normal values for each of the variables used in diagnosis. Pregnants and vegans are excluded for our study, as their specific conditions have great impact on the level of indicators, such as hemoglobin.

The steps of the proposed approach follow:

- Step 1: Fuzzification of Medical Data.
- Step 2: Apply Qualitative Comparative Analysis.
  - Produce the truth table of all possible permutations of the terms considered.
  - Calculate membership degrees for each combination.
- Step 3: Calculate Consistency and Coverage of the solutions.
- Step 4: Suggest final diagnosis.

The following sections exemplify the steps of the proposed approach.

A. Fuzzification of Medical Data

The vector Exam-Data (XD) models every set of medical data that is available and represents a person whose case for anemia is considered. The Exam-Data vector is an (1×n) vector, which considers the same variables with the same order as in the first row of the Anemia-Matrix.

The values in the vector are the membership function values that result from the fuzzification process, which is performed for each one of the variables of the medical examinations before storing it in the vector. The membership functions of the Triangular Fuzzy Numbers (TFN) used in this research are the following in the case of hemoglobin:

$$\mu_{LOW} = \begin{cases} 1, & 0 \le x \le 30 \\ \frac{(34-x)}{4}, & 30 \le x \le 34 \\ 0, & 34 < x \end{cases} \quad (1)$$

$$\mu_{HIGH} = \begin{cases} 0, & 0 \le x \le 38 \\ \frac{(x-38)}{4}, & 38 \le x \le 42 \\ 1, & 42 < x \end{cases} \quad (2)$$

$$\mu_{NORMAL} = \begin{cases} \frac{(x-28)}{5}, & 28 \le x \le 33 \\ 1, & 33 \le x \le 40 \\ \frac{(-x-44)}{4}, & 40 < x < 44 \\ 0, & 44 < x \end{cases} \quad (3)$$

Similarly, membership functions are defined for all the variables.

B. Apply Qualitative Comparative Analysis.

Produce the truth table of all possible permutations of the terms considered. Each permutation is a possible causal combination. Calculate membership degrees for each combination. Its calculation is performed drawing on the fuzzy sets operations theory. Assume two fuzzy sets $\tilde{A}$ and $\tilde{B}$ then:

The fuzzy union, is defined as

$$\mu_{(A \cup B)} = \text{MAX}(\mu_A, \mu_B) \quad (4).$$

The fuzzy intersection is defined as

$$\mu_{(A \cap B)} = \text{MIN}(\mu_A, \mu_B) \quad (5)$$

and the fuzzy complement is calculated as

$$\mu_{-A} 1 - \mu_A \quad (6).$$

All variable expect hemoglobin, are fuzzified using the TFN formula (7).

$$f_a(x) \begin{cases} \frac{(x-a)}{(m-a)}, & a \le x \le m, m \ne a \\ \frac{(x-b)}{(m-b)}, & m \le x \le b, m \ne b \\ 0, & othrwise \end{cases} \quad (7)$$

where a, m, b are real numbers. During fuzzification calculations, the appropriate linguistic scale is identified and then the corresponding mean of the fuzzy number is considered to represent the level of each variable.

TABLE I. LINGUISTIC SCALES AND CORRESPONDING TFNS FOR AGE, MCV, MCH, FERRITIN, COMORBIDITY TESTS USED IN THIS STUDY

Linguistic scale	**Triangular fuzzy scale**	**Mean of fuzzy numbers**
Very High	(0.75, 1.00, 1.00)	1.00
High	(0.50, 0.75, 1.00)	0.75
Medium	(0.25, 0.50, 0.75)	0.50
Low	(0.00, 0.25, 0.50)	0.25
Very Low	(0.00, 0.00, 0.25)	0.00

C. *Calculate Consistency and Coverage of the solutions*

Calculate the consistency and the coverage of the solutions using formulas (8) and (9), respectively:

$$Consistency\ (X \prec Y) = \frac{\sum MIN(X,Y)}{\sum x} \quad (8)$$

$$Coverage = \frac{\sum MIN(X,Y)}{\sum x} \quad (9)$$

where *(X)* is the membership degree of each causal combination and *(Y)* is the membership degree of the outcome set.

D. *Simplify Causal Combinations and Suggest final diagnosis*

Identify best combinations in terms of consistency and coverage. Thus, this study considers a consistently rate above a threshold that is set at 0.8 and the highest possible coverage. The produced causal combinations that satisfy consistency and coverage thresholds are then simplified into the final set of causal combinations, which can be used for anemia diagnosis.

III. DATA ANALYSIS AND RESULTS

This paper analyses the data set shown in Table 2. This data refers to the women data set, showing the values for each medical test as they are produced after fuzzification. For hemoglobin, fuzzification is per-formed by applying formulas (1)-(3). For the rest of the variables fuzzification id used by taking the mean value of the appropriate fuzzy set as shown in Table 1. Similar calculations are performed for the men data set.

TABLE II. THE WOMEN PATIENT DATA SET

Patient	Age	Hg	MCV	MCH	Fr	Como/ty	Outcome
P1	0.75	0.75	0.5	0.5	0.5	1	0
P2	0.5	0.5	0	0	0.25	0	1
P3	1	0.5	0.5	0.5	0.75	1	1
P4	0.5	0.25	0.25	0.25	0	1	1
P5	0.5	0.5	0.75	0.75	0.25	1	1
P6	0.5	0.25	0.5	0.25	0	1	1
P7	0.5	0.75	0.25	0	0.25	1	1
P8	0	0.75	0.25	0.25	0.25	0	1
P9	1	0.75	0.5	0.5	0.5	1	0
P10	0.75	0.75	0.5	0.5	0.5	1	0
P11	0.25	0.5	0.5	0.5	0.75	0	1
P12	0.25	0	0	0	0	1	1
P13	0.5	0.5	0.5	0.5	0.5	1	1
P14	0.75	0.75	1	1	0.25	1	1
P15	0.25	0.25	0.5	0.5	0	1	1
P16	0.75	0.25	0.5	0.5	1	1	1
P17	0.25	0.5	0.5	0.5	0.75	0	1
P18	0.25	0	0	0	0	1	1
P19	0.5	0.5	0.5	0.5	0.5	1	1

The outcome set indicates whether the patient is diagnosed with anemia or not, coded with 1 and 0 respectively. Table 3, shows part of the total of 2^5=64 possible truth table permutations.

TABLE III. THE TRUTH TABLE (PART OF) SHOW ALL POSSIBLE PERMUTATIONS OF THE TERMS

Causal Permutation	Age	Hg	MCV	MCH	Fr	Comorbidity
1	0	0	0	0	0	0
2	0	0	0	0	0	1
3	0	0	0	0	1	0
4	0	0	0	0	1	1
5	0	0	0	1	0	0
6	0	0	0	1	0	1
7	0	0	0	1	1	0
8	0	0	0	1	1	1
9	0	0	1	0	0	0
10	0	0	1	0	0	1
11	0	0	1	0	1	0
12	0	0	1	0	1	1
13	0	0	1	1	0	0

Causal Permutation	Age	Hg	MCV	MCH	Fr	Comorbidity
14	0	0	1	1	0	1
15	0	0	1	1	1	0

TABLE IV. CAUSAL COMBINATIONS' CONSISTENCY AND COVERAGE FOR SEVEN PATIENTS

Causal Permutation	P1	P2	P3	P4	P5	P7	P8
1	0.25	0	0	0.5	0.25	0.5	0.25
2	0.25	0	0	0.5	0.25	0.5	0.25
3	0.25	0	0	0.5	0.25	0.5	0.25
4	0.25	0	0	0.5	0.25	0.5	0.25
5	0.25	0	0	0.5	0.25	0.5	0.25
4	0.25	0	0	0.5	0.25	0.5	0.25
5	0.25	0	0	0.5	0.25	0.5	0.25
6	0.25	0	0	0.5	0.25	0.5	0.25
7	0.25	0	0	0.5	0.25	0.5	0.25
8	0.25	0	0	0.5	0.25	0.5	0.25
9	0.25	0	0	0.5	0.25	0.5	0.25
…							
33	0.25	0	0	0.5	0.25	0.5	0.25
34	0.25	0	0	0.5	0.25	0.5	0.25
35	0.25	0	0	0.5	0.25	0.5	0.25
36	0.25	0	0	0.5	0.25	0.5	0.25
37	0.25	0	0	0.5	0.25	0.5	0.25
38	0.25	0	0	0.5	0.25	0.5	0.25
39	0.25	0	0	0.5	0.25	0.5	0.25
40	0.25	0	0	0.5	0.25	0.5	0.25
41	0.25	0	0	0.5	0.25	0.5	0.25
42	0.25	0	0	0.5	0.25	0.5	0.25
43	0.25	0	0	0.5	0.25	0.5	0.25
44	0.25	0	0	0.5	0.25	0.5	0.25
45	0.25	0	0	0.5	0.25	0.5	0.25
46	0.25	0	0	0.5	0.25	0.5	0.25
47	0.25	0	0	0.5	0.25	0.5	0.25
48	0.25	0	0	0.5	0.25	0.5	0.25
49	0.25	0	0	0.5	0.25	0.5	0.25
50	0.25	0	0	0.5	0.25	0.5	0.25
51	0.25	0	0	0.5	0.25	0.5	0.25
52	0.25	0	0	0.5	0.25	0.5	0.25
53	0.25	0	0	0.5	0.25	0.5	0.25
…							
60	0.25	0	0	0.5	0.25	0.5	0.25
61	0.25	0	0	0.5	0.25	0.5	0.25
62	0.25	0	0	0.5	0.25	0.5	0.25
63	0.25	0	0	0.5	0.25	0.5	0.25
64	0.25	0	0	0.5	0.25	0.5	0.25

The cells in the truth table take the value (1) or (0) representing true or false. Thus, permutation number 7 is read (Age=false, AND Hemoglobin=false, AND MCV=false, AND MCH=true, AND Ferritin=true, AND Comorbidity=false). Next, the membership degrees for all combinations for each patient are calculated drawing on the fuzzy sets operations theory, i.e., formulas (4,5,6). Table 4 shows the membership degrees for only a selected set of combinations, for simplicity.

The membership degree of combination number 7, for patient 1, see cell (Causal permutation1, P1) in Table 4, is calculated as follows by using formulas (5) and (6): Consider combination number 7 membership degree = (Age=false Hemoglobin =false MCV=false MCH=true Ferritin=true Comorbidity =false) = (not (Age), not (Hemoglobin), not (MCV), MCH, Ferritin, not (Comorbidity)). Thus, drawing on data shown in Table 2 for patient P1, the (Age=false) = ((1- (Age)) = (1-0.75) =0.25. Similar calculations are performed for all terms. Thus, for P1, =min (0.7; 0.25; 0.5; 0.5; 1; 1)=0.25. After all membership degrees are calculated, for all causal combinations for all patients, the consistency and coverage degrees are determined. Table 5 shows the results for a selected set of causal combinations.

TABLE V. CAUSAL COMBINATIONS' CONSISTENCY AND COVERAGE

Causal Permutation	Consistency	Coverage
1	1.000	0.077
2	0.929	0.250
3	1.000	0.077
4	0.833	0.096
5	1.000	0.038
…	…	…
33	1.000	0.058
34	0.846	0.212
35	1.000	0.038
36	0.800	0.154
37	1.000	0.019
38	0.778	0.135

Causal Permutation	Consistency	Coverage
39	1.000	0.019
40	0.778	0.135
41	1.000	0.019
42	0.900	0.173
43	1.000	0.019
44	0.889	0.154
45	1.000	0.019
46	0.900	0.173
47	1.000	0.019
48	0.889	0.154
...		
60	0.778	0.135
61	1.000	0.019
62	0.846	0.212
63	1.000	0.019
64	0.778	0.135

The consistency for combination number 2 is calculated, by applying formula (8) as follows:

Consider the outcome column shown in Table 2. Also consider the variables' membership degrees of combination number 2, for all patients as shown in Table 4.

Then,

min{min(0.25;0)+min(0.25;1)+min(0.25;0)+…+min(0.25;1)= min(0.25+0.25+0.25+…+0.25)=3.25 (0.25+0+0+0.5+0.25+…+0)=3.5.

Therefore, the consistency for combination number 2= =0.928.

Regarding the coverage, by applying formula (9), 3.5 and 14 thus coverage=0.25. The FsQCA theory assumes that the best causal combinations exhibit as high as possible consistency and coverage. However, the higher the consistency is, the lower the coverage becomes. By selecting the causal combinations with a consistency higher than the threshold value of 0.8, the final set is defined by selecting those combinations that exhibit the higher possible coverage as well. The selected set of causal combinations (i.e., combination 2, 34, 42, 46 and 62) are highlighted in Table 5. Table 6 shows the selected combinations.

TABLE VI. THE TWO NECESSARY AND SUFFICIENT CAUSAL COMBINATIONS

Causal Permutation	Age	Hg	MCV	MCH	Fr	Comorbidity
2	0	0	0	0	0	1
34	1	0	0	0	0	1
42	1	0	1	0	0	1
46	1	0	1	1	0	1
62	1	1	1	1	0	1

The closer look of Table 6, may lead to the elimination of the Ferritin test from the causal combinations since it seems it does not affect the results. Thus, by restructuring the causal combinations, the results show that the following alternative paths lead to anemia diagnosis.

- ✓ Comorbidity OR
- ✓ Age AND Comorbidity OR
- ✓ Age AND MCV AND Comorbidity OR
- ✓ Age AND MCV AND MCH AND Comorbidity OR
- ✓ Age AND Hemoglobin AND MCV AND MCH AND Comorbidity.

Furthermore, Hemoglobin can also be omitted, since Hemoglobin appears in only one combination (number 62) and it is the only additional factor to combination number 46. Thus, the set of causal combinations is as follows:

- ✓ Comorbidity OR
- ✓ Age AND Comorbidity OR
- ✓ Age AND MCV AND Comorbidity OR
- ✓ Age AND MCV AND MCH AND Comorbidity OR

IV. CONCLUSION AND FUTURE RESEARCH

This paper suggests the use of FsQCA in medical diagnosis and supports its use with the development of the necessary models and a prototype that was put to practice with real world test data. Data is collected from a hospital in Athens, Greece. The data protection act is satisfied in the sense that no personal data is held in the database. It only contains examinations results and diagnoses. FsQCA are used as a decision support method in order to assist physicians with manipulating and interpreting borderline cases such as the handling of the upper or lower normal limits of medical data that may raise ambiguity in problem formulation thus leading to faulty diagnoses. For future research, this paper suggests the testing of the model with more data. Large data sets will assist in evaluating the approach. Further, the analysis of large data sets may increase the complexity of applying the FsQCA method, thus FsQCA may be applied at a second stage after pruning an initial set of causal combinations. In addition, the method can be applied in other areas of medical problems.

REFERENCES

[1] L. A. Zadeh, "Fuzzy sets", Information and control, vol. 8, no. 3, pp. 338-353, 1965.
[2] P. Craiger and M.D. Coovert, "Modeling dynamic social and psychological processes with fuzzy cognitive maps" In Fuzzy Systems, IEEE World Congress on

Computational Intelligence. Proceedings of the Third IEEE Conference, pp. 1873-1877, 1994.
[3] H.J. Zimmermann (1991). "Fuzzy Set Theory and its Applications", Kluwer Academic Publishers.
[4] M. Graber, R. Gordon, and N. Franklin, Reducing diagnostic errors in medicine: what's the goal? Academic Medicine, vol 77, no. 10, pp. 981-992, 2002.
[5] K. Polat and S. Güneş, "An expert system approach based on principal component analysis and adaptive neuro-fuzzy inference system to diagnosis of diabetes disease", Digital Signal Processing, vol. 17, no. 4, pp. 702-710, 2007.
[6] A. Keleş, A. Keleş, and U. Yavuz, "Expert system based on neuro-fuzzy rules for diagnosis breast cancer", Expert systems with applications, vol. 38, no. 5, 5719-5726, 2011.
[7] S. Muthukaruppan and M.J. Er., "A hybrid particle swarm optimization based fuzzy expert system for the diagnosis of coronary artery disease", Expert Systems with Applications, vol. 39, no. 14, pp. 11657-11665, 2012.
[8] V. Pabbi, "Fuzzy Expert System for medical diagnosis", Internatinal Journal of Scientific and Research Publications, vol. 5 no. I, pp. 1-3, 2015.
[9] N. Allahverdi, "Design of fuzzy expert systems and its applications in some medical areas" International Journal of Applied Mathematics, Electronics and Computers, vol. 2, no. 1, pp. 1-8, 2014
[10] N. Allahverdi, A. Tunali, H. Işik, H. Kahramanli, "A Takagi–Sugeno type neuro-fuzzy network for determining child anemia", Expert Systems with Applications, vol. 38, no. 6, pp. 7415-7418, 2011.
[11] L. Azarkhish, M.R. Raoufy and S. Gharibzadeh, "Artificial intelligence models for predicting iron deficiency anemia and iron serum level based on accessible laboratory data", Journal of medical systems, vol. 36, no. 3, pp. 2057-2061, 2012.
[12] M.J. Cascio and T.G. DeLoughery, "Anemia" Medical Clinics, vol. 101, no. 2, pp. 263-284, 2017.
[13] S. Chari, A. Tarkiainen, H. Salojärvi, "Alternative pathways to utilizing customer knowledge: A fuzzy-set qualitative comparative analysis", J Bus Res, vol 69, pp. 5494–5499, 2016.
[14] B. Rihoux and C.C. Ragin, "Configurational comparative methods: Qualitative comparative analysis (QCA) and related techniques", Sage Publications, 2008.
[15] D. Skarmeas, C.N. Leonidou, C. Saridakis "Examining the role of CSR skepticism using fuzzy-set qualitative comparative analysis", J Bus Res, vol. 67, pp. 1796–180, 2014.

A Modeling Tool for Equipment Health Estimation Using a System Identification Approach

Alexander Dementjev, Ilkay Wunderlich, Klaus Kabitzsch
Department of Computer Science, Technical University of Dresden
01062 Dresden, Germany
Email: *firstname.lastname*@tu-dresden.de

Germar Schneider
Infineon Technologies Dresden GmbH
01099 Dresden, Germany
Email: germar.schneider@infineon.com

Abstract —**In high-technology manufacturing industries like pharmaceuticals, semiconductors or photovoltaics, best and stable yields are very important. This can only be reached if the appropriate equipment is still operating in the specified working ranges according to the current recipes or process steps. Because of the high complexity of the corresponding equipment and processes, monitoring solutions like fault detection and classification or predictive maintenance are already established. The combination of such techniques with advanced process control leads to a mechanism for avoiding product scraps and, finally, to the maximization of the production efficiency and business competitiveness. The equipment health factor is an important index of the status of a processing equipment and at the same time a key enabler for advanced monitoring and control strategies. Three families of estimation techniques will be briefly explained in this paper: physics-inspired, statistical-based and data-driven. Then, the focus will be set on the system identification-based approach as the most promising and emerging equipment health estimation strategy. Its backgrounds and advantages will be explained and illustrated. At the end, a universal tool for investigation and modeling of the equipment health factor will be described and discussed.**

Keywords —Equipment Health; Data-Driven Modeling; System Identification; Predictive Maintenance; Time Series Analysis.

I. Introduction

The Equipment Health Factor (EHF) (also known as equipment health index [1]) is a quantitative factor of the status of a processing equipment or a tool, which can be estimated from observable equipment parameters, e.g., on the basis of the history data of the process.

For a sustainable application, the EHF calculation should also be supported by the use of available metrology data (including virtual metrology data) and maintenance information. So, the appropriate data integration of different information sources like process control system, metrology or maintenance is essential for the overall production success. In the literature, there are other similar equipment health definitions under terms like "equipment condition", "tool health" or "machine health condition".

In this article, we focus on the following EHF application fields:

- **Predictive Maintenance** [2] is based on condition monitoring [3]. With Predictive Maintenance (PdM), maintenance actions are performed only if needed and offer cost savings compared to time-based Preventive Maintenance (PvM) [4]. Another advantage towards to PvM is to avoid equipment breakdown by performing proactive maintenance. EHF can be used as a main indicator to predict equipment status.
- **Dynamic Sampling** avoids expensive measuring operations on lots of products (e.g. wafers) without increasing the "material at risk" in production [5]. In case of dynamic sampling, EHF can supply the sampling system with information about current equipment condition for avoiding the metrology actions [6].
- **Equipment Prioritization and Production Scheduling** by giving each equipment a certain priority according to its current EHF. If critical tasks with a high quality demand occurs, the equipment with the highest EHF is recommended to be used [7]. This technique motivates to include the EHF into global production scheduling [1].

In the following, an overview of the already existing methods for equipment health estimation will be given (Section II). Then, a system identification-based approach will be introduced and its advantages underlined in Section III. An appropriate software tool for investigation of the identification-based EHF estimation will be presented in Section IV. Achieved results will be discussed in Section V and, in the end, a short conclusion with an outlook will be given.

II. Methods for Equipment Health Estimation

In this section several families of EHF techniques, which can be classified as follows, are discussed:

- **Physics inspired:** These methodologies are considered to be the most complex to transfer between different equipment types, as they entirely rely on what is known (and can be modeled) of the equipment's behavior [8]. This family of techniques usually consists of very ad-hoc approaches to tackle a specific use case and is therefore the most expensive [9].
- **Statistical or forecast-based:** In this case, relevant time series coming from the target equipment are predicted by exploiting their statistical properties. Their probabilistic future outcome is compared with a preset failure threshold [10]. Notable examples of problems easily solved with this kind of technique include helium flow prediction for edge ring consumption by plasma etching in semiconductor production [11] and health monitoring of electronics under shock loads in packaging and manufacturing [12]. While such techniques can be extremely

powerful in targeting specific problems, it must be said that they lack generality and most of the time cannot be directly transferred between equipment classes and problems.

- **Data-driven:** in contrast to the aforementioned techniques, this class of methods allows quick transfer of methodology between different equipment and processes [13]. The appropriate EHF models will be estimated from the input data using supervised machine learning algorithms like linear or nonlinear regression [14], neural networks [15] or system identification algorithms with gradient-based optimization. Also, classification methods (support vector machines, decision trees, etc.) can be used for equipment health assessment.

  The required training, validation and test data sets could be obtained in a semi-automatic way (for instance by exploiting associated metrology information) as well as in a manual manner, by manually selecting a subset of important parameters to be controlled based on the actual knowledge of the process engineer [16]. It should be noted that such methodologies still require some expert knowledge in order to provide proper results and minimize the false positive rate.

Depending on the use case, each of the approaches may prove itself useful, but no tool is capable for solving every issue in the whole "EHF galaxy" [17]. For this reason, since the beginning of the planning stage, much emphasis has been put on the modularity of the system in order to be able to accommodate a wide variety of mathematical techniques with minimal effort.

III. EHF Estimation Using a System Identification Approach

Most popular statistical-based and data-driven EHF estimation methods presume that changes in the process data can be adequately described with standard statistical functions like variance, mean value, standard deviation or linear regression models. But this limits their applicability to narrow process windows. System identification methods do not rely on that steady-state assumption and characterize processes based on identified physical properties, especially on typical responses to well-defined step changes.

Many equipment signal charts represent in fact responses after control actions like "Heater On", "RF Power On" or "N_2 Primary Valve On" with characteristic trends in according to sensor readings [18]. These trends can be compared with each other or with trends from a reference model to detect process anomalies or, indirectly, decreasing of the equipment health.

By using of a system identification approach, an automatic identification of the reference models should be performed for each existing process context (e.g. different recipes) to describe the characteristic trends in signals not only in steady-state mode. Then, based on an identified reference model, the reference time series should be calculated and compared to the new measurements from the same production context. In the last step, well-known metrics like Mean Squared Error (MSE) can be used to characterize the current equipment health. Finally, the calculated MSE values will be applied to an already existing Fault Detection and Classification (FDC) or EHF software to track the estimated EHF parts.

The proposed common approach consists of 5 steps, as shown Figure 1. The first three steps are performed offline during EHF system deployment:

1) Selection of relevant process variables,
2) Preliminary estimation of the model parameters for the reference time series and
3) Parameter estimation for different model structures.

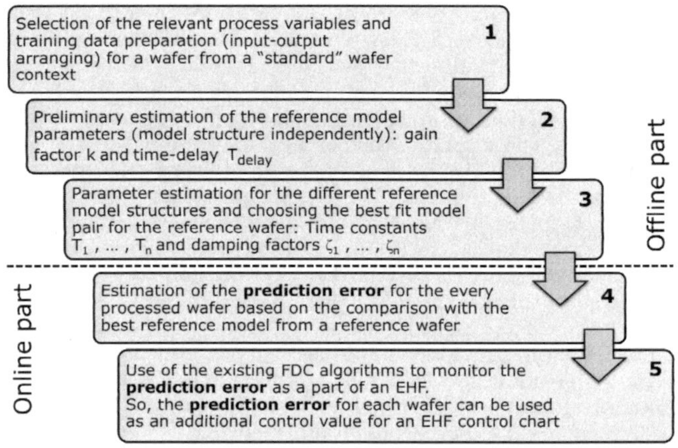

Figure 1. Steps of the proposed approach at a wafer manufacturing example divided into offline and online part.

The system identification based EHF estimation occurs in the two remaining steps which will be executed during an online operation of the EHF modeling tool:

4) EHF online estimation on the basis of model identification on process data and
5) Use of the existing FDC algorithms to monitor and control the EHF (like control charts etc.).

The fourth step can alternatively be performed by identification of the model parameters for each measured time series. In this case the EHF metrics are the differences in the model parameters form different modeled time series according to the reference model.

Figure 2 shows the most popular structures for reference models.

In Figure 3, an example of a reference time series generated by a dynamic second order reference model is given. Figure 4 shows the identified time shift in time series caused by equipment malfunction, respectively.

For the second order model, the estimated model parameters are time delay T_{delay}, gain factor k and two time constants T_1 and T_2. Such models can adequately describe relatively slow processes like heating. Note that for successful and meaningful identification, the measurement frequency must

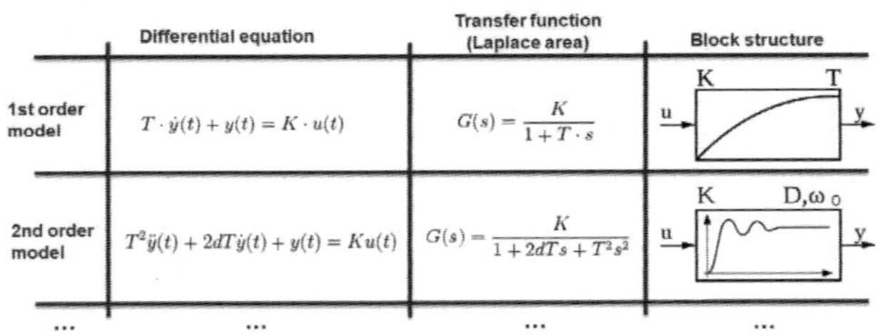

Figure 2. Most popular reference model structures.

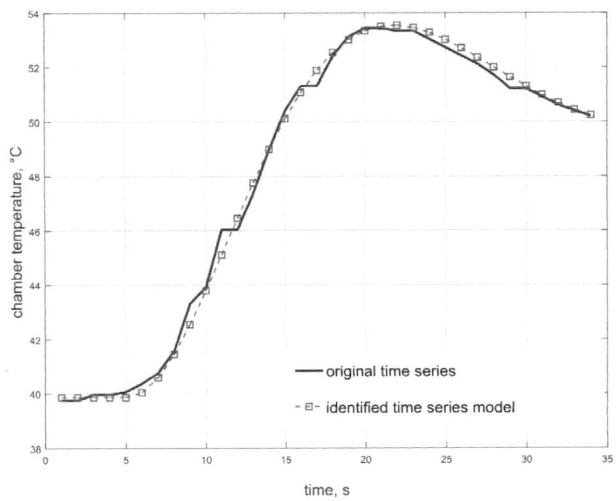

Figure 3. An example of a reference time series.

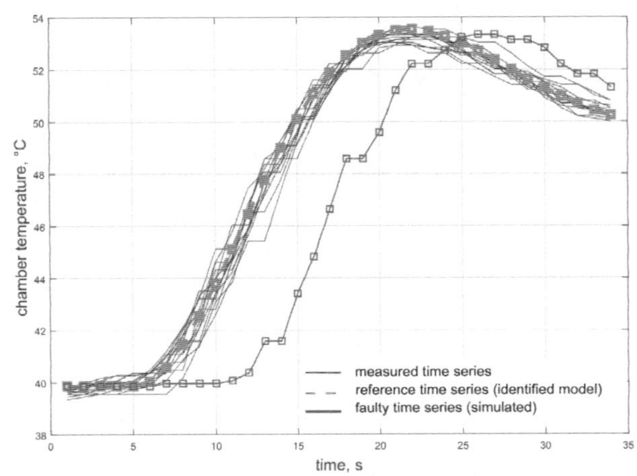

Figure 4. An example for the identified time shift in time series which can be caused by equipment malfunction.

meet the sampling theorem.

Among the common approach (Figure 1), the model identification occurs only on process data from the reference product (e.g., wafer etc.), then generate the reference time series and calculate the MSE on the residuals for the next processed products. In this case the monitored EHF is the MSE.

IV. A Tool for Investigation of the System Identification-Based Equipment Health Estimation

The following section introduces a tool for EHF estimation based on system identification. The tool is programmed in MATLAB using the MATLAB GUIDE environment for the Graphical User Interface (GUI).

A. Structure of the Tool

The EHF estimation tool consists of five GUI panels. The functionality of the first two panels is shortly described in the following:

- **Visualization**: In the first panel the time series can be loaded and displayed. (Ideally the corresponding time series are collected in a data set beforehand)
- **Data Preprocessing**: In case of inhom6ogeneities, e.g., dead time delays, of certain time series can be processed by changing start or end time.

B. Model Identification

Figure 5 shows the third panel after the model identification process is completed. At the top of the figure the settings area can be seen. The following preferences can be changed:

- Selection of the appropriate **model type** (e.g., second order model)
- Choice of the **reference time series** corresponding to the specified course of the process.
- Pick the (virtual) **input signal** of your system (either positive/negative unit step or positive/negative impulse).

The model identification is performed by the MATLAB function for Prediction Error Estimate for Linear and Nonlinear Model (PEM). After identifying the reference model, which is denoted with $m_{ref}(k)$, the estimated model parameters and the fitting quality (in percent) of the model (Figure 5 right) are displayed. In the diagram a comparison of the model and the reference time series is plotted.

C. Reference Based Approach

After finishing the model identification step, one can continue with the reference based approach, which is the implementation of the EHF algorithm introduced Section III. In order to suppress noise components of the signals the model of the reference time series is used to calculate the MSE.

$$MSE(i) = \sum_{k=1}^{K} (x_i(k) - m_{ref}(k))^2 \qquad (1)$$

with i corresponding to the ith time series of the data set and K the length of the each time series $x(k) = [x_1, x_2, ...x_K]$.

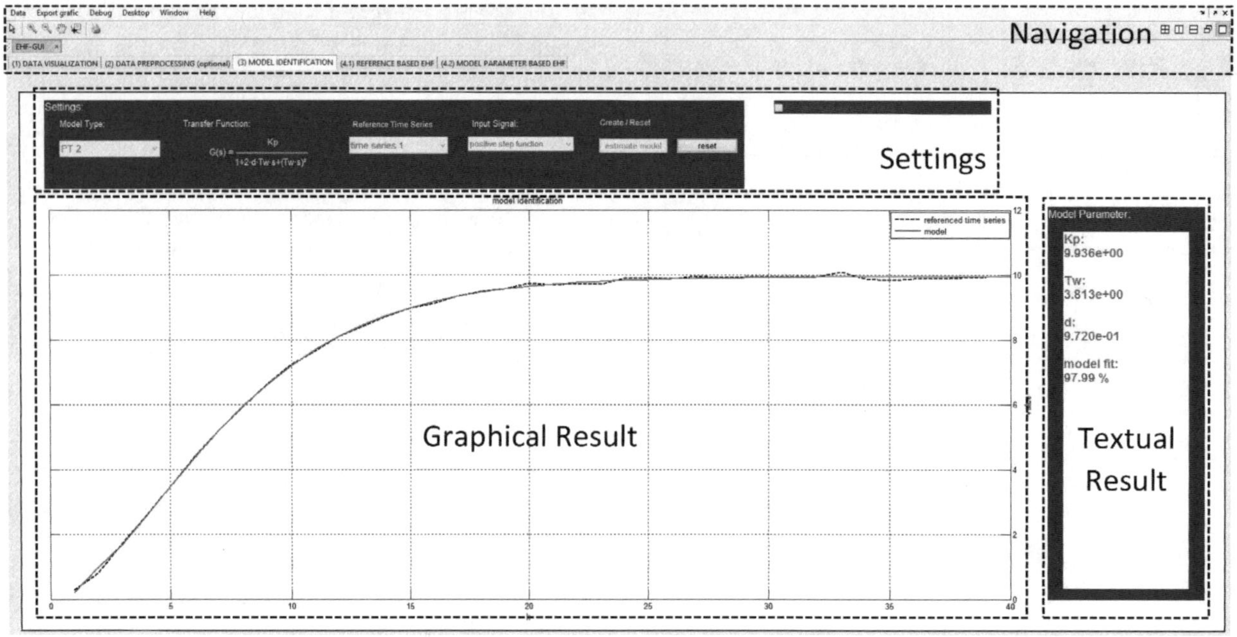

Figure 5. Panel 3 - Model Identification: At the top of the GUI the menu, tool bar and the panel navigation are located. In the middle, the settings for the model identification can be changed. The diagram and the text box at the bottom show the results of the model identification.

Additionally it is possible to set an alert limit in multiples of the standard deviation of the MSE σ_{MSE} (Figure 8, dashed line).

D. Model Parameter Based Approach

The model parameter based approach was introduced in Section III. In order to obtain a normalized EHF between 0% and 100% the identified parameter of the reference model are defined as 100%.

The parameters of the remaining time series are estimated with the same settings which are chosen for the reference model in the third panel. The calculation of the EHF will be introduced in the following steps:

1) Estimation of the reference model parameters $P_{j,ref}$ with $j = 1, \ldots, J$ different parameters (excluding the fitting percentage)
2) Estimation of the parameters of all time series $P_j(i)$ (i corresponding to the ith time series)
3) Calculation of the absolute deviation between each parameter and the corresponding reference parameter:

$$\Delta_j(i) = \frac{|P_j(i) - P_{j,ref}|}{P_{j,ref}} \tag{2}$$

Note that the absolute deviation at the index $i = ref$ (reference time series) is always zero and therefore does not need to be calculated:

$$\Delta_j(i = ref) = \frac{|P_j(i = ref) - P_{j,ref}|}{P_{j,ref}} \equiv 0, \ \forall j$$

4) Summation of the absolute deviations:

$$\Delta_{total}(i) = \frac{1}{J}\sum_{j=1}^{J} \Delta_j(i) \tag{3}$$

5) Mapping of the total deviation to the EHF:

$$EHF(i) = 100\% \cdot (1 - \Delta_{total}(i)) \tag{4}$$

(Negative values will be mapped to 0%.)

E. Validation of the Identification Procedure

In order to validate the estimation process and to further investigate on noise tolerance, data sets are generated with MATLAB SIMULINK and analyzed by the tool.

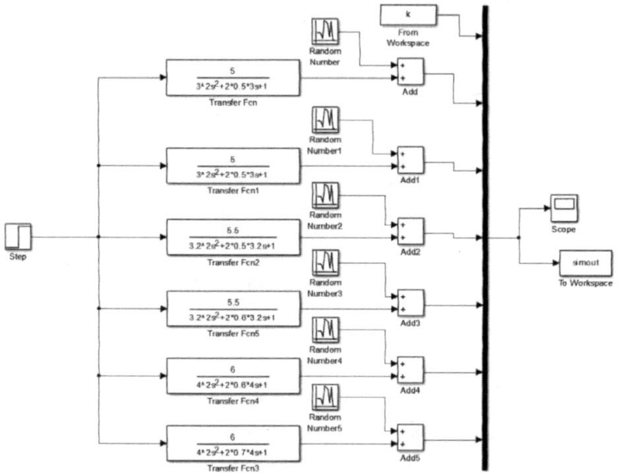

Figure 6. SIMULINK structure for test data generation.

One example data set, which is generated by the structure shown in Figure 6, consists of 6 time series created by a second order system with varying parameters and a unit step as input-signal. These time series are appended with an additive white Gaussian noise component.

The estimated model parameters of the time series are displayed in Table I. Deviations from the generated second

TABLE I. ESTIMATED MODEL PARAMETERS AND THEIR DEVIATION FROM THE GENERATED SECOND ORDER PARAMETERS AT A SIGNAL TO NOISE RATION OF $SNR \approx 27dB$.

time series	1	2	3
K_p	5 (+0)	5 (+0)	5.5 (+0)
T_w	2.9 (−0.1)	3.1 (+0.1)	3.5 (+0.3)
d	0.48 (−0.02)	0.48 (−0.02)	0.51 (+0.01)
fitting:	74.4%	74.8%	76.8%

time series	4	5	6
K_p	5.5 (+0)	6 (+0)	6 (+0)
T_w	3.1 (−0.1)	3.8 (−0.1)	3.7 (−0.3)
d	0.52 (−0.08)	0.61 (+0.01)	0.69 (−0.01)
fitting:	78.4%	81.6%	83.1%

order parameters are denoted in brackets. With this comparison it is shown, that the identification procedure still works for time series with additive white Gaussian noise components.

F. Application Example

The following generated data set consists of 15 generated time series, which can be seen in Figure 7.

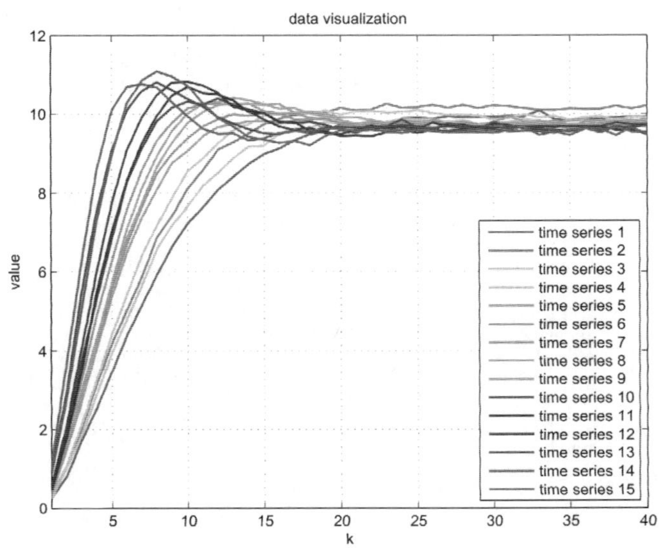

Figure 7. Visualisation of the data set, consisting of 15 time series.

The first time series is selected as the reference time series and is modeled with a second order model type. In Figure 8 the result of the reference based EHF estimation is shown. One can see that the time series 13, 14 and 15 exceed the deviation of $2.5 \cdot \sigma_{MSE}$ (highlighted in red). Figure 9 illustrates the model parameter based approach, which is calculated with the given in Section IV-D. The reference time series, which is highlighted with a green bar, corresponds to an EHF of 100%.

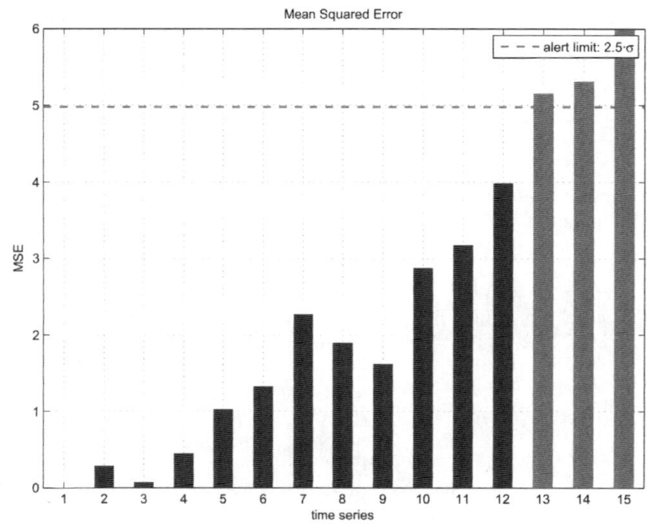

Figure 8. Reference based EHF estimation.

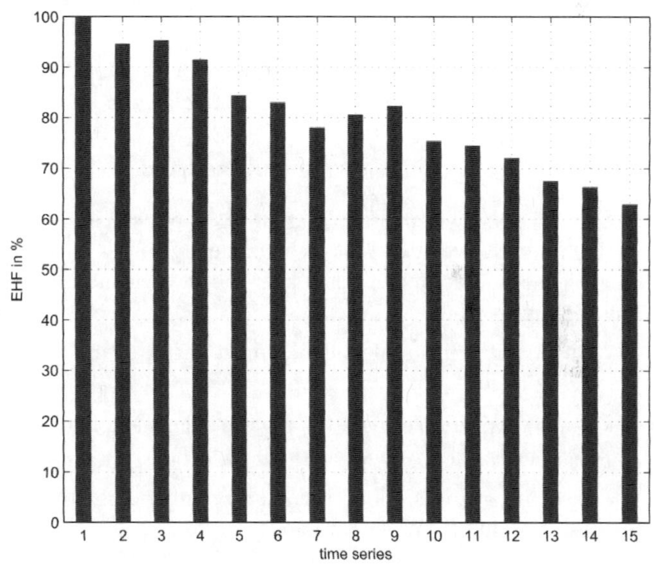

Figure 9. Model parameter based EHF estimation.

It is observable, that the critical time series from the reference based EHF estimation (Figure 8) are corresponding to an EHF below 70%.

V. RESULTS AND DISCUSSION

This section compares the approaches reference based and model parameter based with respect to calculation time and error prediction.

A. Calculation Time

Compared to the the PEM-function the other arithmetic operations such as MSE or absolute deviations are negligible.

With this negligence the two algorithms can be evaluated with respect to the calculation time as follows:

- **Reference based approach:**
  This approach needs one execution of the PEM algorithm for determining the reference model
- **Model parameter based approach:**
  The PEM algorithm has to be executed for each time series in the data set.

⇒ The reference based approach has lower calculation time, which can be critical if there are limited calculation capacities or real-time demands.

B. Error Prediction

- **Reference based approach:**
  With the MSE, high deviations between reference model and time series can be detected. However, the cause of the high deviations cannot be analyzed any further.
- **Model parameter based approach:**
  It is possible to detect which individual parameter is causing the deviation from the reference parameters and as a result the low EHF. This information can be helpful for more precise maintenance work.

⇒ The model parameter based approach provides more information for predicting the equipment health decrease.

VI. Conclusion and Future Work

A tool for the system identification-based equipment health modeling was developed. The EHF modeling tool was tested both on the real equipment data sets and on generated ones. The highlights of the tool are:

- Support for EHF system deployment in offline mode (i.e. using history data),
- Parameterization of the EHF models occurs automatically after the model type selection,
- In-depth analysis of the process background is not necessary (but still welcome!) and
- Processes in "out of steady-state" mode can be considered.

As a future work the application of the developed approach on other processes will be tested, including the preciseness analysis of the EHF estimation. Also the use cases from a process engineer's point of view should be investigated and possibly adapted.

Acknowledgment

The investigation of the described system identification-based EHF estimation method was a part of the EU cooperative project "Enhanced Power Pilot Line" (EPPL) which was co-funded by grants from Austria, Germany, The Netherlands, France, Italy, Portugal and the ENIAC Joint Undertaking.

References

[1] Y.-T. Kao, S. Dauzère-Pérès, J. Blue, and S.-C. Chang, "Impact of integrating equipment health in production scheduling for semiconductor fabrication," *Computers & Industrial Engineering*, vol. 120, pp. 450 – 459, 2018.

[2] R. K. Mobley, *An introduction to predictive maintenance.* Butterworth-Heinemann, 2002.

[3] S. Alaswad and Y. Xiang, "A review on condition-based maintenance optimization models for stochastically deteriorating system," *Reliability Engineering & System Safety*, vol. 157, pp. 54 – 63, 2017.

[4] R. Ahmad and S. Kamaruddin, "An overview of time-based and condition-based maintenance in industrial application," *Computers & Industrial Engineering*, vol. 63, no. 1, pp. 135 – 149, 2012.

[5] J. N.-M. et al., "A literature review on sampling techniques in semiconductor manufacturing," *IEEE Transactions on Semiconductor Manufacturing*, vol. 26, no. 2, pp. 188–195, May 2013.

[6] C. Yugma, J. Blue, S. Dauzère-Pérès, and A. Obeid, "Integration of scheduling and advanced process control in semiconductor manufacturing: review and outlook," *Journal of Scheduling*, vol. 18, no. 2, pp. 195–205, Apr 2015.

[7] C. Krauel and L. Weishäupl, "Multivariate approach for equipment health monitoring," *IFAC-PapersOnLine*, vol. 49, no. 12, pp. 716 – 720, 2016, 8th IFAC Conference on Manufacturing Modelling, Management and Control MIM 2016.

[8] H. M. Hashemian and W. C. Bean, "State-of-the-art predictive maintenance techniques*," *IEEE Transactions on Instrumentation and Measurement*, vol. 60, no. 10, pp. 3480–3492, Oct 2011.

[9] C. S. Kulkarni, J. R. Celaya, K. Goebel, and G. Biswas, "Physics based electrolytic capacitor degradation models for prognostic studies under thermal overstress," *in Proc. of the First European Conference of the Prognostics and Health; Dresden; Germany*, 2012.

[10] X.-S. Si, W. Wang, C.-H. Hu, and D.-H. Zhou, "Remaining useful life estimation a review on the statistical data driven approaches," *European Journal of Operational Research*, vol. 213, no. 1, pp. 1 – 14, 2011.

[11] A. Schirru, S. Pampuri, and G. D. Nicolao, "Particle filtering of hidden gamma processes for robust predictive maintenance in semiconductor manufacturing," in *2010 IEEE International Conference on Automation Science and Engineering*, Aug 2010, pp. 51–56.

[12] P. Lall, P. Choudhary, S. Gupte, and J. Hofmeister, "Statistical pattern recognition and built-in reliability test for feature extraction and health monitoring of electronics under shock loads," *IEEE Transactions on Components and Packaging Technologies*, vol. 32, no. 3, pp. 600–616, Sept 2009.

[13] P. O'Donovan, K. Leahy, K. Bruton, and D. T. J. O'Sullivan, "An industrial big data pipeline for data-driven analytics maintenance applications in large-scale smart manufacturing facilities," *Journal of Big Data*, vol. 2, no. 1, p. 25, Nov 2015.

[14] T. Le, M. Luo, J. Zhou, and H. L. Chan, "Predictive maintenance decision using statistical linear regression and kernel methods," in *Proceedings of the 2014 IEEE Emerging Technology and Factory Automation (ETFA)*, Sept 2014, pp. 1–6.

[15] S. j. Wu, N. Gebraeel, M. A. Lawley, and Y. Yih, "A neural network integrated decision support system for condition-based optimal predictive maintenance policy," *IEEE Transactions on Systems, Man, and Cybernetics - Part A: Systems and Humans*, vol. 37, no. 2, pp. 226–236, March 2007.

[16] S. S. Biswas, A. K. Srivastava, and D. Whitehead, "A real-time data-driven algorithm for health diagnosis and prognosis of a circuit breaker trip assembly," *IEEE Transactions on Industrial Electronics*, vol. 62, no. 6, pp. 3822–3831, June 2015.

[17] D. An, N. H. Kim, and J.-H. Choi, "Practical options for selecting data-driven or physics-based prognostics algorithms with reviews," *Reliability Engineering & System Safety*, vol. 133, pp. 223 – 236, 2015.

[18] A. Dementjev, A. Gellrich, A. Schirru, and A. Kästner, "System identification based equipment health estimation," in *in Proc. of the 15th APCM Conference, Freising, Germany*, 2015.

Shine on Transport Model Simulation Data: Web-based Visualization in R using Shiny

Antje von Schmidt, Rita Cyganski, Matthias Heinrichs
Institute of Transport Research
German Aerospace Center (DLR)
Germany, Berlin
e-mail: antje.vonschmidt@dlr.de, rita.cyganski@dlr.de, matthias.heinrichs@dlr.de

Abstract-**Microscopic transport demand models often use a large amount of data as input and provide detailed information for each individual trip as simulation output. Exploring this data can become very complex. Usually, several types of aggregation and disaggregation are performed on a spatial, temporal or demographic level. Consequently, often a combination of different tools is used for analyzing, communicating and validating the data. This paper introduces an interactive, user-friendly and scalable web application, which integrates different types of evaluations. Guidance and recommendations are given on how to implement such an application in R using Shiny.**

Keywords-transport demand model; simulation data; visualization; R; Shiny.

I. INTRODUCTION

Transport models are used to provide a realistic picture of the current traffic situation, to predict future development of transport demand or to make scenario-based analysis of various possible development paths, such as an aging population, changed prices or new mobility trends. The microscopic transport demand model TAPAS [1][2], which is addressed in this paper, reflects the individual mobility behavior. A large amount of different input data is required for this purpose. Within a simulation run, TAPAS calculates daily mobility patterns for each individual in the analysis area. Thereby, it provides individual trip chains with specific spatial and temporal information as well as a detailed description of each person and the associated household as simulation output. The sum of these gives an overall picture of the transport demand within a specified study area and timescale.

Not only the validation of input and output data, but also the analysis and communication of simulation results are not an easy task, especially if the target audience is heterogeneous and several output media have to be covered. There are many visualization types available, and which one to choose strongly depends on the research question and the domain of interest. In the field of transport research, different types of aggregation and disaggregation are performed, may they be on a spatial, temporal, or demographic level. A wide range of visualization tools are available [3]. Some of them can be used out of the box, and others require programming skills or are only intended for a certain type of visualization, spatial or non-spatial. Consequently, often a combination of these tools is used, also because commercial software solutions or eye catching animations are usually too expensive for being applied within research projects. In general, a flexible and extensible approach is preferable, which allows adaptation to the respective needs. The aim of this paper is to introduce the application "Transport Visualizer" (TraVis). It is an interactive, user-friendly and scalable web-based solution for analyzing, communicating and validating the simulation data of a transport model, such as TAPAS. The simulation data include both the input and the output data of the model. The application is implemented in R and Shiny. R is a popular, flexible and powerful programming language for statistical computing, data analysis and visualization, which is widely used in the scientific field [4]. With the help of the Shiny framework [5] it is possible to convert R analyses to an interactive web application. While TraVis is currently intended for internal use only, it is planned to make the application available as open source in the near future.

The paper is organized as follows: Related work is discussed in Section II, followed by an introduction of the simulation data used with TAPAS in Section III. Section IV describes the implementation requirements. The realization of the TraVis application is outlined in Section V. Finally, Section VI summarizes this paper and gives some ideas for future work.

II. RELATED WORK

For a long time, the role of visualization in transport modelling was largely limited to the static presentation of aggregated final results, primarily through statistical tables and simple graphs or the provision of key indicators describing the development of transport demand [6][7]. In recent years, map-based representations where increasingly used within the transport domain. In particular, an increase in the level of detail can be seen: from a general overview of the study area, over a certain part, time or topics down to the visualization of individual travel behavior [8]-[11]. Modern web technologies [12]-[14] and the growing availability of data have contributed to a significant increase in dynamic and interactive forms of visualization. In transport, as in other research fields, it is necessary to analyze the visualization requirements and consider the type of data to be visualized, the audience to be addressed, the purpose of the visualization, the appropriate level of detail, the aspects of the data that should be transmitted, and the target medium for which the visualization is generated. A general framework for the visualization of transport data and models is defined in [15].

However, the type of visualization is also important. Charts are often used to represent information on a high or intermediate level of detail. Which one should be used depends on the data type and on what is to be shown. In [16], a chart selector guide and four basic methods of data analysis are defined that can help to choose the right chart type for comparison, composition, distribution, and relation. The comparison of single values, such as totals or means, is best shown with regular bar or column charts, while line charts are more suitable for identifying distributions of continuous values or the development of a measure over time. Stacked charts can be used to represent the absolute or relative changes within the composition of categorical variables. Scatter and bubble charts are suitable for representing correlations between two respective three numerical variables, whereas parallel coordinates can be used to point out relationships between multivariate data. A chord diagram is a common way to illustrate interrelation between data in a matrix, whereas data with a spatial context are typically represented by suitable maps. For example, a choropleth map can help to identify regional varieties, while flow maps show the quantity of movements between geographical units. Spatial changes between scenarios are usually achieved by difference maps, whereas animated maps can be used to represent differences over time. There are many more ways for visualizing data, and not all of them can be given here. Hence, only a brief insight into the diversity is given. A good overview can be found at [17].

Although many visualization concepts and tools are available, the challenge remaining is to integrate these different approaches and to enable the users to perform their analyses without mastering programming languages or using a variety of tools.

III. Simulation Data

Microscopic transport demand models usually require a variety of different input data, such as population, locations, network, transport offers, timetable, land use and property data. All this data is very heterogeneous in terms of format and time frame. TAPAS, for instance, requires a highly differentiated synthetic population as main input for the simulation, which is generated by the SYNTHESIZER [18]. Within such transport models, household information plays an important role in the choice of destination and means of transport. Therefore, a synthetic population contains information at both the person and household level. A TAPAS simulation needs for each individual the age, sex and a status variable. The latter is set to one of the following values: child under 6 years, pupil, student, employed (fulltime or halftime), unemployed, or retired. In addition, information on possible mobility options is required, such as driving license, public transport ticket, bike or the mobility budget. Household information comprises the number of persons, the total household income, the number and type of vehicles that belong to the household as well as the spatial reference of the address. The simulation results, on the other hand, provide detailed information for each individual trip, including, among other, trip purpose, transport mode chosen, start and end time of the trip as well as of the activities, and the coordinates of the visited location. Table I provides an excerpt of the simulation output. Overall, data associated with an average simulation run is quite vast, reaching roughly 13 million trips for the city of Berlin for the current population forecast of 3.8 million inhabitants in 2030 [19].

IV. Implementation Requirements

Exploring the simulation data of a transport model can become very complex. Which information should be provided depends on the story to tell. Furthermore, the tabular representation of the simulation data in Section III is understandable for machines but not easily readable by humans, especially when handling large amounts of data. Most of all, the spatial context will be lost. Based on related work, the following aspects were selected as requirements for the implementation.

A. Data type

As mentioned before, the simulation data include a variety of heterogeneous data types, which all have to be taken into account for exploring the data in a disaggregated or aggregated manner. Besides the data with a spatial context like activity location (point), traffic flow (line), vehicle density (polygon) or origin-destination matrices (line and point), there are also descriptive variables. These can be further subdivided into continuous, discrete and categorical data, such as the trip length, person age, or the activity selected.

TABLE I. Generated Individual Daily Activity Plan For A Sample Person

P-ID	HH-ID	Trip						Purpose				
		Start time	*Duration*	*Mode*	*Distance*	*Zone*		*Activity*	*Start time*	*Duration*	*Location*	
						Start	*End*				*Start*	*End*
1	1	7:15	10 min	bike	2 km	200	202	shopping	7:25	5 min	lon/lat	lon/lat
1	1	7:30	30 min	public transport	10 km	202	232	working	8:00	8:30 h	lon/lat	lon/lat
1	1	16:30	15 min	bike	3 km	232	230	sport	16:45	1:00 h	lon/lat	lon/lat
1	1	17:45	45 min	bike	9 km	230	200	home	18:30	12:00 h	lon/lat	lon/lat

B. Target audience and purpose

The visualizer shall help modelers to review the model values and disseminate the results to a wider audience, including both the scientific community and the public. Therefore, different media, including scientific publications, static presentations or interactive visualizations is intended.

C. Level of detail

The target application should contain all levels of detail of spatial, temporal, and demographic dimensions. It shall be possible to aggregate simulated data at both levels – for the complete study area or parts of it. This can be used, e.g., to validate the applied synthetic population, including the vehicle fleet and mobility options. The simulation result should be used for computing common key indicators of the transport demand (e.g., modal split) by aggregation. At the most detailed level, the individual travel behavior should be extracted from the simulation output and visualized. In addition, the stationary transport (parking vehicles) should be included in the analysis, as it can provide useful information for future urban planning. This can be taken into account, for example, if autonomous driving is offered within the simulation, as it is assumed that the space required for parking will change considerably [20].

D. Output medium and interactivity

According to the different audience and purpose, both static as well as dynamic media have to be addressed. To understand changes, for example between different scenario parameters or time frames, it is essential to provide the possibility to compare the corresponding simulation results. To take a closer look at certain aspects of the simulation output, the use of filters should be supported, including the following filter types: specific groups of persons or households, mode choice, location, trip purpose, time of traveling, distance, trip type and specific part of the study area. Detailed filter options are shown in Table II.

TABLE II. FILTER OPTIONS

Filter	Elements
Region type	agglomeration, urban, sub urban, rural, zone IDs
Household size	1, 2, 3, 4, 5+
Number of cars	0, 1, 2
Person group	kids (< 6), pupil, student, employed, unemployed, pensioner
Transport mode	walk, bicycle, car, car (co-driver), cab, public transport, other
Activities	education, free time, private matters, shopping, work, other
Locations	education, free time, private matters, shopping, work, other
Trip type	local people, commuters, origin, destination
Time of traveling	early (0 - 6), morning (7- 12), afternoon (13 - 18), evening (19 - 24)
Distance	1000m, 2000m, 3000m, 4000m, 5000m, 5000m+

Another essential aspect is the opportunity to adjust the resolution of the spatial aggregation, where travel analysis zones or the European wide standardization for geographically grids [21] may be applied. To address the various target media, it is required to export appropriate figures and to show the results on screen.

E. Visualization type and customization

With regards to the different types of data and the various target media, the application should contain suitable visualizations, such as different charts, maps and animations. This is necessary for presenting the simulation data according to the desired level of detail. Furthermore, the application should be scalable so that new types of reporting can be integrated immediately. Besides the choice of the right visualization type, it is also very important to have the opportunity to change their appearance. Therefore, it is required to customize layout related attributes, such as the color of the bars, the chart background, and the position of labels or of the legend as well as the appropriate font type and size. With the focus on internationalization, it is also necessary to supply different languages in order to automatically generate the required labels for the visualization.

V. REALIZATION IN R USING SHINY

All simulation data are stored in a PostgreSQL/PostGIS database. A corresponding view lists all existing simulations of a research project and several SQL functions were written for data preparation. This would also make it possible to parse the data with conventional programs. However, the aim is to enable users to perform their analyses automatically and without the use of alternative tools. Because of the popularity, flexibility, as well as the computational power of R and the possibility of combining it with the interactivity of modern web user interfaces by using Shiny, this application architecture was chosen for TraVis. The functionality of Shiny can be easily enhanced by including HTML widgets for interactive visualization types, requiring usually no further web development skills.

A. Application structure

A basic Shiny application is usually structured either in one script (*app.R)* or split into two: a user-interface script (*ui.R*) and a computational script (*server.R)*. This is most likely sufficient for small applications, but the programming code can quickly become unwieldy in larger ones. Therefore, it is recommended to split these main scripts further to make the code easier to maintain for developers. This can be additionally supported by a modular application design. Currently, there are no suggestions or best practices for organizing R scripts within large applications. Therefore, the file structure shown in Table III was developed and is used within TraVis.

TABLE III. USED FILE STRUCTURE

Folder/File	Description
/data	stored evaluated data (*.rdata)
/documentation	application documentation
/scripts	
/functions	outsourced functions including: database connection, text formatter, conversion functions of geometry types
/modules	includes subfolder for each module, which contains the corresponding ui.R and server.R files
/server	computational snippets
/settings	application settings, e.g, used packages, properties (de/en), database config
/ui	user-interface snippets
/www	
/css	Stylesheets
/js	JavaScript functions
global.R	global objects, with reference to /settings, /scripts
server.R	main computational file, with reference to /server
ui.R	main user-interface file, with reference to /ui

B. Modularizing

The aim is to implement a flexible and scalable application. For this purpose, it is important to keep the programming code clear and manageable. Recently, the capability to use modules was added to Shiny as a new feature [22]. Shiny modules can be used to capture functionality and avoid name collisions by using name spaces for the input and output elements. This is especially important as element ids must be unique within a Shiny application. The following module functions for the evaluation part were defined so far:

- Include a tab set with three tabs, in order to avoid information and visual overlays.
- Show a table in one tab.
- Render a chart in one tab and supply a setting panel to adjust the chart layout individually. This includes customization options, such as the type of the chart, an adoptable color scheme for matching the respective project's corporate design, text alignment and legend position. Furthermore, provide the possibility to export the generated chart as a printable image.
- Render a map in one tab, enabling support for panning, zooming and switching layer on/off, as well as for exporting the map as a printable image. Supply a settings panel to adjust the map layout individually. This includes customization options, such as the color scheme and legend position.
- Supply a panel with elements to filter the simulation output according to the filter options given in Table II.
- Send aggregated data for the whole study area to the tab with the chart.
- Send data on the selected spatial unit to the visualization tab that shows the table respectively the map.

For flexibility reasons and further usage within other applications, these defined functions have been split into several Shiny modules, which are separated into individual R files. The *tableModule* includes an interactive table by using the HTML widget "DT" [23], which is a wrapper of the JavaScript library "DataTables". The *chartModule* contained a chart and a corresponding setting panel, which is shown in Figure 1 (b). For this purpose, the "highcharter" [24] widget is used, which is a wrapper for the "Highcharts" [13] JavaScript library. This library contains a large number of different interactive chart types and supports the export of charts in different output formats (e.g., png, svg or jpeg). The *mapModule* contains a map and a corresponding settings panel, as illustrated in Figure 1 (c). For rendering the map, both the "leaflet" [25] widget, related to the JavaScript "Leaflet" [14] library, and the "highcharter" widget, which includes also maps, is integrated within this module. "Leaflet" is ideal for displaying maps within a web browser, as all the interactive features, such as panning, zooming and switching layer on/off come into use. Within static media, however, these maps are not as well suited as maps from "Highcharts", especially since they have no built-in export interface. To support the different defined output media, both possibilities have been integrated in TraVis. Furthermore, a *filterModule* was created, which includes a panel with the defined filter options and the functionality of filtering the data accordingly. The *tableModule, chartModule* and *mapModule* are wrapped within the higher-level *analysisModule* module. This module includes the tab set panel, where each tab represents the settings of one of the sub-modules, and additionally the interface to the data aggregation functionality for the *chartModule*. The corresponding data to be displayed is then transferred to all sub-modules as parameters. The *analysisModule* is used several times in the application, currently for evaluating the population, mobility options, vehicle fleet and stationary traffic. Further, an *analysisPlusModule* has been created for evaluating the transport demand. The *analysisPlusModule* additionally contains the *filterModule* and is used many times as well in the application. This modular design makes the application easily expandable. Finally, the elements of the user-interface and the related computational parts can be organized better, which makes it also easier for the developer to maintain such an application.

C. Data managagement

Analyzing large amounts of data within the R environment can slow down the performance, because all data is kept in the working memory. For this reason, the disaggregated simulation data is not loaded directly into R. Instead, some data preparation steps are done within the database before, e.g., filtering, mapping or aggregation to the target spatial resolution, to reduce the amount of data.

The simulation results generated by TAPAS are not overwritten when simulation parameters are adjusted, but new result data is generated. Once generated, the data is static and can be stored in corresponding R objects. This has the advantage that the data does not have to be retrieved from the database again for a new simulation evaluation.

D. *Internationalisation*

Results of research projects often have to be presented in different languages. Therefore, it is necessary to adjust the labels of the figures, e.g., titles, axes or legends, accordingly. This can be done automatically in the TraVis application. Switching between English and German is currently implemented. A general approach for multi-language support within a Shiny application can be found at [26].

E. *Application frontend*

The user-interface of TraVis is built with a dashboard for Shiny applications [27]. It includes three parts: header, sidebar and body. The header is currently used for displaying the application name and to toggle the sidebar. Further elements can be integrated. The sidebar contains the navigation of the application. The top menu item is related to the main settings. Here, it is possible to select one or more simulation runs belonging to a chosen research project. Furthermore, the target spatial resolution can be defined. The spatial scope can be further restricted using the study area menu item. The main setting panel is shown in Figure 1 (a). All other menu items refer to evaluation tasks and currently relate to population, mobility options, vehicle fleet, stationary traffic, and transport demand. The sidebar also offers the possibility to define the target language, which will be used within the entire session. The body includes the main panel. Depending on the chosen evaluation task, the corresponding module *analysisModule* or respective *analysisModulePlus* will be shown. At present, evaluations can be performed for the entire study area and parts thereof on a spatial, temporal and demographic level.

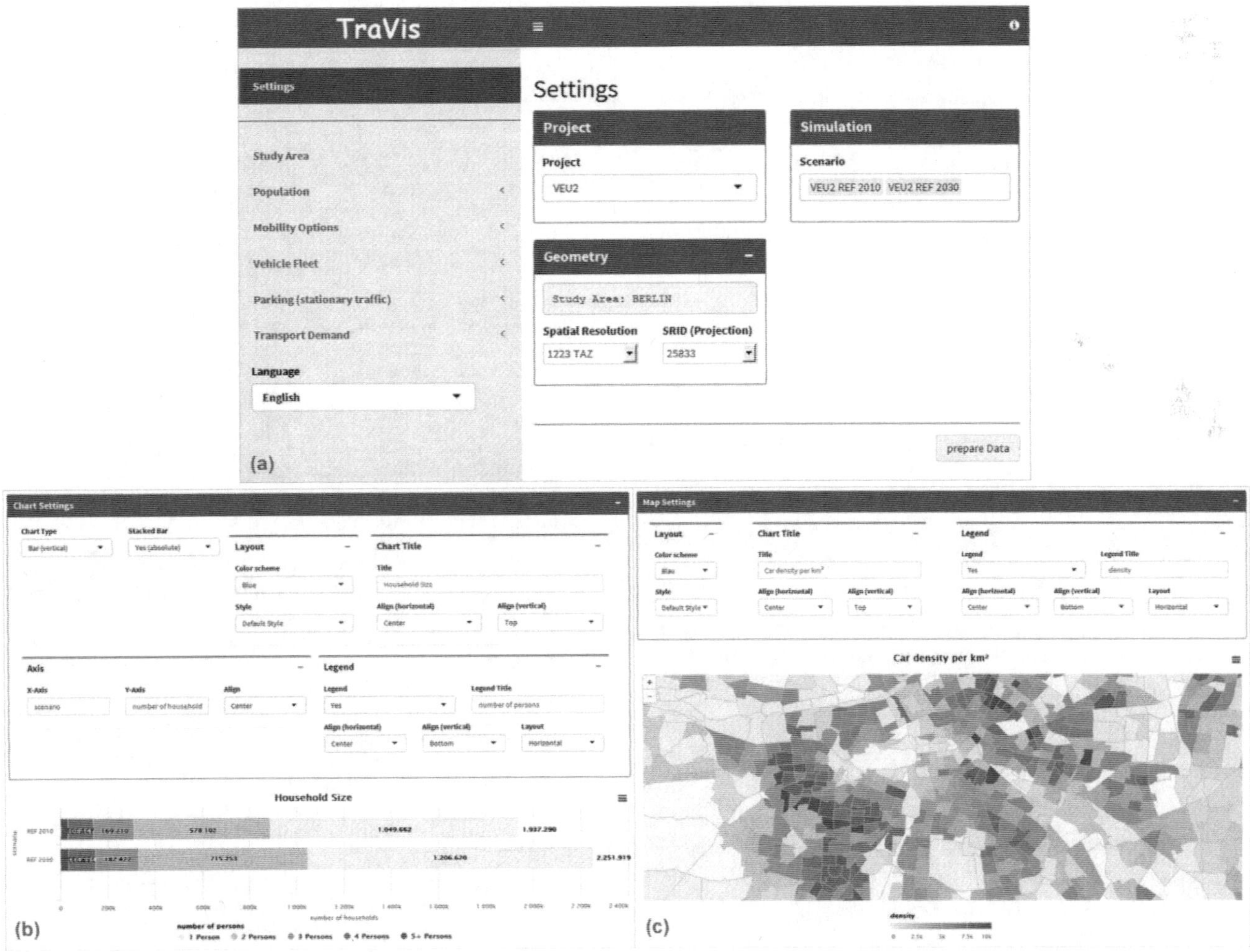

Figure 1. TraVis user-interface showing the main setting panel (a), the chart view (b) with aggregated household data for 2010 versus 2030 of Berlin and the map view (c) with a regional zoom of the city of Berlin representing the predicted car density per km^2 for 2030.

VI. Conclusion And Future Work

This paper introduces a flexible and scalable approach for developing an interactive, user-friendly and scalable web-based application for analyzing, communicating and validating the simulation data of a microscopic transport model with R and Shiny. But the development of such a tool is not always straightforward. If a comprehensive application has to be created, the implementation can quickly become complex and time-consuming. It is therefore recommended to create readable and reusable code. This includes creating a suitable file structure within the R workspace, splitting the programing code into multiple files, deploying functions or even packages, and the use of Shiny modules. This approach could also be used to analyze research results within a different domain.

Upcoming work will focus on the visualization of time-space-related data, such as the individual travel behavior or the computed transport volume. The aim will be to provide such visualizations within R and extend the presented TraVis application accordingly. Furthermore, it is planned to make the application available as open source.

References

[1] M. Heinrichs, D. Krajzewicz, R Cyganski, and A. von Schmidt, "Disaggregated car fleets in microscopic travel demand modelling," 7th International Conference on Ambient Systems, Networks and Technologies, pp. 155-162, 2016, doi: https://doi.org/10.1016/j.procs.2016.04.111, accessed: 2018.09.18

[2] M. Heinrichs, D. Krajzewicz, R Cyganski, and A. von Schmidt, „Introduction of car sharing into existing car fleets in microscopic travel demand modelling," Personal and Ubiquitous Computing, Springer, pp. 1055-1065, 2017 doi: https://doi.org/10.1007/s00779-017-1031-3, accessed: 2018.09.18

[3] N. Yau, „Visualize this: the flowingdata guide to design, visualization, and statistics," Wiley Publishing, 2011, ISBN: 978-0-470-94488-2

[4] R Core Team, "R: A language and environment for statistical computing. R Foundation for Statistical Computing, Vienna, Austria, 2017, http://www.R-project.org, accessed: 2018.09.18

[5] W. Chang, J. Cheng, JJ. Allaire, Y. Xie, and J. McPherson, "Shiny: Web Application Framework for R," 2017 https://CRAN.R-project.org/package=shiny, accessed: 2018.09.18

[6] J. L. Bowman, M. A. Bradley, and J. Gibb, "The Sacramento Activity-based Travel Demand Model: Estimation and Validation Results," presented at the European Transport Conference, 2006

[7] R. M. Pendyala, R. Kitamura, A. Kikuchi, T. Yamamoto, and S. Fujii, "Florida Activity Mobility Simulator: Overview and Preliminary Validation Results," Transportation Research Record (1921), pp. 123-130, 2005

[8] X. Liu, W. Y. Yan, and J. Y. Chow, "Time-geographic relationships between vector fields of activity patterns and transport systems," Journal of Transport Geography, 42, pp. 22-33, 2015

[9] O. Klein, "Visualizing Daily Mobility: Towards Other Modes of Representation," A. Banos, and T. Thevenien (Eds.), Geographical Information and Urban Transport Systems, Wiley Online Library, pp. 167-220, 2013

[10] H. Guo, Z. Wang, B. Yu, H. Zhao, and X. Yuan, "Tripvista: Triple perspective visual trajectory analytics and its application on microscopic traffic data at a road intersection," Visualization Symposium (PacificVis), IEEE Pacific, pp. 163-170, 2011, ISBN: 978-1-61284-935-5

[11] R. Cyganski, A. von Schmidt, and D. Teske, "Applying Geovisualisation to Validate and Communicate Simulation Results of an Activity-based Travel Demand Model," GI_Forum - Journal for Geographic Information Science. pp. 575-578, 2015

[12] M. Bostock, V. Ogievetsky, and J. Heer, "D3: Data-Driven Documents", IEEE Transactions on Visualization and Computer Graphics, IEEE Press, 17 (12), pp. 2301–2309, 2011, doi: https://doi.org/10.1109/TVCG.2011.185, accessed: 2018.09.18

[13] Highsoft, "Highcharts: interactive JavaScript charts for your webpage," 2009, https://www.highcharts.com, accessed: 2018.09.18

[14] V. Agafonkin, "Leaflet: a JavaScript library for interactive maps," 2011, https://leafletjs.com, accessed: 2018.09.18

[15] M. Loidl et al., "GIS and Transport Modeling-Strengthening the Spatial Perspective," ISPRS International Journal of Geo-Information, Bd. 5, pp. 84, 2016

[16] A. Abela, "Advanced Presentations by Design: Creating Communication That Drives Action," Pfeiffer, edition 2th, 2013, ISBN: 978-1-118-34791-1

[17] Ferdio, "Data Viz Project," http://datavizproject.com, accessed: 2018.09.18

[18] A. von Schmidt, R. Cyganski, and D. Krajzewicz, „Generation of synthetic populations for transport demand models, a comparison of methods taking Berlin as an example", "Generierung synthetischer Bevölkerungen für Verkehrsnachfragemodelle, ein Methodenvergleich am Beispiel von Berlin" (original title), In HEUREKA'17 - Optimierung in Verkehr und Transport, FGSV-Verlag, pp. 193-210, 2017

[19] Berlin Senate Department for Urban Development and Housing, "Population Forecast for Berlin and the Districts 2015 - 2030" https://www.stadtentwicklung.berlin.de/planen/bevoelkerungsprognose, accessed: 2018.09.18

[20] D. Heinrichs, „Autonomous Driving and Urban Land Use," in Autonomous Driving. Technical, Legal and Social Aspects, Springer Open, pp. 213-231, 2016, ISBN: 978-3-662-48845-4

[21] INSPIRE, http://inspire.ec.europa.eu, accessed: 2018.09.18

[22] J. Cheng, "Modularizing Shiny app code," 2017, https://shiny.rstudio.com/articles/modules.html, accessed: 2018.09.18

[23] X. Yihui, "DT: A Wrapper of the JavaScript Library 'DataTables', " R package version 0.4, 2018, https://CRAN.R-project.org/package=DT, accessed: 2018.09.18

[24] J. Kunst, "highcharter: A Wrapper for the 'Highcharts' Library," R package version 0.5.0, 2017, https://CRAN.R-project.org/package=highcharter, accessed: 2018.09.18

[25] J. Cheng, B. Karambelkar, and Y. Xie, "leaflet: Create Interactive Web Maps with the JavaScript 'Leaflet' Library," R package version 2.0.2, 2018, https://CRAN.R-project.org/package=leaflet, accessed: 2018.09.18

[26] C. Ladroue, "Multilingual Shiny App," 2014, https://github.com/chrislad/multilingualShinyApp, accessed: 2018.09.18

[27] W. Chang and B. Borges Ribeiro, "shinydashboard: Create Dashboards with 'Shiny'," R package version 0.7.0, 2018, https://CRAN.R-project.org/package=shinydashboard, accessed: 2018.09.18

Machine Learning for Cyber Defense and Attack

Manjeet Rege
Graduate Programs in Software
University of St. Thomas
St. Paul, MN, USA
Email: rege@stthomas.edu

Raymond Blanch K. Mbah
Graduate Programs in Software
University of St. Thomas
St. Paul, MN, USA
Email: kong1343@stthomas.edu

***Abstract*—The exponential advancements in processing, storage and network technologies have led to the recent explosive growth in big data, connectivity and machine learning. The world is becoming increasingly digitalized - raising security concerns and the desperate need for robust and advanced security technologies and techniques to combat the increasing complex nature of cyber-attacks. This paper discusses how machine learning is being used in cyber security in both defense and offense activities, including discussions on cyber-attacks targeted at machine learning models. Specifically, we discuss the applications of machine learning in carrying out cyber-attacks, such as in smart botnets, advanced spear fishing and evasive malwares. We also explain the application of machine learning in cyber security, such as in threat detection and prevention, malware detection and classification, and network risk scoring.**

Keywords- Cyber Security; Machine Learning; Malware; Thread Detection and Classification; Network Risk Scoring.

I. INTRODUCTION

Digital security remains a top concern as the world is becoming increasingly digitalized. With advances in network technologies, such as the Internet, access to cutting edge technology and research findings has never been this easy with research papers being made public daily and the digital world becoming increasingly open sourced. Unfortunately, cutting edge research and breakthroughs in technology are both available to the security analyst and cybercriminals who have various interests in making use of these technologies and information. Research and advances in the field of machine learning has resulted in algorithms and technologies for improving security solutions that help in identifying and decisively dealing with security threats. However, this also makes it possible for cybercriminals to use this knowledge in crafting and launching bigger and more sophisticated attacks.

Cybercriminals have a huge advantage in the cyber war since, out of many attempts, they need to be right just once. For security, on the other hand, the desired success rate needs to be 100%. Research shows that in 2017, multiple organizations, business, individuals and applications were victimized by cybercriminals [1]. Stolen information included sensitive classified intelligence data, financial records, and personally identifiable information. The use of these kinds of information can be catastrophic, especially when it is made publicly available or sold on the black market. Some research statistics with regards to the impact of cyber security to businesses, organizations, and individuals include:

- In recent years, cybercrime has been responsible for more that $400 billion in funds stolen and costs to mitigate damages caused by crimes [2].
- It has been predicted that a shortage of over 1.8 million cybersecurity workers will be experienced by 2022 [3].
- It's been predicted that organizations globally will spend at least $100 billion annually on cybersecurity protection [4].
- Attackers currently make over $1 billion in annually revenue from Ransomware attacks, such as Wannacry and CryptoWall attacks [5].

Keeping up and countering the increasing sophistication of cyber-attacks is becoming increasingly challenging, as defense tools quickly become obsolete. In fact, on average, it can take up to 240 days to detect an intrusion [6]. The sophistication of cyber-attacks is growing both in scale and complexity making it increasingly challenging to keep up and respond to the constant emergence of new threats and vulnerabilities. One major area that is currently having a high impact on cyber security is machine learning, which will be the focus of this paper.

The rest of the paper is structured as follows. In Section II, we present an overview of machine learning, including its various categories (supervised and unsupervised learning). Section III describes the applications of machine learning in cybersecurity, such as in network risk scoring and in malware detection and prevention. In section IV, we discuss the applications of machine learning in cyber-attacks, such as in smart botnets, advanced spear fishing and evasive malwares. Section V discusses cyber-attacks targeted at machine learning models.

II. OVERVIEW OF MACHINE LEARNING

Machine learning is a sub-field of artificial intelligence that aims to empower systems with the ability to use data to learn and improve without being explicitly programmed [7]. It relies on mathematical models derived from analyzing patterns in datasets, which are then used to make predictions on new input data. Applications of machine learning span across a vast set of domains including e-commerce, where machine learning applications are used to make recommendations based on customer behavior and preferences, and health care, where machine learning is used to predict epidemics or the likelihood of a patient having certain diseases, such as cancer, based on their medical records.

Machine learning algorithms can be categorized as Predictive (Supervised Learning) or Pattern Discovery (Unsupervised Learning) [39]. In supervised learning, there is always a target variable, the value of which the machine learning model learns to predict using different learning algorithms e.g., based on an IP address location, frequencies of Web requests and times of request, a machine learning model can predict if a given IP address was part of a Distributed Denial of Service (DDOS) attack. A variety of Machine learning algorithms fall under the umbrella of supervised learning, including Linear and Logistic Regression, Decision Tree and Support Vector Machine (SVM) [40]. On the other hand, in unsupervised learning, there is no prediction of a target variable, rather, unsupervised algorithms learn to find interesting associations or patterns in datasets e.g., identifying computer programs, such as malwares with similar operating/behavioral patterns using clustering and association algorithms.

One particular domain where machine learning is seeing wide adoption is that of cybercrime and security which has multiple use cases for machine learning, such as in malware and log analysis. The power of machine learning is leveraged by cybercriminals as well as security experts. We will now discuss how machine learning is being used for cybercrime as well as cyber security.

III. Applications of Machine Learning in Cyber Security

With the growing threat of cybersecurity, studies are focusing on machine learning and its vast set of tools and techniques to identify, stop and respond to sophisticated cyber-attacks [21]. Machine learning can be leveraged in various domains of cyber security to provide analytical-based approaches for attack detection and response. It can also enhance security processes by automating routine tasks and making it easy for security analysts to quickly work with semi-automated tasks. Some popular applications of machine learning in cyber security are presented below.

A. Threat detection and classification

Machine learning algorithms can be implemented in applications to identify and respond to cyber-attacks before they take effect [8]. This is usually achieved using a model developed by analyzing big data sets of security events and identifying the pattern of malicious activities. As a result, when similar activities are detected, they are automatically dealt with. The models' training dataset is typically made up of previous identified and recorded Indicators of Compromise (IOC), which are then used to build models and systems that can monitor, identify and responds to threats in real time. Also, with the availability of IOC datasets, we can use machine learning classification algorithms to identify the various behaviors of malwares in datasets and classify them accordingly. Studies have been made on behavioral-based analysis frameworks that make use of machine learning clustering and classification techniques to analyze the behaviors of thousands of malwares [14]. This makes it possible to use the learned patterns to automate the process of detecting and classifying new malware. This can help security analysts or other automated systems to quickly identify and classify a new type of threat and respond to it accordingly using a data driven decisions. For example, by using a historic dataset containing detailed events of WannaCry ransomware attacks, a machine learning model can learn to identify similar attacks, thereby making it possible to automate the identification and response process of similar attacks. Machine learning techniques have also been used in IP traffic classification [15][16] which can help automate the process of intrusion detection systems that can be used to identify behavioral patterns as in the case of DDOS attacks. With the increasing number of machine learning techniques, other studies have been focused on analyzing multiple machine learning solutions for intrusion detection systems including single, hybrid and ensemble classifies [17].

B. Network risk scoring

This refers to the use of quantitative measures to assign risk scores to various sections of a network, thereby helping organizations to prioritize their cyber security resources accordingly with regards to various risk scores. Machine learning can be used to automate this process by analyzing historic cyber-attack datasets and determining which areas of networks were mostly involved in certain types of attacks. Using machine learning is advantageous in the sense that the resulting scores will not only be based on domain knowledge of the networks but most importantly, the scores will be data driven. This score can help quantify the likelihood and impact of an attack with respect to a given network area and can thus help organizations to reduce to risk of being victimized by attacks.

Studies have been carried out on the use of machine learning algorithms such K-Nearest Neighbor, Support Vector Machines, and Random Forest algorithms to analyze and cluster network assets based on their connectivity [18]. Other studies have focused on how IOT devices connected to small and Medium Sized Enterprises (SMEs) can be used to lunch attacks on SMEs [19]. Machine learning powered systems have been developed that make use of the mutual reinforcement principle to analyze massive volumes of alerts in organization networks to determine risk scores by taking into account the associations of various network entities [20].

C. Automate routine security tasks and optimize human analysis

Machine learning can be used to automate repetitive tasks carried out by security analysts during security activities. This can be done through analyzing records/reports of past actions taken by security analysts to successfully identify and respond to certain attacks and using this knowledge to build a model that can identify similar attacks and respond accordingly without human intervention. Though it is difficult to automate the full security process and replace the human security analyst, there are some aspects of the analysis that machine learning can automate including malware detection, network log analysis, and vulnerability assessments, such as network risk analysis. By incorporating machine learning in the security work flow, 'man and machine' can join forces and accomplish things at a degree of speed and quality that will have been otherwise impossible.

With the exponential growth of artificial intelligence, we see an increasing number of tasks being automated. It is tempting to think that artificial intelligence will increase automation, and certain tasks that are currently performed by humans will be taken over by machines. This might be true in some cases, however there are numerous cases where the combination of artificial intelligence and human intelligence produce far better results than each will produce by itself. It is for this reason that we are currently seeing the rise of artificial intelligence companies with a focus on not only creating AI product for automating tasks, but creating products that enhancing and complement the productivity of human analysts. A well-known example of such a company is Palantir [9], which creates products that make it easy for analysts to aggregate and make use of massive volumes of data.

In other to enhance security analysts activities, studies have been carried out on the use of machine learning algorithms, such as genetic algorithms and decision tries to create applications that generate rules for classifying network connections [22]. Other approaches go far as to implement a cognitive architecture to create an automated cyber defense decision-making system with expert-level ability inspired by how humans reason and learn [23]. Cybersecurity analysts typically have to spend time responding to multiple events, which sometimes include false positives, which mostly turn out to be a waste of their time. Studies have been done to show that machine learning classifiers can be trained on alert data to identify and distinguish between false positives and true positives, thereby making it possible to create an automated system that will alert the analyst only on scenarios that include true positives [24].

IV. APPLICATIONS OF MACHINE LEARNING IN CYBER CRIME

Just as machine learning is a promising tool to deal with the growing cyber threats, as shown in the previous section, it also acts as a tool that can be leveraged by malicious attackers. For instance, there have been studies that show the possibility of cybercriminals leveraging machine learning to create intelligent malware that can outsmart current intelligent defense systems [25]. Hence, as the field of machine learning progresses at a rapid rate while offering promising solutions for cyber defense, it also makes it possible for cybercriminals to use it in carrying out more sophisticated attacks at scale as well as lunch attacks targeted at machine learning models. Everyone including security analysts and cybercriminals are actively seeking new innovative AI techniques/technologies to add to their arsenal of cyber weapons. For instance, just like cyber defense specialist are actively analyzing data to better understand an attackers' patterns, the attackers themselves can also steal data about users and analyze it to better craft their attacks. An example includes illegally accessing and analyzing a targeted users' emails with the aim of having a better understanding of their email patterns and leveraging that to craft better phishing emails.

Some popular categories of machine learning based attack techniques include:

A. *Unauthorized Access*

Machine learning can be used to gain unauthorized access to systems, such as those involving captchas. One field that has been hugely impacted by machine learning is that of machine vision, whereby a machine is trained to identify objects. This is the same technology being used in self driving cars where cars rely on machine learning to identify and avoid obstacles. With machines being capable of identifying objects in images, they can be trained to bypass captcha-based system that relies on a user to identify the objects in an image before being authorized [10]. Also, machine learning algorithms, such as neural networks that attempt to mimic the human brain can be trained to speed up and automate social engineering techniques, such as guessing user passwords by training the model with big datasets containing data of previously hacked user information including their usernames and passwords and any kind of information that can be used to enhance the guessing process.

Multiple studies have been carried out on how machine learning can be leverage to gain unauthorized access to systems. Examples include PassGANs that can generate high quality password guesses by using Generative Adversarial Networks (GAN) and real password leaks to learn the distribution of real passwords [26]. Some studies focus on using machine learning to generate passwords for real time broot force attacks that rely on testing different variants of passwords with the aim of successfully gaining unauthorized access to a system [27]. Other studies focus on using Deep learning to bypass CAPTCHAs without human intervention [28][29], while others focus on leveraging machine learning to clone human voices. Applications exists that leverage machine learning techniques to clone voices [30], making it possible to impersonate people.

B. *Evasive Malware*

Typically, the creation of malware involves writing a malicious program which in most basic cases can be identified by security programs which have records of the malwares' signature. However, there have been cases where machine learning has been used to generate malware code that other security programs could not detect including machine learning based systems [11]. Another example includes DeepLocker, an AI powered malware developed by IBM researchers that is capable of leveraging facial recognition, voice recognition and geolocation to identify its target before launching its attack [12]. There's a lot of research on using machine learning to generate computer code with the goal of replacing computer programmers with AI systems in scenarios where an AI can write the code without human intervention. Examples include a recent research carried out at Microsoft to create AI systems that can generate code without human intervention [13].

C. Spear Phishing

Machine learning can be leveraged to carryout advanced spear phishing attacks for example, by illegally collecting genuine email data of targeted individuals and feeding the data to a machine learning model which can then learn from the data, derive context from the data and generate emails that look similar and genuine to those it learned from. This can then be incorporated into an automated process thereby speeding up the efficiency and speed in which cybercriminals can launch targeted phishing attacks. Some phishing attacks leverage social engineering to illegally acquire information about their targeted users.

Social engineering is a popular kind of attack technique that uses deception to manipulate individuals to get their personal information. There have been studies on using machine learning to carry out sophisticated social engineering attacks. Examples include studies that used long short-term memory (LSTM) neural network and recurrent neural network that are trained on social media post extracted from a targets time line with the aim of manipulating users into clicking on deceptive URLs [31][32]. Similar approaches can also be used to carry out email based phishing attacks.

V. SECURITY THREADS TO MACHINE LEARNING PRODUCTS

From the beginning of the computer revolution, cybercriminals have always been on the lookout for ways to exploit software vulnerabilities and carry out malicious activities. With the explosive growth of artificial intelligence technology, cybercriminals are beginning to look for ways to exploit vulnerabilities in this domain. Attacks on machine learning systems are typically discussed in the context of adversarial machine learning which is concerned with the security of applying machine learning techniques to security-related tasks, such as biometric recognition, spam filtering, network intrusion and malware detection. Attacks on machine learning algorithms can be categorized into three domains: attacks targeted at altering training datasets and introducing vulnerabilities in the final model [33]; attacks targeted at increasing the error rate of the final model [34]; attacks aimed at making it possible for a specific set of records to be classified or interpreted by the model as desired by the attacker [35].

Like we earlier said, a machine learning model is built by feeding data into a computer algorithm which then learns patterns from the data and can then use the learned patterns to predict or classify unseen data. The final product of a machine learning model can be a simple equation which is then translated as a computer code that receives input and produces output in the form of a classification or prediction. With this simple intuition of machine learning models, it can be seen that cybercriminals can interfere with a machine learning product by tempering with the training and test data or altering the final parameters of the model:

- *Poisoning the training data*: It is well known by machine learning practitioners that the success of machine learning projects relies heavily on quality of the data. This is usually called 'garbage in garbage out' meaning if you train your model on garbage data, it will produce garbage results, regardless of how advanced your model is. A possibility is that a cybercriminal gains access to the training set of a machine learning model and alters the data before the training begins without the knowledge of the machine learning engineers. Clearly, we can see that the data will already be tampered with and has lost its original quality which will result in modeling on wrong data. Hence, our final model will no longer be a reliable one since it was trained on bad data and it doesn't matter how good the modeling process goes, our predictions or model classifications will surely not be appropriate. Also, another scenario can be in a situation where a model is made to re-train itself every time it receives new records. In this case, a cybercriminal can feed the model with bad data and the model can learn from this bad data and as a result, negatively impact its performance. Multiple studies have been carried out on understanding and defending against poisoning attacks [36][37].
- *Altering a machine learning model*: In this case, a cybercriminal can illegally access a machine learning model and alter its parameters and thereby influence how it produces results. For example if after training, the final machine learning model deployed to production can be represented mathematically as $y = 1 + 2x$, where x is the input parameter and y is the output from the model, then if a cybercriminal can access the system and alter the equation to $y = 1 - 2x$, then it can clearly be seen that this can lead to wrong prediction and might result in catastrophic decisions if the results of the predictions were being used to make key business decisions.
- *Evading detection by machine learning models*: This refers to attacks that aimed at avoiding detection. This can happen in situations where an attacker alters data used during the testing phase with the aim of avoiding being classified as a threat during regular system operations. Biometric systems have been used as examples in studies to show how such attacks can be done [38].

From the points mentioned above, it can be seen that it is of vital importance that machine learning projects take security seriously. Appropriate measures should be taken to monitor machine learning models and their datasets.

VI. CONCLUSION

In this paper, we have seen how machine learning can be applied in a security context from both a defense and attack perspective as well as the potential threats targeted at machine learning models. Clearly it can be seen that machine learning is a powerful tool that can be used for automating complex defense and offense cyber activities. Hence, with cybercriminals also leveraging machine learning in their arsenal of cyber weapons, we are expected to experience more sophisticated and big attacks powered by AI. It is therefore of vital importance that security specialists as well as machine learning practitioners stay abreast with the recent advancements in machine learning including adversarial machine learning so as to constantly be on the lookout to make use of potential AI related security applications.

This paper can act as basis for future research that can focus on analyzing existing security solutions and the various challenges of leveraging machine learning to develop and deploy scalable cybersecurity systems in production environments.

REFERENCES

[1] S. Larson. 10 biggest hacks of 2017. 2017, December 20. Retrieved: November 3, 2018, from https://money.cnn.com/2017/12/18/technology/biggest-cyberattacks-of-the-year/index.html

[2] T. Rimo and M. Walth, "McAfee and CSIS: Stopping Cybercrime Can Positively Impact World Economies", McAfee, June 9, 2014.

[3] "2017 Global Information Security Workforce Study", Frost and Sullivan, May 2017.

[4] Worldwide Revenue for Security Technology Forecast to Surpass $100 Billion in 2020, According to the New IDC Worldwide Semiannual Security Spending Guide. 2016, October 12. Retrieved: September 21, 2018, from https://www.businesswire.com/news/home/20161012005102/en/Worldwide-Revenue-Security-Technology-Forecast-Surpass-100.

[5] A. Cuthbertson. Ransomware attacks have risen 250 percent in 2017, hitting the U.S. hardest. 2017, May 28. Retrieved: September 21, 2018, from http://www.newsweek.com/ransomware-attacks-rise-250-2017-us-wannacry-614034.

[6] B. M. Cooper. Resiliency and Recovery Offset Cybersecurity Detection Limits. 2015, January 16. Retrieved: September 21, 2018, from https://www.afcea.org/content/resiliency-and-recovery-offset-cybersecurity-detection-limits.

[7] S. Dolev and S. Lodha, "Cyber Security Cryptography and Machine Learning", In Proceedings of the First International Conference, CSCML 2017, Beer-Sheva, Israel, June 29-30, 2017.

[8] S. Dolev and S. Lodha, "Cyber Security Cryptography and Machine Learning", In Proceedings of the First International Conference, CSCML 2017, Beer-Sheva, Israel, June 29-30, 2017.

[9] About. (n.d.). Retrieved: November 03, 2018, from http://www.palantir.com/.

[10] G. A. Wang, M. Chau, and H. Chen. Intelligence and Security Informatics: 12th Pacific Asia Workshop, PAISI 2017, Jeju Island, South Korea, May 23, 2017, Proceedings. Cham, Switzerland: Springer.

[11] H. Weiwei., and Y. Tan. Generating Adversarial Malware Examples for Black-Box Attacks Based on GAN. 2017, February 20, Retrieved: November 03, 2018, from https://arxiv.org/abs/1702.05983v1.

[12] M. P. Stoecklin. DeepLocker: How AI Can Power a Stealthy New Breed of Malware. 2018, August 13. Retrieved: September 20, 2018, from https://securityintelligence.com/deeplocker-how-ai-can-power-a-stealthy-new-breed-of-malware/

[13] D. Gershgorn. Microsoft's AI is learning to write code by itself, not steal it., 2017, March 1. Retrieved: November 03, 2018, from https://qz.com/920468/artificial-intelligence-created-by-microsoft-and-university-of-cambridge-is-learning-to-write-code-by-itself-not-steal-it/

[14] K. Rieck, P. Trinius, C. Willems, and T. Holz. Automatic analysis of malware behavior using machine learning. Journal of Computer Security, 19(4), 639-668, 2011.

[15] T. Nguyen, and G. Armitage. A survey of techniques for Internet traffic classification using machine learning. *IEEE Communications Surveys and Tutorials*, *10*(4), 56-76. 2008.

[16] S. Zander, T. Nguyen, and G. Armitage. Automated traffic classification and application identification using machine learning. In *Local Computer Networks, 2005. 30th Anniversary. The IEEE Conference on* (pp. 250-257). IEEE, 2005, November.

[17] C. F. Tsai, Y. F. Hsu, C. Y. Lin, and W. Y Lin. Intrusion detection by machine learning: A review. *Expert Systems with Applications*, *36*(10), 11994-12000, 2009.

[18] D. Arora, K. F. Li, and A. Loffler. Big data analytics for classification of network enabled devices. In *Advanced Information Networking and Applications Workshops (WAINA), 2016 30th International Conference on*(pp. 708-713). IEEE, 2016, March.

[19] J. Saleem, B. Adebisi, R. Ande, and M. Hammoudehs A state of the art survey-Impact of cyber attacks on SME's. In *Proceedings of the International Conference on Future Networks and Distributed Systems* (p. 52). ACM, 2017, July.

[20] X. Hu, T. Wang, M. P. Stoecklin, D. L. Schales, J. Jang, and R. Sailer. Asset risk scoring in enterprise network with mutually reinforced reputation propagation. In *2014 IEEE Security and Privacy Workshops (SPW)* (pp. 61-64). IEEE, 2014, May.

[21] J. B. Fraley, and J. Cannady. The promise of machine learning in cybersecurity. In *SoutheastCon, 2017* (pp. 1-6). IEEE. 2017, March.

[22] C. Sinclair, L. Pierce, and S. Matzner. An application of machine learning to network intrusion detection. In *Computer Security Applications Conference, 1999.(ACSAC'99) Proceedings. 15th Annual* (pp. 371-377). IEEE, 1999.

[23] D. P. Benjamin, P. Pal, F. Webber, P. Rubel, and M. Atigetchi. Using a cognitive architecture to automate cyberdefense reasoning. In *Bio-inspired Learning and Intelligent Systems for Security, 2008. BLISS'08. ECSIS Symposium on* (pp. 58-63). IEEE, 2008, August.

[24] L. Zomlot, S. Chandran, D. Caragea, and X. Ou. Aiding intrusion analysis using machine learning. In *Machine Learning and Applications (ICMLA), 2013 12th International Conference on* (Vol. 2, pp. 40-47). IEEE, 2013, December.

[25] R. Price. Artificial intelligence-powered malware is coming, and it's going to be terrifying. 2016, October 08. Retrieved: September 19, 2018, from https://www.businessinsider.com/darktrace-dave-palmer-artificial-intelligence-powered-malware-hacks-interview-2016-10?r=UK&IR=T.

[26] B. Hitaj, P. Gasti, G. Ateniese, and Perez-Cruz, F. Passgan: A deep learning approach for password guessing. arXiv preprint arXiv:1709.00440, 2017.

[27] K. Trieu, and Y. Yang. Artificial Intelligence-Based Password Brute Force Attacks, 2018.

[28] F. Stark, C. Hazırbas, R. Triebel, and D. Cremers. Captcha recognition with active deep learning. In GCPR Workshop on New Challenges in Neural Computation, 2015.

[29] H. Gao, W. Wang, Y. Fan, J. Qi, and X. Liu. The Robustness of" Connecting Characters Together" CAPTCHAs. J. Inf. Sci. Eng., 30(2), 347-369, 2014.

[30] Lyrebird Ultra-Realistic Voice Cloning and Text-to-Speech. (n.d.). Retrieved: September 20, 2018, from https://lyrebird.ai/

[31] J. Seymour, and P. Tully. Generative Models for Spear Phishing Posts on Social Media. *arXiv preprint arXiv:1802.05196.* 2018.

[32] J. Seymour, and P. Tully. "Weaponizing data science for social engineering: Automated E2E spear phishing on Twitter." *Black Hat USA* , 2016: 37.

[33] L. Huang, A. D. Joseph, B. Nelson, B. Rubinstein, and J. D. Tygar. "Adversarial machine learning". In 4th ACM Workshop on Artificial Intelligence and Security, AISec, 2011, pages 43–57, Chicago, IL, USA, October 2011.

[34] M. Barreno, B. Nelson, R. Sears, A. D. Joseph, and J. D. Tygar. Can machine learning be secure? In ASIACCS '06: Proceedings of the 2006 ACM Symposium on Information, computer and communications security, pages 16–25, New York, NY, USA, 2006. ACM.

[35] M. Barreno, B. Nelson, A. Joseph, and J. Tygar. "The security of machine learning". Machine Learning, 81:121–148, 2010.

[36] B. I. P. Rubinstein, B. Nelson, L. Huang, A. D. Joseph, S. h. Lau, S. Rao, N. Taft, and J. D. Tygar. "Antidote: understanding and defending against poisoning of anomaly detectors". In Proceedings of the 9th ACM SIGCOMM conference on Internet measurement conference, IMC '09, pages 1–14, New York, NY, USA, 2009. ACM.

[37] B. Biggio, B. Nelson, and P. Laskov. "Poisoning attacks against support vector machines". In J. Langford and J. Pineau, editors, 29th Int'l Conf. on Machine Learning. Omnipress, 2012.

[38] R. N. Rodrigues, L. L. Ling, and V. Govindaraju. "Robustness of multimodal biometric fusion methods against spoof attacks". J. Vis. Lang. Comput., 20(3):169–179, 2009.

[39] A. Dey. Machine Learning Algorithms: A Review. *vol*, *7*, 1174-1179, 2016.

[40] S. B. Kotsiantis, I. Zaharakis, and P. Pintelas. Supervised machine learning: A review of classification techniques. *Emerging artificial intelligence applications in computer engineering*, *160*, 3-24, 2007.

Algorithms for Electrical Power Time Series Classification and Clustering

Gaia Ceresa, Andrea Pitto,
Diego Cirio, Emanuele Ciapessoni

Ricerca sul Sistema Energetico RSE S.p.A.
via Rubattino 54, 20134 Milano, Italy
Email: gaia.ceresa@rse-web.it
andrea.pitto@rse-web.it
diego.cirio@rse-web.it
emanuele.ciapessoni@rse-web.it

Nicolas Omont

Réseau de Transport d'Électricité RTE
92932 Paris la Défense Cedex, France
Email: nicolas.omont@rte-france.com

***Abstract*—The EU-FP7 project iTesla developed a toolbox aimed to assess dynamic security of large electrical power systems, taking into account the forecast uncertainties due to renewable energy sources and load. Important inputs to the toolbox consist in the forecasts and the realizations of thousands of active power injections from renewable generators, and of active and reactive power absorption of the load, in the high voltage French transmission grid, collected into hourly historical time series. Data show a deep variety of distribution functions and profiles in the time domain. In this context, the statistical analysis of historical dataset is very important in order to characterise and manage such a large variability of distributions. In particular, the potential multimodality of the variables has to be identified in order to adapt the sampling technique developed in the iTesla toolbox, thus assuring accurate results also for this subset of variables. Moreover, clustering some variables can help reduce the dimensionality of the problem, which represents an important advantage while analysing security on very large power systems. The paper describes four algorithms: one looks for the number of distribution's peaks and classifies the variables into unimodal or multimodal; the second and the third cluster and combine multimodal variables to obtain unimodal ones, because they are more suitable for the subsequent computation. All of them are part of an advanced tool for automatic data description, that pre-processes the raw data and produces descriptive statistics on them. The Separation Algorithm is the last one, it back-projects the sum of two series into the original components.**

Keywords*—*Multimodality; Gaussian Mixture; Cluster; Time series.

I. Introduction

Power system security assessment is a theme of great interest for the Transmission System Operators (TSO), because they have to operate the system under the uncertainties due to renewable not programmable sources, load, and unexpected events due to climate change. The EU FP7 project iTesla [1] [2] led by the French TSO, Réseau de Transport d'Électricité, and co-funded by the European Commission, developed a tool to perform dynamic security assessment in an on-line environment, where uncertainties are dealt with by analysing the historical series of forecasts and realizations of the electrical power grid in an off-line environment. The project's output is a free toolbox, described in [3], available on GitHub [4] and usable to assess the security of any network.

The testing phase suggested further activities concerning two aspects: the choice of the most suitable set of data to train the model in the off-line part, in order to assure the most accurate result when applied in the on-line case; and an in-depth statistical description on the forecast errors. This last activity leads to a twofold consequence: the modification of the iTesla model to consider the peculiarity of some input series; the clustering of some input series, that are combined into a smoother one that is evaluated with higher accuracy by the model, together with a dimensionality reduction of the problem [5]–[7]. In any case, in order to perform security analysis on the grid, the tool needs plausible samples for the original variables before clustering, so it requires a Separation Algorithm that divides the combined variables into their original components.

This paper is organized as follows: Section II gives an idea of the entire algorithm for the data analysis; Section III accurately describes the time series classification into unimodal and multimodal; Section IV proposes two clustering algorithms and the Separation Algorithm; Section V shows one application; Section VI draws the conclusion.

II. Preprocessing

The input data are composed of two sets: snapshots of active and reactive powers related to thousands of injections/absorptions in the French electrical High Voltage (HV) and Extra High Voltage (EHV) transmission grid, hourly values over one month (or more), and their forecasts done the day before. The variables under statistical analysis are time series of forecast errors computed by

$$error_{hour,node} = snapshot_{hour,node} - forecast_{hour,node} \quad \forall hour \in \{hour_{min}, hour_{max}\} \tag{1}$$

Each time series refers to an injection or absorption, that often has different characteristics from others, in both profile and distribution: some are continuous, others focus their values on a finite number of levels. Several peculiar features can be detected, such as the presence of outliers and/or of a seasonal smooth profile.

Furthermore, there are many problems that have to be solved before starting the algorithm: first, it is necessary to remove the variables not significant from a statistical point of view (with too many missing values, or too many constant values, or with a variance too low); then, the outliers are detected and deleted; finally, some overall statistical information are computed, like moments and linear correlation [5].

III. Multimodality Detection

The proposed algorithm for separating multimodal variables from the unimodal ones is composed of four steps, as in Fig. 1: detection of the peaks, fitting by using a Gaussian Mixture, comparison with conventional asymmetric unimodal distributions, application of bimodal index. The algorithm is applied to each forecast error variable independently.

A. Find Peaks

For each time series, the first algorithm step constructs a histogram with more than 10 average samples per equidistant bin, and then it detects all the bins that are local maxima; one local maximum is considered a *peak* only if its previous and its next local maxima are lower than it. The peaks lower than 10% of the highest one are not considered. The result is a too numerous set of peaks, where usually some of them are not significant: it is necessary to better define the number of modes of the variable's density distribution.

B. Gaussian Mixtures

The model tries to fit the variable's distribution function with a Gaussian Mixture [8], that is a combination of two or more unimodal Gaussian components, each one with a mean, a variance and proportion. A loop tests the best mixture, changing the number of components from 1 until the number of peaks detected in the previous step; the best solution has lowest Bayesian Information Criterion (BIC) [9]. During each fitting, the Expectation-Maximization (EM) algorithm [10] finds the best set of the k parameters of each mixture components in an iterative way, maximizing the *Likelihood* (L) function by applying the Maximum Likelihood Estimation method (MLE); repeating three times each fitting, the best case has lowest Akaike's Information Criterion (AIC) [11]. Being n the number of variable's elements,

$$BIC = -2ln(L)+k\cdot ln(n); \qquad AIC = -2ln(L)+2k. \quad (2)$$

The EM algorithm stops when it converges, i.e., when the error between L and real data is lower than a given tolerance; if 100 iterations are reached without convergence, the Mixture is discarded and another one with different number of components is tested. If the best fit is a Normal distribution, the algorithm stops and analyses the next variable.

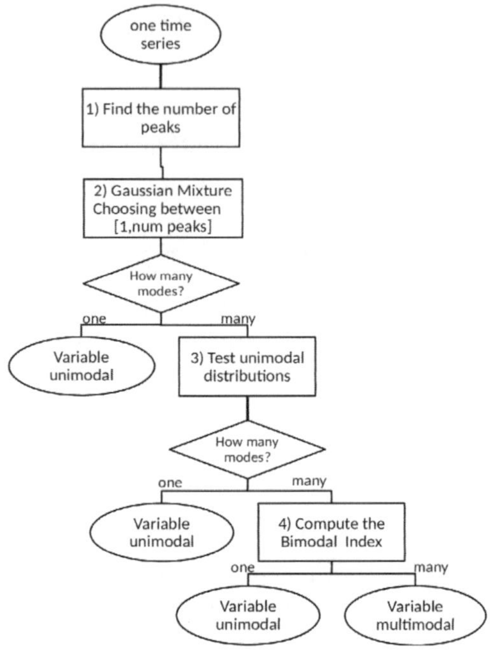

Fig. 1. Algorithm for Multimodality Detection.

C. Comparison with Unimodal Distributions

Many variables, up to this point classified among the multimodal ones, have a platykurtic and skewed distribution, and they are approximated by a Mixture composed of two or more components that are not well separated at a visual inspection. This step looks for a unimodal asymmetrical distribution that fits the variable in a better way than the Gaussian Mixture, choosing between six distributions: Weibull, Logistic, Gamma, Log-Normal, Generalized extreme value and T-location scale. The best fitting is obtained by the MLE method until convergence.

If the BIC index of one unimodal distribution is lower than the BIC of the best mixture, the algorithm classifies the variables as unimodal and analyses the next variable.

D. Bimodal Index

Variables classified as multimodal up to this point are subjected to a final step: the computation of a bimodality index, Ashman's D index [12]. It is used with the mixture of two distributions with unequal variances, σ_1^2 and σ_2^2. Let μ_1 and μ_2 their averages, the mixture is unimodal if and only if

$$D = \sqrt{2}\frac{|\mu_1 - \mu_2|}{\sqrt{\sigma_1^2 + \sigma_2^2}} \leq 2 \quad (3)$$

It means that if the components are not well separated, the distribution could be better fitted by a unimodal distribution. If a mixture contains three or more components, the Ashman's D index is computed for each pair of components, and the global distribution is multimodal if at least one D index is higher than 2.

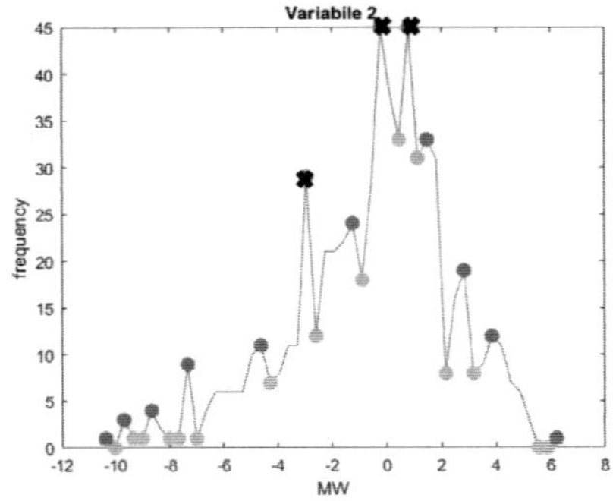

Fig. 2. Local maxima (red points) and peaks (black crosses) detected by the module *Find Peaks*.

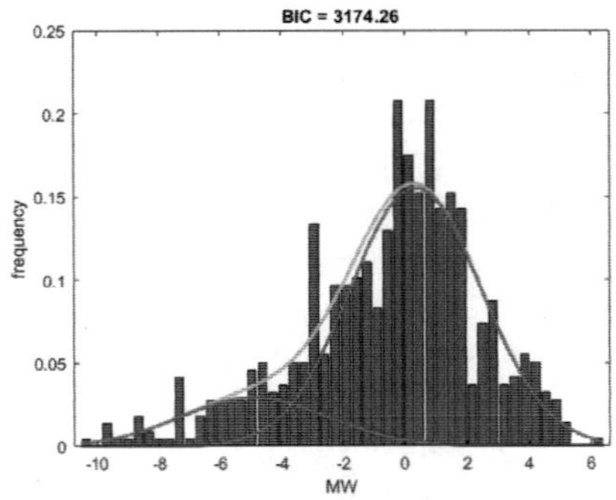

Fig. 3. Mixture with two components detected by the module *Gaussian Mixture*.

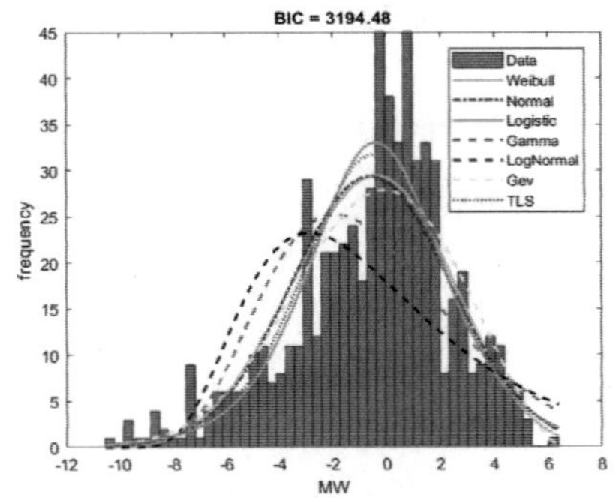

Fig. 4. Seven distributions detected by the module *Unimodal distributions*. Ashman's index $= D < 2$.

One example explains how the multimodality algorithm works: Fig. 2 displays 13 local maxima of which 3 peaks; Fig. 3 presents the best Gaussian Mixture with 2 components; Fig. 4 shows that one unimodal distribution fits the variable almost as good as the Mixture (their BICs differ for only 20 points); finally, the Ashman's D index is lower than 2, so the variable is classified among the unimodal set.

IV. Clusterization

The original iTesla tool provides very accurate results in case of unimodal variables identified in the previous section. Two consecutive developments have been achieved: the former is to modify the iTesla tool to manage the multimodal variables, as described in [5]–[7], the latter is to combine the multimodal variables to get a unimodal one, as proposed in this section. Two clusterization algorithms are described, one based on correlation and distance concepts and the other on the physical connection of the variables: for each specific application, the selected algorithm is the one which produces the highest number of clusters. In the iTesla tool, the multimodal not clustered variables are treated by a specific module.

Each clustering algorithm can generate some cluster, each one with two or three variables, and transform them into one unimodal variable, reducing the problem dimensionality. In its final part, the iTesla module applies new simulated realizations of the original variables on the grid to compute a new system states: to this purpose a Separation Algorithm decomposes the samples of the aggregated variables into the original ones.

A. Algorithm Based on Hierarchical Clustering

Each variable comes from an electrical node, that has a specific geographical position; different events can happen and induce two nodes to have a similar behaviour: the linear correlation identifies this kind of relationship. But only if two correlated nodes are close, it is probable that this liaison is physically justified by the operational practice on the system.

Fig. 5 shows the algorithm to select the variables, cluster them and check the clusters. The algorithm works separately two times, once on the active power variables and once on the reactive power ones. The first step is always to group together all the multimodal variables.

The distance function is based on the linear correlation Pearson index: two variables X and Y are close if they are highly correlated:

$$dist(X,Y) = 1 - |corr(X,Y)| \,. \tag{4}$$

Then, the hierarchical clustering produces a set of clusters composed of two variables at most; the next step verifies if they are *equal* in a particular meaning: X and Y are *equal* if their difference is higher than 1 MW (Mvar) for at most the 3% of their records. Given N the number of variable elements,

$$\begin{aligned} given\ J = \{1,2,..,N\}\,,\ I = \{j_1, j_2, ..j_{3\%N}\} \subset J \\ if\ |X_j - Y_j| < 1\ \forall j \in J \setminus I \\ \Rightarrow X = Y \end{aligned} \tag{5}$$

The reason of this *equality* is the sensitivity of measurement instruments, 1 MW (Mvar), together with the error propagation from measurement to this elaboration. Furthermore, there could be some outliers in the time series differences, that are estimated at most in the 3% of each variable's population.

The next step applies the nearest neighbour algorithm to verify the geographical distances: if variable Y falls between the k nodes closest to variable X, the cluster remains, otherwise it is filtered out. A *trial and error* approach sets parameter k equal to 50 because it is a good trade off between the neighbour's number of the urban nodes, where they are very concentrated, and the countryside where they are rare. When k decreases, also the number of good clusters gets lower.

In the final step, the time series clustered together are added: if the sum's distribution function is multimodal, the cluster is

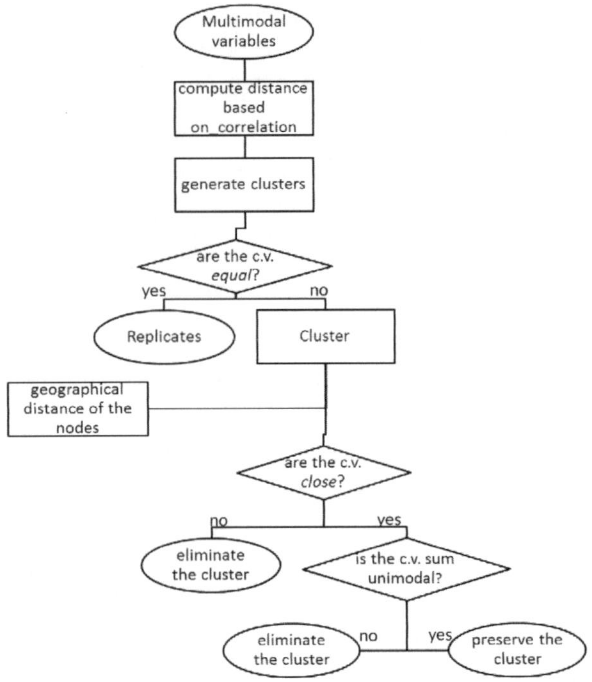

Fig. 5. Clusterization Algorithm.

eliminated, otherwise it remains and the clustered variables are treated as one smoother unimodal variable.

B. Algorithm Belonging to the Same Substation (ABSS)

In the electrical grid, a substation can be represented by busbars containing switches. When the switch is closed, all the busbars work like a unique electrical node; when it is open, the busbars are split into two half-busbars, each one working like an independent electrical node; the power injection or absorption at the substation level at each instant is the power at all the busbars. The combination of switch statuses in the entire grid, called grid topology, impacts the values because they are not always measured and the state estimator arbitrarily splits the overall substation injection/absorption when no individual data is available: the right value is unpredictable at single node level, but foreseeable at substation level. The variables belonging to the same substation have the same first 7 characters in their names.

From a mathematical point of view, the forecast errors of the electrical nodes that lie in a substation are large, with generally an irregular distribution and many peaks, but the forecast error at the substation level has better statistical properties, often showing a unimodal distribution.

The strategy adopted is to cluster the multimodal variables in the same substation, adding their time series in order to obtain one unique time series with a smoother distribution. The algorithm:

1) Considers separately the variables of active and reactive power.
2) Groups the variables (usually two or three) that are in the same substation.
3) Removes the clusters containing *equal* variables, like defined in Equation 5.
4) Sums the two or three time series of clustered together variables.
5) For each group, it checks if the resulting sum is unimodal: if yes, the cluster remains, otherwise, it is eliminated.

C. Separation Algorithm

In the iTesla work flow, the clustered variables are sent to the sampling module, aimed to generate plausible realisations of the same variables. However, in order to perform studies on the grid, it is necessary to back-project these samples of clustered variables into the samples of original variables, one for each electrical node of the system.

Given the sum of clustered variables in the overall system, the Separation Algorithm have to split them to assign a value to each single variable, preserving the cluster sum. The physical aspect is the most important: it must preserve the overall variability of the system, avoiding that one variable has a too high variance, because it can lead to a computational problem of system stability without any correspondence in the reality. It is important to preserve also the correlation between variables, if present.

Two splitting algorithms are proposed, respectively for two and three clustered variables.

The fundamental formula at the base of all the reasoning is the variance of the sum of two variables.

$$Var(X+Y) = Var(X) + Var(Y) + 2Cov(X,Y) \quad (6)$$

Suppose that the historical time series are X_o and Y_o, their unimodal sum is Z_o. The iTesla platform has to simulate new values for the system variables, preserving the original distributions: it estimates a new sum Z_n; the Separation Algorithm tries to split Z_n in X_n and Y_n, with both variances not too high and with linear correlation similar to the original series: it estimates X_n, and computes Y_n like difference between the sum and X_n, in order to not modify the sum $Z_n = X_n + Y_n$. For the sake of simplicity, in this explication $Z_o = Z_n$. So it remains

$$\begin{aligned} Var(X_o) + Var(Y_o) + 2Cov(X_o, Y_o) = \\ Var(X_n) + Var(Y_n) + 2Cov(X_n, Y_n) \end{aligned} \quad (7)$$

Since the variable X_n will be calculated considering its dependence from Z_n, its variance decreases, while the remaining sum increases:

$$\begin{aligned} Var(X_o) \geq Var(X_n) \\ Var(Y_o) + 2Cov(X_o, Y_o) \leq Var(Y_n) + 2Cov(X_n, Y_n) \end{aligned} \quad (8)$$

Separation Algorithm for Two Variables: Given:

- X_o, Y_o the original variables
- $Z_o = X_o + Y_o$
- Z_n the new sum generated inside the iTesla tool, for testing model it is $Z_n = Z_o$.

The algorithm works as follows:

- if $|corr(X_o, Y_o)| \leq 0.9$ then
  - it calculates average $\mu_{X|Z}$ and variance $\sigma_{X|Z}$ of X_n conditioned to Z_n
  - it generates the distribution $\mathcal{N}_{X|Z}(\mu_{X|Z}, \sigma_{X|Z})$
  - it extracts randomly one realization of X_n from $\mathcal{N}_{X|Z}$
  - it computes $Y_n = Z_n - X_n$
- if $|corr(X_o, Y_o)| > 0.9$ then
  - $ratio = \frac{|X_o|}{|X_o|+|Y_o|}$
  - $X_n = sign(corr(X_o, Z_o)) \cdot ratio \cdot Z_n$
  - compute $Y_n = Z_n - X_n$

Separation Algorithm for Three Variables: Given:

- X_o, Y_o, V_o the original variables
- $Z_o = X_o + Y_o + V_o$
- Z_n the new sum generated inside the iTesla tool, for testing model it is $Z_n = Z_o$.

The algorithm works as follows:

- $ratio1 = \frac{|X_o|}{|X_o|+|Y_o|+|V_o|}$
- $X_n = sign(corr(X_o, Z_o)) \cdot ratio1 \cdot Z_n$
- $ratio2 = \frac{|Y_o|}{|X_o|+|Y_o|+|V_o|}$
- $Y_n = sign(corr(Y_o, Z_o)) \cdot ratio2 \cdot Z_n$
- $V_n = Z_n - X_n - Y_n$

V. CASE STUDY

The implementation and the testing phase are done with Matlab 2017b.

The analysed dataset is composed of the time series of forecast and realizations of 3194 withdrawal/injections in the electrical French transmission grid, each one with 654 records collected once per hour from 2013/03/01 00:30 to 2013/03/01 23:30, concerning loads and renewable sources. The variables under study are the forecast errors, obtained by the Equation 1.

The preprocessing keeps 3122 significant variables, 80% of the original dataset.

A. Multimodality

Fig. 6 reports the results of the application of the algorithm for the multimodality detection. It can be noticed that the number of detected multimodal variables (700 out of 3122) is significant, which justifies the need for a proper management of the multimodal variables in the iTesla tool.

B. Clusters

The two Clustering Algorithms find different numbers of clusters. The Clustering ABSS finds 42 clusters with 2 variables and 11 with three variables, while the other algorithm finds 28 clusters with two variables: in this application case the ABSS is preferable to reduce the problem dimensionality because it clusters 117 variables. An example of cluster is in Fig. 7: the histograms of three multimodal variables related to the same substation are shown in blue, while their unimodal sum, that is the total production or absorption of the substation, is shown in magenta.

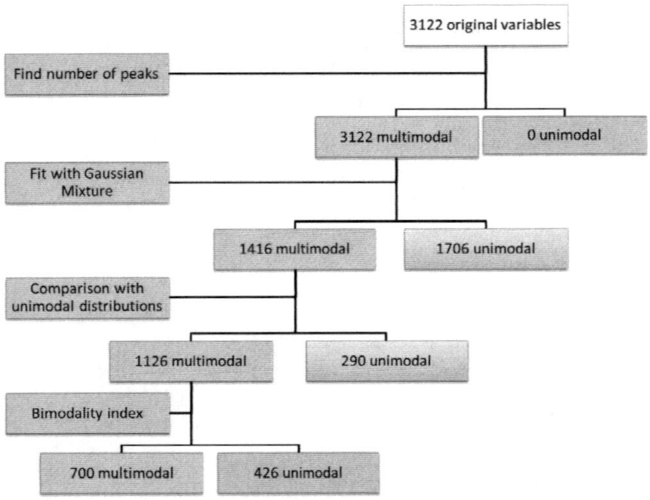

Fig. 6. Classification process operated by the Multimodality Algorithm on the test case.

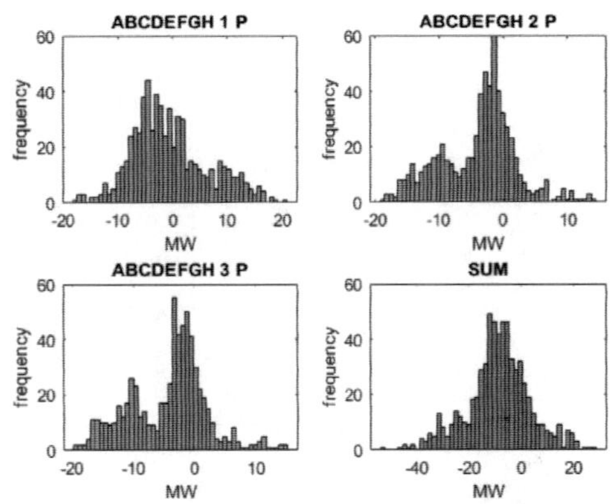

Fig. 7. Example of three clustered variables within same substation.

C. Separation Algorithm

Given the 42 clusters composed of two variables, 11 clusters with three variables, the sum's decomposition into the contributions of two (or three) variables has to preserve the total variability caused by the clustered stochastic variable in the system, i.e., each component does not have a too big variance with respect to the original variables. Table I shows the statistical description of three examples of new variables obtained with the decomposition method described above. The last column is the difference between total standard deviation of the original variables and those of new variables: $total\ variation = (\sigma_A + \sigma_B)_{new} - (\sigma_A + \sigma_B)_{orig}$; if this value is negative, the original variables have an overall variability higher than the new case, so the decomposition algorithm does not add variability to the system. If the total variation is positive, the new variables have higher standard deviations compared to the original ones; in these cases, it is

TABLE I. COMPARISON BETWEEN ORIGINAL VARIABLES AND NEW ONES, OBTAINED BY DECOMPOSITION OF THEIR SUM. MW FOR ACTIVE POWER AND Mvar FOR REACTIVE POWER.

	Var	μ_A	μ_B	σ_A^2	σ_B^2	Cov_{AB}	σ_A	σ_B	$corr_{AB}$	$\sigma_A^2+\sigma_B^2$	$\sigma_A+\sigma_B$	total variation
1	original	3.26	-1.54	84.4	134.1	-35.4	9.2	11.6	-0.3	218.5	20.8	1.04
1	new	3.25	-1.58	60.6	196.7	-54.7	7.8	14	-0.5	257.3	21.8	-
2	original	0.84	-2.61	36.7	32	-20.7	6.1	5.7	-0.6	68.7	11.7	0.5
2	new	0.91	-2.70	26.8	49.4	-24.5	5.2	7	-0.7	76.2	12.2	-
3	original	2.66	-1.50	182.2	125.3	-126	13.5	11.2	-0.8	307.5	24.7	-1.46
3	new	3.17	-0.98	116.3	155	-108	10.8	12.5	-0.8	271.3	23.3	-

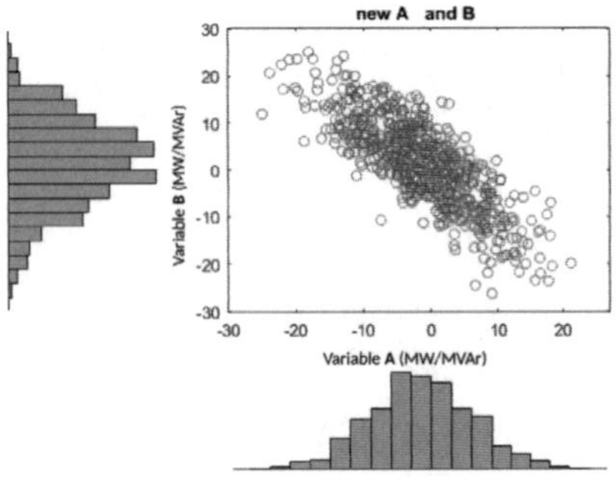

Fig. 8. Histograms and scatter plots of the original variables A and B. v1 is variable A, v2 is variable B.

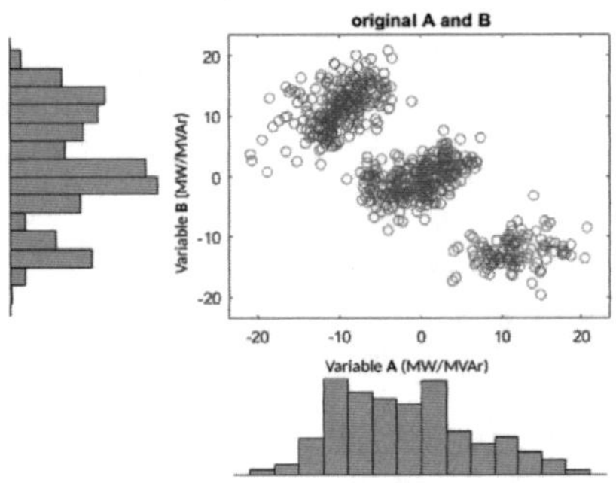

Fig. 9. Histograms and scatter plots of variables obtained by the separation of the sum A+B. A3 si variable A, B3 is new variable B.

desirable a low value. Looking at the results, the averages of original and new variables are very similar, the variances of variable A decreases while those of B increase; considering the standard deviations, they increase a little and their sum in original variables have a very small difference from their sum in new variables. One graphical comparison is shown in Fig. 8 (original variables) and Fig. 9 (splitted variables): the distributions of the splitted variables are smoother than those of the original ones, but they preserve the direction of the correlation and the standard deviations.

Considering all the 53 clusters, in 17 cases the variation is positive, but the worst case is 4.15 MW/Mvar, while all the other differences are lower than 2 MW/Mvar. These values demonstrate the goodness of this Separation Algorithm considering its objective.

VI. CONCLUSION

The paper has presented some algorithms to detect the multimodality of power system forecast errors and to cluster multimodal variables into aggregated variables with smoother statistical properties. The need for these algorithms comes from the application of an advanced toolbox for power system security assessment developed in the EU project iTesla. The results of the application of the first algorithm show that it is effective in identifying the set of multimodal variables, which can be a significant fraction of the total amount of variables, in a real life operational environment in power systems. Moreover, the tests on the clusterization techniques show that few pairs or triples of multimodal variables can be reduced into unimodal aggregated variables. The last simulations also show that the back-projection techniques used to go back from the samples of clustered variables to the original components are effective in generating reasonable samples of each individual original component without altering the variability in the system. The proposed techniques are general and can be applied to any kind of data.

REFERENCES

[1] "iTesla Project," Sep 2016, URL: http://www.itesla-project.eu/.

[2] M. H. Vasconcelos et al., "Online security assessment with load and renewable generation uncertainty: The itesla project approach," in 2016 International Conference on Probabilistic Methods Applied to Power Systems (PMAPS), Oct 2016, pp. 1–8.

[3] "iTesla Power System Tools description," May 2018, URL: http://www.itesla-pst.org/.

[4] "iTesla Power System Tools code," Sep 2018, URL: https://github.com/itesla.

[5] A. Pitto, G. Ceresa, D. Cirio, and E. Ciapessoni, Power system uncertainty models for on-line security assessment applications: developments and applications. Rapporto RdS RSE 17001186, Feb 2017.

[6] A. Pitto and G. Ceresa, Automated techniques for the analysis of historical data and improvement accuracy of uncertainty models for security assessments of the electrical power grid. Rapporto RdS RSE 17007093, Feb 2018.

[7] G. Ceresa, E. Ciapessoni, D. Cirio, A. Pitto, and N. Omont, "Verification and upgrades of an advanced technique to model forecast uncertainties in large power systems," in 2018 International Conference on Probabilistic Methods Applied to Power Systems (PMAPS), Jun 2018, pp. 1–8.

[8] D. Reynolds, Gaussian Mixture Models. Springer US, 2009, pp. 659–663.

[9] Bayesian Information Criteria. New York, NY: Springer New York, 2008, pp. 211–237.

[10] Y. Chen and M. R. Gupta, "EM Demystified: An Expectation-Maximization Tutorial," UWEE Technical Report, vol. UWEETR-2010-0002, Feb 2010.

[11] H. Akaike, Akaike's Information Criterion. Berlin, Heidelberg: Springer Berlin Heidelberg, 2011, pp. 25–25.

[12] K. Ashman, C. Bird, and S. Zepf, "Detecting bimodality in astronomical datasets," Astronomical Journal, vol. 108, pp. 2348–2361, 1994.

An Integration Module for Mining Textual and Visual Social Media Data

Mohammed Ali Eltaher
Dept. of Computer Science, Faculty of Education-Ubari
University of Sebha
Sebha, Libya
E-mail: bineltaher@gmail.com

***Abstract*—In social media networks, visual data, such as images, co-exist with text or other modalities of information. In order to benefit from different data modalities, further research is obligatory. This paper introduces the first step towards an integration module, which is based on visual and textual data available in social media. We utilized tags and images of users with a novel approach of information fusion in order to enhance the social user mining. Here, two different approaches were applied to enhance social user mining: (1) content based image fusion, and (2) semantic based image fusion. Our approaches were applied to a gender classification mining application and showed the performance of our methods to discover unknown knowledge about the user.**

Keywords- social media mining; content based integration; semantic based integration.

I. INTRODUCTION

By combining features of image and textual attributes that are generated by the user, interesting properties of social user mining are revealed. These properties serve as a powerful tool for discovering unknown information about the user. However, there is a minimum amount of research reported on the combination of images and texts for social user mining.

Textual and visual information are rich sources of social user mining. It is highly desired to integrate one media with another for better accuracy. Gallagher et al. [1] use both textual and visual information to find geographical locations of Flickr images. Their model builds upon the fact that visual content and user tags of a picture can be useful to find the geo-location. Another example, in order to determine the gender of a user, a profile image and its description can be more effective than a single media, such as image itself or description only. The progress of data mining techniques makes it possible to integrate different data types in order to improve the mining tasks of social media, and thus make them more effective.

Labeling the semantic content of multimedia objects such as images with a set of keywords is known as image tagging. More details about different types of image tagging can be found in [2]. The social user mining task mainly depends on the availability and quality of tags. Furthermore, a semi-automatic tagging process, that helps to tag multimedia objects, would improve the quality of tagging and thus the overall social user mining process.

As a mining application, the gender classification problem in Flickr is one of the applications that our approach addresses. Popescu and Grefenstette [3] introduced a gender identification technique for Flickr's users based only on tags. However, the existing studies show that tags are few, impressive, ambiguous, and overly personalized [4]. In addition, recent studies reveal that users do annotate their photos with the motivation to make them better accessible to the general public [5]. In our approach, we apply tags and images to address the gender classification problem. For a user u, given his d_u (tags and images) from Flickr, we predict the gender of u based on tags, images, and a combination of both tags and images.

In this paper, we propose a novel approach for integrating Flickr's data by combining multiple types of features. We utilize tags and images of users by using two different approaches to enhance social user mining: (1) content based image fusion, and (2) semantic based image fusion. Our approaches were applied to the gender classification problem. For the classifier, we use a Naive Bayes algorithm with multinomial distributed data, where the integrated data are typically represented as feature vector, as well as Support Vector Machine (SVM). In order to evaluate the proposed algorithm, we downloaded 148,511 users profile information with 300 tags and up to 50 photos for each user from Flickr.com.

The rest of this paper is organized as follows. Section II describes the novel approach of information fusion by combined textual and visual information using image contents. Section III describes the second approach for semantic based image fusion, using a semi-automatic image tagging system. Section IV addresses the classification algorithms and the experimental result. Finally, Section V concludes the paper.

II. CONTENT BASED IMAGE FUSION

Through the content based image fusion, we combined textual and visual information by using image contents. We proposed a data integration method between the user's tags and image contents. For the image contents, we used a hue histogram and a hue in bag of words. We implemented the tags with hue histogram as a feature vector, as well as tags with hue in bag of words. Figure 1 shows the proposed module of content based image fusion.

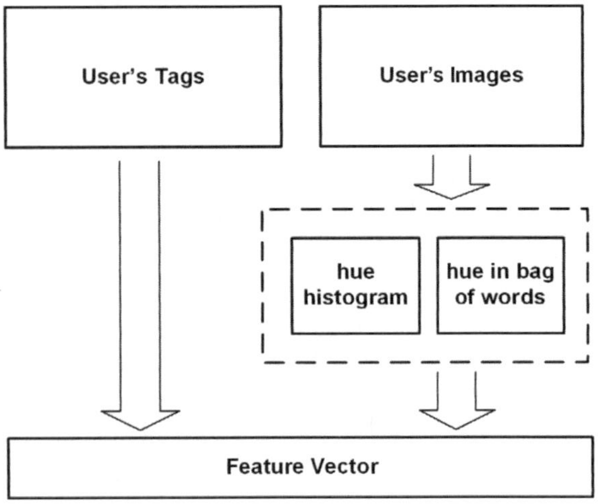

Figure 1. Content based image fusion

A. *Integrated Data Units*

Flickr allows their users to annotate their photos with textual labels called "tags". In many social media sites, tags are accurate descriptors of content, and could be used in many mining applications [6]. This section captured the content of users' Flickr photos through the user-generated tags. The first element of our content based data integration module is the user's tags. For each user u, we utilized up to 300 tags T_u, whereby each tag is represented as a word denoted as:

$T_u = \langle t_1, t_2, \ldots, t_n \rangle$, where n is the number of tags for each user.

For the second element of the proposed content based data integration module, we use the user's images as visual data. Specifically, we represent the images through two features known as hue histogram and hue in bag of words. Hue histogram is based on the hue value of all the pixels in the user's images. Hue, Saturation, Value (HSV) and Hue, Saturation, Lightness/Luminance (HSL) represent other color models that are used in multimedia mining. In HSV, the brightness of a pure color is equal to the brightness of white. In HSL the lightness of a pure color is equal to the lightness of a medium gray. Each hue value in the HSL or the HSV color space represents an individual color. For the hue in bag of words feature, we selected the top two colors by assigning "1" to the feature value for these top colors and "0" to the others. The hue histogram and hue in bag of words can be denoted as follows:

$HS_u = \langle hs_1, hs_2, \ldots, hs_n \rangle$,

$HBW_u = \langle hbw_1, hbw_2, \ldots, hbw_n \rangle$, where n represents the number of colors for each user u.

B. *Integration Scheme*

We continued to implement the users' tags with the hue histogram and the hue in bag of words as a feature vector. Figure 2 shows the scheme of the content based image fusion. For the tag features, each user u has a feature vector F_t that corresponds to all the users' tags. This feature vector can be defined as:

$F_t = \langle T_u \rangle$, where T_u is the users' tags.

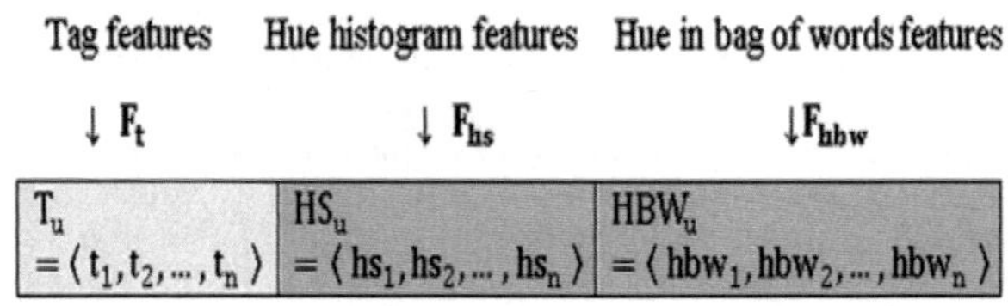

Figure 2. Feature vector of content based data integration

For the hue histogram, each user had up to 50 images. We calculated the hue histogram for each user based on their images, and determined the average based on 50 images for each color. For the hue in bag of words, we selected the top two colors for each user based on the images. The feature vectors of the hue histogram and the hue in bags of words can be defined as:

$F_{hs} = \langle HS_u \rangle$, where HS_u is hue histogram per user.

$F_{hbw} = \langle HBW_u \rangle$, where HBW_u is a hue in bag of words per user.

III. SEMANTIC BASED IMAGE FUSION

In this section, we address the problem of integrating textual and visual data semantically to perform the social user mining tasks. We determined that the integration of the two data types will be more beneficial than using an individual data type. We proposed a data integration module that combined both textual and visual information. First, we applied a semi-automatic image tagging system called *Akiwi* to suggest keywords for images. *Akiwi* uses an enormous collection of 15 million images tagged with keywords. Basically, *Akiwi* retrieves images that are visually very similar to the query image. Based on the keywords of these images, *Akiwi* tries to predict the keywords for the unknown image. Then, we integrated these keywords for individual users' tag. Figure 3 illustrates the data integration module for the sematic based image fusion.

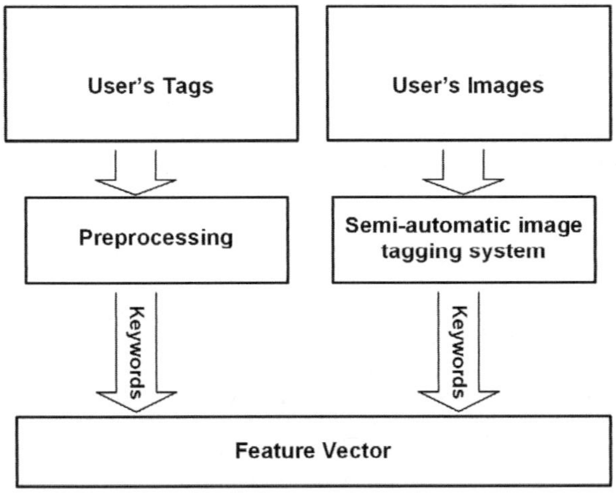

Figure 3. Semantic based image fusion

A. *Integrated Data Units*

Social media networks provide their users with the ability to describe any photos' contents by manually annotating the photos. Similar to the above represented content based integration module, our first element of the semantic based data integration module is users' tags. Some users' tags are unreliable due to excess noise in tags provided by users. These tags prove to be irrelevant or incorrectly spelled.

For example, only about 50% of the tags provided by Flickrs' users are in fact related to the images [7]. Due to tagging inaccuracies, we use a semi-automatic image tagging system to suggest keywords for our images. These keywords are considered as the second element of our proposed semantic based data integration module. We applied *Akiwi* to suggest keywords for the images. *Akiwi* uses an enormous gathering of 15 million images tagged with keywords. Essentially, *Akiwi* retrieves images that are visually precise similar to the query image. Based on the keywords of these images, *Akiwi* tries to predict the keywords for the unknown image.

B. *Integration Scheme*

For the semantic based data integration module, we implemented the users' tags with the keywords retrieved from *Akiwi* as a feature vector. The main difference in this module focuses on tags and keywords generated by users, as opposed to keywords generated by *Akiwi*. Figure 4 shows the scheme of the semantic based image fusion. These feature vectors of tags and keywords for each user can be defined as:

- $F_t = <T_u>$, where T_u is users' tags.
- $F_k = <K_u>$, where K_u is users' keywords.

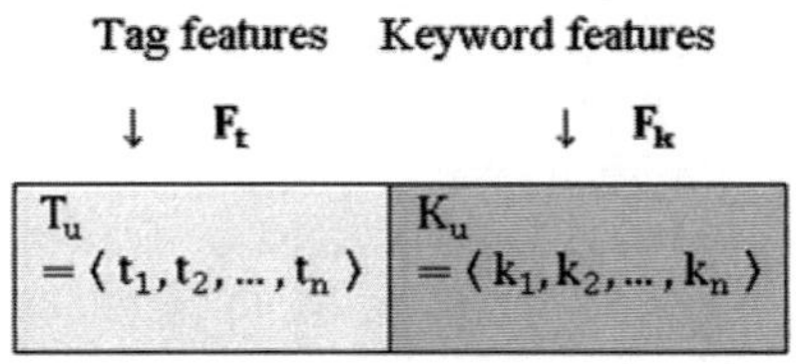

Figure 4. Feature vector of semantic based data integration

IV. CLASSIFICATION ALGORITHMS

Generally, there are various mining techniques that can be used in evolving social user mining. To apply our approaches for the gender classification problem, we selected two popular classifiers: the Naive Bayes and the SVM.

The Naive Bayes classifier is one of the most efficient and effective inductive learning algorithms for machine learning and data mining [8]. Naive Bayes methods are a set of supervised learning algorithms based on applying Bayes' theorem with the "naive" assumption of independence between every pair of features. In this experiment, we adopted a multinomial Naive Bayes model. This model implements the Naive Bayes algorithm for multinomial distributed data, where the data is typically represented as vector. Given the gender classification problem having G classes $\{g_1, g_2\}$ with probabilities $P(g_1)$ and $P(g_2)$, we assign the class label G to a Flickr user u based on the feature vector $D_u = (d_1, d_2, \dots, d_N)$, where d_N represent the user data, such as tags and images:

$$g = arg \max_g P(g|D_u) \quad (1)$$

The above equation is to assign a class with the maximum probability given the feature vector of user data D_u. This probability can be formulated by using Bayes theorem as follows:

$$P(g|D_u) = \frac{P(g) \times \prod_{i=1}^{N} P(d_i|g)}{P(D_u)} \quad (2)$$

Here, the objective is to predict the most probable class to the user u giving the feature vector D_u that contains N features to the most possible class.

The SVM is a popular machine learning method for classification and other learning tasks [9]. In our experiment, we adopted the C-Support Vector Classification (SVC), which is implemented based on libsvm [10]. The main idea of applying SVM on classification is to find the maximum-margin hyperplane to separate classes in the feature vector space. Given a set of Flickr data D_u, that is relevant to a user u and class labels for training $\{(d_u, g_u)|u = 1, \dots, N\}$, where d_u represent the feature vectors of user data and g_u

is the target class label, the SVM will map these feature vectors into a high dimensional space.

A. Content Based Classification

As the amount of social media content grows, researchers should identify robust ways to discover unknown knowledge about users, based on these contents. In this section, we explain how the contents of tags and images are used for gender classification.

Tags reflect what users consider important in their images and also reveal the users' interest. We assume that male and female tagging vocabularies are different, and this difference can be used to identify their gender. To test our assumption, we built a dictionary containing female and male tagging vocabularies. In order to determine the importance of tags, we compute the gender tagging vocabulary by counting the number of different gender users who used the respective tag. Then, we calculated the probability of a gender given the utilized tags.

The color histogram is a representation of color distribution in an image. For image data, a color histogram represents the number of pixels that have colors in each of a fixed list of color ranges that span the color space for the image. The color histogram can be built for any kind of color space. The hue histogram is based on the hue value of all the pixels in an image. Each hue value in HSL or HSV color space represents a color by itself.

The hue in bag of words approach is motivated by an analogy of learning methods that applies the bag-of-words representation for text categorization [11], visual categorization with bags of keypoints [12], and bags of features [13]. For this approach, we selected the top two colors by assigning "1" to the feature value for these top colors and "0" to the other colors.

B. Semantic Based Classification

Using the semantic content of multimedia data added by the user could be beneficial to the social user mining research. However, manually annotating images requires time and effort, and it is difficult for users to provide all relevant tags for each image. Thus, a semi-automatic image tagging system emerged and has recently involved in different task. To improve the quality of tags, we applied a semi-automatic image tagging system *Akiwi* to suggest keywords for images. The goal of using semi-automatic image tagging system is to assign a few relevant keywords to the image to reflect its semantic content. This process improves the quality of tags by utilizing image content. For the gender classification problem, the semantic based approach is conducted based on the collected keywords from *Akiwi*.

Similar to the tags data in the content based classification, the assumption is that male and female keyword vocabularies are different. This difference can be used to classify their gender. To test our assumption, we built a dictionary containing female and male keyword vocabularies. In order to determine the importance of keywords, we computed the gender tagging vocabulary by counting the number of different gender users who used the respective keywords. Then, we calculated the probability of a gender given the utilized keywords.

In addition, we proposed a data integration module to combine both semantic based and content based data. Particularly, we utilized this module for the gender classification problem by combining the keywords of the user with his/her tags. We used a feature vector to merge both the keywords and the tags of the user.

V. EXPERIMENT RESULT

This experiment utilizes Scikit-Learing tools in Python [14]. Two different classification methods, i.e., Naive Bayes and SVM were used. In this experiment, we adopted the multinomial Naive Bayes model. This model implements the Naive Bayes algorithm for multinomial distributed data, where the data are typically represented as feature vector. For the SVM, we adopted SVC, which is implemented based on libsvm. For both classifiers, we use the fit (X, Y) method. This method fit the classifier according to the given training data. Next, we used predict (X) method to perform the classification in a sample of X. In our case, X represents the feature matrix of the data, while Y represents the user label.

A. Data Set

One of the greatest online photo management and sharing application is Flickr. In this site, user can shares their photos and organize them in many ways. Textual and visual data can be obtained through the Flickr public API, which allows us to download information with the user's authorization. We downloaded 148,511 user's tags and images. Table 1 shows more details about our data set. To evaluate the proposed algorithms, we build a ground truth data based on 215k users. Precisely, we collected the Flickr users' profile information using crawler. For the gender attribute, we were able to collect 148,511 users with known gender.

TABLE I. DATA SET

Data Category	**Size**
Tags	Up to 300 tags per user
Images	Up to 50 images per user
Ground truth	148,511 user

B. Experiment Result for Content Based Classification

For the content based experiment, we implemented a multinomial Naive Bayes classifier. We examined the performance of different features, and we observed the difference that appeared in the classification. Table 2 shows the result of different features, such as tags, hue histogram, and hue in bag of words.

TABLE II. EXPERIMENT RESULT OF CONTENT BASED CLASSIFICATION

Features	Accuracy	F1
tags	0.7362	0.7349
huehist	0.6141	0.6140
huebow	0.5866	0.5786
tags+huebow	0.7365	0.7351
tags+huehist	0.7251	0.7228
huehist+huebow	0.6151	0.6150
tags+huehist+huebow	0.7181	0.7141

To assess the performance of our model, we used the standard classification accuracy (*Acc*) and F1 score as defined in the equations 3 and 4, shown below. For evaluation purposes, all classes are grouped into four categories: 1) true positives (TP), 2) true negatives (TN), 3) false positives (FP), and 4) false negatives (FN). For instance, the true positives are the users that belong to the positive class and are in fact classified to the positive class, whereas the false positives are the users not belonging to the positive class but incorrectly classified to the positive class.

$$ACC = \frac{TP + TN}{TP + TN + FP + FN} \tag{3}$$

$$F1 = \frac{2TP}{(2TP + FP + FN)} \tag{4}$$

C. *Experiment Result of Semantic Based Classification*

To compare the performance of our approach, we use the classification accuracy (*Acc*) as defined in equation 3, precision (*Pre*), and recall (*Rec*) metrics, as well as F1 score as defined in the following equations:

$$\mathrm{Pr}e = \frac{TP}{TP + FP} \tag{5}$$

$$\mathrm{Re}c = \frac{TP}{TP + FN} \tag{6}$$

$$F1 = 2\left(\frac{\mathrm{Pr}e \times \mathrm{Re}c}{\mathrm{Pr}e + \mathrm{Re}c}\right) \tag{7}$$

where TP represents true positives, TN true negatives, FP false positives, and FN false negatives.

We performed the experiments by sampling of the data set for different features and classifiers, and then tested the performance of each classifier and each feature. The results are presented in Table 3. As seen in the table, the results show over 80% in terms of accuracy for gender classification when using keywords with both classifiers. This indicates that the proposed semantic based approach outperforms the content based one. In terms of classifier, we observed that Naive Bayes is slightly better than SVM, specifically with tags. This is because the Naive Bayes classifier can work better even if there is some missing data.

TABLE III. EXPERIMENT RESULT OF SEMANTIC BASED CLASSIFICATION

Features	Approach	Acc	Pre	Rec	F1
keywords	NB	0.82	0.81	0.82	0.81
	SVM	0.82	0.83	0.82	0.80
Tags	NB	0.78	0.82	0.78	0.78
	SVM	0.74	0.55	0.74	0.63
Keywords +Tags	NB	0.80	0.80	0.80	0.79
	SVM	0.78	0.61	0.78	0.68

VI. CONCLUSION

In this paper, we proposed a new data integration method that integrates textual and visual data. Unlike the previous approaches that used a content based approach to merge multiple types of features, our main approach is based on image semantic through a semi-automatic image tagging system. Our method was applied to gender classification mining application and showed the performance of our method to discover unknown knowledge about user. For gender classification, we performed the experiments with the data set, and the results for the semantic based approach indicate over 81% accuracy for gender classification, which outperforms the content based approach by 10%.

REFERENCES

[1] A. Gallagher, D. Joshi, J. Yu, and J. Luo, "Geo-location inference from image content and user tags," in Proc. IEEE Computer Society Conf. Computer Vision and Pattern Recognition Workshops CVPR Workshops 2009, pp. 55–62.

[2] C. Marlow, M. Naaman, D. Boyd, and M. Davis, "Ht06, tagging paper, taxonomy, flickr, academic article, to read," in Proceedings of the Seventeenth Conference on Hypertext and Hypermedia, ser. HYPERTEXT '06. New York, USA: ACM, 2006, pp. 31–40.

[3] A. Popescu and G. Grefenstette, "Mining user home location and gender from flickr tags." in ICWSM, 2010.

[4] L. S. Kennedy, S.-F. Chang, and I. V. Kozintsev, "To search or to label?: Predicting the performance of search-based automatic image classifiers," in Proceedings of the 8th ACM International Workshop on Multimedia Information Retrieval, ser. MIR '06. New York, USA: ACM, 2006, pp. 249–258.

[5] M. Ames and M. Naaman, "Why we tag: Motivations for annotation in mobile and online media," in Proceedings of the SIGCHI Conference on Human Factors in Computing Systems, ser. CHI '07. New York, USA: ACM, 2007, pp. 971–980.

[6] P. Heymann, D. Ramage, and H. Garcia-Molina, "Social tag prediction," in Proceedings of the 31st Annual International ACM SIGIR Conference on Research and Development in Information Retrieval, ser. SIGIR '08. New York, USA: ACM, 2008, pp. 531–538.

[7] B. Sigurbjornsson and R. van Zwol, "Flickr tag recommendation based on collective knowledge," in Proceedings of the 17th International Conference on World Wide Web, ser. WWW '08. New York, USA: ACM, 2008, pp. 327–336.

[8] H. Zhang, "The optimality of Naive Bayes," A A, vol. 1, no. 2, p. 3, 2004.

[9] N. Cristianini and J. Shawe-Taylor, An introduction to support vector machines and other kernel-based learning methods. Cambridge university press, 2000.

[10] C.-C. Chang and C.-J. Lin, "Libsvm: A library for support vector machines," ACM Trans. Intell. Syst. Technol., vol. 2, no. 3, pp. 27:1–27:27, May 2011.

[11] N. Cristianini, J. Shawe-Taylor, and H. Lodhi, "Latent semantic kernels," J. Intell. Inf. Syst., vol. 18, no. 2-3, pp. 127–152, Mar. 2002.

[12] G. Csurka, C. R. Dance, L. Fan, J. Willamowski, and C. Bray, "Visual categorization with bags of keypoints," in In Workshop on Statistical Learning in Computer Vision, ECCV, 2004, pp. 1–22.

[13] S. Lazebnik, C. Schmid, and J. Ponce, "Beyond bags of features: Spatial pyramid matching for recognizing natural scene categories," in Computer Vision and Pattern Recognition, 2006 IEEE Computer Society Conference on, vol. 2, 2006, pp. 2169–2178.

[14] F. Pedregosa et al. "Scikit-learn: Machine Learning in Python ," Journal of Machine Learning Research, vol. 12, pp. 2825–2830, 2011.

A Predictive Data Analytic for the Hardness of Hamiltonian Cycle Problem Instances

Gijs van Horn*, Richard Olij†, Joeri Sleegers‡ and Daan van den Berg§

* Indivirtual and University of Amsterdam, The Netherlands
† University of Amsterdam, The Netherlands
‡ Olisto and University of Amsterdam, The Netherlands
§ Docentengroep IvI, Faculty of Science, University of Amsterdam, The Netherlands

contact@gijsvanhorn.nl*, richard.olij@student.uva.nl†, joeri.sleegers@olisto.com‡, d.vandenberg@uva.nl§

***Abstract*—In their landmark paper "Where the *Really* Hard Problems Are", Cheeseman et al. describe the relative instance hardness, measured in computation time, of three decision problems (Hamiltonian Cycle, Vertex Coloring, K-satisfiability) and one optimization problem (Traveling Salesman). For these four problems, they identify a single property, an "order parameter" related to specific instance characteristics, for predicting computational hardness. One such characteristic is the probability of a random graph being Hamiltonian (having a Hamiltonian Cycle): it depends on its average vertex degree, which is its order parameter. This Hamiltonian probability goes through a sudden phase transition as the order parameter increases and the hardest problem instances, algorithmically speaking, are found close to this phase transition. As such, the order parameter can be seen as an analytic on instance data useful for predicting runtimes on (exponential time) algorithms. In this study, we replicate the original experiment and extend it with two more algorithms. Our countribution is as follows: first, we confirm their original results. Second, we show that an inversion of their heuristic significantly improves algorithmic performance on the same graphs, at zero extra cost. Third, we show that an advanced pruning algorithm by Vandegriend and Culberson further improves runtimes when run on the same graphs. We conclude that the order parameter based on problem instance data analytics is useful across different algorithms. Fourth, we produce high-resolution online interactive diagrams, which we make available for further research along with all the source code and input data.**

Keywords*—*Hamiltonian Cycle; exact algorithm; exhaustive algorithm; heuristic; phase transition; order parameter; data analytics; instance hardness; replication.

I. Introduction

The "Great Divide" between P and NP has haunted computer science and related disciplines for over half a century. Problems in P are problems for which the runtime of the best known algorithm increases polynomially with the problem size, like calculating the average of an array of numbers. If the array doubles in size, so does the runtime of the best known algorithm - a polynomial increase. A problem in NP however, has no such algorithm and it is an open question whether it will ever be found. An example hereof is "satisfiability" (sometimes abbreviated to SAT), a problem in which an algorithm assigns values 'true' or 'false' to variables in Boolean formulas like $(a \vee \neg b \vee d) \wedge (b \vee c \vee \neg d)$ such that the formula as a whole is satisfied (becomes 'true'), or making sure that no such assignment exists. Algorithms that do this, and are guaranteed to give a solution whenever it exists and return no otherwise, are called *complete* algorithms.

Being complete is a great virtue for an algorithm, but it comes at a hefty price. Often, these algorithms operate by *brute-force*: simply trying all combinations for all variables until a solution is found, which usually takes vast amounts of time. Smarter algorithms exist too; clever pruning can speed things up by excluding large sections of state-space, at the cost of some extra computational instructions, an investment that usually pays off. Heuristic algorithms are also fast but not necessarily complete - so it is not guaranteed a solution is found if one exists. After decades of research, runtimes of even the most efficient complete SAT-algorithm known today still increases exponentially with the number of variables – much worse than polynomial, even for low exponents. Therefore, SAT is in NP, a class of "Notorious Problems" that rapidly become unsolvable as their size increases. In practice, this means that satisfiability problems (and other problems in NP) with only a few hundred variables are practically unsolvable, whereas industries such as chip manufacture or program verification in software engineering could typically employ millions [1] [2].

So, the problem class NP might be considered "the class of dashed hopes and idle dreams", but nonetheless scientists managed to pry loose a few bricks in the great wall that separates P from NP. Most notably, the seminal work "Where the *Really* Hard Problems Are" by Cheeseman, Kanefsky and Taylor (henceforth abbreviated to 'Cetal'), showed that although runtime increases non-polynomially for NP-problems, some *instances* of these hard problems might actually be easy to solve [3]. Not every formula in SAT is hard – easily satisfiable formulas exist too, even with many variables, but the hard ones keep the problem as a whole in NP. But Cetal's great contribution was not only to expose the huge differences in instances hardness within a single NP-problem, they also showed *where* those really hard instances are – and how to get there. Their findings were followed up numerous times and truly exposed some of the intricate inner anatomy of instance hardness, and problem class hardness as a whole.

So, where *are* these notorious hard problem instances then? According to Cetal, they are hiding in the phase transition. As their constrainedness increases, the problem instances suddenly jump from having many solutions to having no solutions. For an example in satisfiability, most randomly generated SAT-formulas of two clauses and four variables such as our formula $(a \vee \neg b \vee d) \wedge (b \vee c \vee \neg d)$ are easily satisfiable; they have many assignments that make them true. But as soon as the order parameter, the ratio of clauses versus variables α, passes 4.26, (almost) no satisfiable formulas exist [4] [5]. So, if we randomly generate a formula with 20 or more clauses on these same four variables, it is almost certainly unsatisfiable and those rare formulas that *are* satisfiable beyond the phase transition have very few solutions – which counterintuitively enough makes them easy again. So, for most complete algorithms, both extremes are quickly decided: for the highly satisfiable formulas in $\alpha << 4.26$, a solution is quickly found, and unsatisfiable formulas in $\alpha >> 4.26$ are quickly proven as such. But in between, just around $\alpha = 4.26$, where the transition from satisfiable to unsatisfiable takes place, are formulas that take the longest to decide upon. This is where the really hard problem instances are: hiding in the phase transition. But Cetal identify this order parameter not only for SAT; the Hamiltonian cycle problem (explained in detial in Section II) has one too, and so does Vertex Coloring. Again, the phase transition is where the really hard problem instances are and although their rather coarse seminal results on these problems have been followed up in more detail, they are solid [5]–[8]. Or to put it in a later quote by Ian Gent and Toby Walsh: "[Indeed, we have yet to find an NP-complete problem that *lacks* a phase transition]" [9].

In hindsight, but only in hindsight, the ubiquity of phase transitions throughout the class is not a complete surprise. Satisfiability, Vertex Coloring and the Hamiltonian cycle problem are NP-complete problems; a subset of problems in NP that with more or less effort can be transformed into each other [10]. This means a lot. This means that if someone finds a polynomial complete algorithm for just one of these problems, all of them become easy and the whole hardness class will simply evaporate. That person would also be an instant millionaire thanks to the Clay Mathematics Institute that listed the P$\stackrel{?}{=}$NP-question as one of their Millenium Problems [11]. But the intricate relations inside NP-completeness might also stretch into the properties of phase transitions and instance hardness. Or, to pour it into another fluid expression by Ian Gent and Toby Walsh "[Although any NP-complete problem can be transformed into any other NP-complete problem, this mapping does *not* map the problem space uniformly]" [9]. So, a phase transition in say, satisfiability, does *not* guarantee the existence of a phase transition in Hamiltonian Cycle or in Vertex Coloring. The fact is though, that Cetal do find them for all three.

In the next section, we will look at the Hamiltonian cycle problem, how it depends on the average vertex degree of a graph, and give an overview of the available algorithms for the problem so far. In Section III, we will explain the algorithm from Cetal's original experiment, and the two algorithms we've added as an extension. In Section IV, the experimental details and results are laid out in detail. In Section V, we conclude that the Cetal's findings are replicable, but also that the order parameter serves as a predictive data analytic on other algorithms. We also discuss the implications. Section VI contains acknowledgements, and a small tribute to Cetal's original work.

II. The Hamiltonian Phase Transition

The Hamiltonian cycle problem comes in many different varieties, but in its most elementary form it involves finding a path (a sequence of distinct edges) in an undirected and unweighted graph that visits every vertex exactly once, and forms a closed loop. The probability of a random graph being Hamiltonian (i.e., having a Hamiltonian Cycle), has been thoroughly studied [12]–[14]. In the limit, it is a smooth function of vertex degree and therefore the probability for a random graph of V Vertices and E edges being Hamiltonian can be calculated analytically:

$$P_{Hamiltonian}(V, E) = e^{-e^{-2c}} \quad (1)$$

in which

$$E = \frac{1}{2}\, V ln(V) + \frac{1}{2}\, V ln(ln(V)) + cV \quad (2)$$

Like the phase transition around α in SAT, the Hamiltonian phase transition is also sigmoidally shaped across a threshold point, the average degree of $ln(V) + ln(ln(V))$ for a graph of V vertices (also see Figure 1). The phase transition gets ever steeper for larger graphs, until it becomes instantaneous at the threshold point as V goes to infinity. For this (theoretical) reason, the probability of being Hamiltonian at the threshold point is somewhat below 0.5 at $e^{-1} \approx 0.368$,

The probability of being Hamiltonian is one thing, deciding whether a given graph actually *has* a Hamiltonian cycle is quite another. A great number of complete algorithms have been developed through the years, the earliest being exhaustive methods that could run in $O(n!)$ time [15]. A dynamic programming approach, quite advanced for the time, running in $O(n^2 2^n)$ was built by by Michael Held & Richard Karp, and by Richard Bellman independently [16] [17]. Some early pruning efforts can be found in the work of Silvano Martello and Frank Rubin whose algorithms could still run in $O(n!)$ but are in practice probably much faster [18] [19]. Many of their techniques eventually ended up in the algorithm by Vandegriend & Culberson (henceforth 'Vacul'), which we rebuilt as part of this replication, and can be found in Section III [20]. Algorithms by Bollobás and Björklund run faster than Bellman–Held–Karp, but are technically speaking not complete for finite graphs [21] [22]. The 2007 algorithm by Iwama & Nakashima [23] runs in $O(2^{1.251n})$ time on cubic graphs, thereby improving Eppstein's 2003 algorithm that runs

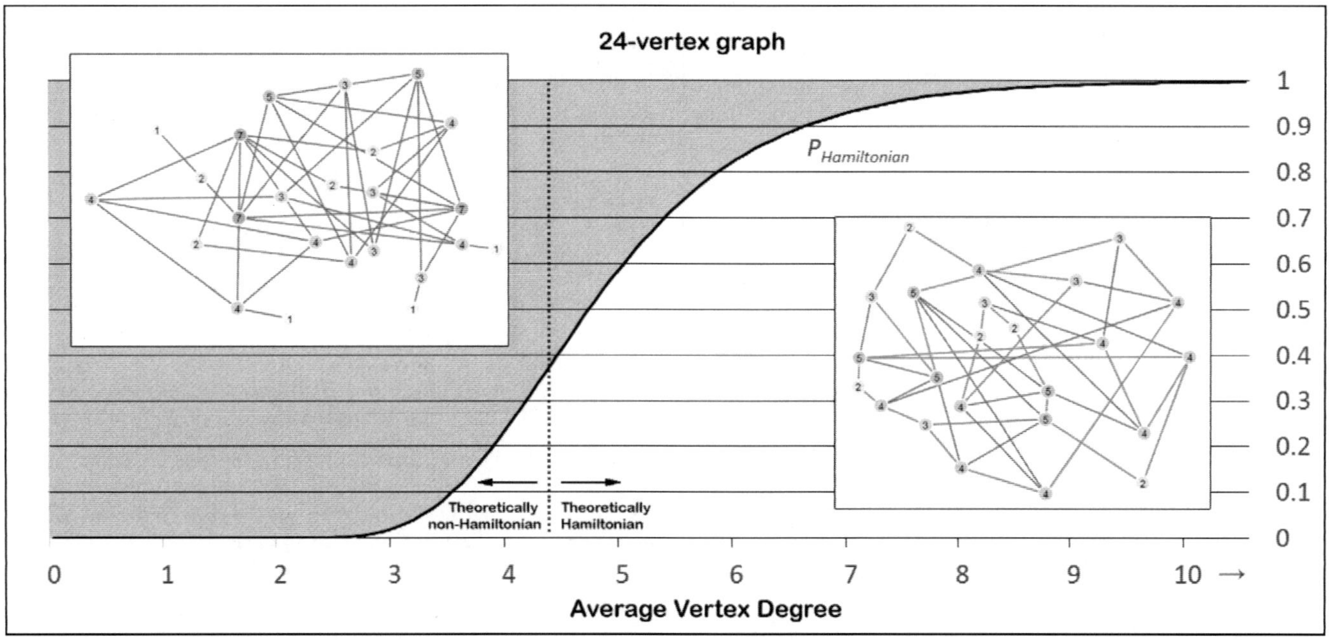

Fig. 1. The probability of a randomly generated graph being Hamiltonian depends on the average vertex degree, and is sigmoidally shaped around the threshold point of $ln(V) + ln(ln(V))$. Top-left inset is a non-Hamiltonian random graph, bottom-right inset is a Hamiltonian graph with the Hamiltonian cycle itself being highlighted.

in $O(2^{1.260n})$. While these kind of marginal improvements on specialized instances are typical for the progress in the field, these two actually deserve some extra attention.

The cubic graph, in which every vertex has a maximum degree of three, is of special importance in the generation of 3D computer images. Many such images are built up from triangle meshes, and as specialized hardware render and shade triangles at low latencies, the performance bottleneck is actually in feeding the triangular structure into the hardware. A significant speedup can be achieved by not feeding every triangle by itself, but by combining them into triangle strips. An adjacent triangle can be defined by only one new point from the previously fed triangle, and therefore adjacent triangles combined in a single strip can speedup the feeding procedure by a maximum factor three for each 3D object. Finding a single strip that incorporates all triangles in the mesh is equivalent to finding a Hamiltonian cycle through the corresponding cubic graph in which every triangle is a vertex, which makes both Eppstein's and Iwama&Nakashima's result of crucial importance for the 3D imagery business (see Figure 2).

So, concludingly, none of the complete algorithms on finding Hamiltonian cycles runs faster than exponential on all instances (with vertices of any degree), and the Bellman–Held–Karp "is still the strongest known", as Andreas Björklund states on the first page of his 2010-paper [22]. Cetal's algorithm however, is much closer related to the depth-first approach by Rubin and Martello and runs in $O(n!)$ time, as do the other algorithms in the next section.

III. Three Hamiltonian algorithms

Naked depth-first-search is a complete and exhaustive method, but Cetal mount the algorithm with "two heuristics": 1) the starting vertex is the vertex with the highest degree and 2) when recursing, always prioritize a higher degree vertex over a lower degree vertex. It should be very clearly understood though, that Cetal's "heuristics" are just speedup procedures expected to boost the algorithm's performance by reducing runtimes but do not compromise its completeness like a 'heuristic algorithm' such as Simulated Annealing would.

For this replication, two more algorithms were implemented: Van Horn's algorithm (named after the first author) which is identical to Cetal's, except that it *inverts* the heuristic, starting at the lowest degree vertex, and prioritizing lower degree adjacent vertices over higher ones when recursing. Inspiration for this inversion came from an almost prophetic statement by James Bitner and Edward Reingold from their famous '75-paper that "In general, nodes of low degree should occur early in the search tree, and nodes of high degree should occur later." [24]. They were guessing at the time, but it turns out they were right and their intuition has later been formalized in a more generalized way [25], but still it is baffling to see how much performance is gained from such a simple inversion – at zero extra cost.

Thirdly, we replicated Vacul's somewhat more sophisticated algorithm intentionally programming it from scratch for the sake of replicability. It is also a depth-first-search and it also prioritizes vertices of lower degree over higher degree but additionally, it has an iterated-restart feature and three pruning

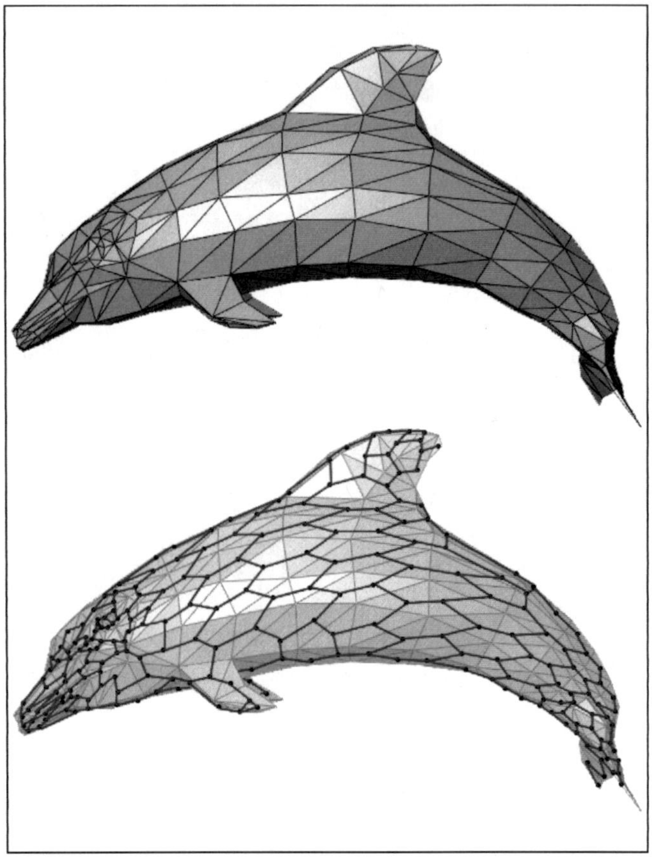

Fig. 2. Fast rendering of triangle mesh 3D images critically depends on finding Hamiltonian cycles through the corresponding 'cubic' graphs, in which every vertex has a maximum degree of three.

techniques, employed in preprocessing and during recursion. A preprocessing stage first runs an iterated pruning routine that chips away edges that cannot be in any Hamiltonian cycle. Any vertex v that has two neighbours (adjacent vertices) n_1 and n_2 which both have degree 2 only keeps those edges to n_1 and n_2; all its other edges are pruned off because they cannot be in any Hamiltonian cycle. It also looks for a forced path, and prunes the edge between the first and last vertex if it exists. Since any pruning activity can lead to new vertices of degree 2, the procedure needs to be run again until no more edges are pruned off. Then, the graph is checked for non-Hamiltonicity-properties: degrees smaller than 2 and articulation points (a.k.a "cut vertices"). If it has neither of those two, the preprocessing stage is finished and the depth-first recursion starts. During recursion, the exact same pruning methods and one more take place: whenever a vertex is added to the path, all edges from the previous node are pruned, except for the two in the path. As is common for depth-first, all pruned edges get placed back when backtracking. Finally, Vacul set an upper bound on the number of recursions for their algorithm. When exceeded, the bound is upped and a random restart is launched. An interesting technique, but we omitted it simply because Cetal's original graph sizes are small enough to do an exhaustive search – Vacul's go up to 1500 vertices, Cetal's only to 24. A peculiar detail to keep in mind is that these kinds of small randomnesses often improve runtimes in exact algorithms on large inputs, but also make them non-deterministic: experiments may vary from trial to trial - even for two runs on the same input. By omitting this option, runtimes (such as in Figure 3) are consistent, exactly reproducible and non-variable on their input.

IV. Experiment & Results

In Cetal's study, 20 graphs were generated for "a given connectivity", and analyzed for Hamiltonian Cycles and the computation times (in iterations) recorded. Some runs are cut off at "a prespecified maximum". The average is taken, but it "[severely underestimates the true costs, as it also contains those saturated values]". So, although of the exact experimental parameters are left undefined, Cetal state: "[The existence of the phase transition is clear]".

This left us with some choices. Generally, we tried to stick to Cetal's work as closely as possible, generating two sets of graphs, one with 16 vertices and one with 24 vertices and employed the full range of 0 to the maximum $\frac{1}{2}n^2 - \frac{1}{2}n$ edges. We generated 20 random graphs for every number of edges, resulting in 2400 random graphs for the 16-vertex graphs, and 5520 random graphs for the 24-vertex graphs. We could not consult Cetal's source data, but judging by their figures, our numbers might be higher than Cetal's original work, which makes our replication a little more rigourous. In the remainder of the paper, we will discuss results on the 24-vertex graphs, but results for the 16-vertex graphs are comparable and the reader is encouraged to try our online interactive diagrams when interested.

We ran Cetal's algorithm, Van Horn's algorithm, and Vacul's algorithm all on the same input data and recorded the number of iterations for each algorithm on each random graph. We set our cutoff point at 10^9 iterations, which was reached 65 times by Cetal's algorithm and 57 times by Van Horn's algorithm (but not on the same graphs). Van Horn's algorithm, with its inverted heuristic, performs better with shorter runtimes on 4627 out of the 5520 graphs (83.8%), but nonetheless peaks in runtime near the Hamiltonian phase transition. Vacul's algorithm with advanced pruning outperformed both other algorithms on 3334 out of the 5520 graphs (61.3%). It did not reach the cutoff point even once, even though its hardest graphs are still near the Hamiltonian phase transition, roughly between vertex degrees 4 and 7 for 24 vertices. Note that the vertical axis is logarithmic, so the computational difference between easy and hard graphs is astoundingly large, even for these small instances.

V. Conclusion and Discussion

It seems fair to say that Cetal's results on the Hamiltonian cycle problem are reproducible and valid. Harder graphs do reside around the Hamiltonian phase transition for their algorithm and the average vertex degree indeed functions as

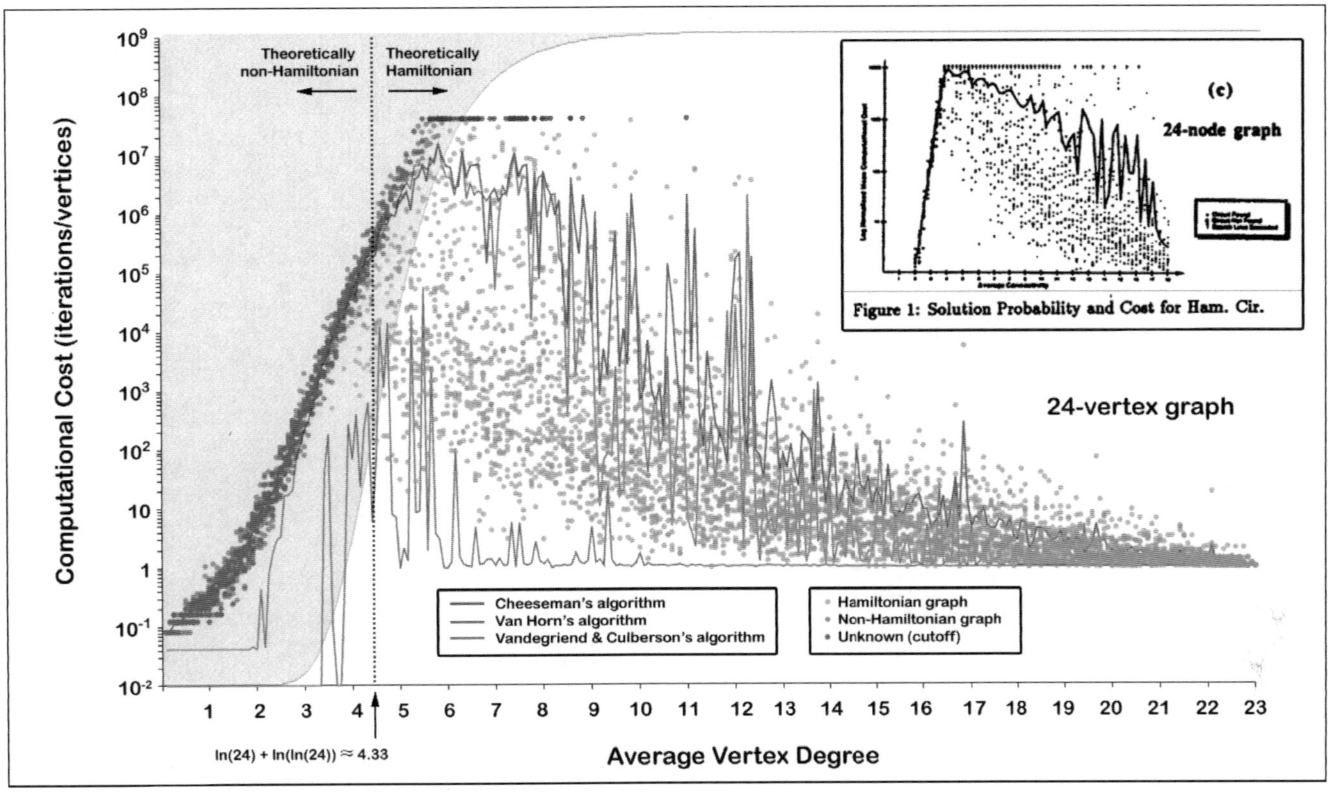

Fig. 3. Results of a replicated study by Cetal, which we extended with algorithms by Van Horn and Vacul. The top-right inset is Cetals original figure, and it covers no data points. Note how the order parameter is a useful predictive data analytic for all three algorithms.

an order parameter, and is to some degree useful for predicting runtimes. Furthermore, the same order parameter also seems to hold for Van Horn's algorithm, which largely outperforms Cetal's with shorter runtimes simply by inverting the heuristic from prioritizing higher degree vertices to prioritizing lower degree vertices.

Finally, Vacul's algorithm of sophisticated pruning lives up to its promise and outperforms both other algorithms, being so effective it practically erases the phase transition for our problem instances. Still, the harder graphs are near the phase transition and the average vertex degree might still be seen as an order parameter. Much of this is due to the pruning done during preprocessing and recursing. This procedure however, is quadratic-time and gets executed during every iteration in an exponential algorithm. So, even though the number of iterations may be much lower, the amount of wall clock time per iteration is likely to be higher. To what extent this is a purely theoretical issue remains to be seen; the cost-benefit tradeoff of such 'intermediate speedup procedures' is classically related to constructive algorithms, and we would like to quantitatively investigate the details for these specific algorithms in future work.

For now, these pruning procedures appear quite beneficial and firmly instantiate Steven Skiena's famous take-home lesson "[Clever pruning can make short work of surprisingly hard problems.]" [26]. Furthermore, Bitner & Rheingold's early observation that nodes with tighter constraints should be prioritized over looser constraints seems like a good guiding principle for designing these kinds of complete algorithms – at least for Hamiltonian cycle detection, but possibly for a much wider class of problems because after all, it (still) is NP-complete.

With the seminal work of Peter Cheeseman, Bob Kanefsky and William Taylor, the field of instance hardness has seen the light. Ever since, principles such as solution backbones, complexity cores and algorithm selection have all emerged as important scientific concepts, scraping ever more plaster off the wall that separates P from NP. We think these concepts, and their paper, should be part of any serious curriculum in computer science or artificial intelligence.

VI. Acknowledgements

Many thanks to Richard Karp, Edward Rheingold, Andreas Björklund and Joseph Culberson for answering questions over email, and to Marcel Worring and Hans Dekkers from University of Amsterdam for granting some research time.

References

[1] R. E. Bryant, "On the complexity of vlsi implementations and graph representations of boolean functions with application to integer multiplication," IEEE transactions on Computers, vol. 40, no. 2, pp. 205–213, 1991.

[2] F. Ivančić, Z. Yang, M. K. Ganai, A. Gupta, and P. Ashar, "Efficient sat-based bounded model checking for software verification," Theoretical Computer Science, vol. 404, no. 3, pp. 256–274, 2008.
[3] P. C. Cheeseman, B. Kanefsky, and W. M. Taylor, "Where the really hard problems are." in IJCAI, vol. 91, 1991, pp. 331–340.
[4] T. Larrabee and Y. Tsuji, Evidence for a satisfiability threshold for random 3CNF formulas. Citeseer, 1992.
[5] S. Kirkpatrick and B. Selman, "Critical behavior in the satisfiability of random boolean expressions," Science, vol. 264, no. 5163, pp. 1297–1301, 1994.
[6] I. P. Gent and T. Walsh, "Easy problems are sometimes hard," Artificial Intelligence, vol. 70, no. 1-2, pp. 335–345, 1994.
[7] T. Hogg and C. P. Williams, "The hardest constraint problems: A double phase transition," Artificial Intelligence, vol. 69, no. 1-2, pp. 359–377, 1994.
[8] T. Hogg, "Refining the phase transition in combinatorial search," Artificial Intelligence, vol. 81, no. 1-2, pp. 127–154, 1996.
[9] I. P. Gent and T. Walsh, "The tsp phase transition," Artificial Intelligence, vol. 88, no. 1-2, pp. 349–358, 1996.
[10] M. R. Garey and D. S. Johnson, Computers and intractability. wh freeman New York, 2002, vol. 29.
[11] A. M. Jaffe, "The millennium grand challenge in mathematics," Notices of the AMS, vol. 53, no. 6, pp. 652–660, 2006.
[12] P. Erdos and A. Rényi, "On the evolution of random graphs," Publ. Math. Inst. Hung. Acad. Sci, vol. 5, no. 1, pp. 17–60, 1960.
[13] L. Pósa, "Hamiltonian circuits in random graphs," Discrete Mathematics, vol. 14, no. 4, pp. 359–364, 1976.
[14] J. Komlós and E. Szemerédi, "Limit distribution for the existence of Hamiltonian cycles in a random graph," Discrete Mathematics, vol. 43, no. 1, pp. 55–63, 1983.
[15] S. Roberts and B. Flores, "Systematic generation of Hamiltonian circuits," Communications of the ACM, vol. 9, no. 9, pp. 690–694, 1966.
[16] M. Held and R. M. Karp, "A dynamic programming approach to sequencing problems," Journal of the Society for Industrial and Applied Mathematics, vol. 10, no. 1, pp. 196–210, 1962.
[17] R. Bellman, "Dynamic programming treatment of the travelling salesman problem," Journal of the ACM (JACM), vol. 9, no. 1, pp. 61–63, 1962.
[18] S. Martello, "Algorithm 595: An enumerative algorithm for finding Hamiltonian circuits in a directed graph," ACM Transactions on Mathematical Software (TOMS), vol. 9, no. 1, pp. 131–138, 1983.
[19] F. Rubin, "A search procedure for Hamilton paths and circuits," Journal of the ACM (JACM), vol. 21, no. 4, pp. 576–580, 1974.
[20] B. Vandegriend and J. Culberson, "The gn, m phase transition is not hard for the Hamiltonian cycle problem," Journal of Artificial Intelligence Research, vol. 9, pp. 219–245, 1998.
[21] B. Bollobas, T. I. Fenner, and A. M. Frieze, "An algorithm for finding Hamilton paths and cycles in random graphs," Combinatorica, vol. 7, no. 4, pp. 327–341, 1987.
[22] A. Bjorklund, "Determinant sums for undirected Hamiltonicity," SIAM Journal on Computing, vol. 43, no. 1, pp. 280–299, 2014.
[23] K. Iwama and T. Nakashima, "An improved exact algorithm for cubic graph tsp," in International Computing and Combinatorics Conference. Springer, 2007, pp. 108–117.
[24] J. R. Bitner and E. M. Reingold, "Backtrack programming techniques," Communications of the ACM, vol. 18, no. 11, pp. 651–656, 1975.
[25] Gent et al., "The constrainedness of search," in AAAI/IAAI, Vol. 1, 1996, pp. 246–252.
[26] S. S. Skiena, "The algorithm design manual," p. 247, 1998.

Predictive Analytics in Utility Vehicle Maintenance

Jürgen Prinzbach, Stephan Trahasch
Electrical Engineering and Information Technology
Offenburg University of Applied Sciences
Offenburg, Germany
email: {juergen.prinzbach, stephan.trahasch}@hs-offenburg.de

Abstract—**In public transportation, the motor pool often consists of various different vehicles bought over a duration of many years. Sometimes, they even differ within one batch bought at the same time. This poses a considerable challenge in the storage and allocation of spare parts, especially in the event of damage to a vehicle. Correctly assigning these parts before the vehicle reaches the workshop could significantly reduce both the downtime and, therefore, the actual costs for companies. In order to achieve this, the current software uses a simple probability calculation. To improve the performance, the data of specific companies was analysed, preprocessed and used with several modelling techniques to classify and, therefore, predict the spare parts to be used in the event of a faulty vehicle. We summarize our experience running through the steps of the Cross Industry Standard Process for Data Mining and compare the performance to the previously used probability. Gradient Boosting Trees turned out to be the best modeling technique for this special case.**

Keywords-maintenance; utility vehicle; spare parts; data analysis; predictive analytics.

I. INTRODUCTION

For service providers in the field of public transportation or waste disposal in particular, it is important to be able to optimally manage their own vehicle fleet in the area of maintenance and to minimize downtimes as much as possible. Unfortunately, the vehicles purchased over the years sometimes differ so much even within a single batch that many different spare parts have to be kept in stock. In addition to the enormous storage costs, this makes the assignment of a new part to a faulty vehicle more difficult than one would hope for [1]. Therefore, software is used in the areas of fleet management, workshop and logistics, to help traffic companies meet these challenges. However, cases still exist when a defect reported by a driver is checked upon arrival at the depot of the company by a shop assistant. In the worst case, when creating a repair order, the mechanic realizes that not all spare parts needed are in stock, which means that the downtime of the vehicle will be extended by the respective delivery time taking at least six to eight hours, even with special express delivery, depending on the industry and supplier. If the workshop manager were to receive a well-founded proposal on the material to be installed ahead of time, it could be ready at the point of entry to the workshop and both the time and cost could be reduced enormously.

For that reason, this work focuses on analysing and processing the data of several traffic companies ranging from the vehicle data to the respective repair processes. In particular, data quality should be taken into account, as the data basis of the software could be used by the respective company in the most diverse ways. The knowledge gained from this should make it possible, based on the Cross Industry Standard Process for Data Mining [2], to improve an already implemented software by creating and evaluating different models for the prediction of the corresponding spare parts.

This paper is organized as follows. Section 2 puts this paper in the context of related works, whereas Section 3 explains the current implementation of the mentioned probability in the application and the data this is based upon. Data analysis and preprocessing are explained in Section 4, whereas Section 5 describes the actual modelling. Section 6 summarizes the evaluation criteria and results, and the final section concludes this paper.

II. RELATED WORK

In the field of maintaining machines or plants, predictive maintenance is often used when talking about data analytics. This usually means the prediction of faults or failures of said machines in order to avoid larger failures through planned repairs or servicing. As described in [3], this is about the observation of the current state of the machine in the execution of its tasks. The bottom line is therefore the evaluation of log-based sensor data and the possible prediction of failures. Another elaboration [4] also attempts to improve their maintenance planning by detecting error signatures in environment variables in significant data sets containing machine records. Even though this paper deals with the avoidance of vehicle failures, such a preventive approach is currently not possible, which is partly due to the fact that the vehicle manufacturers do not make the data available during operation.

Rather, one could think about it as using predictive analytics techniques as a kind of "management tool" to reduce the planned and unplanned downtime of the respective machine [5] – in this case the vehicles. Detecting the correct and needed spare parts before the vehicle arrives in the depot could at least partially eliminate unnecessary activities, such as inspecting the vehicle or adjusting incorrect parts, thereby dramatically reducing the overall cost of the vehicle. In the optimal case, for example, the repair could be planned so that it lies between two uses of the vehicle. This would make the vehicle practically not fail.

Breaking down the required task down to its core one realizes that it is ultimately about the classification of the respective spare part based on relevant attributes of the existing data sets. Which attributes in addition to the error message of the driver or vehicle are relevant or which algorithms are suitable in this case for determining the parts is therefore part of this work. In addition to Support Vector Machines (SVM) or simple decision trees, Gradient Boosted Trees could also be an option. A future relevant approach could also be "Gradient Boosted Decision Tables" using a novel method of storing the decision tables and a more efficient prediction algorithm [6].

III. CURRENT IMPLEMENTATION

In the area of public transportation, the software used here offers extensive functions for the administration and support of buses and their maintenance. It has a modular structure and supports a large number of vehicle types and their technical infrastructure. Among other things, vehicles can be planned, timetables managed, defects recorded and spare parts ordered. The last two points belong to the process of maintenance, which is triggered in the event of a fault on the vehicle. As soon as a defect is created in the system, possible spare parts are displayed with the respective usage probabilities. However, this is only possible with correspondingly good data and with reference to the vehicle and the work to be performed.

Due to the individual adaptability of the software, the various supported business areas as well as the high degrees of freedom in the administration of the data by the users, it may be difficult to obtain sufficient data. Furthermore, the number of processes, after which meaningful suggestions for spare parts can be generated, increases due to the variety of different vehicles of each company. However, if all prerequisites are met, it is possible to confirm everyday knowledge and gain new insights with the calculation of the probability of using specific parts. This already implemented probability is calculated from the ratio of the number of processes executed using a particular spare part to the total number of executions of that process. In this way, one obtains a simpler way of calculating the conditional probability of using a material, assuming that a particular process is applied to a defect. However, the probability also always depends on the particular vehicle, which – in simple terms – is defined by its brand and model. Thus, formula (1) can be used to calculate the probability of using a replacement part, where the individual components can be formalized as such that I_v represents the parts used and O_v the individual processes:

$$P(I_v \mid O_v) = P(I_v \cap O_v) \,/\, P(O_v) \quad (1)$$

This could lead to a result like the one shown in Table I. So, because of the probability in this particular case one would probably order item 1536 for the corresponding process and vehicle.

TABLE I. CALCULATION OF THE PROBABILITY OF THE USAGE OF ONE PARTICULAR ITEM FOR EACH PROCESS AND VEHICLE

Item	Process	Vehicle	P [%]
1536	82-1203	EVO-O530-BJ08	47.15
1531	82-1203	EVO-O530-BJ08	29.27
1539	82-1203	EVO-O530-BJ08	13.01
1537	82-1203	EVO-O530-BJ08	2.85
1529	82-1203	EVO-O530-BJ08	1.22

IV. DATA FOUNDATION

The required data is stored in a relational database management system. On this basis, the attributes needed to calculate the explained probability are simply merged via joins in a view. However, there is the question of how much the results can be trusted and business decisions to be made on that basis. On the one hand, some users may sometimes make very far-reaching changes to the data; on the other hand, they must also be appropriately maintained, and the processes carefully recorded. Here, one can probably assume that given freedoms are often exploited, which may corrupt the data quality and thus the results. In addition, it turns out that the recalculation and update of the probability is not always enabled for all processes. It should also be noted that the probability of use is based on purely historical observations and that no model for future events is included or can be derived.

Moreover, direct feedback on errors is just as impossible as basic testing of the quality of the process in the event of emerging defects. For the practical application of the method, with a few exceptions, it is still necessary to have a person with relevant specialist knowledge. So important decisions should not depend on this calculation – but it can help in assessing the situation at hand. To improve this situation, predictive analytics methods have been tested and their results analysed in further sections.

A. Data Understanding

In order to better understand the vehicle and deficiency data needed to predict spare parts and thus create different models, it is first necessary to understand the context of the data by generating it. Furthermore, the quality of the preliminary data has to be considered more closely so that the attributes used in the modelling can be selected. After that the data may be preprocessed for further usage. In this work, R [7] and R Studio [8] have been used with various packages, such as "caret" [9], "ROSE" [10] or "doParallel" [11] for all analysis and modelling work.

B. Data Analysis

For further analysis of the data, database backups are used of two companies who use the same software in different ways and to varying degrees. On closer inspection, the big difference between the existing data records has become clear. The first database (DB1) has more than 25 times as many lines with 862,350 defect entries as the second database (DB2), which is also reflected in the number of different attributes.

TABLE II. DISTRIBUTIONS AND CHARACTERISTICS OF SELECTED ATTRIBUTES

Attribute	Range	Mean	Median	Skew	Deviation
ManufacturerTypeKey	325	100.07	59	1.01	76.06
Manufacturer	44	29.33	34	-0.35	6.55
Model	103	60.54	73	-0.88	18.98
Process	1317	510.25	485	0.27	403.10
Fault	368	161.83	178	0	107.75
Material	1109	499.90	410	0.39	311.03

Thus, the first company with 57 vehicle manufacturers and more than 140 models has almost 30 times as many different vehicles in use as the other one. However, this stark difference or this high number of different manufacturers seems to be exceedingly unrealistic, since there are not so many brands in the area of buses in the local market. This could either be a mixture of different categories, such as passenger cars or some data may not have been recorded correctly. It is also noticeable that the granularity of work processes and defects differ greatly. For example, with 584 to 369, DB1 has more than 1.5 times more defects and 2,567 to 1,234 more than twice as many processes than DB2. These observations can also be demonstrated in the usable spare parts. While a larger number of different vehicles can be expected to have an increasing number of different replacement parts, the differences in granularity present show how fundamentally different the two companies deal with defects and workflows. Fig. 1 illustrates these observations by the different occurrences of the key attributes "ManufacturerTypeKey", an artificial primary key, which is composed among other things of the two attributes "Manufacturer" and "Model" which are also shown. Furthermore, the attributes "Process", "Fault" and "Material", which corresponds to the spare parts, are displayed. Note that the illustration assumes a minimum occurrence of defects and attributes of 50 each. Even though the two most common deficiencies in DB1 have been removed, as explained in the preprocessing section, it promises significantly better results.

Therefore, further investigations are being concentrated on this database. For example, the attributes "performance" and "weight" have a proportion of missing values (NAs)

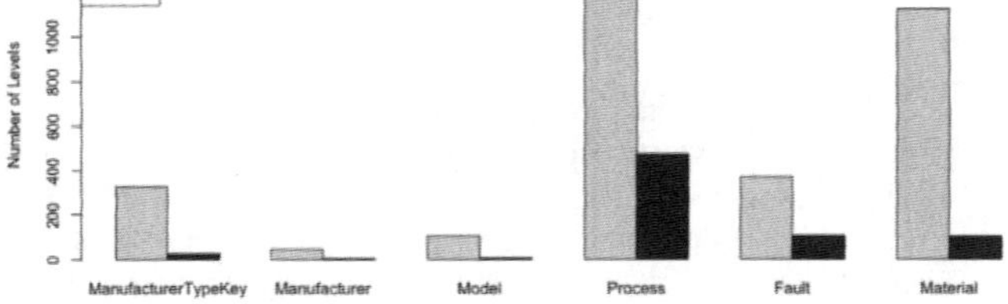

Figure 1. Number of different characteristics in key attributes with a minimum occurrence of the deficiencies and attributes of 50 each and the exclusion of the two most prevalent deficiencies in DB1

between 70% and 80%, which makes them completely useless due to the lack of possibilities for recalculation. For the other attributes, on the other hand, the number of NAs is so small that the respective rows could simply be removed. Thus, after the clean-up of the missing values, a number of 861,026 supposedly usable rows are obtained. However, when looking at the three most common deficiencies, it turns out that this unfortunately is not the case. For example, one can see from the descriptions "additional work and maintenance" and "lack, please more specific" of the fault types "Z1111" and "Z9999" that in the first case simple maintenance work has been carried out. Thus, there was no defect of the vehicle. In the second case, the clerk simply did not know what was really broken. So, both manifestations should not be used in the given context, as this could distort the result in case of doubt. This means that with 485,489 lines that make up these two most common deficiencies, nearly 60% of the total database is unusable for the process of learning which spare parts to use in which situation.

For further analysis, the distributions and characteristics of individual attributes of the resulting data set can now be considered. This information is presented in Table II, noting that only those datasets have been used in which both the feature of the spare part and the defect have occurred at least 50 times. Furthermore, the attributes have been numbered prior to the calculations. It can be seen that, for example, the months in which a deficiency occurred are distributed fairly evenly, whereas the affected vehicle models appear to be affected very differently. Therefore, if necessary, the data should be normalized in preprocessing.

Calculating a correlation matrix and looking at it by using a heat map, the correlation of 0.27 shows that the manufacturer-type key seems to have some connection with the target class of parts, while the day or month when the deficiency was reported appears to be completely insignificant (0.01 to 0.02). Whether this is actually the case will be demonstrated by the various experiments in creating the models. What seems logical, however, are the obvious links between the manufacturer and the model (0.71) or the age and miles driven (0.28).

C. Data Preprocessing

In the following, the activities performed in the field of data preparation are explained. Here, not only separately performed steps are mentioned, but also those which have been run through during the model creation with the help of the respective packages. First, approximately 15 attributes like "weight" and "performance" that have been found to be unhelpful during each experiment have been removed because, for example, they contain too many missing values [12]. Following this, the errors for non-specific problems "Z1111" and "Z9999" were removed due to their low information content.

After this clean-up, some transformations of the data and generation of new attributes from existing columns were performed. This includes, for example, the generation of the age in years, which is derived from the first registration and the current date. The age of the vehicles can therefore be very important, as some parts become more susceptible to defects over time. This also means that certain repairs and thus also certain spare parts, for example, are needed after 5 years, rather than after just one year.

Furthermore, from the date of the defect notification, the corresponding month was extracted to obtain a seasonal component. From this, temporal correlations of potential failures of the heating can be obtained, which are more likely to occur in winter than in summer. In addition to this characteristic, the mileage since the last inspection has been roughly obtained from the kilometers travelled so far. This was only possible because the vehicles in the public transport industry are always maintained every 30,000 km. After calculating this information, the kilometer-based attributes are categorized according to the experiment. For example, the total mileage of the vehicles could be divided into 5,000 km classes.

In the next step, the attributes were converted to numerical factors and those columns were removed that had become unnecessary by generating additional information. Theoretically, a scaling or transformation at this point would be useful. However, a number of experiments have shown that performing these activities manually produces worse results than running them by the respective package just prior to the modelling. Now the data was prepared in such a way that further experiments could be carried out on the basis of it. Other possible steps at this point included both splitting the data into training and test data by a fixed percentage or performing a Principal Component Analysis (PCA). For example, the former would have specified that 70% of the data would be used to learn a model, while 30% would be used for later evaluation [12]. The PCA tries to further reduce the number of currently 11 attributes at this time by calculating artificial properties to reduce complexity while maintaining the same quality [12]. Furthermore, PCA offers other benefits, such as decorrelating the attributes. Ultimately, however, all attempts at optimization were doomed to failure, as the various deficiencies and materials occur in very different frequencies, which can be seen, for example, in the respective skewness in Table 2. Thus, there was a bias in the direction of the most prevalent manifestations, which will be shown by the experiments presented in the next section.

V. MODELLING

At the beginning, we performed experiments with various algorithms and various combinations of attributes and split ratios of the training and test data. For the latter, 70:30 and 80:20 were first investigated, while Naive Bayes [12] and Support Vector Machines (linear, radial, and polynomial) were mainly used with their default settings. It quickly became clear that a holistic prediction of the many different, very unevenly distributed target classes of the attribute "material" is not possible. For this reason, according to the number of different spare parts, we have to generate databases with all data records but binary target classes. Each database therefore stands for a single spare part and its use, which is why the target attribute "material" only indicates whether or not it is used – in other words, a "yes" or a "no". This created significantly better results. However, in some cases a few positive cases were faced with some 10,000 negative cases, which meant that some materials could be predicted extremely well and others extremely badly. Therefore, we tried to approximate the uneven classes with the help of packages like ROSE and thus to improve the results, which finally succeeded. We were also able to largely confirm the results of the correlation matrix for the individual attributes with some experiments. However, there was also one or the other surprise. While the matrix did not see any correlation with the day the defect was reported, this property proved helpful in determining the required spare part. In order to give a small but concrete overview of the modellings carried out, three of them are described below. First, however, we explain how the individual parameters of the respective packages were determined. For the modelling itself, mainly the Caret package [8] with different algorithms was used.

A. Parameter Settings

To determine the best possible parameters, models were created for 10 to 20 previously randomly selected spare parts and the respective results compared. Through this reduction, the calculation time could be minimized. However, with a more powerful production system, integration into the actual modelling process would be desirable. Finally, the following steps for parameter determination were carried out – here exemplified at the *k*-fold cross validation:

1. Definition of the possible values for the tuning parameters.
2. Execution of the modelling process including resampling of the data and prediction of the respective spare parts using the test data.
3. Creation of an evaluation matrix for all results meaning that the results of the respective predictions have been collected in a confusion matrix and the sensitivities have been read out.
4. Determination of the final tuning parameters by ordering the sensitivities in descending order of magnitude and frequency.

B. Naive Bayes vs. GBM and C5.0

After the initial experiments, it turned out that the generated data sets with binary target classes using Naive Bayes provided the best results so far. In this series of experiments, tree-based models, such as Gradient Boosting Trees (GBM) [12] or C5.0 Trees were tested. GBM should hereby maximize the Receiver Operating Characteristic (ROC), while C5.0 used a cost function to try and improve the results by increasing the cost of incorrect predictions.

Furthermore, it should be noted that only parts that were used more than 1000 times were evaluated, resulting in 84 models. Added to this is the restriction to defects that occurred more than 50 times. Finally, after some experiments a split ratio of 75:25 was calculated as the mean of the previous experiments.

C. Gradient Boosting Trees

With the aforementioned experiment, we found that Gradient Boosting Trees in our context enable the better models, which is why they were used as a priority thereafter. Added to this was the described determination of optimal parameters, which should further improve the results. Here are some of the parameters and options used in the Caret Package:

- Scaling and centering of the data
- Repeated *k*-fold cross validation with 5 folds and 2 repeats
- Between 400 and 500 trees at a depth of 7

However, at this time it was first noticed that the most prevalent shortage, which accounts for more than one-third of the data, is for maintenance and remanufacturing only and, therefore, does not represent a defect. For this reason, these samples did not contribute to the determination of the target class and were therefore not considered. The remaining shortcomings and materials have now been assumed to occur at least 100 times, ultimately using just over 200,000 samples and creating 788 models.

D. Gradient Boosting Trees without the two most common defects

In this experiment, only models were created using Gradient Boosting Trees. However, only those records were used that do not represent the two most common shortcomings "Z1111" and "Z9999". In addition, both the respective defects and the target class should total at least 50 times in the data, leaving 231,363 lines remaining. Following this, binary training and test data with a ratio of 75:25 were generated for each of the 1110 spare parts. In the modelling itself, the following parameters were used:

- Preprocessing:
  - Center and scale
  - Principal Component Analysis
- Train Control:
  - Repeated cross validation with 6 folds and no repetition
- Grid Settings:
  - 700 trees with a depth of 13
  - Shrinkage of 0.1

It should be noted at this point that this experiment was performed once with and once without the information of the work process. This is because the usage probability used so far includes this, while in the future it will work without this information. The tests carried out thus permit estimates of the quality of the individual models in both cases.

VI. Evaluation

After the experiments presented in the previous section and the training of different models for the classification of spare parts, the criteria for determining the model quality and the performance are explained below. Afterwards, the results are presented and conclusions drawn for future applications.

A. Underlying Criteria

In principle, the probability of using spare parts already implemented sets the standard for all new processes. Furthermore, it is especially important for companies to recognize the cases in which a spare part is really needed. This means that it is far less dramatic to get a material out of the warehouse for repair or to order and then not need it, as if the vehicle is already in the workshop and it is found that parts are missing. On the one hand, one can conclude that some of the known quality measures should be weighted more heavily than others, on the other hand, the relevant measures for the used probabilities must be calculated. The latter is relatively easy since it already covers or predicts the positive cases. This also coincides with the requirement to determine really needed parts.

Thus, the evaluation strategy is quite simple: For the predictive algorithms, the known criteria listed below are used, with the ultimate focus being on sensitivity and the possible comparison with the probabilities. For these measurements, a 2x2 confusion matrix is first calculated, which makes it possible to compare the actual classes to test data predicted with the respective model. This simple matrix is usable because the data has been converted into binary sets as described. From this, mainly criteria like sensitivity, accuracy and others were calculated [13].

Although other measures such as False Positive Rate or Positive Predictive Value have been calculated, they will not be listed here due to the lack of relevance to the results.

B. Results

Despite the poor accuracy of 20 to 30% achieved in first experiments with Naive Bayes, this algorithm is used again and again as a comparison. Looking at the average values for sensitivity, specificity and accuracy (see Fig. 2), the three algorithms compared here seem to work similarly well. Furthermore, it can be seen that the optimization towards the spare parts actually needed has an effect and, therefore, the

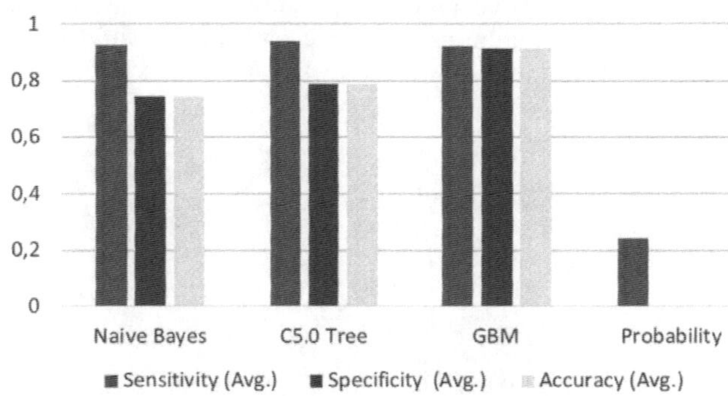

Figure 2. Average modelling results by criteria

true positive rate (TPR) is higher than the other values. The Gradient Boosting Trees, with the two most common defects removed, are an exception. With more than 90% on all criteria they provide very good results. Comparing these with the average sensitivity of the currently implemented probability reveals its seemingly blatant weaknesses. This also confirms the assumption that the modeling techniques of predictive analytics should provide better results. However, this diagram does not disclose some important information. First and foremost, only the average of the respective quality measure is indicated across all models and thus across all spare parts. This means that outliers, i.e., binary models for the respective spare parts that deliver bad classifications, are not recognizable in Section V (D). Another important point is that the probability is not calculated in all cases, which makes a scientifically sound comparison almost impossible. This is because the function may have been disabled due to other deficiency evaluations or set calculation limits. Nonetheless, these benchmarks can be seen as indicative, suggesting that better ways could be found to provide automatic suggestions for replacement parts to be installed in the event of vehicle defects.

VII. Conclusions

First, it must be noted that despite the problems during the experiments, it is in principle possible to predict the required spare part with predictive analytics in case of a defect in a vehicle. Based on the underlying criteria, this also worked better than the currently implemented probability.

However, in order to make an actual recommendation and to be able to compensate for variations in the quality of the forecast, a few points should be noted. First, care should be taken to improve the quality of the data. For this purpose, it would be useful to standardize the basic vehicle data across all companies using the software and at least to explain the information of the vehicle registration certificate to mandatory information. Furthermore, a uniform catalog of shortcomings should be drawn up in cooperation with the customer in order to avoid, for example, different granularities in case of defects. This would allow more attributes or even more databases from multiple customers to be used to create the models, which should allow them to be more accurate and less subject to fluctuations. Whether Gradient Boosting Trees still deliver the best results after that will have to be reevaluated. However, it may also be beneficial to use the probability calculation to validate the results of the models if the results are not too bad, which would be the case for accuracies of less than 60%.

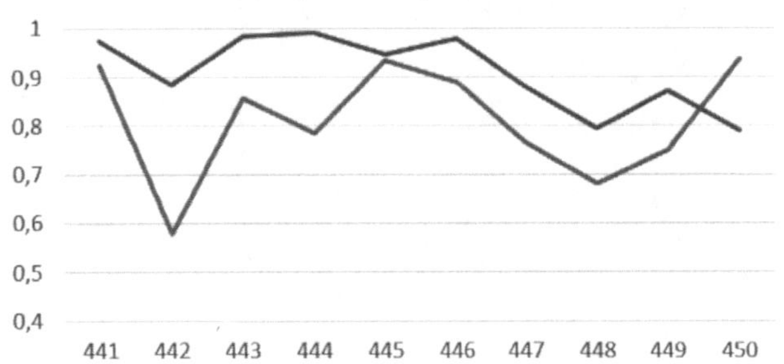

Figure 3. Results from ten randomly selected models created with GBM

These improvements will be addressed in future activities in this area and an integrated service in the cloud for companies in public transportation will be created, which then stores information about the work processes in case of emerging defects and can create models on the common data. Then, it should also be able to answer inquiries about new processes and make suggestions or make predictions about spare parts. This work has thus paved the way for far-reaching improvements to the repair of utility vehicles.

Acknowledgment

This work was supported by COS GmbH in Oberkirch (Germany) and the Federal Ministry of Education and Research.

References

[1] J. Prinzbach, Predictive Analytics in der Instandhaltung, Master Thesis, Offenburg University of Applied Sciences, 2017.

[2] P. Chapman et al., CRISP-DM 1.0: Step-by-step data mining guide, 2000.

[3] L. Spendla, M. Kebisek, P. Tanuska, and L. Hrcka, "Concept of Predictive Maintenance of Production Systems in Accordance with Industry 4.0," IEEE 15th International Symposium on Applied Machine Intelligence and Informatics (SAMI), 2017 2017 Jan 26 IEEE Press, Jan. 2017.

[4] B. Cline, R. S. Niculescu, D. Huffman, and B. Deckel, Predictive Maintenance Applications for Machine Learning, 2017 Annual Reliability and Maintainability Symposium (RAMS), IEEE Press, Jan. 2017.

[5] R. K. Mobley, *An introduction to predictive maintenance*, Butterworth-Heinemann, Amsterdam, New York, 2002.

[6] Y. Lou and M. Obukhov, "BDT: Gradient Boosted Decision Tables for High Accuracy and Scoring Efficiency," Proc. 23rd ACM SIGKDD International Conference on Knowledge Discovery and Data Mining - KDD '17, ACM Press, Aug. 2017.

[7] The R Foundation, "The R Project", [Online] Available from https://www.r-project.org [retrieved: Oct. 2018]

[8] RStudio, "RStudio" [Online] Available from https://www.rstudio.com [retrieved: Oct. 2018]

[9] The R Foundation, "caret", [Online] Available from https://cran.r-project.org/package=caret [retrieved: Oct. 2018]

[10] The R Foundation, "ROSE", [Online] Available from https://cran.r-project.org/package=ROSE [retrieved: Oct. 2018]

[11] The R Foundation, "doParallel", [Online] Available from https://cran.r-project.org/package=doParallel [retrieved: Oct. 2018]

[12] M. Kuhn and K. Johnson, Applied predictive modeling, New York: Springer, 2016.

[13] J. Han, M. Kamber, and J. Pei, Data mining: Concepts and techniques, Amsterdam: Elsevier/Morgan Kaufmann, 2012.

Evaluation of Ship Energy Efficiency Predictive and Optimization Models Based on Noon Reports and Condition Monitoring Datasets

Spandonidis Christos, Themelis Nikos, Christopoulos George, Giordamlis Christos
Prisma Electronics, Athens, Greece
emails: {c.spandonidis, nikos.themelis, g.christopoulos, christos}@prismael.com

Abstract - **For a long time, the shipping industry has relied on Noon Reports to extract the main parameters required to define both the ship's performance and fuel consumption, despite the fact that these reports have low sampling frequency (approx. 24 hours. Nowadays, satellite communications, telemetries, data collection, and analytics are making possible to treat a fleet of ships as a single unit. Thus, the shipping industry is definitely part of the information business. In the current work, we present a qualitative and quantitative comparison between the models developed from historical trends that are extracted from Noon Reports and the Continuous Monitoring System. The analysis is based on parameters that are reported by both data sources. While effort has been made in order to quantify variances due to the different sampling rate, our main focus was on quantification of uncertainty and the resulted confidence interval in order to clarify the potential and limitations of the resulting predictive models. The paper aims to contribute to the areas of tools and mechanisms of data analytics, in the specific area of maritime intelligence.**

Keywords - Continuous Monitoring; Noon Report; Performance Assessment; Trim Assessment.

I. INTRODUCTION

Today's ships are equipped with numerous sensors and advanced systems which help to operate vessels more efficiently. Any decision making inside a shipping company must be based on accurate and verifiable data and not just on feelings, instincts, or intuition. Managing a fleet of vessels involves complex processes. The ability to utilize data to obtain actionable knowledge, predictions and insights allows for continuous process improvements and optimal performance throughout the lifetime of assets.

The ability to manage all data and information from different systems onboard in a safe and efficient manner enables a new level of possibility to analyze and monitor situations, critical operations and adverse conditions as well as to increase performance awareness. Integration of performance indicators across systems is vital for getting the full overview of actual asset operation. Aggregation of lower level performance indicators into top-level Key Performance Indicators (KPIs) is a proven approach to performance management as the condition and operation of sub-systems is crucial for the total system operational predictability and the need for maintenance. Knowing how the vessel and its systems perform in real operation is a cornerstone for optimizing the fuel efficiency and technical maintenance of the vessel and its systems.

Aldous [1] provides a comprehensive review of the recent developments in performance monitoring based on data derived either by Noon Reports or by Continuous Monitoring System. In this work, an extensive review of the models, namely theoretical, statistical and hybrid used in ship performance assessment is provided. Additionally, the author refers to eight categories of application of ship performance models: *i)* Operational real-time optimization (e.g Armstrong [2], Psaraftis & Kontovas [3]), *ii)* Maintenance trigger (e.g. Walker & Atkins [4]), *iii)* Evaluating technological interventions (e.g. Stulgis [5]), *iv)* Operational delivery plan optimization (e.g. Rakke et al. [6]), *v)* Fault analysis (e.g. Spandonidis & Giordamlis [7], Djeziri et al. [8]), *vi)* Charter party analysis, vii) Vessel benchmarking (e.g. Bazari [9]) and *viii)* Inform policy (e.g. Smith et al. [10]). In that framework, Aldous et al. [11] provide a method for quantifying the uncertainty in reported fuel consumption between two months and one year's worth of data from 89 ships. The subsequently calculated confidence is then compared to the uncertainty in the data acquired from an onboard continuous monitoring system. Furthermore, ISO [12] describes the uncertainty entered into the measurement from various sources as well as proposes a data handling methodology. Nevertheless, utilizing data from ships in order to support the decision-making process of shipping companies, and to provide insight for cost-efficient operations, is not a new idea. This has been previously mentioned as part of traditional methods based on Noon Reports data, which are quite popular within the marine industry.

In the current work, we take the first step towards quantifying the statistical trustworthiness of different methods of data collection, as obtained by Noon Reports (NR) and from LAROS Continuous Monitoring System (L-CMS). Our aim is to examine the capabilities of each method to provide reliable input in performance assessments, by presenting a case study based on real obtained datasets from NR and L-CMS.

The rest of the paper is structured as follows. In Section II, we present briefly the basic architecture of the LAROS Continuous Monitoring System. In Section III, verification, validation, and software modules of the L-CMS platform are presented. Test results and corrective actions taken are also discussed. In Section IV, we present the methodology used in the current work for the quantification of performance based on a standard indicator as well as the tested ship and methods of data acquisition. Statistical measures for the quantification of the reliability level of each method are utilized. A study on how differences in the frequency of the reporting could affect trim optimization is also included. Finally, in Section V, we discuss the key results of the study.

II. SYSTEM DESCRIPTION

For the Continuous Monitoring System, we relied on LAROS system.

- Smart Collectors are connected using the appropriate interface to analog or digital signals coming from different sensors and instruments of the vessel.
- Smart Collectors analyze the signals and calculate the required parameters. The sampling rate, as well as the rate of the parameters calculations, can be set from 100 msec up to 30 minutes.
- Smart Collectors set up a wireless secure network inside the vessel to transmit the processed data to the Gateway with a user-defined sampling rate and ability to maintain and customize them remotely. The wireless protocol is based on IEEE 802.15.4 MESH (Adams [13]) with additional layers and data format to cover the requirements of the vessel environment and increase the network Quality of Service.
- Through the Gateway, all the measured and processed parameters are stored in Central Server (onboard). The Server periodically produces binary files and compresses them in order to reduce the size of the data to be sent via normal satellite broadband.
- The compressed files are transmitted through File Transfer Protocol (FTP) to the HQ database.
- In the data center, there is a service that decompresses the incoming files and stores the new measurements in the main database.

TABLE I. INDICATIVE FUNCTIONAL MODULES - SHIPPING

Module	***Needed signals***	***Connection points***
Propeller – Hull Performance	Vessel Speed, Shaft Revolutions per Minute (RPM), Shaft Power.	Speed log, Torque-meter- RPM Indicator.
Engine Performance	Fuel Oil Consumption (FOC), Power (Specific Fuel Oil Consumption - SFOC), Diesel Generator (DG) Output	Flowmeters [Fuel Oil (FO) flow], FO temp, FO density, DG Power Analyzer
FO Consumption	FOC, Vessel Speed through water, Shaft RPM, Boiler Status	Flowmeters (FO flow), FO temp, FO density, Boiler status indicator
On-line bunkering	Tank level, FO temperature	Cargo Control Console, Engine Control Room (ECR)/ Cargo Control Room (CCR) Indicators.
Maintenance managementt	Pressures, Temperatures, Alarms from critical systems	Alarm Monitor System (AMS), ECR Indicators
Power management	DG Output, Reefers Power Consumption	DG/Reefer Power Analyzers
Environmental conditions	Wind speed & direction, Water depth, Ambient temperature & Pressure	Anemometer, Echo-Sounder, weather station
Operational profile	Ground Speed, Drafts, Trim, Rudder angle	GPS, strain gage, Inclinometer

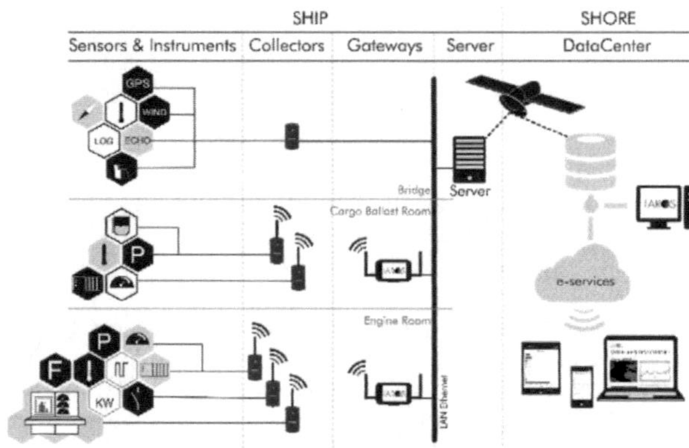

Figure 1. Operational data flow

Table I summarizes the main functionality modules, the needed signals, and the collection points onboard. In Figure 1, the aggregation of data needed for indicative functional modules is schematically illustrated.

III. SOFTWARE (SW) SYSTEM TESTING

The test plan followed can be briefly described as follows:

A. SW Module Verification

In order to verify our results, that is, to ensure that the code runs correctly given the equations of the model, two kinds of reliability tests were performed:

a) Evaluation of conservation principles and the subsequent execution of SW algorithms;

b) Monitoring of the systematic and the statistical error.

B. SW Validation

SW validation should involve comparison of characteristically obtained results with the same data obtained by other systems or sensors. However, there was lack of data during the implementation phase, as the vessel was at port/berth and main systems were inactive. In addition, Trim/List sensor was not mounted. To overcome this difficulty, two different kinds of validation tests were performed by different testing groups:

a) Regression testing. This represents the evaluation of data quality in the long term. The crew was instructed to report daily both LAROS measurements and sensor measurements of critical systems. Measurements were noted on regular periods (e.g. every 3 hours). Regression models (linear) were applied in order to estimate any deviation.

b) Performance testing. Performance testing was done by performing system and regression testing with a smaller sampling rate during both transient and steady-state conditions.

C. Test results

Testing procedure was performed according to the initial plan. Minor difficulties faced during the process were resolved ad hoc. The calculated uncertainties are standard deviations of the average (e.g. Speed over ground, Torque, etc.) at a 95% confidence level. The software module performs very well with a standard deviation of less than 1% in the steady state. Furthermore, for transient state validation showed the deviation of measured results from experimental data is less than 2%. This deviation was judged to be of acceptable level and is mainly caused by the sampling rate (60 sec) of hardware equipment. During the test period, based on data measured by the crew, onboard support engineers identified that main engine's fuel oil temperature presented a nonlinearity compared to actual measurements. Figure 2 presents some samples of the collected data: The issue resolved upon calibration of the collector with the appropriate linear function. Table II summarizes the results of system testing.

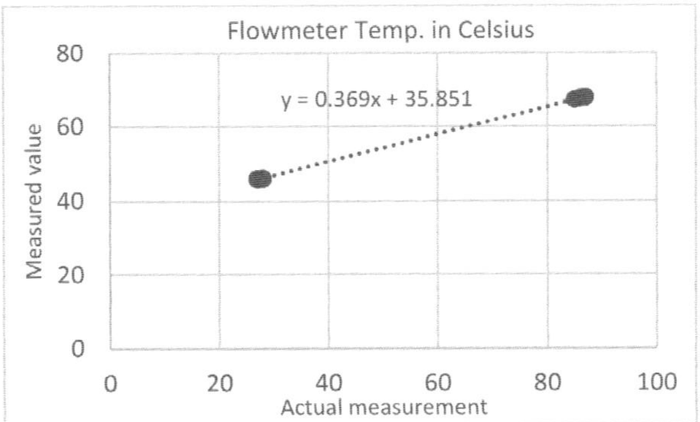

Figure 2. Correction factor and offset for the calibration of hardware

TABLE II. RESULTS OF SYSTEM TESTING

Test Case	*Pass/Fail*	*Deviation*
Conservation Principles	Pass	Deviation <0.5%
Statistical error	Pass	Reproducible averages within statistical uncertainties
Systemic error	Pass	Different OS Different web browser
Steady state	Pass	N/A
Transient state	Pass	N/A

IV. METHODOLOGY AND CASE STUDY RESULTS

We focus on a time period of 9 months for the performance assessment of hull and propeller, targeting mainly hull fouling degradation. The ship that provided the data for the comparison study is a 170000 DWT Bulk Carrier. In a first instance, we choose to use average values per hour from the L-CMS. The ship sailed about 60.5% of the considered time.

A. Evaluation based on power deviation

The targeted performance indicator is the increase of the required power, which affects significantly the ship's fuel consumption. The performance indicator is calculated as (ISO [12]):

$$\%Power\ increase = \frac{P_{measured} - P_{expected}}{P_{expected}} \quad (1)$$

where $P_{expected}$ corresponds to the expected delivered power needed to maintain a given speed at a specific loading condition and with no effect from environmental conditions. For the estimation of the expected power, we use as a model the reference power – speed curves obtained from sea trials, corresponding to the ballast and full load condition. We apply a correction on the power values for displacement deviation of the actual values from the reference ones using the Admiralty formula, according to the next equation:

$$P_e = P_{e(ref)} \left(\frac{\Delta_{act}}{\Delta_{d(ref)}}\right)^{2/3} \quad (2)$$

Furthermore, no extrapolation of speed-power curves is allowed, thus we utilize data only for the speed range of the trial tests. In addition, we are not considering measurements that correspond to values of displacement and trim that deviate more than 5% Δ and 0.5% L_{BP} from the respective values of the reference conditions. Furthermore, the performance index presented before is calculated by filtering data that exceeds various upper bounds of wind force (e.g. 4 Beaufort Force (BF), 5 BF etc.).

Different data acquisition methods are available for carrying out the assessment. The first is based on NR filled out by the crew on a daily basis and the second one relies on the L-CMS, in which several reporting frequencies have been examined (hourly, 15 and 5 min). We test the capability of the trend prediction over time using the 2 methods. The key idea for this comparison study is to use a fraction of the available information as hindcast data and the remaining period to play the role of the forecast period. The first three months are used as the hindcast period. The forecast trend is calculated based on hindcast (or trained) data using a linear regression model. The actual trend is calculated by the known data of the "forecast" period using the same model. In the framework of this study, we assume that the linear regression model is capable of providing the trend, as we focus on the comparison between the 2 methods.

Figure 3 shows the results when an upper bound of wind force of 5 BF is applied. In order to quantify the comparison between the actual and the forecast trend, we calculate the standard error of the estimate for the "forecast" period and we average over the whole wind force range (Figure 4). In this graph, we have also included the respective values of the various reporting periods. As expected, the frequent periods result in smaller estimate errors for the forecasting period.

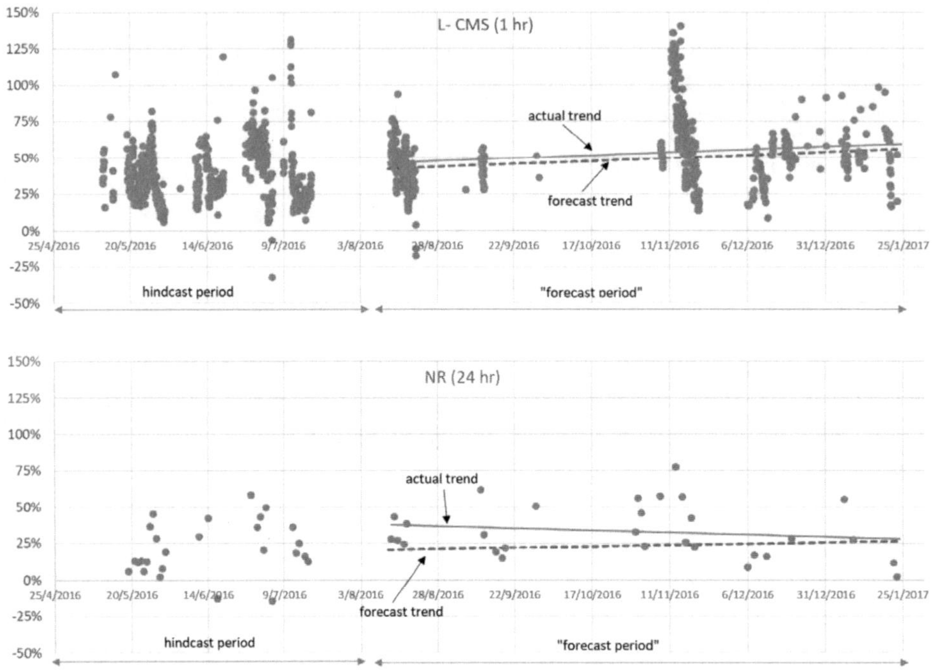

Figure 3. Actual and forecast trend for the CMS (upper graph) and NR (lower graph) methods for wind force lower than 5 BF.

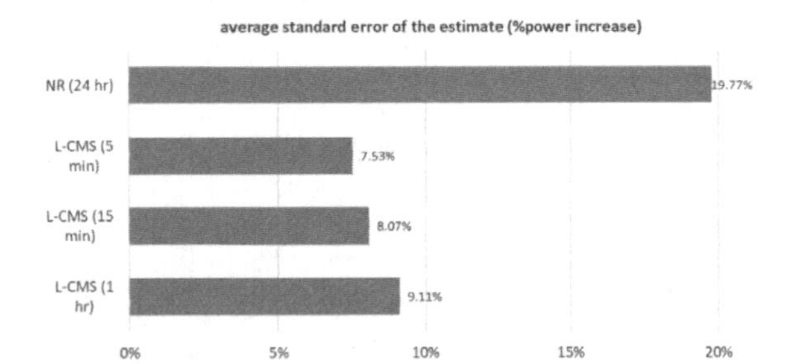

Figure 4. Sensitivity of the reporting periods on the average standard error of the estimate.

B. *Trim optimization based on Heickel coefficient*

Trim is defined as the difference between the draughts at ship's aft and forward, with positive trim to the aft. Being one of the usual methods for improving ship performance and energy efficiency optimization, trim optimization refers to minimization of the required power at vessel specific displacement and specific speed, thus reducing the hull resistance and/or increasing the total propulsive efficiency. Normally, the procedure demands dedicated model tests and/or computational fluid dynamics (CFD) modeling [14]. Next, we are using a traditional and reliable measure for the assessment of the hull and propulsion efficiency, such as the well-known Heickel coefficient that reflects the hydrodynamic efficiency of ship's hull form [15] in order to evaluate the ability to optimize the trim based on L-CMS and NR data. Heickel coefficient is defined as:

$$Heickel\ Coef. = V \cdot \left(\frac{\sqrt{\Delta}}{P}\right)^{1/3} \tag{3}$$

where Δ is the displacement, P the engine power, and V the ship's speed. Figure 5 illustrates Heickel coefficient propagation for the 9-month period under evaluation.

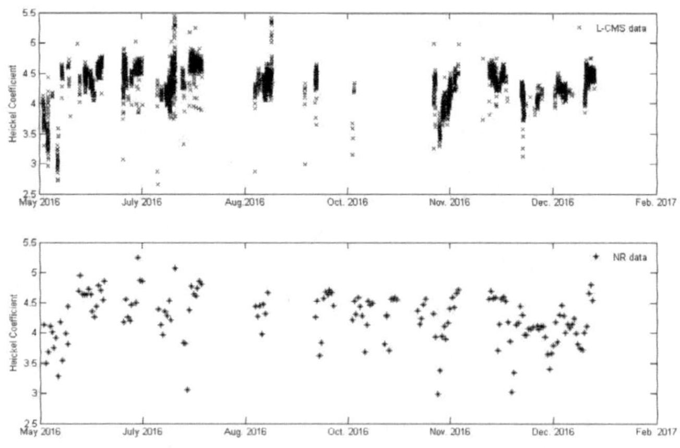

Figure 5. Heickel Coefficient propagation for L-CMS (up) and NR (down) data.

In general, the Heickel coefficient is operational speed and displacement dependent. In order to overcome this dependence, we evaluate the coefficient against the Froude number given by the equation:

$$Fn = \frac{V}{\sqrt{g \cdot L_w}} \tag{4}$$

where g is the gravity acceleration and L_w is the ship's waterline length. Figures 6 and 7 illustrate the contour plots for Heickel coefficient with respect to Froude number and trim distributions for ballast and full load condition, respectively. The same filters and operational conditions were used for both cases (L-CMS and NR). Visual evaluation of the plots produced by L-CMS data (up) and NR data (down) prove that the limited number of sampling point from the latter make it almost impossible to produce any constructive result. In contrast, the plurality of data acquired from the former gives a good navigation map for delicate trim optimization. As shown, Heickel coefficient is directly related to trim, hence optimal trim with respect to the Froude number should be selected in order to reduce ship resistance.

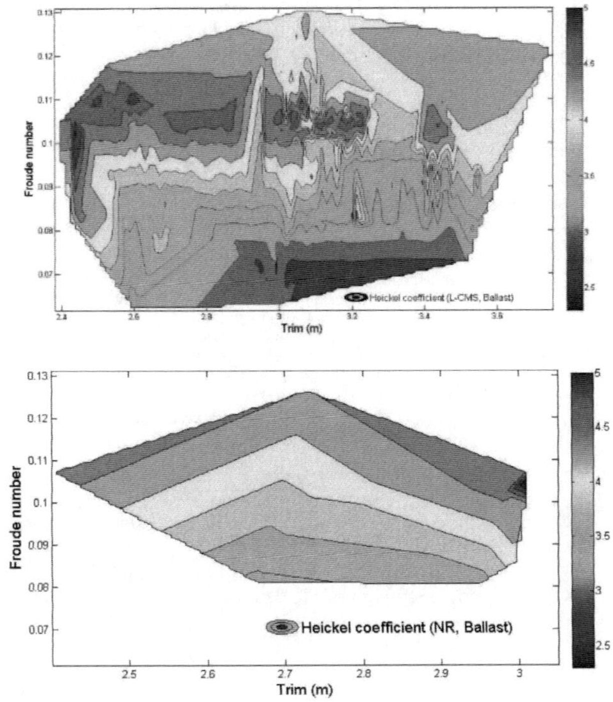

Figure 6. Heickel coefficient distribution vs Froude number and trim for ballast condition. L-CMS (up) and NR (down) data.

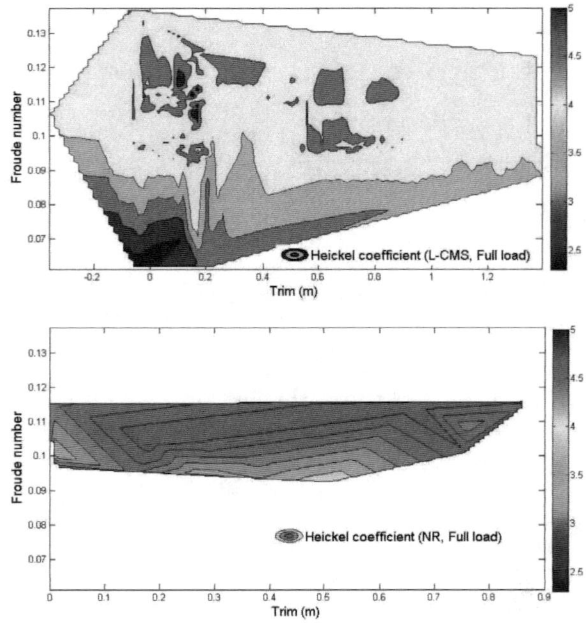

Figure 7. Heickel coefficient distribution vs Froude number and trim for full load condition. L-CMS (up) and NR (down) data.

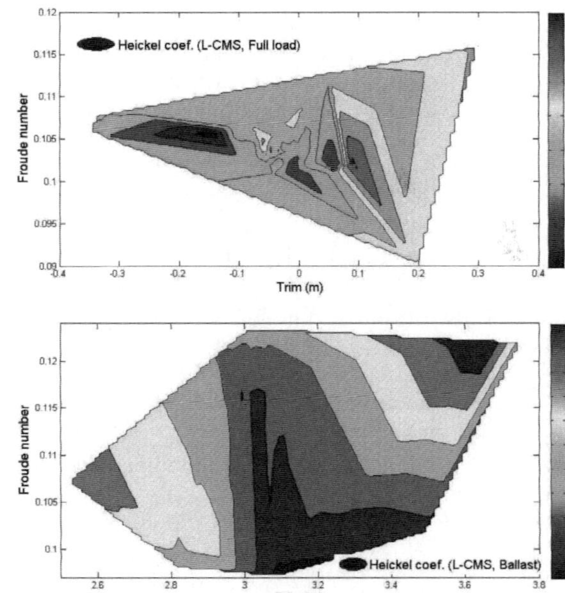

Figure 8. Heickel coefficient distribution vs Froude number and trim for ballast (up) and full loading (down) condition for wind force below 2 BF.

TABLE III. INDICATIVE FUEL GAIN

Loading condition	*Froude Number*	*Fuel reduction*	*Potential profit ($) for 20 days trip*
Ballast	0.12	1.3%	4.400
Ballast	0.1	2.6%	8.800
Full load	0.105	4%	16.600
Full load	0.1	3.4%	14.000

Working in that direction and based on L-CMS data, we evaluated the potential gain of trim optimization for specific operational conditions. Thus, we considered only data for wind force below 2 BF and Froude number between 0.09 and 0.125, which proved to be the normal value limits for normal operation. Figure 8 illustrates the contour plots for trim values with respect to Heickel coefficient and Froude number distribution for ballast (up) and full load (down) conditions. As shown in both cases and for Froude number close to 0.105, a correction to the trim value of the order of half a meter may result in a 4% reduction of fuel consumption. Table III presents some indicative results for the estimation of fuel and cost reduction on the assumption of half meter trim correction from ordered trim.

V. CONCLUSION AND FUTURE WORK

A step towards the assessment of the trustworthiness level of different data collection methods used in performance assessments was presented. For the current work, we restricted our efforts only to parameters that are reported by both sources: Noon Reports and LAROS Continuous Monitoring System. Power increase (%) was used as an evaluated performance indicator, while a trim assessment study was also carried out. Special attention was given to the quantification of our comparison study and especially to the frequency of the reporting period by examining the capability of prediction potential through the standard error of the estimate in each case.

The results indicated that NR data provide less statistically reliable data than the L-CMS. Of course, this depends also on the quality of the NR, which according to our analysis, in this specific case was quite sufficient. It is also derived that the high-frequency data of the L-CMS method provide a more detailed insight, as shown in the trim assessment study.

A logical next step in our research would be the systematic evaluation of the impact of the sampling rate on energy/emissions efficiency and key performance indicators, as well as of the learning procedure of predictive algorithms.

REFERENCES

[1] L. Aldous, "Ship Operational Efficiency: Performance Models and Uncertainty Analysis, "Ph.D. Thesis, University College London, 2015.

[2] V. N. Armstrong, "Vessel optimization for low carbon shipping," Ocean Engineering, vol 73, pp. 1-13, 2013.

[3] H. N. Psaraftis and C. A. Kontovas, "Ship speed optimization: Concepts, models and combined speed-routing scenarios," Transportation Research Part C: Emerging Technologies, vol. 44, pp. 52-69, 2014.

[4] M. Walker and I. Atkins, "Surface Ship Hull and Propeller Fouling Management," Warship 2006 - The Affordable Warship, pp. 131-138, 2006.

[5] V. Stulgis, T. Smith, N. Rehmatulla, J. Powers, and J. Hoppe, "Hidden Treasure: Financial Models for Retrofits," Research Report, Carbon War Room and UCL Energy Institute, 2014.

[6] J. G. Rakke et al., "A rolling horizon heuristic for creating a liquefied natural gas annual delivery program," Transportation Research Part C: Emerging Technologies, vol. 19(5), pp. 896-911, 2011.

[7] C. C. Spandonidis and C. Giordamlis, "Data-centric Operations in Oil & Gas Industry by the Use of 5G Mobile Networks and Industrial Internet of Things (IIoT)," In Proceedings of Thirteenth International Conference on Digital Telecommunications (ICDT 2018), pp. 1-5, 2018.

[8] M. A. Djeziri, B. Ananou, and M. Ouladsine, "Data-driven and model-based fault prognosis applied to a mechatronic system", International Conference on Power Engineering, Energy and Electrical Drives, IEEE, pp. 534-539. 2013.

[9] Z. Bazari, "Ship energy performance benchmarking/rating: methodology and application," Journal of Marine Engineering and Technology, vol. 6(1), pp. 11-18, 2007

[10] T. Smith et al., "Reduction of GHG Emissions from Ships: Third IMO GHG Study 2014. I. M. O.," IMO, London, UK, 2014.

[11] L. Aldous, T. Smith, and R. Bucknall, "Noon report data uncertainty," In Proceedings of Low Carbon Shipping, London, pp. 1-13, 2013.

[12] ISO 19030-1, "Ships and marine technology - Measurement of changes in hull and propeller performance. Part 1 – Basic principles," 2016.

[13] J. T. Adams, "An Introduction to IEEE 802.15.4," IEEE Press, vol. 2, pp. 1-8, 2006.

[14] H. Hansen and K. Hochkirch, "Lean ECO-Assistant Production for Trim Optimisation," 11th International Conference on Computer and IT Applications in the Maritime Industries, COMPIT 2013, Cortona, Italy, pp. 76-84, 2013.

[15] E. K. Boulougouris, A. D. Papanikolaou, and A. Pavlou, "Energy efficiency parametric design tool in the framework of holistic ship design optimization," Proc. IMechE Part M: J. Eng. Marit. Environ., vol. 225, pp. 242–260, 2011.

Forecasting Burglary Risk in Small Areas via Network Analysis of City Streets

Maria Mahfoud[1], Sandjai Bhulai[2], Rob van der Mei[1], Dimitry Erkin[1], and Elenna Dugundji[1]

[1] CWI National Research Institute for Mathematics and Computer Science
[2] Vrije Universiteit Amsterdam, Faculty of Science, Department of Mathematics
Email: M.Mahfoud@cwi.nl, S.Bhulai@vu.nl, R.D.van.der.Mei@cwi.nl, Dimitry.Erkin@gmail.com, E.R.Dugundji@vu.nl

Abstract—**Predicting residential burglary can benefit from understanding human movement patterns within an urban area. Typically, these movements occur along street networks. To take the characteristics of such networks into account, one can use two measures in the analysis: betweenness and closeness. The former measures the popularity of a particular street segment, while the latter measures the average shortest path length from one node to every other node in the network. In this paper, we study the influence of the city street network on residential burglary by including these measures in our analysis. We show that the measures of the street network help in predicting residential burglary exposing that there is a relationship between conceptions in urban design and crime.**

Keywords–predictive analytics; forecasting; street network; betweenness centrality; closeness centrality; residential burglary

I. INTRODUCTION

Residential burglary is a crime with high impact for victims. Substantial academic research has accordingly been dedicated to understanding the process of residential burglary in order to prevent future burglaries. In this attempt, several studies have focused on the role of the urban configuration in shaping crime patterns; this is regarded as one of the fundamental issues in environmental criminology, e.g., [1].

According to [2], environmental criminology is based on three premises. The first premise states that the nature of the immediate environment directly influences criminal behavior, thus a crime is not only reliant on criminogenic individuals, but also on criminogenic elements in the surroundings of a crime. The second premise states that crime is non-randomly distributed in time and space, meaning that crime is always concentrated around opportunities which occur on different moments in a day or week, or different places in a given geographical area. The third premise argues that understanding the criminogenic factors within a targeted environment, and capturing patterns and particular characteristics of that area, can reduce the number of crimes within that area.

Understanding human movement patterns within an urban area is essential for determining crime patterns [3]. These movements occur along a street network consisting of roads and intersections. Throughout the city street network, various places are connected, allowing transportation from one point to the next. Within the network, a street segment can be described as the road, or edge, linking two intersections, or nodes. In their study, [4] found that crime is tightly concentrated around crime hotspots that are located at specific points within the urban area. The urban configuration influences where these hotspots are located, suggesting that it is possible to deal with a large proportion of crime by focusing on relatively small areas. They found that crime hotspots are characterized by being stable over time, and that the hotspots are influenced by social and contextual characteristics of a specific geographical location. To be able to understand and prevent crime, it is important to examine these very small geographic areas, often as small as addresses of street segments, within the urban area. In an analysis of crime at street segment level, [5] reveal that crime trends at specific street segments were responsible for the overall observed trend in the city, emphasizing the need for understanding the development of crime at street segment level.

In urban studies, betweenness is a measure used to determine popularity or usage potential of a particular street segment for the travel movements made by the resident or ambient population through a street network [6], [7]. In criminology, betweenness represents the collective awareness spaces developed by people, including offenders, during the course of their routine activities. This metric provides a means to represent concepts, such as offender awareness, in empirical analysis [8]. Several studies have been conducted to uncover the effects of betweenness on crime. [8] investigated whether street segments that have a higher user potential measured by the network metric betweenness, have a higher risk of burglary. Also included in their research was the geometry of street segments via a measure of their linearity and different social-demographic covariates. They concluded that betweenness is a highly significant covariate when predicting burglaries at street segment level. In another study conducted by [9], a mathematical model of crime was presented that took the street network into account. The results of this study also show an evident effect of the street network.

In this research, we examine for small urban areas (4-digit postal codes: PC4) what the influence of the city street network is on residential burglary by applying betweenness as well as another centrality measure, closeness. These two centrality measures give different indications of the accessibility of an area and we study whether a more accessible area has a higher risk of residential burglary compared to a less accessible area. For comparison, we consider the same areas defined in our previous research [10]. In this earlier study, we predicted residential burglaries within different postal code areas for the district of Amsterdam-West. We extend the model of our earlier research by including the centrality measures closeness and betweenness as explanatory variables. Furthermore, we investigate which of the two centrality measures gives better outcomes, closeness or betweenness.

This paper is organized as follows. Section II describes

the dataset and the data analysis. Section III provides the methodological framework of this research. The results of the analysis are discussed in Section IV. In Section V, conclusions and recommendations for further research are presented.

II. DATA

The data used for this research is collected from three different data sources. The first dataset is provided by the Dutch Police and ranges from the first of January 2009 to 30 April 2014. The original dataset includes all recorded incidents of residential burglaries in the city of Amsterdam recorded at a monthly level and grouped into grids of 125 $\times$ 125 meters resulting in 94,224 records. Next to residential burglary, the dataset includes a wide range of covariates. These covariates provide information on the geographic information of the grid such as the number of Educational Institutions (EI) in the grid. In addition to these covariates, the data includes also spatial-temporal indicators of the following crime types: violation, mugging, and robbery. These spatial-temporal indicators measure the number of times a crime type happened within a given grid cell for a given time lag. The second dataset is obtained from the Statistics Netherlands (CBS) and includes various demographic and socio-economic covariates such as the average monthly income. This data is provided on a six alphanumeric postal code level where the first two digits indicate a region and a city, the second two digits indicate a neighborhood and the last two letters indicate a range of house numbers usually a street or a segment of a street. The third dataset is an internal dataset containing different centrality measures calculated on the street network of Amsterdam.

As this research focuses on explaining and predicting residential burglaries at the four-digit postal code level (PC4), the data should be aggregated at this level. Before aggregating the data we perform some pre-processing steps. First, we check the crime records for missing postal codes: if the postal code is missing then all linked data from CBS and the street network will be missing. We observed that 309 of the total 1,812 grid cells had a missing postal code (PC6). Some of these grid cells (34) were subsequently updated manually; other grid cells referred to industrial areas, bodies of water, railroads, grasslands, and highways. As a double check, we also confirmed whether there were residential burglaries in the remaining grid cells with missing postal codes; in our case, there were indeed none. These grid cells were further removed from the dataset and the data were aggregated based on PC4 conditioning on the district as some postal codes (PC4) can cover different police districts. Discrete covariates were aggregated by taking the sum of the covariate on all PC6. For continuous covariates, this was done by taking the average on all PC6. Exploring the data is done in a similar way as discussed in [10], where an extensive data analysis is applied to the crime data and the CBS data. To analyze this data we extend the final set of covariates by the different centrality measures and repeat the same step again. The dataset was assessed for outliers and collinearity. The presence of outliers was graphically assessed by the Cleveland dot plot and analytically by the Local Outlier Factor (LOF) with 10 neighbors and a threshold of 1.3. Results of this analysis show that the training data exhibits a percentage of outliers of 7.6. The majority of these occurred in December and January. Due to the high percentage of outliers in the training set, we decided to apply the analysis initially without outliers then apply the analysis with the outliers.

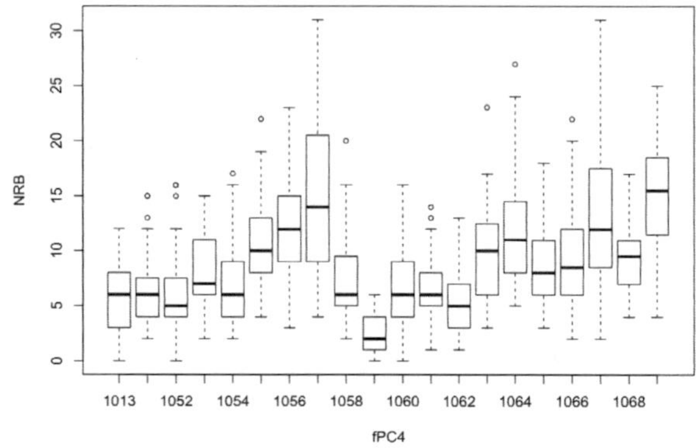

Figure 1. Boxplot of the number of burglaries conditional on the postal code indicating heterogeneity of variance in the number of burglaries within the different postal codes.

The collinearity was assessed by the calculating the variance inflation factor values (VIF) that measures the amount by which the variance of a parameter estimator is increased due to collinearity with other covariates rather than being orthogonal, e.g., [11]. A VIF threshold of 2 is used to assess collinearity [10]. This analysis results in the following set of covariates: the temporal covariate MONTH; the number of educational institutions (sEI), the number of restaurants (sRET), percentage of single-person households (aSH), the number of persons that generate income (sNPI), the total observed mugging incidents in the grid and its direct neighborhood in the last three months (sMuGL3M) and finally, the average monthly income (aAMI).

Furthermore, the relationship between residential burglaries and the categorical covariates was assessed using conditional box plots. Results show a temporal monthly effect and a spatial postal code effect on the burglaries. The effect of the postal codes on the burglaries is illustrated in Figure 1 where a clear difference in the mean and in the variance of the monthly number of burglaries is observed between the different postal codes.

III. METHODOLOGY

A. *Centrality measures*

Before discussing the centrality measures, we first need to introduce some important concepts of graph theory. A network represented mathematically by a graph is defined as a finite non-empty set V of vertices connected by edges E. A graph is usually written as $G = (V, E)$ where V is the set of vertices and E represents the set of edges where the number of vertices in G is called the order and the number of its edges is called the size. Two vertices u and v are said to be adjacent if there is an edge that links them together. In this case, u and v are also neighbors of each other. If two edges share one vertex then these edges are called adjacent edges. Using this concept of adjacency between all vertices represented in a matrix form results in an adjacency matrix that summarizes all information describing a network.

Another concept for understanding centrality measures is the one of paths and shortest paths. Informally, a path is a way of traveling along edges from vertex u to vertex v without repeating any vertices [12]. Formally, a path P in a graph G is a subgraph of G whose vertices form an ordered sequence, such that every consecutive pair of vertices is connected by an edge. A path P is called an $u-v$ path in G if $P=(u=x_0,x_1,\ldots,x_j=v)$ s.t. $x_0x_1,x_1x_2,\ldots,x_{j-1}x_j$ are all edges of P. The number of edges in a path is called its length. The path $u-v$ with the minimum length is called the shortest path between u and v.

In the context of our analysis, a vertex represents an intersection between streets and an edge is a transport infrastructure supporting movements between the two intersections.

Paths can be considered as the key elements in defining centrality measures. In a transportation network, these centrality measures describe the flow of traffic on each particular edge of the network identifying the most important vertices in it. Some of these centrality measures that we will use in this paper are the closeness (CC) centrality and the betweenness centrality (BC).

Closeness is a very simple centrality measure to calculate. It is a geometric measure where the importance of a vertex depends on how many nodes exist at every distance. Closeness centrality can be defined as the average of the shortest path length from one node to every other node in the network and is given by:

$$\mathrm{CC}(\nu)=\frac{1}{\sum_{d(u,\nu)<\infty}\mathrm{d}(\mathrm{u},\nu)}, \tag{1}$$

where $d(u,\nu)$ is the distance between u and ν. Informally, closeness centrality measures how long it will take to spread information from node ν to all other nodes in the network and it is used to identify influential nodes in the network.

The closeness of an edge $u-v$ can be calculated by taking the average closeness values of the nodes u and v.

The betweenness centrality BC is a path-based measure that can be used to identify highly influential nodes in the flow through the network. Given a specific node ν, the intuition behind betweenness is to measure the probability that a random shortest path will pass through ν. Formally, the betweenness of node ν, $\mathrm{BC}(\nu)$ is the percentage of shortest paths that include ν and can be calculated as follows:

$$\mathrm{BC}(\nu)=\sum_{u\neq w\neq\nu\in \mathrm{V}}\frac{\sigma_{u,w}(\nu)}{\sigma_{u,w}}, \tag{2}$$

where $\sigma_{u,w}$ is the total number of shortest paths between node u and w. And $\sigma_{u,w}(\nu)$ is the total number of shortest paths between node u and w that pass through ν. The betweenness of an edge e can be regarded as the degree to which an edge makes other connections possible and can be calculated in the same way by replacing the node ν by an edge e. An edge with high betweenness value forms an important bridge within the network. Removing this edge will severely hamper the flow of the network as it partitions the network into two large subnetworks.

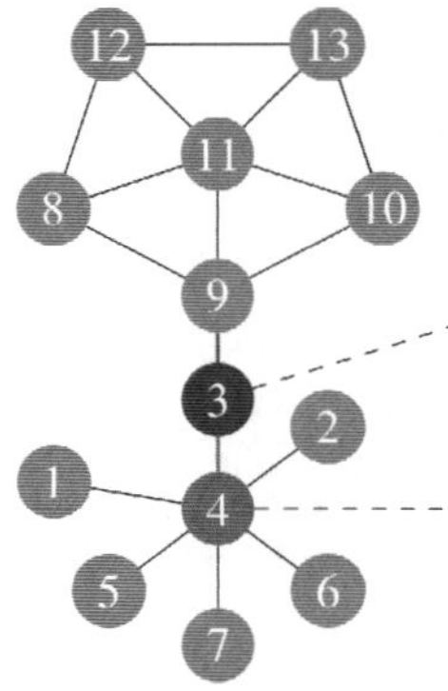

Figure 2. Illustration of high node (edge) betweenness and closeness.

High betweenness or closeness values indicate that a vertex or an edge can reach other vertices or edges, respectively, on relatively short paths. An example of a network is illustrated in Figure 2. In this example, node 3 has the highest closeness and node 4 the highest betweenness. The edge connecting the nodes 3 and 9 has the highest closeness within this network. This edge has also the highest betweenness together with the edge connecting the nodes 3 and 4.

In practice, it is almost impossible to calculate the exact betweenness or closeness scores. To make the calculations feasible, one can set a cut-off distance d and allow only paths that are at distances shorter or equal to d.

B. GAMM including centrality measures

In our paper [10], we used generalized additive mixed-effect models with different structures of the random component and showed that the one-way nested model with postal code as a random intercept has the optimal structure of the random component. Further, we showed that using the population as offset captures the most variation in the data. Moreover, the covariates month and the average monthly income seem to be the most important predictors for the number of burglaries within postal codes. In this paper, the optimal model discussed in [10] will be extended by two different centrality measures as covariates. We assess the effect of these centrality measures on explaining and forecasting the number of burglaries within the postal code. This model is given by:

$$\begin{aligned}\mathrm{y}_{i,t}&\sim \mathrm{Poisson}(\mu_{i,t}),\\ \mu_{i,t}&=\exp(\mathrm{base}_{i,t}+\mathrm{CM_i}+\mathrm{a}_i),\\ \mathrm{a}_i&\sim N(0,\sigma^2_{PC4}),\end{aligned} \tag{3}$$

where a_i is a random intercept for the postal code and $\mathrm{CM_i}$ represents the closeness $\mathrm{CC_i}$ or the betweenness $\mathrm{BC_i}$. The $\mathrm{base_{i,t}}$ is given by:

$$\begin{aligned}\mathrm{base}_{i,t}=&1+\mathrm{sEI}_i+\mathrm{sRET}_i+\mathrm{aSH}_i+\mathrm{sNPI}_i+\\&\mathrm{sMugL3M}_{i,t}+f_1(\mathrm{aAMI}_i)+f_2(\mathrm{Month}_t).\end{aligned} \tag{4}$$

Figure 3. Betweenness of the street segments in Amsterdam West. The betweenness is calculated using the average speed on the street segment and a time threshold of four minutes.

Figure 4. Closeness of the street segments in Amsterdam West. The closeness is calculated using the average speed on the street segment and a time threshold of four minutes.

The models were fitted using the Laplace approximate maximum likelihood [13]. This allows comparing the models based on the Akaike Information Criterion (AIC). All analyses were conducted using the `gamm4` package [14].

To assess the predictive performance of the models, the Root Mean Squared Error (RMSE) is calculated for an out-of-sample test. If $\mathrm{y}_{i,t}$ denotes the realization in postal code i and in month t, and $\hat{\mathrm{y}}_{i,t}$ denotes the forecast in the same postal code and in the same month, then the forecast error is given by $\mathrm{e}_{i,t} = \mathrm{y}_{i,t} - \hat{\mathrm{y}}_{i,t}$ and the RMSE is given by:

$$\mathrm{RMSE} = \sqrt{\frac{1}{NT}\sum_{i=1}^{N}\sum_{t=1}^{T}\mathrm{e}_{i,t}^2}. \tag{5}$$

IV. RESULTS

In this section, we first present the results of the centrality measures. Then, we will discuss the results of the model including these centrality measures as covariates.

As discussed in Section III-A, in practice it is computationally very expensive to calculate the exact betweenness and closeness scores. In general, these can be estimated by setting up a buffer zone using a cut-off distance d and calculating these centrality measures by considering only the paths at a shorter length than d. Using historical data, the average speed per street segment was calculated and five different time cut-offs were used. Segments that are reachable within one to five minutes are used to calculate the centrality measures. Note that these averages make sense because the centrality measures are calculated for the whole city and not for each area separately.

The betweenness and the closeness on the street segment level using a cut-off of four minutes are illustrated in Figure 3 and Figure 4, respectively. The corresponding average betweenness and closeness per area are illustrated in Figure 5 and Figure 6, respectively. Figures 3 and 4 show a wide red road running from top to bottom. This road corresponds with the A10, which is the ring road of Amsterdam. Figure 3 also shows that the roads with high betweenness correspond to the main access roads within this district. Figure 4 reveals that the roads within the areas situated on the right-hand side of the A10 have a higher closeness in general. This part of the city was built mainly before the Second World War [15] and has a higher density due to enclosed building blocks creating a more finely meshed network of roads when compared to the left-hand side of the ring road. This part was built after the Second World War and is characterized by a lower density due to more open building blocks with an emphasis on more green areas and better enclosure of the residential area via main access roads. The blank areas in the district correspond with green areas, such as parks, lakes and agricultural land.

Adding a centrality measure to the GAMM model results in a better prediction based on the RMSE. The RMSE of the GAMM model without centrality measure was about 4.5519 and as can be seen from Table I, extending the model with the betweenness or the closeness results in a generally lower RMSE. It is noteworthy that the closeness leads to better predictions when using lower thresholds (lower or equal 3 min); see Figures 7 and 8. If the threshold is four minutes or higher including the betweenness in the model results in better predictions. This can be explained by the average time an offender might need to flee from the scene of the crime on a residential street to the nearest main access road. In this case, the closeness describes the number of different routes the offender can take during his flight. Within 4 or 5 minutes, the offender can be traveling on the main access road in order to create as much distance as possible from the crime scene.

The results in the area with the postal code 1067 differ from the other areas. Including the closeness and betweenness does not improve the model, the error on the other hand increased. Taking a closer look at this area revealed that this area mainly consists of green areas with few roads. With less alternative routes available, the closeness gives a higher error.

When looking at the other areas, it is possible to say that the

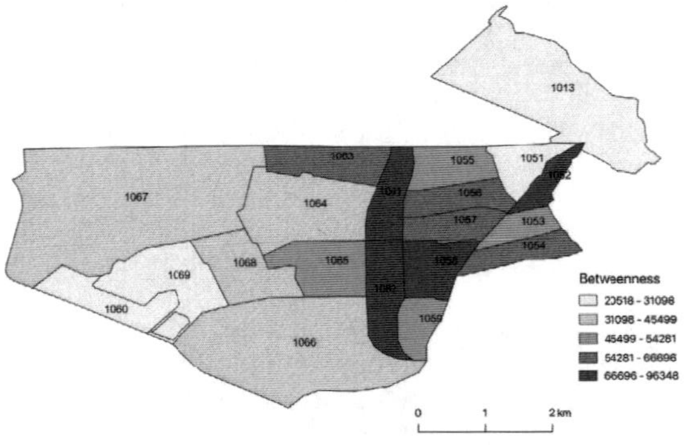

Figure 5. Average betweenness per postal code.

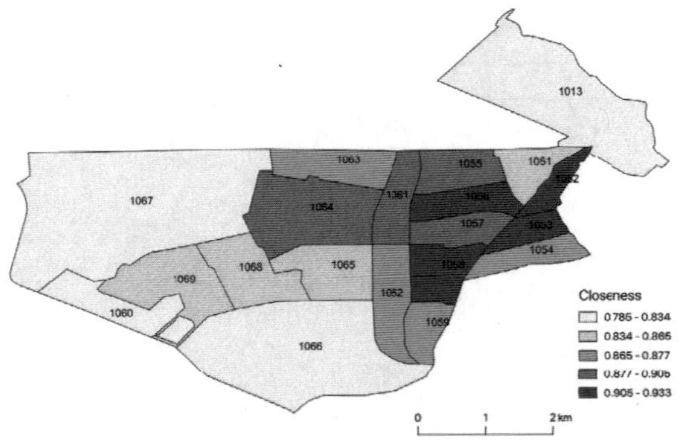

Figure 6. Average closeness per postal code using a threshold of four minutes.

building density influences the effectiveness of the centrality measures on the models. In areas with a lower density, the centrality measures have almost no influence on the outcomes, whereas in the urban areas with a high building density adding the centrality measures to the model improves the outcomes of the model.

Most studies use betweenness as a centrality measure, however, these studies focus on social networks. Given our results, we believe that the closeness is a better centrality measure for modeling crime based on small geographic areas. However, as shown there is a difference in effectiveness of this centrality measure related to the building density of the area.

Table I. ROOT MEAN SQUARED ERROR (RMSE) VALUES FROM FITTING THE GAMM MODEL WITH CLOSENESS AND BETWEENNESS USING DIFFERENT THRESHOLDS.

Model	1 min	2 min	3 min	4 min	5 min
GAMM + CC	4.5297	4.5323	4.5366	5.5437	4.5478
GAMM + BC	4.5562	4.5497	4.5405	4.5279	4.5326

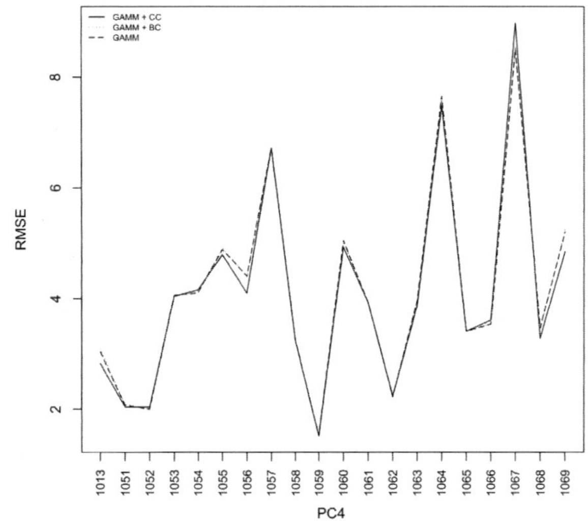

Figure 7. RMSE per PC4 base on an out-of-sample for the GAMM model, the GAMM + CC and the GAMM + BC using a threshold of 1 minute.

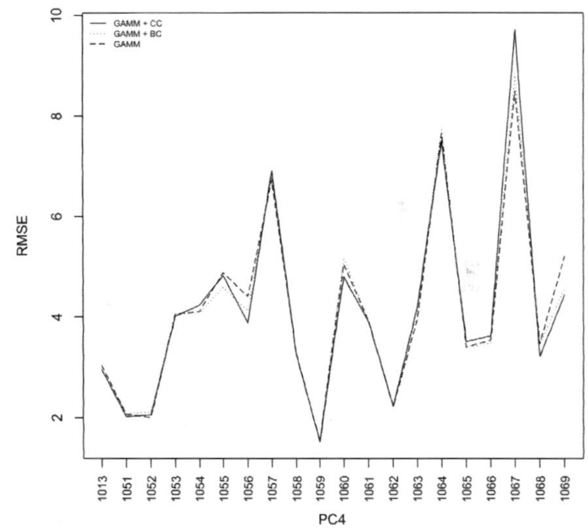

Figure 8. RMSE per PC4 base on an out-of-sample for the GAMM model, the GAMM + CC and the GAMM + BC using a threshold of 4 minutes.

V. CONCLUSION AND FUTURE WORK

During this research, we have tried to determine the influence of accessibility of the street network within small urban areas on residential burglary by applying the centrality measures closeness and betweenness. We have found that adding the centrality measures as a variable to our model has improved the performance of this model as can be concluded from the lower RMSE. Furthermorem we have shown that there is a relation between the different conceptions in urban design over time and residential burglary. Our results show that the pre-world War II neighborhoods suffer from more residential burglary than the neighborhoods built after the Second World War. Also, differences in the performance of the two centrality measures were found. Closeness as a centrality measure gives better predictions when taking into consideration a threshold smaller than 4 minutes. If the threshold is 4 minutes or larger, the betweenness gives better predictions. We can also conclude that the centrality measures perform better when applied to geographic areas with a high density, for example, a city center.

Our study has shown that there is a relationship between the conceptions in urban design and crime. Neighborhoods built under a certain conception of urban design tend to have a higher risk of residential burglary, which can be explained by how the public space is designed. Further research is necessary to confirm this hypothesis.

REFERENCES

[1] P. J. Brantingham, and P. L. Brantingham, Environmental criminology. Sage Publications Beverly Hills, CA, 1981.

[2] R. Wortley and M. Townsley, Environmental criminology and crime analysis. Taylor & Francis, 2016, vol. 18.

[3] P. Brantingham and P. Brantingham, "Crime pattern theory," in Environmental criminology and crime analysis. Willan, 2013, pp. 100–116.

[4] D. Weisburd, E. R. Groff, and S.-M. Yang, The criminology of place: Street segments and our understanding of the crime problem. Oxford University Press, 2012.

[5] D. Weisburd, S. Bushway, C. Lum, and S.-M. Yang, "Trajectories of crime at places: A longitudinal study of street segments in the city of Seattle," Criminology, vol. 42, no. 2, 2004, pp. 283–322.

[6] L. C. Freeman, "Centrality in social networks conceptual clarification," Social networks, vol. 1, no. 3, 1978, pp. 215–239.

[7] P. Crucitti, V. Latora, and S. Porta, "Centrality measures in spatial networks of urban streets," Physical Review E, vol. 73, no. 3, 2006, p. 036125.

[8] T. Davies and S. D. Johnson, "Examining the relationship between road structure and Quantitative Criminology, vol. 31, no. 3, 2015, pp. 481–507.

[9] T. P. Davies and S. R. Bishop, "Modelling patterns of burglary on street networks," Crime Science, vol. 2, no. 1, 2013, p. 10.

[10] M. Mahfoud, S. Bhulai, and R. van der Mei, "Spatio-temporal modeling for residential burglary," in Proceedings of the 6th International Conference on Data Analytics. IARIA, 2018, pp. 59–64.

[11] D. Liao and R. Valliant, "Variance inflation factors in the analysis of complex survey data," Survey Methodology, vol. 38, no. 1, 2012, pp. 53–62.

[12] A. Benjamin, G. Chartrand, and P. Zhang, The fascinating world of graph theory. Princeton University Press, 2015.

[13] R. H. Baayen, D. J. Davidson, and D. M. Bates, "Mixed-effects modeling with crossed random effects for subjects and items," Journal of memory and language, vol. 59, no. 4, 2008, pp. 390–412.

[14] S. Wood and F. Scheipl, GAMM4: Generalized additive mixed models using mgcv and lme4, 2014, r package version 0.2-3. [Online]. Available: http://CRAN.R-project.org/package=gamm4

[15] G. Amsterdam. De groei van Amsterdam. [Online]. Available: https://maps.amsterdam.nl/bouwjaar/?LANG=nl (2018)

Optimal Taxi Fleet Management

a Linear Programming Approach to the Taxi Capacity Problem

Jacky P.K. Li and Sandjai Bhulai

Vrije Universiteit Amsterdam,
Faculty of Science,
Amsterdam, The Netherlands
Email: {jacky.li, s.bhulai}@vu.nl

Abstract—**This paper develops a model to determine the optimal number of taxis in a city by examining the trade-off between the overall profitability of the taxi service versus the customer satisfaction. We provide a data analytic investigation of taxi trips in New York City. We model the taxi service strategy by a fleet management model that can handle arrivals and deterministic travel times. Under this model, we examine the number of taxis in a particular period of time and measure the maximum profit in the overall system and the minimum number of rejected customer requests. We observe that the maximum profit of the overall system can be reduced significantly due to reducing the cost of driving without passenger(s). We present a case study with New York City Taxi data with several experimental evaluations of our model with a different period of time during the day and also with a realistic and a heuristic model. The results provide a better understanding of the requirement to satisfy the demand in a different period of time. These data may have important implications in the field of self-driving vehicles in the near future.**

Keywords–New York taxi service; revenue optimization; optimal routing; linear programming; min-cost network flow problem.

I. INTRODUCTION

Taxis are an essential component of the transportation system in most urban centers. The ability to optimize the efficiency of routing represents an opportunity to increase revenues for taxi services. Vacant taxis on the road waste fuel, represent uncompensated time for the taxi drivers, and create unnecessary carbon emissions while also generating additional traffic in the city. In the not-too-distant future, fully autonomous vehicles will be the norm rather than the exception. Taxis could eventually work together to satisfy the demand of the customers versus compete against each other to make revenue individually. This can reduce the amount of traffic on the road and the overall fuel cost significantly. Based on these ideas, creating a model in which all the taxis work together to satisfy all the customers would be an interesting endeavor to explore the number of taxis necessary to satisfy all the demand.

Previous studies have focused on developing recommendation systems for taxi drivers [1]–[6]. Several studies use the global positioning system (GPS) to create recommendations for both the drivers and the passengers to increase profit margins and reduce seek times [3] [5]–[7]. Ge et al. [8] and Ziebart et al. [9] gather a variety of information to generate a behavioral model to improve driving predictions. Ge et al. [1] and Tseng et al. [10] measure the energy consumption before finding the next passenger. Castro et al. [7], Altshuler et al. [11], Chawla et al. [12], Huang et al. [13], and Qian et al. [14] learn knowledge from taxi data for other types of recommendation scenarios, such as fast routing, ride-sharing, or fair recommendations.

In terms of Linear Programming research, Liang et al. [15] propose a method of automated vehicle operation in taxi systems that addresses the problem of associating trips to automated taxis; however, this research paper is based on a small case study. It does not provide a feasible model. Roling et al. [16] describe an ongoing research effort pertaining to the development of a surface traffic automation system that will help controllers to better coordinate surface traffic movements related to arrival and departure traffic in airport traffic planning. Bsaybes et al. [17] developed framework models and algorithms for managing a fleet of Individual Public Autonomous Vehicles with a heuristic model.

In this paper, we are confronting the problem within the context of managing New York City (NYC) taxis to serve customers who request a ride. We are investigating a realistic model with 15 km x 15 km grid combined with a demand of 20,000 rides in 30 minutes. We assume the total business time is equal to the sum of the total occupancy time plus the total seeking time. Fundamentally, if we can satisfy the ride requests with deterministic travel times and minimize the seeking time, this would provide the maximum profit in the overall system.

The deterministic version of this problem is the min-cost/max-profit integer problem. The linear and integer versions for the min-cost "multi-commodity-flow" problem have been studied extensively in [18] and [19]. In this paper, we also examine both a realistic and a heuristic model to explore the difference between the two models with real New York City Taxi data that is provided to the public. Figure 1 shows that there are consistent patterns in demand between certain periods of the day and certain days of the week during June 2013.

The paper is structured as follows. In Section II, we analyze

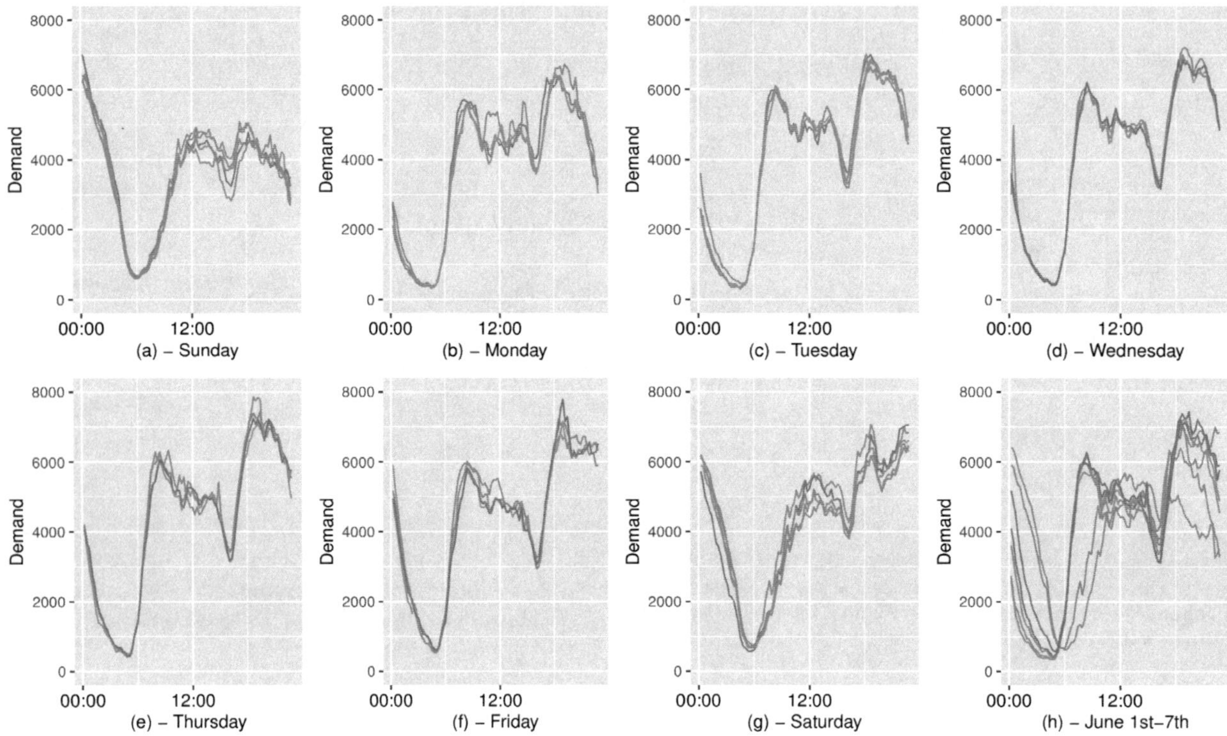

Figure 1. (a) to (h) display the day of the week in June. (i) displays the first week of June.

the New York Taxi dataset in 2013. This provides the input for our linear programming model, which is explained in Section III. We assess the performance of the linear programming model in Section IV, where we conduct numerical experiments with the realistic model and also the heuristic model. Finally, the paper is concluded in Section V.

II. DATASET

In our research, we are investigating NYC taxi demand patterns of a particular day of the week. From each ride record, we use the following fields: pick-up time, pick-up longitude, pick-up latitude, drop-off time, drop-off longitude, drop-off latitude, and traveling time. We omit the records containing missing or erroneous GPS coordinates. Records that represent trip durations longer than 1 hour and trip distances greater than 100 kilometers are omitted.

We are interested in observing a consistent demand during a period of a month. According to timeanddate.com [20], only three days in the month of June recorded a rainfall. We believe the weather and temperature can be a factor of the demand. Figure 1 displays the days of the week in June from Sunday (Figure 1a) to Saturday (Figure 1g), respectively, and also the first week of June in Figure 1h.

During the weekday, the lowest demand of the day is from approximately 04:00 to 05:00, and the highest demand is from approximately 18:00 to 19:00 followed by 08:00 to 08:30 and the 12:00 to 12:30 period. Based on this observation, we choose the four different time slots, the lowest demand of the day 04:00-04:30, the morning traffic 08:00-08:30, the lunch break 12:00-12:30, and the dinner traffic 18:30-19:00. Table I displays the maximum, the average, the minimum demand and the coefficient of variation per minute during four different time periods in June. The coefficient of variation is consistent especially for Tuesday and Wednesday. Based on this observation, we choose June 4th, 2013, the first Tuesday of June as our main focus.

The analysis of the dataset of the New York Taxi service is focused on the island of the Manhattan area in New York, USA. This area imposes a rectangular grid of avenues and streets. We discretized the grid into a 50×50 grid, making each block in the grid approximately 300 meters $\times$ 300 meters. The choice for a block size of 300 meters is based on the assumption that a taxi can traverse this distance within 1 minute. Due to the calculation time, we also created a heuristic model with a 10×10 grid, making each block in the grid approximately 1,500 meters $\times$ 1,500 meters and a taxi can traverse this distance within 5 minutes.

The state of a taxi can be described by two parameters: the current location, which is an element of the set $L = \{(1,1), \ldots, (50,50)\}$ grid and the current time, which comes from the set $T = \{1, \ldots, 30\}$. We will denote the system state in our model as $s = ((i,j),t) = (i,j,t)$, which we will elaborate on in Section III.

We select June 4th, 2013 as the date to analyze with an average of 36.47 requests per minute from 04:00-04:30, an average of 581.37 requests per minute from 08:00 to 08:30, an average of 472.43 requests per minute from 12:00 to 12:30, and an average of 661.90 requests per minute from 18:30 to

TABLE I. THE TOTAL DEMAND PER MINUTE IN JUNE 2013.

		Sunday	Monday	Tuesday	Wednesday	Thursday	Friday	Saturday
04:00-04:30	Max	314	63	56	72	80	116	304
	Average	233.22	39.22	35	49.21	56.86	83.56	55.95
	Min	145	20	18	31	40	53	102
	% Coefficient of variation	16.50%	18.75%	19.48%	15.45%	16.41%	11.17%	28.09%
08:00-08:30	Max	174	588	631	643	679	637	284
	Average	130.07	516.43	562.88	567.71	575.06	539.53	186.95
	Min	80	418	502	506	477	439	134
	% Coefficient of variation	14.44%	7.42%	5.51%	5.48%	6.96%	7.42%	7.20%
12:00-12:30	Max	485	562	551	560	568	570	586
	Average	435.21	462.97	495.86	502.38	501	489.47	477.51
	Min	382	389	419	441	420	432	399
	% Coefficient of variation	6.10%	8.33%	5.26%	4.17%	6.90%	7.06%	8.06%
18:30-19:00	Max	526	686	760	735	739	709	722
	Min	380	552	563	559	575	565	497
	Average	456.81	622.58	654.07	642.47	664.57	637.41	593.03
	% Coefficient of variation	7.37%	4.33%	5.56%	5.78%	5.34%	5.57%	7.53%

19:00.

III. LINEAR PROGRAMMING

The deterministic version of the taxi routing problem is by solving a max-profit integer "multi-commodity-flow" problem for each time period. These problems tend to get large easily with the number of possible states and resource types, and their multi-commodity nature presenting an unwelcome dimension of complexity. Due to this reason, we present both a realistic and a heuristic model for comparison.

For notational convenience, we denote (x, y) by i and denote (x', y') by j. We are required to serve every customer demand. However, if there are not enough vacant taxis within the same grid, the unsatisfied customer demands are not served. To handle this, we assume that the unsatisfied demands are lost, and we take the profit from serving a higher revenue demand to be the incremental profit from serving the demand with a taxi.

In [21], we assumed that all taxis take a single time period to travel and all customers have the same taxi preferences. In this model, we extend our formulation to cover cases where there are multi-period travel times. For notational convenience, we assume that demand at a certain location can be served by a taxi at the same location at the same time and the demand can be served by the vacant taxi that is able to arrive at the same location at the same time. For the rest of the section, we adopt the terminology that an empty taxi driving toward the next customer is "seeking".

A. Parameters of the Linear Programming Model

In this subsection, we state the parameters used in the rest of the model.

Location – realistic $(i, j) \in L = \{1, \ldots, 50\} \times \{1, \ldots, 50\}$: the area is divided into a grid of 50×50 grid cells;

Location – heuristic $(i, j) \in L = \{1, \ldots, 10\} \times \{1, \ldots, 10\}$: the area is divided into a grid of 10×10 grid cells; we implement a smaller grid compared to the realistic model in order to simplify the calculation process.

Time $t \in T = \{1, \ldots, 30\}$: we use minutes as the interval of a time slot, and a total of 30 minutes as time horizon.

- $D_{i,j,t}$ describes the number of **demand** that need to be carried from grid cell i to grid cell j at time period t from the original dataset on June 4th, 2013.
- $S_{i,j,t}$ describes the number of **empty** taxis moving from grid cell i to grid cell j at time period t from the original dataset.
- $\mathcal{T}_{i,j,t}$ describes the **traveling time** from a taxi moving from grid cell i to grid cell j. We assume the traveling time is the same at any period of time t. In the heuristic model, the **traveling time** is multiplied by 5 to match the travel time for both models since the grid size is also increased by a factor of 5.
- $x^{\mathrm{l}}_{i,j,t}$ describes the number of **loaded** taxis moving from grid cell i to grid cell j at time period t.
- $x^{\mathrm{e}}_{i,j,t}$ describes the number of **empty** taxis moving from grid cell i to grid cell j at time period t.
- $c^{\mathrm{l}}_{i,j}$ describes the net **reward** from an occupied taxi moving from grid cell i to grid cell j. We assume the profit is the same at any period of time t. In the heuristic model, the $c^{\mathrm{l}}_{i,j}$ is multiplied by 5 to match the realistic model.
- $c^{\mathrm{e}}_{i,j}$ describes the **cost** of a vacant taxi moving empty from grid cell i to grid cell j. We assume the cost is the same at any period of time t. (Remark: In order to simplify the model, the **cost** is half of the **reward** and the heuristic model is multiplied by 5 to match the realistic model.)
- $R_{i,t,t'}$ describes the number of taxis in operation that are inbound to location i at time period t and will arrive at location i at time period t'.
- $\mathcal{R}$ describes the number of taxis in the system.

The deterministic version of the problem we are interested in can be written as:

$$\max \sum_{t \in T} \sum_{i,j \in L} (-c^{\mathrm{e}}_{i,j} x^{\mathrm{e}}_{i,j,t} + c^{\mathrm{l}}_{i,j} x^{\mathrm{l}}_{i,j,t}) \quad (1)$$

TABLE II. DEMAND AND SEEKING ON JUNE 4TH, 2013

	Realistic (50×50)					Heuristic (10×10)				
	Actual Demand	# of Vehicles	Demand / # of Vehicles	Driving empty	Missed demand	Actual Demand	# of Vehicles	Demand / # of Vehicles	Driving empty	Missed demand
04:00-04:30	1,094	650	1.68	628	10	1,035	600	1.73	240	16
08:00-08:30	17,441	8,000	2.18	5,469	7	15,982	7,350	2.17	2,185	30
12:00-12:30	14,173	5,400	2.62	5,213	11	12,800	5,050	2.53	1,699	36
18:30-19:00	19,857	8,200	2.42	5,015	12	18,203	7,650	2.38	1,124	13

subject to

$$
\begin{aligned}
&R_{i,1,t'} = \mathcal{R}, && i \in L, t \in \{1\}, t' \in T,\\
&\sum_{j\in L}(x^{e}_{i,j,t} + x^{l}_{i,j,t}) = R_{i,t',t}, && i \in L, t, t' \in T,\\
&R_{j,t',t+1} = \sum_{i\in L} I_{(t'-t)=\tau_{i,j}}(x^{e}_{i,j,t} - x^{l}_{i,j,t}) + R_{j,t',t}, && \\
& && j \in L, t, t' \in T,\\
&x^{l}_{i,j,t} \le D_{i,j,t}, && i, j \in L, t \in T,\\
&x^{e}_{i,j,t}, x^{l}_{i,j,t} \in \mathbb{Z}_{+}, && i, j \in L, t \in T.
\end{aligned}
\tag{2}
$$

which is a special case of the max-profit integer multi-commodity flow problem.

We evaluate the linear programming approach based on the New York Taxi dataset on June 4th, 2013 on four particular times 04:00-04:30, 08:00-08:30, 12:00-12:30, and 18:30-19:00. In our deterministic case study experiment, we formulate the problem as a max-profit integer problem (1). From the dataset, we generate the data of $D_{i,j,t}$, which is the number of demand from location i to location j at time t. We also generate the data of $S_{i,j,t}$, which is the number of empty taxis driving from location i to location j at time t to seek for the next passenger(s).

In order to provide a better understanding of our result, we calculate:

- Demand $= D_{i,j,t}$,
- Actual seeking $= S_{i,j,t}$,
- Seeking from our model $= c^{e}_{i,j}$,
- Missing demand $= D_{i,j,t} - x^{*,l}_{i,j,t}$,
- Actual revenue $= c^{l}_{i,j} \times D_{i,j,t}$,
- Revenue from our model $= c^{l}_{i,j} \times x^{*,l}_{i,j,t}$,
- Actual cost $= c^{e}_{i,j} \times S_{i,j,t}$,
- Cost from our model $= c^{e}_{i,j} \times x^{*,e}_{i,j,t}$,
- Actual profit = actual revenue − actual cost,
- Profit = revenue − cost,
- Lost revenue $= c^{l}_{i,j} \times [D_{i,j,t} - x^{*,l}_{i,j,t}]$,

where $x^{*,e}_{i,j,t}$ and $x^{*,l}_{i,j,t}$ are the optimal solutions for $x^{e}_{i,j,t}$ and $x^{l}_{i,j,t}$, respectively.

One thing to note is that the initial location of the vehicle was set up based on $R_{i,1,t'} = \mathcal{R}$, which means the vehicles are located to the highest demand profit at the start.

IV. CASE STUDIES AND OBSERVATIONS

In this section, we concentrate on the programming and the results. We use `Rcplex` [22] to run our model. In the realistic model we calculate the result based on the 50×50 grid and a 30-minute interval. Due to the constraints and variables, the matrix size is approximately 377 million x 188 million. This requires an approximate 250 GB of memory according to [22], it took over three hours per calculation. This model is do-able in terms of calculation, but not scalable making it intractable for larger problem sizes. Due to this reason, we create the heuristic model with 10×10 grid to decrease the size such that it can be handled on a standard desktop computer with 8 GB of memory. We also increase the travel time in the heuristic model by 5 to match the increase in size of the grid. The calculation time with the heuristic model is approximately 10 seconds.

Table II displays the results of four different time periods using both the realistic and the heuristic model. The heuristic model has less demand due to having no demand within the same grid which eliminates just under 10% of the requests each time period. The demand for the number of vehicles is close in each model under both the realistic and the heuristic models. These results indicate that the simplified heuristic model can still give an accurate approximation of how many taxis we need to satisfy the demand per period of time.

Table III displays the results of each minute for both the realistic and the heuristic model for 12:00-12:30 on June 4th, 2013. We decrease the size of the fleet by 1,000 vehicles and see the percentage difference of the profit. The optimal fleet sizes are 5,400 for the realistic model and 5,050 for the heuristic model. When we increase the fleet size by a 1,000, there will be less driving without the passenger(s) and it does not provide more profit to the system.

Figure 2 provides a view of the profit comparison for the realistic model on June 4th, 2013 from 12:00 to 12:30. A fleet of 5,000 vehicles would satisfy most of the demand and provide the highest demand in the system.

V. CONCLUSION

We use a linear programming to model the taxi service and determine the optimal policy to yield the best profit in the overall system. In Table II, each taxi can cover approximately 1.76, 2.17, 2.60, and 2.40 demand at 04:00-04:30, 08:00-08:30, 12:00-12:30 and 18:30-19:00 time periods, respectively, for both models.

Table III displays the profit for both the realistic and the heuristic model. The optimal solution for the realistic model requires 5,400 vehicles which provide an increased profit of 25,844.50 units to the actual profit and is unable to satisfy

TABLE III. TABLE OF DEMAND, SEEKING, ACTUAL PROFIT AND DIFFERENCE OF PROFIT WITH DIFFERENT SIZE OF THE FLEET FOR 12:00-12:30 TIME PERIOD FOR BOTH THE REALISTIC AND THE HEURISTIC MODEL TO COMPARE BETWEEN THEM.

	Realistic Model (50×50)						Heuristic Model (10×10)					
Minute	Demand $D_{i,j,t}$	Seeking $S_{i,j,t}$	Actual Profit	$6,400$ Vehicles	$5,400$ Vehicles	$4,400$ Vehicles	Demand $D_{i,j,t}$	Seeking $S_{i,j,t}$	Actual Profit	$6,050$ Vehicles	$5,050$ Vehicles	$4,050$ Vehicles
1	464	409	3,826.5	+917.5	+917.5	+917.5	415	251	3,725	+935	+935	+920
2	490	416	3,951.5	1,021	1,021	1,021	439	277	3,830	+1,060	+1,060	+1,060
3	476	411	4,110	+934.5	+934.5	+934.5	433	255	3,977.5	+932.5	+932.5	+922.5
4	484	374	4,139	+842	+842.5	+842.5	441	219	4,125	+810	+810	+810
5	461	373	3,819	+920.5	+923	+923	417	217	3,892.5	+892.5	+892.5	+892.5
6	462	385	3,777	+956	+959	+959.5	418	243	3,747.5	+962.5	+972.5	+870
7	471	401	4,012	+968	+971	+970.5	423	246	3,902.5	+957.5	+960	+925
8	475	369	4,212.5	+819	+824	+816.5	434	207	4,122.5	+777.5	+777.5	+697.5
9	491	363	4,483.5	+769	+791	+790	456	213	4,532.5	+752.5	+752.5	+722.5
10	479	341	4,224	+828.5	+850.5	+831.5	438	198	4,292.5	+777.5	+777.5	+682.5
11	470	372	4,088.5	+896	+918	+877.5	434	215	4,052.5	+822.5	+820	+622.5
12	441	367	3,479	+882	+915	+871.5	393	221	3,350	+850	+895	+790
13	418	359	3,373.5	+871.5	+923	+789	378	201	3,397.5	+797.5	+857.5	+632.5
14	453	353	3,766	+825	+873	+638.5	406	198	3,662.5	+757.5	+772.5	+410
15	490	326	4,409	+725.5	+777.5	469	454	193	4,365	+695	+690	+340
16	505	342	4,752	+762	+818.5	+414	463	206	4,727.5	+747.5	+767.5	-217.5
17	482	346	4,324.5	+809.5	+865	+485.5	436	201	4,360	+750	+767.5	-97.5
18	500	390	4,206.5	+905.5	+964	+287.5	453	228	4,212.5	+862.5	+902.5	+2.5
19	493	372	4,164	+825.5	+866	+189.5	439	211	4,120	+800	+912.5	-55
20	490	342	4,079.5	+776	+831	+79.5	431	195	3,887.5	+707.5	+737.5	+52.5
21	453	394	3,569.5	+913.5	+996	+422.5	398	220	3,497.5	+797.5	+860	+165
22	437	359	3,758	+813	+892	+322	397	201	3,792.5	+702.5	+800	+167.5
23	504	360	4,509.5	+790.5	+876	+332.5	450	202	4,442.5	+717.5	+747.5	-105
24	479	335	4,262	+746	+827	+158	438	184	4,190	+645	+717.5	+85
25	458	332	3,593	+789.5	+861	+231.5	392	196	3,387.5	+737.5	+822.5	+527.5
26	469	301	4,232.5	+657	+747.5	+240.5	410	167	4065	+605	+600	+170
27	504	319	4,804	+694.5	+759	+298.5	461	179	4715	+635	+625	+50
28	440	344	4,116	+719.5	+768	+516	404	194	4115	+660	+655	+350
29	466	337	3,830	+739.5	+740	+498	433	201	3837.5	+702.5	+687.5	+227.5
30	468	299	3,988	+593	+593	+489	416	179	3942.5	+622.5	+622.5	+402.5
Total	14,173	10,791	121,860	+24,710.5	+25,844.5	+17,616.5	12,800	6,318	120,267.5	+23,472.5	+24,130	+13,022.5
Missing Demand	-	-	-	0	11	1,469	-	-	-	0	36	139

11 demands. In the heuristic model, it requires 5,050 vehicles to satisfy 12,800 demands and it misses 36 demands in that period. The table also shows that more vehicles to satisfy all the demand does not provide the highest profit.

As for future discussion, our current model is based on a 50×50 grid with a 30-minute time period, which is 2,500 $\times$ 2,500 $\times$ 30 = 375 million data points on one dimension, this requires a supercomputer with 2 TB memory and it takes over three hours per calculation. This is not a feasible method to solve the model. Creating a model that uses dynamic programming with value function approximation will reduce the calculation time and the memory use.

Secondly, having stochastic demand would provide an even more realistic model, especially when traffic accidents occur in real time. Lastly, ride sharing is an obvious next step toward taxi routing research. Can we satisfy all the demand with limited vehicles and maximize the profit?

REFERENCES

[1] Y. Ge et al., "An energy-efficient mobile recommender system," in Proceedings of the 16th ACM SIGKDD international conference on Knowledge discovery and data mining - KDD '10. New York, New York, USA: ACM Press, 2010, p. 899. [Online]. Available: http://dl.acm.org/citation.cfm?doid=1835804.1835918

[2] H. Rong, X. Zhou, C. Yang, Z. Shafiq, and A. Liu, "The rich and the poor: A Markov decision process approach to optimizing taxi driver revenue efficiency," in Proceedings of the 25th ACM International on Conference on Information and Knowledge Management. ACM, 2016, pp. 2329–2334.

[3] J. Yuan, Y. Zheng, L. Zhang, X. Xie, and G. Sun, "Where to find my next passenger," in Proceedings of the 13th international conference on Ubiquitous computing. ACM, 2011, pp. 109–118.

[4] Y. Zheng, J. Yuan, W. Xie, X. Xie, and G. Sun, "Drive Smartly as a Taxi Driver," in 2010 7th International Conference on Ubiquitous Intelligence & Computing and 7th International Conference on Autonomic & Trusted Computing. IEEE, Oct 2010, pp. 484–486.

[5] M. Qu, H. Zhu, J. Liu, G. Liu, and H. Xiong, "A cost-effective recommender system for taxi drivers," in Proceedings of the 20th ACM SIGKDD international conference on Knowledge discovery and data mining - KDD '14. New York, New York, USA: ACM Press, 2014, pp. 45–54.

[6] D. Zhang et al., "Understanding Taxi Service Strategies From Taxi GPS Traces," IEEE Transactions on Intelligent Transportation Systems, vol. 16, no. 1, pp. 123–135, Feb 2015.

[7] P. Castro, D. Zhang, and S. Li, "Urban traffic modelling and prediction using large scale taxi GPS traces," Pervasive Computing, pp. 57–72, 2012.

[8] Y. Ge, C. Liu, H. Xiong, and J. Chen, "A taxi business intelligence system," in Proceedings of the 17th ACM SIGKDD international conference on Knowledge discovery and data mining - KDD '11. New York, New York, USA: ACM Press, 2011, p. 735. [Online]. Available: http://dl.acm.org/citation.cfm?doid=2020408.2020523

[9] B. D. Ziebart, A. L. Maas, A. K. Dey, and J. A. Bagnell, "Navigate like a cabbie: Probabilistic reasoning from observed context-aware behavior," in Proceedings of the 10th international conference on Ubiquitous computing. ACM, 2008, pp. 322–331.

[10] C.-M. Tseng and C.-K. Chau, "Viability analysis of electric taxis using New York city dataset," in Proceedings of the Eighth International Conference on Future Energy Systems. ACM, 2017, pp. 328–333.

[11] T. Altshuler, R. Katoshevski, and Y. Shiftan, "Ride sharing and dynamic networks analysis," arXiv preprint arXiv:1706.00581, 2017.

[12] S. Chawla, Y. Zheng, and J. Hu, "Inferring the Root Cause in Road Traffic Anomalies," in 2012 IEEE 12th International Conference on Data Mining. IEEE, Dec 2012, pp. 141–150.

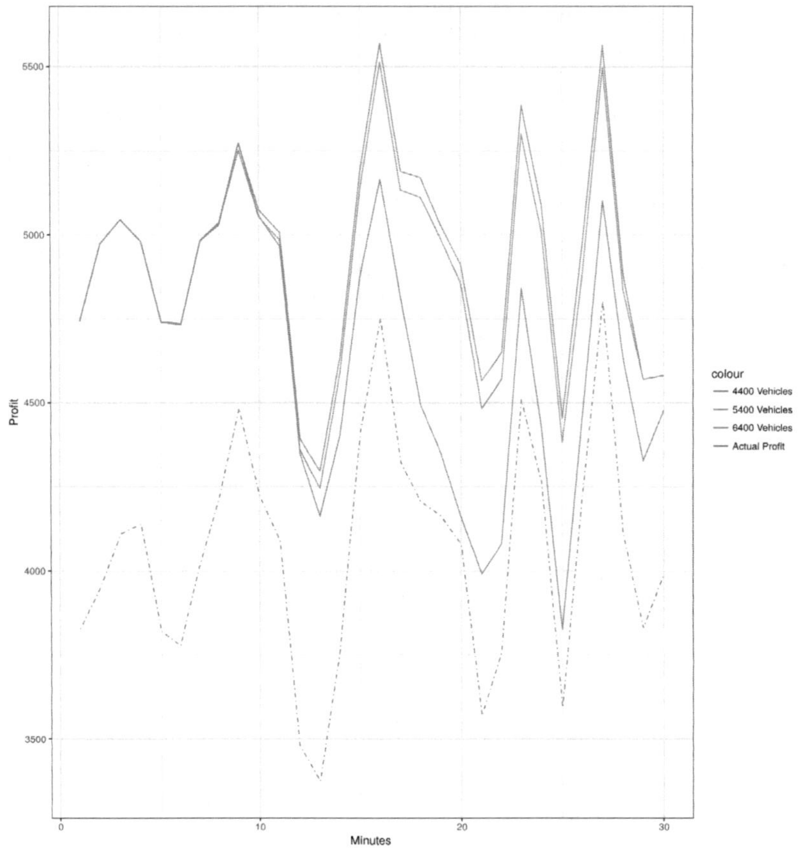

Figure 2. Profit with the different sizes of the vehicles inventory in 30 minutes.

[13] Y. Huang, F. Bastani, R. Jin, and X. S. Wang, "Large scale real-time ridesharing with service guarantee on road networks," Proceedings of the VLDB Endowment, vol. 7, no. 14, pp. 2017–2028, 2014.

[14] S. Qian, J. Cao, F. L. Mouël, I. Sahel, and M. Li, "Scram: a sharing considered route assignment mechanism for fair taxi route recommendations," in Proceedings of the 21th ACM SIGKDD International Conference on Knowledge Discovery and Data Mining. ACM, 2015, pp. 955–964.

[15] X. Liang, G. H. de Almeida Correia, and B. van Arem, "An optimization model for vehicle routing of automated taxi trips with dynamic travel times," Transportation Research Procedia, vol. 27, pp. 736–743, 2017.

[16] P. C. Roling and H. G. Visser, "Optimal airport surface traffic planning using mixed-integer linear programming," International Journal of Aerospace Engineering, vol. 2008, no. 1, p. 1, 2008.

[17] S. Bsaybes, A. Quilliot, and A. K. Wagler, "Fleet management for autonomous vehicles using multicommodity coupled flows in time-expanded networks," in LIPIcs-Leibniz International Proceedings in Informatics, vol. 103. Schloss Dagstuhl-Leibniz-Zentrum fuer Informatik, 2018.

[18] R. Mesa-Arango and S. V. Ukkusuri, "Minimum cost flow problem formulation for the static vehicle allocation problem with stochastic lane demand in truckload strategic planning," Transportmetrica A: Transport Science, vol. 13, no. 10, pp. 893–914, 2017.

[19] D.-P. Song and J. Carter, "Optimal empty vehicle redistribution for hub-and-spoke transportation systems," Naval Research Logistics (NRL), vol. 55, no. 2, pp. 156–171, 2008.

[20] CustomWeather. (2013) Past weather in New York, New York, USA June 2013. [Online]. Available: https://www.timeanddate.com/weather/usa/new-york/historic?month=6&year=2013

[21] J. Li, S. Bhulai, and T. van Essen, "Dynamic coordination of the New York city taxi to optimize the revenue of the taxi service," to appear in International Journal On Advances in Intelligent Systems, 2018.

[22] Technote. (2012) Guidelines for estimating CPLEX memory requirements based on problem size. [Online]. Available: https://www-01.ibm.com/support/docview.wss?uid=swg21399933

Dynamic Models for Knowledge Tracing & Prediction of Future Performance

Androniki Sapountzi[1] Sandjai Bhulai[2] Ilja Cornelisz[1] Chris van Klaveren[1]
[1]Vrije Universiteit Amsterdam, Faculty of Behavioral and Movement Sciences, Amsterdam Center for Learning Analytics
[2]Vrije Universiteit Amsterdam, Faculty of Science, Department of Mathematics
Email addresses: a.sapountzi@vu.nl, s.bhulai@vu.nl, i.cornelisz@vu.nl, c.p.b.j.van.klaveren@vu.nl

Abstract— **Large-scale data about learners' behavior are being generated at high speed on various online learning platforms. Knowledge Tracing (KT) is a family of machine learning sequence models that are capable of using these data efficiently with the objective to identify the likelihood of future learning performance. This study provides an overview of KT models from a technical and an educational point of view. It focuses on data representation, evaluation, and optimization, and discusses the underlying model assumptions such that the strengths and weaknesses with regard to a specific application become visible. Based on the need for advanced analytical methods suited for large and diverse data, we briefly review big data analytics along with KT learning algorithms' efficiency, learnability and scalability. Challenges and future research directions are also outlined. In general, the overview can serve as a guide for researchers and developers, linking the dynamic knowledge tracing models and properties to the learner's knowledge acquisition process that should be accurately modeled over time. Applied KT models to online learning environments hold great potential for the online education industry because it enables the development of personalized adaptive learning systems.**

Keywords- big data applications; educational data mining; knowledge tracing; sequential supervised machine learning.

I. INTRODUCTION

Big Data Analytics (BDA) is becoming increasingly important in the field of online education. Massive Open Online Courses (i.e. Coursera), Learning Management Systems (i.e. Moodle), social networks (i.e. LinkedIn Learning), online personalized learning platforms (i.e. Knewton), skill-based training platforms (i.e. Pluralsight), educational games (i.e. Quizlet), and mobile apps (i.e. Duolingo) are generating various types of large-scale data about learner's behaviors and their knowledge acquisition [1]–[3]. To illustrate this with an example, the 290 courses offered by MIT and Harvard in the first four years of edX produced 2.3 billion logged events from 4.5 million learners. The emerging scientific fields of educational neuroscience [4] and smart-Education [5][6], which hopefully are going to provide new insights about how people acquire skills and knowledge, indicate new big data sources in education.

Artificial Intelligence (AI), Learning Analytics (LA), and Educational Data Mining (EDM) are three areas under development oriented towards the inclusion and exploration of big data analytics in education [2][7]–[9]. EDM considers a wide variety of types of data, practices, algorithms, and methods for modeling and analysis of student data, as categorized by [1][2][10][11]. EDM, LA, AI and Big Data technologies are well-established and have progressed rapidly, however advanced analytic methods suited for large, diverse, streaming or real-time data are still being under development. A critical question in this area is whether more advanced learning algorithms or data of higher quality [12] and well pre-processed [1], or bigger datasets [8][13]–[15] are more important for achieving better analysis results. For all the above reasons, the implementation of BDA in education is considered to be both a major challenge and an opportunity in education [2][3][7]–[11][13][16][17].

Knowledge Tracing (KT) is widely applied in intelligent tutoring systems, and to other modal sources of big data [11] such as online standardized tests, Massive Open Online Courses (MOOC's) data, and educational apps. KT is an EDM framework for modeling the acquisition of student knowledge over time, as the student is observed to interact with a series of learning resources. The objective of the model is either to infer the knowledge state for the specific skill being tutored or to predict the performance on either the next learning resource in the sequence or all the learning resources. KT can be considered as a sequence machine learning model that estimates a hidden state, that is the probability that a certain concept of knowledge is acquired, based on a sequence of noisy observations, that are the interaction-performance pairs on different learning resources at consecutive trials. The estimated probability is then considered a proxy for knowledge mastery which is leveraged in recommendation engines to dynamically adapt the feedback, instruction or learning resource returned to the learner. Furthermore, KT models are applied in mastery learning frameworks which are used to estimate the moment that a certain skill is acquired by the learner [18]. These components empower the development of adaptive learning systems.

The literature distinguishes two representations of KT models: the probabilistic and the deep learning. The former models the knowledge of a learner as a binary hidden state with a level of uncertainty attached to it. The latter models the knowledge of a learner with distributed continuous hidden states that are updated in non-linear, deterministic ways. Graphical probabilistic models of Hidden Markov Models and Dynamic Bayesian Networks can be considered as the baseline models, while deep Recurrent Neural Networks models with Long Short-Term Memory (LSTM) units have only recently been employed. Throughout the paper, the differences between these modeling approaches and their impact on the educational purposes are discussed.

This study provides an overview of currently existing representations of KT models from both an educational and a technical angle. It discusses the underlying model assumptions such that the strengths and weaknesses of the reviewed models are revealed. The review can serve as a guide for researchers and developers, in that when the objective is to predict future performance in online learning environments, the review is informative for which dynamic KT models should be chosen. In addition to that, we hope that by highlighting their strengths and similarities, inspiration for more sophisticated algorithms or richer data sources would be created, capable of accurately capturing the process of knowledge acquisition.

This study proceeds as follows. Section II describes the representation for the knowledge tracing along with a brief introduction behind the probabilistic and recurrent neural network sequence models. Section III introduces the baseline KT model and the other three models, after which the strengths, weaknesses, differences, and similarities are highlighted together with their intrinsic behaviors. Section IV discusses the Item Response Theory (IRT), as it is the alternative family of models for modeling and predicting knowledge acquisition. Section V discusses the prospects and challenges, and Section VI provides the conclusions.

II. Data Representation For knowledge tracing

Data representation refers to the choice of a mathematical structure with which to model the data or, relatedly, to the implementation of that structure. It turns a theoretical model to a learning algorithm and embodies assumptions required for the generalization [19]. If the assumptions of the representation or the explanatory factors accompanied the data are not sufficient to capture the reality and determine the right model, the algorithm will fail to generalize to new examples. Instances of assumptions could be the linear relationships of factor dependencies or a hierarchical representation of explanatory factors. A good representation is one that can express the available kind of knowledge and hence can be a useful input to the predictor [15], meaning that a reasonably-sized learned representation can capture the structure of a huge number of possible input configurations. Other elements contributing to a good representation are outlined in [19]. An interesting point to note is that predictive analytics that lies in distributed or parallel systems, a common case in BDA, the choice of representation will affect how well the data set can be decomposed into smaller components so that analysis can be performed independently on each component.

A. The Knowledge Tracing Task

In KT, two AI frameworks have been utilized to represent the different kinds of available knowledge and disentangle the underlying explanatory factors: the Bayesian (inspired by Bayesian probability theory and statistical inference) and the connectionist deep learning framework (inspired by neuroscience). Bayesian Knowledge Tracing (BKT) is the oldest and still dominant approach for modeling cognitive knowledge over time while the deep learning approach to knowledge tracing (DKT) is a state-of-the-art model.

KT in its general form is formulated as a supervised learning problem of time-series prediction. Suppose a data set D consisting of ordered sequences of length T, to be exercise-performance observation pairs X = $\{(x_{m,1}, y_{m,1}) \dots (x_{m,T}, y_{m,T})\}$ with $y_{m,t} \in \{0,1\}$ from the m-th student on trial $t \in \{1,..,T\}$. The goal is to compute the posterior probability distribution for the parameters $p(y|x;\theta)$ for student m.

The objective in the Bayesian approach is to estimate the probability that a student has mastered a skill S_1 based on the sequence of observed answers that tap S_1, as determined by the concept map. The prediction task in the deep learning approach is the probability that the student will answer the next exercise correctly in their next interaction while the network is presented with the whole trial sequence for all the skills practiced.

A distinction between the two approaches is located on the existence of the concept map. In BKT, the sequences of X are passed through a pre-determined concept map which is assumed to be accurately labelled by experts. The concept map represents a mapping of an exercise or a step of a learning resource to the related skills. The domain knowledge is divided into a hierarchy of relatively fine-grained component skills, also known as Knowledge Components (KC). This may include skills, concepts, or facts. The concept map is used to ensure that students master prerequisite skills before tackling higher level skills in the hierarchy [18]. In the Bayesian approach, a different model is initiated for each new skill while the prediction serves for drawing inferences about the knowledge state of a student for the skill. In the BKT, a student's raw trial sequence is parsed into skill-specific subsequences that preserve the relative ordering of exercises within a skill but discard the ordering relationship of exercises across skills.

Rather than constructing a separate model for each skill, DKT model all skills jointly. In deep learning though, the sequences are not passed through a concept map, but through featurization, that is the distributed hidden units in the layers that relate the input sequences to the output sequences. This distributed featurization, which is the core of the RNN's generalizing principle, is used to induce features and hence discover the concept map and skill dependencies.

B. Probabilistic Sequence Models

The problem of knowledge tracing was first posed as a special case of Hidden Markov Models (HMM) with a straightforward application of Bayesian inference. DBN employed afterward to solve for the assumption of independence of latent states among the different skills. A DBN is a Bayesian network repeated among multiple time steps.

HMM and DBN are Probabilistic Graphical Models (PGM). In PGMs, two concepts are always present: *i)* the data or random variables are represented as nodes in a graph and *ii)* a probabilistic distribution is attached over the nodes via the edges of the graph [20]. HMM is an undirected PGM while Bayesian networks are Directed Acyclical Graphs (DAG) describing probabilistic influences between the nodes of the graph. To briefly explain the benefits of each representation, DAG are useful for expressing causal relationships between random variables, whereas undirected graphs are better suited to expressing soft constraints between the latent and observed random variables [20].

HMM is used to model sequences of possible events in which the probability of each event depends only on the state attained in the previous event, i.e., *Markov processes*, with unobserved states, also called *hidden* or *latent* states. The latent variables are the discrete variables h_n describing which component of the mixture distribution is responsible for generating the corresponding observation. They can take only one value of all the possible hidden states K where each hidden state has got its own internal dynamics described by a transition matrix A describing stochastic transitions between states. The inference of the probability distribution over the hidden states allow us to predict the next output. The outputs produced by a state are stochastic and hidden, in the sense that there is no direct observation about which state produced an output, much like a student's mental process. However, the hidden states produce as observables the emission probabilities Φ that govern the distribution (i.e., actions of a learner).

The parameters that need to be evaluated and learned in HMM are $\lambda = \{\Pi, A, \Phi\}$, where Π is the initial latent variable z_1 which doesn't depend on some other variable. In HMM, including DBN and all generative models, the inference problem is firstly solved: given the parameters θ and a sequence of observations *(practice attempts)* $X = \{X_t\}$, $t \in \{1,..,T\}$, what is the probability that the observations are generated given the model $P(X|\lambda)$; and secondly the learning problem $P(\lambda|X)$ is solved.

In the DBN, this is equivalent to $P(X, h|\lambda)$, where we marginalize over the hidden states h of the latent variables. Since this is a directed graph and edges carry arrows that have directional significance, the joint distribution is given by the product over all of the nodes of the graph, whose distribution is conditioned on the variables corresponding to the parents of each node. A detailed explanation of the computations in the DBN is provided by [20][21].

C. Recurrent Neural Network Sequence Models

Deep Recurrent Neural Networks and specifically the Long Short-Term Memory (LSTM) unit was only recently employed to the KT task to solve for the binary, highly structured representation of the hidden knowledge state. Recurrent Neural Networks (RNN) are a family of Artificial Neural Networks (ANN) used for modeling sequential data that hold a temporal pattern. ANN relate the input units to the output units through a series of hidden layers, each comprising a set of hidden units. The latter is triggered to obtain a specific value by events found in the input and previous hidden states, a process implemented by a non-linear activation function.

RNNs are layered ANNs that share the same parameters, also called *weights*, through the activation function. This property is illustrated in Fig.3 with the formation of a directed circle between the hidden units. RNNs are very powerful because they combine the two following properties:

i. The distributed hidden state allows them to forget and store a lot of information about the past such that they can predict efficiently.

ii. The non-linear activation functions allow them to update their hidden state in complicated ways which can yield high-level structures found in the data.

LSTM is a type of hidden units in RNN that includes '*gates*' which let the hidden state to act as a memory able to hold bits of information for long periods of time and thus can adjust the flow of information across time. When there is no specific trigger, the unit preserves its state, very similar to the way that the latent state in HMM is sticky—once a skill is learned it stays learned [22].

III. Sequence Models Applied In Knowledge Tracing

A. Standard Bayesian KT: skill-specific discrete states

The BKT [18] includes four binary parameters that are defined in a skill-specific way. The two performance-related variables that are emitted from the model are the following:

i. S-slip, the probability that a student will make an error when the skill has been learned, and

ii. G -guess, the probability that a student will guess correctly if the skill is not learned;

The two latent and learning-related variables are the following:

i. $P(\theta_{t-1}) = P(\theta_0)$ which is the initial probability of knowing the skill a priori, and

ii. $P(T)$ which represents the transition probability of learning after practicing a specific skill on learning activities. The estimated acquired skill-knowledge, which is the probability of $P(\theta_t)$, is updated according to (1c) using the $P(T) = P(\theta_{t+1} = 1|\theta_t = 0)$ and observations from correct or incorrect attempts X computed either by (1a) or (1b), respectively. Equation (1d) computes the probability of a student applying the skill correctly on an upcoming practicing opportunity. The equations are as follows:

$$P(\theta_{t+1}|y_t = 1) \frac{P(\theta_t) * (1 - P(S))}{P(\theta_t) * (1 - P(S)) + (1 - P(\theta_t)) * (P(G))} \quad (1a)$$

$$P(\theta_{t+1}|y_t = 0) = \frac{P(\theta_t) * P(S)}{P(\theta_t) * P(S) + (1 - P(\theta_t)) * (1 - P(G))} \quad (1b)$$

$$P(\theta_{t+1}) = P(\theta_{t+1}|y_t) + (1 - P(\theta_{t+1}|y_t)) * P(T) \quad (1c)$$

$$P(C_{t+1}) = P(\theta_t) * (1 - P(S)) + (1 - P(\theta_t)) * P(G) \quad (1d)$$

At each t, a student m is practicing a step of a learning opportunity that tap a skill S. The step-by step process of a student trying to acquire knowledge about S is illustrated in Fig.1. Given a series of y_t, and t for the student m, the learning task is the likelihood maximization of the given data $P(y|\lambda)$, where $\lambda = \{P(S), P(G), P(T), P(\theta_t)\}$. In the original paper, this is done through Curve Fitting and evaluated via Mean Absolute Error, which is considered an insufficient measure [26]. The key idea of BKT, is that it considers guessing and slipping in a probabilistic manner to infer the current state and update the learning parameter during the practicing process.

Even though BKT updates the parameter estimates based on dynamic student responses, it is assumed that all of the four parameters are the same for each student. In essence, the actual probability of a correct response is averaged across students, and the models predicted probability of a correct response is averaged across skills. Because the data of all students practicing a specific skill are used to fit the BKT parameters for that skill, without conditioning on certain student's characteristics, a big part of the research is focused on adding learner-specific variables by assuming variability among students' process of learning. Yudelson [23] found that the inclusion of student-specific parameters has a significant positive effect on prediction accuracy and interpretability, as well as in dealing with over-fitting. [24] added Dirichlet priors for the initial mastery θ_{t-1}, while [23] extended their work and found that adding variables of learning rates $P(T)$ for individual learners, provides higher model accuracy.

B. BKT with student-specific features of learning rates: Personalized predictions

The Individualized BKT (IBKT) model [23] includes apart from skill-specific, student-specific parameters as well. The model is developed by splitting the skill-specific BKT parameters, substituted by w , into two parameters components *(i)* w^k-the skill-specific and *(ii)* w^u-the student-specific component; and combining them by summing their logit function $l(p) = \log\left(\frac{p}{1-p}\right)$, and sigmoid function $\sigma(x) = \frac{1}{(1+e^{-x})}$. These two procedures are illustrated in (2a)

$$w = \sigma(l(w^k) + l(w^u)) \qquad (2a)$$

Updating the gradients of the parameters is possible using the chain rule, as illustrated in (2b) for the student-specific component of the parameter.

$$\frac{\partial J}{\partial w^u} = \frac{\partial J}{\partial w}\frac{\partial w}{\partial w^u} \qquad (2b)$$

The IBKT models are built in an incremental manner by adding w^u in batches and where the effects of each addition are examined on Cross Validation (CV) performance. It is also possible to improve the overall accuracy by incrementally updating the w^k once a new group of students finishes a course or a course unit.

Figure 1 depicts the structure for the HMM model of both BKT and IBKT. Although the underlying HMM model and hence the process of a student practicing exercises remains the same, the fitting process is different. The parameters λ are spitted into two components and the model is fitted for each student separately by computing the gradients of these parameters.

The blue circular nodes capture the hidden students' knowledge state per skill, while the orange rectangles denote the exercise-performance observations associated to each skill correspondingly. We note that, in the upcoming figures the blue circular nodes and orange rectangles are also used to describe the same meaning. The nodes in the probabilistic models denote stochastic computations whereas in the RNN deterministic ones.

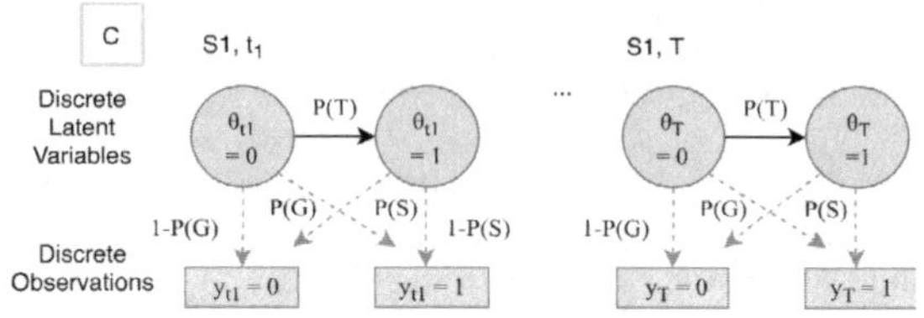

Figure 1. *Baseline and Individualized Bayesian Knowledge Tracing represented as a Hidden Markov Model.* In IBKT, the four parameters $\{G,S,\theta_t,T\}$ are splitted to include student-specific parametrs.

Both the BKT and IBKT assume independent skills sets and cannot deal with hierarchical structures since they are undirected graphs. This assumption is restrictive because it imposes that different skill sets cannot be related and, as a result, observing an outcome for one skill set is not informative for the knowledge level of another skill set. However, the expert model in educational domains, that is the decomposition of the subject matter or set of skills into a set of concepts (KCs) that need to be acquired by a learner, is frequently hierarchical. DAG is the optimal data representation for describing the expert model in traditional and adaptive learning systems that incorporate parallel scalable architectures and BDA [3].

C. Dynamic Bayesian Network: Discrete Skill-Specific Dependencies in KT

DBN is a DAG model allowing for the joint representation of dependencies among skills within the same model. [21] applied DBN in knowledge acquisition modeling in a KT setting.

Again, at each trial t, a student m receives a quiz-like assessment that contains learning opportunities, but this time these belong to different skills S. The Bayesian network is repeated itself at each time step t with additional edges connecting the knowledge state on a skill at t to $t+1$. The set of variables X contains all skill nodes S as well as all observation nodes Y of the model while H denote the domain of the unobserved variables, *i.e.*, learning opportunities that have not yet been attempted by students and hence their corresponding binary skill variables S are also latent. The objective is then again to estimate the parameters θ that maximize the likelihood of joint probability $p(y_m, h_m|\theta)$, where y_m and h_m denote the observed and hidden variables respectively.

The enhancement of the model is that even without having observed certain outcomes for a skill, say y_3 in time step t_2 , is still possible to infer the knowledge state regarding $S3$. To illustrate that, consider the example model depicted in Figure 2. It depicts that, the probability of skill $S3$ being mastered at t_2 depends not only on the state of $S3$ at the previous time-step t_1, but also on the states of S1 and S2 at t_2. Suppose now that a student solves a learning opportunity associated with $S2$ at step t_2; then the hidden variables at t_2 will be $h_m = \{S1, S2, S3, y3, y1\}$ while the observed variables will be $y_m = y_2$.

In KT, the objective function is the log (likelihood) loss. In DBN, it is reformulated using a log-linear model to obtain a linear combination of a lower dimensional representation of features F. Equation (3) shows the log likelihood function of DBN:

$$L(w) = \sum_{m} \ln\left(\sum_{h_m} exp(w^{\mathrm{T}}\varphi(y_m, h_m) - \ln(Z))\right) \quad (3)$$

, where φ: $\mathrm{Y} \times \mathrm{H} \rightarrow \mathbb{R}^F$ denotes a mapping from the latent space H and the observed space Y to an F-dimensional feature vector. Z is a normalizing constant and w denotes the weights that can be directly linked to the parameters of the model θ.

DBNs grapple with the same limitations as HMM: the representation of student understanding is binary and reported per skill, given that each skill can be associated with exactly one observable, and there is the requirement for accurate concept labeling. RNN have only recently tried to model student understanding in order to break the beforementioned assumptions.

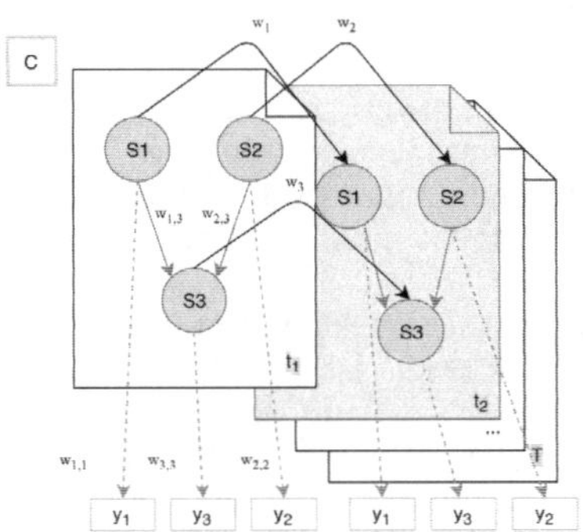

Figure 2. Bayesian Knowledge Tracing represented as a Dynamic Bayesian Network unrolled over T time steps. The hierarchical relationships between the skills are depicted and incorporated to the estimation of knowledge growth, shown by the arrow lines.

D. *Recurrent Neural Networks: Continuous Knowledge States & Skill Dependencies*

In an RNN, the hidden layer provides a continuous and high dimensional representation of the latent knowledge state h_t, which learns the properties of sequences of observations of student responses $x_t = (x_0, .., x_T)$, denoted as a_t in (4c), on learning activities, denoted as q_t in (4c). DKT [25] exploits the utility of LSTM whose fully and recurrent connection allow them to retain information of x_t for many time steps; and use it in a prediction at a much later point in time. The distributed representation allows an RNN to induce features related to skill dependencies or concepts (KCs) associated with exercises. The hidden-to-hidden connections encode the degree of overlapping between skills and exercises. According to (4a), the hidden units are activated via the hyperbolic tangent, which employs information on both the input x_t and on the previous activation h_{t-1} ,

$$h_t = \tanh(W_{hx}x_t + W_{hh}h_{t-1} + b_h) \quad (4a)$$

where b_h is the bias term and W_{hx}, W_{hh} are the weights of units corresponding to the input and hidden layer. The non-linear and deterministic output h_t will be passed to the sigmoid function σ to give the probability of getting each of the learning activities correct $y_t = (y_0, .., y_T)$ in the students' next interaction $t + 1$, as shown in (4b):

$$y_t = \sigma(W_{yh}h_t + b_y) \quad (4b)$$

Finally, the loss for a single student will be the negative log-likelihood, as shown in (4c):

$$L = \sum_{t} l(y^T\delta(q_{t+1}), a_{t+1}) \quad (4c)$$

where l is the binary cross entropy and δ denotes the one hot encoding transformation of the input, a necessary step for ANN and a suitable preprocessing step for small data-sets. Compressing Sensing is suitable for big data sets.

Figure 3 depicts an example architecture of RNN, where X represents the entire sequence of exercises a student receives in the order the student receives them. After feeding X to the network, each time the student answers an exercise, a prediction is made as to whether or not she/he would answer an exercise of each concept (KC) correctly on her next interaction. It's important to note that, in the DKT a deep RNN is employed, whose architecture include many hidden layers.

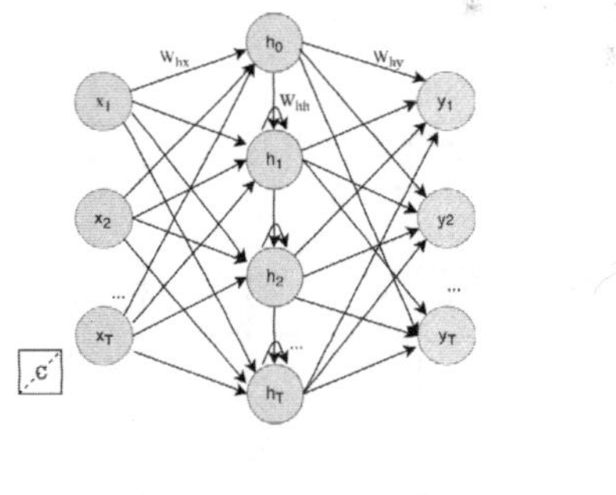

Figure 3. Deep Knowledge Tracing represented as a Recurrent Neural Network unrolled over T time steps. The arrow lines represent the change in the hidden knowledge state which is updated in non-linear

E. *Comparison of the sequence models for KT*

Table I outlines and compares important features of the models described above. The modeling of knowledge acquisition and the prediction of future performance in the BKT are binary and skill-specific without conditioning in individual learning or skill interdependencies. The predictions in the other models allow for individualization, skill dependencies, or continuous latent states and the discovery of the concept map. All models share the assumption that each learning activity is a learning opportunity rather than an opportunity to assess the acquired knowledge.

The criterion of choosing the right algorithm is a combination of the efficiency of the available data along with the learning algorithm's components; these are the representation, evaluation, and optimization [15]. The rows of representation, optimization, evaluation, learnability, and efficiency in Table I comprise the technical-oriented elements whereas the remaining ones reflect the impact on educational settings. In the below paragraphs, we briefly describe each of
these components considering the KT task. The data representation has been already introduced in Section II.

1) Evaluation of the predictions

Model evaluation metrics analyze the performance of the predictive model and are widely discussed in the context of general machine learning applications including educational ones [26]–[28]. In KT, these include the Root Mean Square Error (RMSE), classification accuracy, and Area Under the Curve (AUC). RMSE is the standard performance metric, and it has demonstrated a high correlation to the log-likelihood function and the *'moment of knowledge acquisition'* [26]. AUC should be used only as an additional metric, in order to assess the model's ability to discriminate incorrect from correct performance, since it has several important disadvantages with regard to KT. DKT was criticized in terms of the employment of AUC, because it computes the accuracy on a per-trial basis instead of per-skill.

TABLE I. COMPARISON OF KNOWLEDGE TRACING MODELS

Model	**BKT**	**IBKT**	**DBN**	**DKT**
Extension	Baseline	Personalization	Detailed Skill Estimation	Continuous Knowledge State
Representation	HMM	HMM	DBN	RNN
Optimization	Curve Fitting, Expectation Maximization	Gradient Descent	Constrained Latent Structure	Stochastic Gradient Descent
Learnability-Fitting	158 observations-55 skills	2 datasets: *i.*8,918,054 observations, 3,310 students 515 or 541 skills *ii.* 20,012,498 observations 6,043 students 800-900 skills	5 datasets: Size range: 100-500 observations 3-9 Skills 77- 7265 students	3 datasets: Total size: 65.000 students, 2.000 observations-answers 230 items
Efficiency	4 /skill,	4 /skill + 2 /student *(a)*	4/skill + 2^{n-1} for n skills	250,000 with 200 hidden units & 50 skills. 4((input size+1) * output size + output $size^2$)
Evaluation	MAE	RMSE, Accuracy	RMSE, AUC	AUC
Restrictions	Prone to Bias	Independent Skills	Complex & hard-coded	Highly Complex & not interpretable
Variation in learner ability	X	✓	X	✓
Inclusion of forgetting	X	X	✓	✓
Inter-Skill Similarity	X	X	✓	✓
Exercise ordering effect	X	X	X	✓

a. the initial probability and the learning rate is individualized

2) Optimization, Identifiability and Degeneracy

The optimization function derives the optimal possible values for the parameters of the objective function. Unlike in most other optimization problems, the function that generated the data and should be optimized is unknown and hence training error surrogates for test error [15]. The optimization of the log-likelihood function is performed using Curve Fitting (CF), Expectation Maximization (EM), Constrained optimization, and Gradient Descent methods (GD). All of them with appropriate initialization conditions [18][28]–[30] of the parameters, can solve for the identifiability issue which is considered an issue in the probabilistic approaches [20][28]. The identifiability issue is directly linked with the interpretability of the parameters values computed by the probabilistic models [20], where inferences about knowledge states are being made. It arises when there is more than one combination of parameters that optimizes the objective function. Constrained optimization [21] uses log-linear likelihood to ensure the interpretability of the constrained parameters, and it is suitable for DBNs. GD allows IBKT to introduce student-specific parameters to BKT without expanding the structure of the underlying HMM and hence without increasing the computational cost of fitting [23].

Equally important for the optimization methods is to be robust to degeneracy, where it is possible to obtain model parameters which lead to paradoxical behavior [30]. The standard KT model is susceptible to converging to erroneous degenerate states depending on the initial values of the parameters [28], and many research has focused on this property of the models [29]–[31]. An example in the BKT is the probability that the student acquired the instructed knowledge dropping after three correct answers in a row [29]. An instance in DKT includes the alternation between known and not-yet-known instead of transiting gradually over time [31].

3) Computational & Statistical Efficiency

Learnability comprises statistical efficiency, that is the number of student interaction examples required for good generalization, namely to correctly classify the unseen examples of interactions. The number of examples required to establish convergence, which is related to the number of training data that is used to learn the parameters of the model, is depicted in the table as Learnability-Fitting. The training of BKT model is faster, while deep neural networks and IBKT is relatively slow due to the requirement of large datasets for effective training. Generalization in DBN is inferred by using different learning domains datasets. According to the authors [21], the performance differences between DBN and BKT, especially the influence of the different parameters, need to be investigated further.

Computational efficiency refers to the number of computations during training and during prediction. These include the number of iterations of the optimization algorithm and the number of resources (i.e., the number of hidden units). In the table, we note only the number of model parameters which is not necessarily the most appropriate measure of model complexity. Nonlinear functions and large datasets increase the model complexity which offers flexibility in fitting the data [20]. In DKT, there are high demands regarding computational resources. Nowadays, there are many parallel and distributed computing infrastructures that can be used to boost the efficiency of such data-intensive tasks. IBKT models take the advantage of parallel computing infrastructures. Comparing HMM and DBN, the latter needed 21-86 parameters for the datasets used in the paper. DBN is more computationally expensive due to their complex loopy structure and the skill-dependencies [21].

It is important to note that, the parameter estimates and the behavior of KT models should be researched in scalability cases in either the number of students or the increased number of observations per student [30].

4) Features related to performance and learning

The DKT model allows for differences in learning ability of the student by conditioning on recent performance of the student. By giving the complete sequence trial of performance-exercise pairs to the model, it can condition on the average accuracy of previous trials. DBN and DKT allow for skill-dependencies and can also infer the effect of exercise ordering on learning, which is considered an important element in learning and retention. The probabilistic KT tends to predict practice performance over brief intervals where forgetting the acquired knowledge, *the probability of transitioning from a state of knowing to not knowing a skill*, is almost irrelevant; whereas DKT incorporates recency effects and allows for long-term learning.

The complex representation in DKT is chosen based on the grounds that learning is a complex process [25] that shouldn't rely only on simple parametric models because they cannot capture enough of the complexity of interest unless provided with the appropriate feature space [22]. The assumption embodied in this approach is that the observed data is generated by the interactions of many different factors on multiple levels. DKT is a complex model, and thereby it should be applied to more complex problems and data. Hence, as long as there are sufficient data more behavioral in nature to constrain the model, a shift to connectionist paradigms of modeling will offer superior results when compared to classical approaches [11].

DKT success is attributed to its flexibility and generality in capturing statistical regularities directly present in the inputs and outputs, instead of representation learning [22]. When the performance of the baseline BKT and DKT models is compared [22], it is found that both models perform equally well, when variations of BKT models allow for more flexibility in modeling statistical regularities, that DKT has already the ability to explore. These are forgetting, variability in abilities among students, and skill discovery that allows for interactions between skills.

IV. Item Response Theory For Predicting Future Performance

This review focuses specifically on Knowledge Tracing, thereby ignoring the only available alternative which is Item Response Theory (IRT) [32]. Theoretically, IRT models differ from KT models on that the former is developed for assessment purposes *(i.e., the theory focuses on short tests in which no learning occurs)* or for modeling very coarse-grained skills where the overall learning is slow (i.e., summative rather than formative assessments) [33]. Technically, IRT uses the responses on learning opportunities directly to estimate the learner's ability, while KT models go through the concept map or featurization.

The concept of IRT assumes that the probability of a correct response to an assessment item is a mathematical function of student parameters and item parameters. The latter is better estimated when there is a large amount of data to calibrate them. The student parameters can be used to account for variability in student a priori abilities. It's interesting to note that, (2a) of IBKT incorporates the compensatory logic behind the IRT, when summing the logistic functions to incorporate skill and student-specific parameters [23]. The prediction task in the baseline model is done by mapping a difference between a student knowledge on a skill θ and an item difficulty β into the probability of a correct answer $r_t = 1$ using a logistic function $\sigma(x)$, as depicted in (5). The estimate of ability is continually re-calibrated based on learner's performance.

$$p(r_t = 1|\theta) = \frac{1}{1+\exp\{-(\theta-\beta)\}} \quad (5)$$

The baseline IRT model is a logistic regression based Rasch model, also known as the One Parameter (1PL) IRT while its descendants include the Performance Factor Analysis (PFA) and the Additive and Conjugate Factor Model. The latter model is better estimated when there is a large amount of data available for calibration. The PFA model is highly predictive, but it's not useful for adaptive environments in the sense that it cannot optimize the subset of items presented to students according to their historical performance. The literature has already compared the models of PFA and BKT, both in theoretical [34] and in practical [35] terms *(i.e., predictive accuracy and parameter plausibility)*. Both models are considered difficult to implement in an online environment and are rarely evaluated with respect to online prediction performance [33][36][37].

V. Prospects And Challenges

Predicting future performance through modeling knowledge acquisition is a complex task; as human learning is grounded in the complexity of both the human brain and knowledge. This raises the opportunity to increase our understanding of knowledge prediction by synthesizing methods from various academic disciplines such as human-machine interaction design, machine learning, psychometrics, educational science, pedagogy, and neuroscience.

From a social science perspective, learning is influenced by complex macro-, meso- and micro-level interactions, including affect [38], motivation [39][40], and even social identity [41]. Predicting student knowledge with the mere observation of correct versus incorrect responses to learning activities provides weak evidence since it's not a sufficient data source.

Currently, there are some KT models augmented with non-performance data such as metacognitive [42], affect [43], and other student traits apart from learning rates [44] [45]. As educational apps and smart learning environments increase in popularity, it may be possible to collect valuable, diverse and vast amounts of student learning data, that will capture the reality of learning, and hence they will create opportunities, as well as new challenges, to deepen our understanding of knowledge acquisition and employ these insights to personalize education better.

VI. CONCLUSIONS

Modeling learner's skill acquisition and predicting future performance is an integral part of online adaptive learning systems that drive personalized instruction. Knowledge Tracing is a data mining framework widely used for that purpose because of its capability to infer a student's dynamic knowledge state as the learner interacts with a sequence of learning activities. Embarking from the baseline Bayesian model and based on the principles desired for adaptive learning systems, we outline three of the model's most recent extensions. These include the individualization of learning pace among students, the incorporation of the relationships among multiple skills, and the continuous representation of the knowledge state, which is able to induce both student and skill-specific features.

We show how probabilistic and deep learning approaches are related to the task of modeling sequences of student interactions by outlining their technical and educational requirements, advantages and restrictions. In particular, we investigate the assumptions in representation, the potential pitfalls in optimization, and the evaluation of the predictions. The general idea is that by investigating these aspects, one can gain an understanding why prediction models work the way they do or why they fail in other cases. A crucial question is how efficient and accurate these learning methods are regarding learning and generalization when they are applied to online adaptive learning environments where scalability and computational speed are important elements. The current study is useful both for researchers and developers allowing for a comparison of the different models. In addition, the corresponding citations throughout the paper can be used to provide further guidance in implementing or extending a model for a specific data source, online learning environment, or educational application.

REFERENCES

[1] C. Romero, J. R. Romero, and S. Ventura, "A Survey on Pre-Processing Educational Data," Springer Cham, pp. 29–64, 2014.

[2] C. Romero and S. Ventura, "Educational Data Mining: A Review of the State of the Art," IEEE Trans. Syst. Man, Cybern. Part C Applications Rev., vol. 40, no. 6, pp. 601–618, Nov. 2010.

[3] A. Essa, "A possible future for next generation adaptive learning systems," Smart Learn. Environ., vol. 3, no. 1, p. 16, Dec. 2016.

[4] K. W. Fischer, U. Goswami, and J. Geake, "The Future of Educational Neuroscience," Mind, Brain, Educ., vol. 4, no. 2, pp. 68–80, Jun. 2010.

[5] Z.-T. Zhu, M.-H. Yu, and P. Riezebos, "A research framework of smart education," Smart Learn. Environ., vol. 3, no. 1, p. 4, Dec. 2016.

[6] S. Kontogiannis et al., "Services and high level architecture of a smart interconnected classroom," in IEEE SEEDA-CECNSM, Sep. 2018, unpublished.

[7] Z. Papamitsiou and A. A. Economides, "Learning Analytics and Educational Data Mining in Practice: A Systematic Literature Review of Empirical Evidence," Journal of Educational Technology & Society, vol. 17. International Forum of Educational Technology & Society, pp. 49–64, 2014.

[8] B. K. Daniel, "Big Data and data science: A critical review of issues for educational research," Review, Wiley, Br. J. Educ. Technol., Nov. 2017.

[9] K. Nadu and L. Muthu, "Application of Big Data in Education Data Mining and Learning Analytics -A Literature Review ICTACT J. Soft Comput., vol. 5, no. 4, pp. 1035–1049, Jul. 2015.

[10] C. Romero and S. Ventura, "Educational data science in massive open online courses," Wiley Interdiscip. Rev. Data Min. Knowl. Discov., vol. 7, no. 1, p. e1187, Jan. 2017.

[11] Z. A. Pardos, "Big data in education and the models that love them," Curr. Opin. Behav. Sci., vol. 18, pp. 107–113, Dec. 2017.

[12] I. Taleb, R. Dssouli, and M. A. Serhani, "Big Data Pre-processing: A Quality Framework," in 2015 IEEE International Congress on Big Data, 2015, pp. 191–198.

[13] P. Prinsloo, E. Archer, G. Barnes, Y. Chetty, and D. Van Zyl, "Bigger data as better data in open distance learning" Review, Int. Rev. Res. Open Distrib. Learn., vol. 16, no. 1, Feb. 2015.

[14] D. Gibson, "Big Data in Higher Education: Research Methods and Analytics Supporting the Learning Journey," Technol. Knowl. Learn., vol. 22, no. 3, pp. 237–241, Oct. 2017.

[15] P. Domingos and Pedro, "A few useful things to know about machine learning," Commun. ACM, vol. 55, no. 10, p. 78, Oct. 2012.

[16] K. Colchester, H. Hagras, D. Alghazzawi, and G. Aldabbagh, "A Survey of Artificial Intelligence Techniques Employed for Adaptive Educational Systems within E-Learning Platforms," J. Artif. Intell. Soft Comput. Res., vol. 7, no. 1, pp. 47–64, Jan. 2017.

[17] A. Peña-Ayala, "Educational data mining: A survey and a data mining-based analysis of recent works," Expert Syst. Appl., vol. 41, no. 4, pp. 1432–1462, Mar. 2014.

[18] A. T. Corbett and J. R. Anderson, "Knowledge tracing: Modeling the acquisition of procedural knowledge," User Model. User-Adapted Interact., vol. 4, no. 4, pp. 253–278, 1995.

[19] Y. Bengio, A. Courville, and P. Vincent, "Representation Learning: A Review and New Perspectives," IEEE Trans. Pattern Anal. Mach. Intell., vol. 35, no. 8, pp. 1798–1828, Aug. 2013.

[20] C. M. Bishop, Pattern recognition and machine learning, Editors: M. Jordan J. Kleinberg B. Scholkopf, Springer, 2006.

[21] T. Kaser, S. Klingler, A. G. Schwing, and M. Gross, "Dynamic Bayesian Networks for Student Modeling," IEEE Trans. Learn. Technol., vol. 10, no. 4, pp. 450–462, Oct. 2017.

[22] M. Khajah, R. V. Lindsey, and M. C. Mozer, "How deep is knowledge tracing?," arXiv preprint arXiv:1604.02416, Mar. 2016.

[23] M. V. Yudelson, K. R. Koedinger, and G. J. Gordon, "Individualized Bayesian Knowledge Tracing Models," in International Conference on Artificial Intelligence in Education, 2013, pp. 171–180.

[24] Z. A. Pardos and N. T. Heffernan, "Modeling Individualization in a Bayesian Networks Implementation of Knowledge Tracing," Springer, Berlin, Heidelberg, 2010, pp. 255–266.

[25] C. Piech et al., "Deep Knowledge Tracing," in Advances in Neural Information Processing Systems, NIPS, 2015, pp. 505–513.

[26] R. Pelanek, "Metrics for Evaluation of Student Models.," J. Educ. Data Min., vol. 7, no. 2, pp. 1–19, 2015.

[27] J. P. González-Brenes and Y. Huang, "Your model is predictive-but is it useful? Theoretical and Empirical Considerations of a New Paradigm for Adaptive Tutoring Evaluation," in Proceedings of the 8th International Conference on Educational Data Mining, 2015.

[28] J. E. Beck and K. Chang, "Identifiability: A Fundamental Problem of Student Modeling," pp. 137–146, 2007, Proceedings of the 11th International Conference on User Modeling.

[29] R. S. J. d. Baker, A. T. Corbett, and V. Aleven, "More Accurate Student Modeling through Contextual Estimation of Slip and Guess Probabilities in Bayesian Knowledge Tracing," pp. 406–415, 2008, in International Conference on Intelligent Tutoring Systems.

[30] Z. A. Pardos, Z. A. Pardos, and N. T. Heffernan, "Navigating the parameter space of Bayesian Knowledge Tracing models: Visualizations of the convergence of the Expectation Maximization algorithm.", In Proceedings of the 3rd International Conference on Educational Data Mining pp. 161–170, 2010

[31] C.-K. Yeung and D.-Y. Yeung, "Addressing Two Problems in Deep Knowledge Tracing via Prediction-Consistent Regularization," Jun. 2018, in press, In Proceedings of the 5th ACM Conference on Learning @ Scale,

[32] M. Khajah, Y. Huang, J. P. Gonzales-Brenes, M. C. Mozer, and P. Brusilovsky, "Integrating knowledge tracing and item response theory: A tale of two frameworks", In Proceedings of the 4th International Workshop on Personalization Approaches in Learning Environments, pp. 7–15, 2014

[33] R. Pelánek, "Applications of the Elo rating system in adaptive educational systems," Comput. Educ., vol. 98, pp. 169–179, Jul. 2016.

[34] R. Pelánek, "Bayesian knowledge tracing, logistic models, and beyond: an overview of learner modeling techniques," User Model. User-adapt. Interact., vol. 27, no. 3–5, pp. 313–350, Dec. 2017.

[35] Y. Gong, J. E. Beck, and N. T. Heffernan, "Comparing Knowledge Tracing and Performance Factor Analysis by Using Multiple Model Fitting Procedures," Springer, Berlin, Heidelberg, 2010, pp. 35–44.

[36] C. Ekanadham and Y. Karklin, "T-SKIRT: Online Estimation of Student Proficiency in an Adaptive Learning System.", arXiv preprint arXiv:1702.04282, 2017

[37] K. H. Wilson, Y. Karklin, B. Han, and C. Ekanadham, "Back to the basics: Bayesian extensions of IRT outperform neural networks for proficiency estimation Acknowledgements." arXiv preprint arXiv:1604.02336, 2016.

[38] E. A. Linnenbrink, P. R. Pintrich, and P. R. Pintrich, "Role of Affect in Cognitive Processing in Academic Contexts," pp. 71–102, Jul. 2004.

[39] A. J. Elliot and C. S. Dweck, Handbook of competence and motivation. Guilford Press, 2007.

[40] B. Fogg and BJ, "A behavior model for persuasive design," in Proceedings of the 4th International Conference on Persuasive Technology - Persuasive ', p. 1., Sep. 2009

[41] G. L. Cohen and J. Garcia, "Identity, Belonging, and Achievement: A Model, Interventions, Implications," Current Directions in Psychological Science, vol. 17. Sage Publications, Inc. Association for Psychological Science, pp. 365–369, 2008.

[42] I. Roll, R. S. Baker, V. Aleven, B. M. Mclaren, and K. R. Koedinger, "Modeling Students' Metacognitive Errors in Two Intelligent Tutoring Systems 1 Metacognition in Intelligent Tutoring Systems." In: Proceedings of User Modeling, pp. 379–388, 2005

[43] S. Spaulding and C. Breazeal, "Affect and Inference in Bayesian Knowledge Tracing with a Robot Tutor." Proceedings of the Tenth Annual ACM/IEEE International Conference on Human-Robot Interaction, pp. 219-220, USA 2015

[44] M. Khajah, R. M. Wing, R. V Lindsey, and M. C. Mozer, "Incorporating Latent Factors Into Knowledge Tracing To Predict Individual Differences In Learning." Proceedings of the 7th International Conference on Educational Data Mining, Educational Data Mining Society Press, pp. 99–106, 2014.

[45] J. I. E. Lee, "The Impact on Individualizing Student Models on Necessary Practice Opportunities.," Int. Educ. Data Min. Soc., In Proceedings of the 5th International Conference on Educational Data Mining, pp. 118–125, Jun. 2012

Efficient Use of Geographical Information Systems for Improving Transport Mode Classification

Jorge Rodríguez-Echeverría*†§, Sidharta Gautama*†, Nico Van de Weghe‡, Daniel Ochoa§ and Benhur Ortiz-Jaramillo¶
* Department of Industrial Systems Engineering and Product Design, Ghent University, Gent-Zwijnaarde, Belgium
Email: {Jorge.RodriguezEcheverria, Sidharta.Gautama}@UGent.be
† Industrial Systems Engineering (ISyE), Flanders Make
‡ Department of Geography, Ghent University, Ghent, Belgium, Email: Nico.VandeWeghe@UGent.be
§ Faculty of Electrical and Computer Engineering, ESPOL Polytechnic University, Guayaquil, Ecuador
Email: jirodrig@espol.edu.ec, dochoa@fiec.espol.edu.ec
¶ imec-IPI, Department of Telecommunications and Information Processing, Ghent University, Ghent, Belgium
Email: Benhur.OrtizJaramillo@UGent.be

***Abstract*—Comparison between transport mode classifiers is usually performed without considering imbalanced samples in the dataset. This problem makes performance rates, such as accuracy and precision, not enough to report the performance of a classifier because they represent a cut-off point in the classifier performance curve. Our rule-based method proposes to combine both, the network elements associated with the transport mode to identify, and the elements associated with other means of transport. We performed a comparison between our proposed method and another geospatial rule-based method, by applying a real-world representative dataset with a target class imbalance. We evaluated the performance of both methods with five experiments, using the area under the Receiver Operating Characteristic curve as metric. The results show that the tested methods achieve the same false positive rate. However, our method identifies correctly 84% of the true positive samples, i.e., the highest performance in our test data (data collected in Belgium). The proposed method can be used as a part of the post-processing chain in transport data to perform transport and traffic analytics in smart cities.**

Keywords–Transport mode classification; Crowdsourcing; Tracking data; Receiver operating characteristic.

I. Introduction

Mobility surveys are carried out around the world with the purpose of discovering the behavior of citizens according to the transport mode [1]. Knowing the demand for transport services helps cities to manage and improve their transportation systems. Different strategies, such as questionnaires, interviews or space-time diaries have been used to collect travel data in the past. With the advent of smart-phones, that integrate sensors, such as Global Positioning System (GPS) receivers, crowdsourcing has come to the scene as a new tool to gather mobility data, either using a travel diary app or as a background location-aware service. Hence, automatic public-transport classification becomes the key element to capture user's activity patterns as well as to perform transport and traffic analytics.

Therefore, the identification of public transport modes has become an active research area [2]. For instance, Transmob project [3] provided users with mobility cards as a single payment method to pay bus, tram, subway and train tickets, parking at garages or streets, and shared bike rentals. M-card10 [4] is a smartphone application of De Lijn, the Flemish bus agency, in which commuters can buy up to 10 public transport tickets. The app activates a ticket when getting on a bus or a tram. These ticket-based systems provide information for automatic public transport mode detection. However, users must generate events, check-in and check-out, to identify each mode accurately. Live positioning systems [5][6] take advantage of the capabilities of Geographical Information Systems (GIS) to perform transport-mode classification on tracking data collected through cell phones. Such systems require the integration of tracking data with open access or proprietary GIS layers for generating geospatial data to discover new knowledge.

In several studies, GPS data is used because of the temporal aspects, accurate information about travels and geographical aspects when it is combined with GIS data, such as Open Street Map (OSM) transport network [5][7]–[9]. These studies are aimed to identify transport mode using a rule-based approach. A common factor among those methods is to use network elements related to the transport mode for the automatic transport mode identification, e.g., train segments will only cross railways and train stations. In this paper, we named these kind of elements as Passing Points (PP). Our approach for transport mode classification also considers traffic network elements that do not belong to the transport mode to be identified. We called these elements Non Passing Points (NPP).

Usually, researchers focus only on reporting the success rates of their proposed systems. However, when a representative dataset is used, real case scenarios, this is typically an unbalanced classification problem where it is easy to classify a sample as non-class to get a high accuracy and precision [10]. Hence, we focus on the true positive rate to report our outcomes. Our method performs transport mode classification (e.g., train) using the network elements associated with the transport mode to identify (e.g., train stations and railways), but we also consider elements associated with other means of transport (e.g., motorway junctions) to filter out false positive trip segments. In this paper, we perform a comparison between an improved version of our methodology [6] and the work described by Gong et al. [5]. We evaluated both techniques by applying them on an extensive labeled dataset collected during a mobility campaign. Results show that the probability of falsely rejecting train trips decrease when Non Passing Points are considered into the method.

The remainder of the paper is organized as follows. In Section 2, we present an overview of the works that use the transport network information, and position our approach related to the state-of-the-art. In Section 3, we describe the methodology used to compare the tested methods. In Section 4, we explain the evaluation process used to compare the tested methods. Furthermore, in Section 5, we perform experiments with the tested techniques, followed by the results and discussion at Section 6. The final section includes the concluding remarks.

II. GPS AND GIS TRANSPORT MODE CLASSIFICATION

Nowadays, mobility survey studies are carried on with GPS technology. Transport and traffic analytics require that GPS raw data are post-processed to identify transport modes. Some studies follow a fuzzy logic approach to carry on this task. The study by Schüssler et al. [11] combines GPS data as well as accelerometer data and the locations of public transport stops to derive stage start and end times and transportation modes. They report an accuracy of 92.5%. The study by Rasmussen et al. [12] implemented a three stage method which combines GIS rules and fuzzy logic. The method to identify rail trips was very efficient; however, there are two differences among our studies. First, they use a small dataset to test their method while our is bigger and follows an official statistics distribution. Finally, a dedicated GPS device was used by them during the data collection while in our case data was gathered through crowdsourcing using smartphones, so the resolution and the quality data are different [13]. The study by Biljecki et al. [14] used geographical data to calculate some indicators, such as the proximity of the trajectory to the network to perform the classification of single-mode segments. The accuracy of their method is 91.6%, however they do not report the accuracy by each transport mode.

Another alternative are the rule-based approaches where spatial operations are used for filtering out trip segments that do not correspond to the target transport mode to identify. They can achieve similar results compared to machine learning approaches [15]. The study by Stopher et al. [8] used the contextual information from the user (e.g., if the household has any bicycles), or from the transport network (e.g., most bus stops are located midway along blocks) to build a probability matrix to determine if the user is walking, biking or driving. Then, motorized vehicle trips are identified using street and public transport GIS layers using an elimination process looking for what happens before and after the trip segment analyzed (e.g., public transport trips usually are among walking trips). This study used a dedicated GPS device. Data logging was sporadic in buses or it was non-existent in trains. They classified a segment as a train segment when the starting and/or ending point was on a railway. They do not report the accuracy per transport mode however they report an overall success rate of about 95%. Bohte and Maat [9] also use a similar approach comparing the starting and ending points of a trip against the locations of train stations of the rail network however they apply more rules to these points under the assumption that a train trip take place between the two trips. They report a success rate 34% for train trip classification.

Gong et al. [5] developed a rule-based methodology to identify five transport modes (walk, subway, rail, car and bus). This study was carried in New York city, using a dedicated GPS device. They report the best success rate (35.7%) for train trip classification to the best of our knowledge. Therefore, we will perform a comparison with this method. Our studies have some similarities and differences. The study by Gong et al. was applied over a small dataset which contains data generated by 63 volunteers in one week while our was applied to a large crowdsourcing dataset; however, both dataset are made of multimodal trips. Our studies differ in the data collection method, they used a dedicated GPS device while we used cellphone devices. Regarding to the techniques, both use train station elements from a GIS layer for classifying transport mode of GPS segments likewise the previous studies mentioned, but only both use railway elements to determine alignment between GPS points and the rail network. Our technique exploits traffic network elements that belong to others transport network to improve the elimination process, i.e., those segments that cross elements, such as motorway junctions and train stations will be excluded.

III. METHODOLOGY

This paper presents a comparison among two rule-based methods that perform transport mode classification using GPS and GIS data.

Gong et al. [5] classifies four transport modes: bus, car, foot and train. However, we modified the output to focus only on train classification. This method uses five rules to identify walking segments, four rules to identify train segments, and finally four rules to classify bus and car segments. This method uses rail stations and rail links to establish whether the GPS points that belong to a trip segment follow the railway or not. The rules used to detect train trips in this study are listed as follows:

1) Distance from first point of trip segment to the nearest subway entrance <100 m or to the nearest commuter rail station <200 m; or distance from first point of trip segment to nearest subway or commuter rail link endpoint <200 m
2) Distance from last point of trip segment to nearest subway entrance <100 m or to the nearest commuter rail station <200 m; or distance from last point of trip segment to nearest subway link endpoint <200 m
3) Distance from each point of trip segment to nearest subway or commuter rail link <60 m
4) If possibly elevated train, then distance from each stopped point to nearest subway station <184 m or to the nearest commuter rail station <311m

In our work, the transport mode classification is performed based on the assumption that a train trip segment is a trip segment which along its path includes at least one train station, follows the railway and does not include other transport network elements, such as motorway junctions. We use a set of rules to filter out all those trips that do not comply with these characteristics.

First, we smoothed the segments using a speed-based filter to filtered out GPS point with high speed. We used 300 km/h as threshold due to the high-speed trains that uses part of the railway network. Second, we extracted Passing Points, such as train stations and railways, and Non-Passing Points, such as motorway junctions, from OSM. Then, Non-Passing elements that intercept with Passing elements were excluded (e.g., using a 100 meters buffer around railways, we excluded motorway junctions which were close to railways). Third, we performed spatial operations to filter out non train segments. The smoothed trip segments were intercepted with train station buffers to keep segments which cross train stations. The remaining segments were intercepted with motorway junctions, which are distant from railways, to filter out every possible car segment. Finally, a distance-based filter between the GPS points of the remaining segments and railways was applied to filter out segments that are not following the railway. The remaining trip segments correspond to the train trip segments.

We designed five experiments for testing our proposed method. In each experiment, we built a classifier following the rules of each method. We identified three parameters in common among the methods: the train station buffer radius, the amount of necessary GPS points, and the distance between GPS points and railways.

IV. Experiment Evaluation

A. Dataset

In this study, we used a labeled subset of 4,534 trip segments, which correspond to 178 devices from the dataset collected during the GPSWAL mobility survey, a crowdsourcing travel survey carried out between 2016 and 2017 by the L'Institut Wallon de l'évaluation, de la Prospective et de la Statistique (IWEPS), in Belgium. This dataset was described in our previous work [6]. Figure 1 shows a sample of GPSWAL segments.

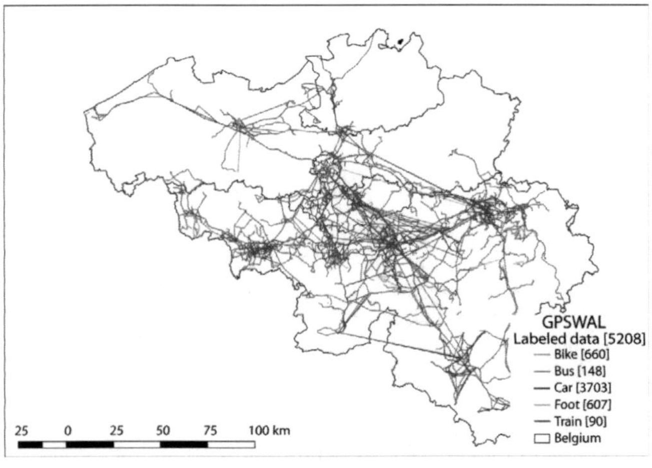

Figure 1. Subset of trip segments collected during the travel survey GPSWAL in Belgium.

The distribution of the trip segments by transport modes follows the modal split described by the Flemish Travel Behavior Survey OVG 5.1 [16] and is depicted in Table I.

TABLE I. Modal split of the trip segments

Transport mode	*OVG 5.1*	*Segments*
Bike	12.41%	660
Bus	2.78%	148
Car	69.62%	3703
Foot	11.41%	607
Train	1.69%	90

To implement both methods, we used four GIS data sources to extract transport network elements. The following layers were created and data transformation and cleaning processes were performed over them:

1) Bus stops from bus agencies: De Lijn, TEC Walloon and MIVB/STIB Brussels
2) Train stations from OpenStreetMap
3) Railways from OpenStreetMap
4) Motorway junctions from OpenStreetMap

B. Evaluation

Each experiment was repeated changing the threshold of the parameters to find the best classifier, i.e., every possible combination of the parameter values was evaluated. We computed a confusion matrix for every operating point to gather information about the classifier's performance. The following rates were calculated using the confusion matrix:

$$\mathrm{ACC} = \frac{(\mathrm{TP} + \mathrm{TN})}{(\mathrm{FP} + \mathrm{FN} + \mathrm{TP} + \mathrm{TN})} \tag{1}$$

$$\mathrm{PRE} = \frac{\mathrm{TP}}{(\mathrm{TP} + \mathrm{FP})} \tag{2}$$

$$\mathrm{TPR} = \frac{\mathrm{TP}}{(\mathrm{TP} + \mathrm{FN})} \tag{3}$$

$$\mathrm{FPR} = \frac{\mathrm{FP}}{(\mathrm{FP} + \mathrm{TN})} \tag{4}$$

where TP is the True Positive, FP is the False Positive, FN is False Negative, and TN is True Negative. Here, ACC and PRE are accuracy and precision, respectively. These rates are valid only for one single operating point. Shifting the decision threshold of the classifier, we plotted values of True Positive Rate (TPR) against False Positive Rate (FPR). The resulting curve is called a Receiver Operating Characteristic (ROC) curve [17]. ROC graphs are useful tools for selecting models for classification based on their performance with respect to the false positive and true positive rates [18]. Figure 2 shows those ROC for the first experiment.

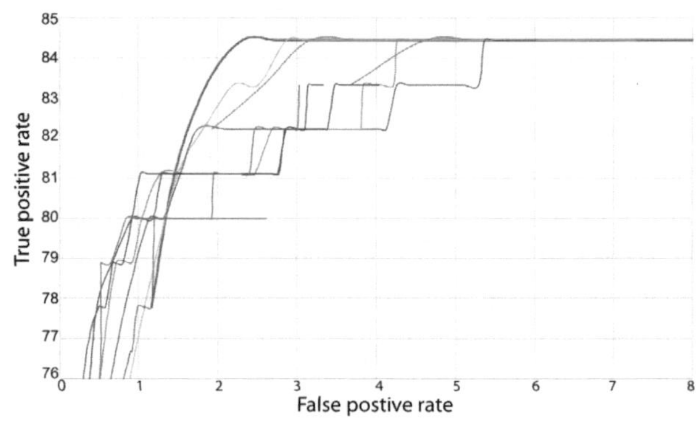

Figure 2. ROC curves for iteration of experiment 1: distance between GPS points and railways is 30 m, train station buffer is 100 m.

The optimal classifier in every experiment was selected using the ROC Area Under the Curve (ROC AUC). In general, a ROC AUC with the highest value identifies the classifier with the best performance. To identify the operating point that represents the combination of parameters with the best performance, we computed the Euclidean distance to the top-left corner of the ROC curve for each cutoff value. This is defined as follows:

$$d = \sqrt{(1 - \mathrm{TPR})^2 + \mathrm{TPR}^2} \quad (5)$$

where TPR is the true positive rate and FPR is the false positive rate. We selected the best operating point based on the lowest distances to the corner. Finally, using the ROC AUC and the Euclidean distance metrics, we perform the comparison between the five classifiers.

V. EXPERIMENTS

Before performing the experiments, we determined the threshold of each parameter.

In the literature, spatial buffer size has been used in other studies to analyze public transport facilities [19], transport classification [5][14] or public transport flow analysis [20]. This parameter usually ranges from 20 to 1000 meters. Gong et al. [5] fixed the radius value in 200 m. Figure 3 shows how many train segments cross the train stations when the buffer radius increases. In our method, it was fixed in 100 m, 93.33% of the train segments cross at a distance less than or equal to this. For the benchmarking, we performed the experiments using these two values to set the buffer radius.

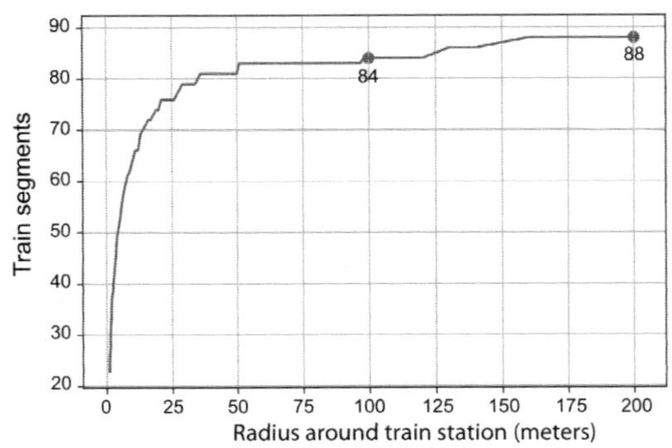

Figure 3. Number of train segments crossing around train stations.

Gong et al. [5] used the total number of GPS-point' segment for classifying, i.e., 100% of GPS points. We wondered which is the minimum amount of GPS points from a train trip segment to classify it as such. We changed this parameter in steps of 5% in each iteration, ranging from 5% to 100%.

The distance between GPS points and railways was fixed to 60 meters in the study by Gong et al. [5]. We analyzed the labeled train segments to determine the appropriated range of values to change the threshold of this parameter. We found that GPS points from train segments were in average 18.19 meters far from rail ways, while the maximum distance was 217.56 meters. Hence, the possible values of this parameter are in a range between 15 and 220 meter, we changed this parameter in steps of 5 meters in each iteration.

The first experiment consisted in applying our method [6] to the labeled dataset. The results have shown that there are misclassified train segments; this occurred when a segment crossed more than one train station, but it does not use railways. Another issue not handled by this version was the non-classification of train segments when they cross only one train station. We improved our method incorporating a stage to filter further non-train segments using the amount of GPS points needed per segment as well as the distance between those points and the rail ways. We compared the performance of both versions computing a confusion matrix in each case. The values of the confusion matrices are shown in Figure 4.

(a) Version I (b) Version II

Figure 4. Confusion matrix of the proposed method.

We evaluated our improved method to determine which are the best parameter values to built the classifier. The parameter values, performance rates, and metrics calculated for the best classifier of this experiment are shown in Table II.

The second experiment consisted in the implementation of the method by Gong et al. [5]. We configured the parameters according to the values established in their method. Figure 5a shows the confusion matrix computed after applying this method on the labeled dataset. Figure 5 shows the confusion matrix of the classifier modified to focus only on train classification. We evaluated the method to determine which are the best parameter values to built the best classifier. The confusion matrix for the best operation point is shown in Figure 6a.

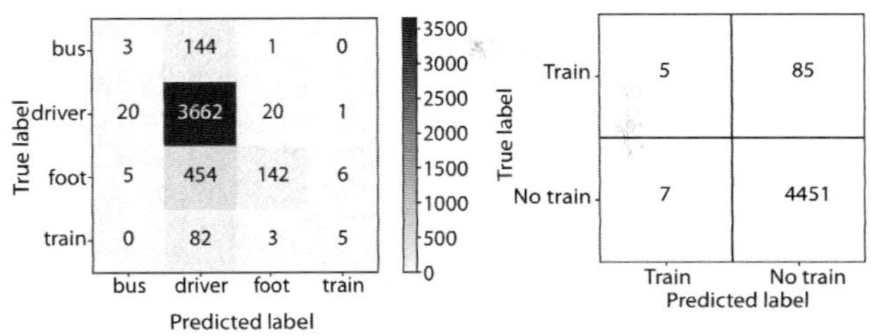

(a) Transport mode classification. (b) Train classification.

Figure 5. Confusion matrix of the Gong et al. method applied to the dataset.

We performed three additional experiments combining the rules used by Gong et al. [5] for detecting train trips. Experiment three consisted in combining rules one and three, so this experiment analyze the starting point and how far the GPS points which belong to a segment are from the railways. Experiment four combines rules two and three. In this case, ending points and how far the GPS points which belong to a segment are analyzed. The last experiment uses rules one or two combined with rule three. Hence, segments that start or end in a train station are analyzed in conjunction with how far their GPS points are from the railways.

The confusion matrices at the best operating point for each experiment performed with Gong et al. [5] method are shown in Figure 6. The parameter values, performance rates, and metrics calculated for the best classifiers are shown in Table II.

TABLE II. PARAMETER VALUES, RATES, AND METRICS FROM THE BEST CLASSIFIER OF EACH EXPERIMENT

Experiment	*ROC AUC*	*Euclidean distance*	*Train station buffer*	*Min GPS points (%)*	*Min rail distance*	*FPR*	*TPR*	*Accuracy*	*Precision*
1	0.0685	0.16	100	30	30	0.02	0.84	97.43	42.46
2	0.0004	0.87	200	20	15	0.01	0.13	97.85	37.50
3	0.0079	0.72	200	25	25	0.01	0.25	97.76	40.32
4	0.0201	0.47	200	25	20	0.01	0.53	97.96	48.49
5	0.0423	0.32	200	25	25	0.02	0.68	97.65	43.89

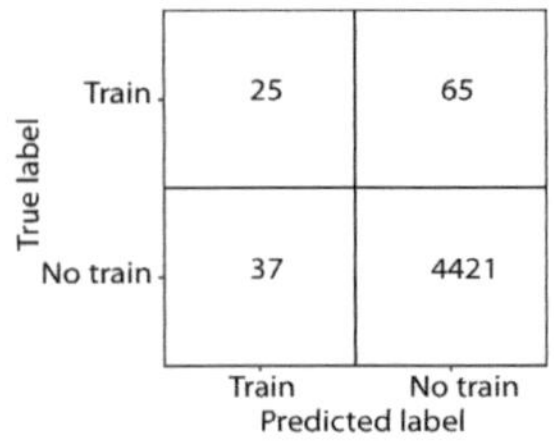

(a) Experiment I

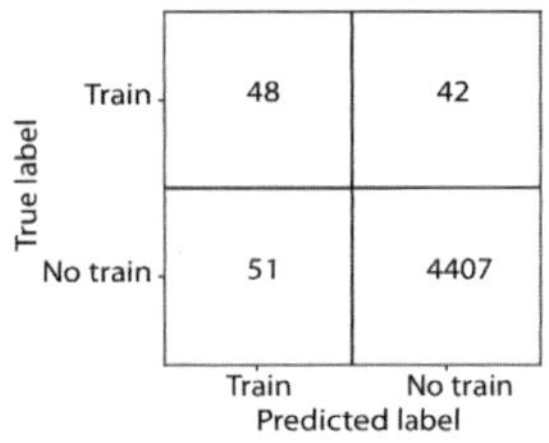

(b) Experiment II

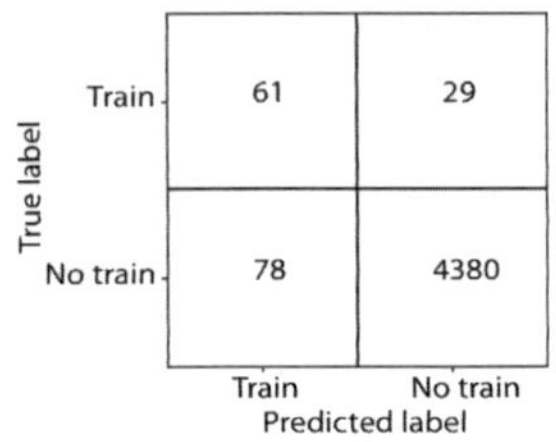

(c) Experiment III

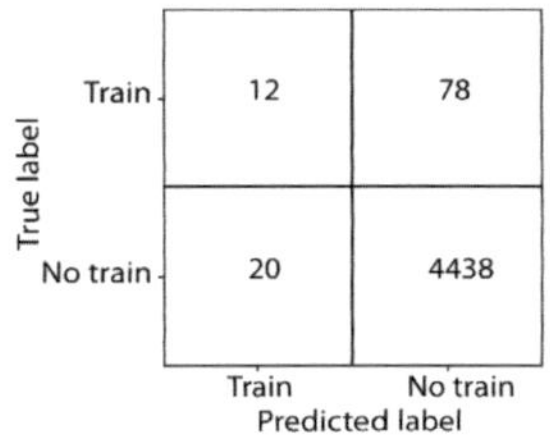

(d) Experiment IV

Figure 6. Confusion matrix of the best operation point for each experiment with Gong et al. method.

VI. RESULTS AND DISCUSSION

This section presents the results of the performed comparisons. We have evaluated two methods through five experiments, one corresponds to our method which uses Passing and Non-Passing Points and four correspond to Gong et al. [5] method which uses only Passing Points. The dataset has an unbalanced set of classes, e.g., the target class represents only 1.69% of the data.

Before benchmarking, we performed the value choice of the three parameters in common between the methods: the train station buffer radius, the amount of necessary GPS points, and the distance between GPS points and railways. In each experiment, we selected the classifiers that maximize the relation between the true positive rate and the false positive rate instead of only considering the accuracy or precision. Figure 7 shows the benchmarking using the ROC AUC as metric. The parameter values, computed rates and metrics of each ROC curves are showed in Table II.

Results showed that the ROC AUC in experiment two had the lowest values. After analyzing this scenario, we realized that rules of the method by Gong et al. [5] were too restrictive for the used railway network and dataset quality [21]. Because of this, we performed three other experiments to test its behavior with less restrictive rules. This classifier has an accuracy of 97.85% while its true positive rate is 0.13, the lowest among the experiments. The results of experiment three showed us an improvement of the method by Gong et al. [5] in the identification of positive cases when only rules one

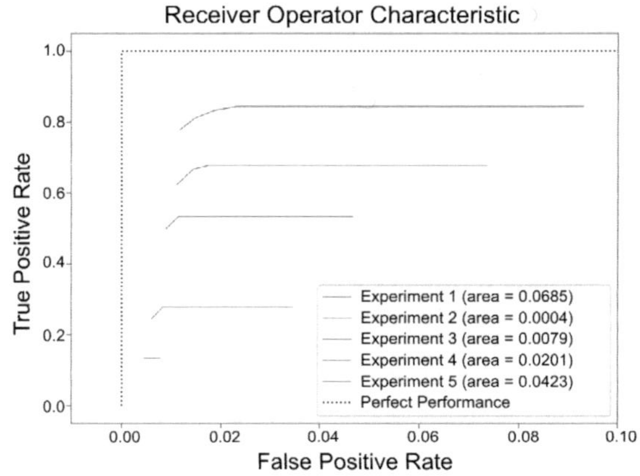

Figure 7. Benchmarking for the five experiment using the ROC AUC metric

and three are combined. In comparison with experiment two, we observed that in this experiment the true positive rate and precision are better, however the accuracy is lower. The results of experiment four showed a good performance, i.e., when only segments and end train stations are used. This experiment had the highest rate values when we applied the method by Gong et al. [5] to the dataset. Nevertheless, the ROC AUC value does not represent the best classifier with this method. Experiment five used a combination between rule number one or two with rule number three used. In this case, the results showed the best ROC AUC value using the method by Gong et al. [5] besides having the best true positive rate among experiments with this method. However, the number of false positive cases increased.

When comparing the results obtained from the benchmarking between the method by Gonzalez and the proposed method, we determined that our classifier presents a better performance in relation with the true positive rate. For instance, we classified correctly 84 trips out of every 100 train trips, while the method by Gong et al. [5] only identified 68 trips. However, both methods misclassified 2 train trips in every 100 trips.

VII. CONCLUSION AND FUTURE WORK

In this paper, we reported a comparison performed among location based methods which aim to classify transport mode. We have also presented the design, execution and results of the experiments performed with each method. Additionally, the influence of the parameters of the tested algorithms has been experimentally studied with the purpose of performing a fair comparison. Finally, we have shown the results of the best classifier according to the ROC curves.

The objective of this paper was to perform a comparison between a methodology that only uses Passing Point elements, and a methodology which uses both Passing and Non-Passing

Points, applying both on a dataset where the transport-mode classes are unbalanced. Previous works in transport mode classification only report successful rate but the results showed that in addition to calculate the accuracy and precision of a method, it is also necessary to calculate the true positive and false positive rates to evaluate the classifier performance. According to the ROC graph, the proposed method has the greatest ROC AUC value, i.e., it has a better performance in comparison with the method by Gong et al. [5]. The true positive rate of the proposed methodology is 84% in comparison with 64% obtained by the best classifier using the method by Gong et al. [5]. For future work, we plan to apply the proposed method to classify other transport modes (e.g., bus) or combining it with other kind of techniques. We also plan to explore transport classification with unbalanced classes using crowdsourcing data.

ACKNOWLEDGMENT

The authors are grateful to IWEPS for research access to data of the GPSWAL mobility survey. This work is funded by the Flanders Agency for Innovation and Entrepreneurship through the FLAMENCO project (FLAnders Mobile ENacted Citizen Observatories). This work is supported by the Escuela Superior Politécnica del Litoral (ESPOL) under the Ph.D. studies 2016 program.

REFERENCES

[1] "GPSWAL: The new IWEPS smartphone mobility survey," URL: https://www.iweps.be/projet/gpswal [accessed: 2018-11-04].

[2] M. Rinne, M. Bagheri, T. Tolvanen, and J. Hollmén, "Automatic recognition of public transport trips from mobile device sensor data and transport infrastructure information," in Personal Analytics and Privacy. An Individual and Collective Perspective, R. Guidotti, A. Monreale, D. Pedreschi, and S. Abiteboul, Eds. Cham: Springer International Publishing, 2017, pp. 76–97.

[3] "Antwerp management school," TransMob project URL: https://www.antwerpmanagementschool.be/en/research/expertise-center-smart-mobility/project/transmob [accessed: 2018-11-04].

[4] "De lijn," URL: https://www.delijn.be/nl/vervoerbewijzen/ticket-op-gsm [accessed: 2018-11-04].

[5] H. Gong, C. Chen, E. Bialostozky, and C. T. Lawson, "A gps/gis method for travel mode detection in new york city," Computers, Environment and Urban Systems, vol. 36, no. 2, 2012, pp. 131 – 139, Special Issue: Geoinformatics 2010", ISSN: 0198-9715.

[6] J. Rodriguez-Echeverría, S. Gautama, and D. Ochoa, "A methodology for train trip identification in mobility campaigns based on smartphones," in Proceedings of the 2017 IEEE First Summer School on Smart Cities (S3C) August 6–11, 2017, Natal, Brazil. IEEE, Aug 2017, pp. 141–144.

[7] H. L. Filip Biljecki and P. van Oosterom, "Transportation mode-based segmentation and classification of movement trajectories," International Journal of Geographical Information Science, vol. 27, no. 2, 2013, pp. 385–407.

[8] P. Stopher, C. FitzGerald, and J. Zhang, "Search for a global positioning system device to measure person travel," Transportation Research Part C: Emerging Technologies, vol. 16, no. 3, 2008, pp. 350 – 369, Emerging Commercial Technologies, ISSN: 0968-090X.

[9] W. Bohte and K. Maat, "Deriving and validating trip purposes and travel modes for multi-day gps-based travel surveys: A large-scale application in the netherlands," Transportation Research Part C: Emerging Technologies, vol. 17, no. 3, 2009, pp. 285 – 297, ISSN: 0968-090X.

[10] P. Evangelista, "The unbalanced classification problem: detecting breaches in security," Ph.D. dissertation, Rensselaer Polytechnic Institute, Troy, New York, Nov. 2006, URL: https://www.cs.rpi.edu/ szymansk/theses/evangelista.phd.06.pdf [accessed: 2018-11-04].

[11] N. Schüssler, L. Montini, and C. Dobler, "Improving post-processing routines for GPS observations using prompted-recall data," [Working paper Transport and Spatial Planning], vol. 724, 2011.

[12] T. K. Rasmussen, J. B. Ingvardson, K. Halldórsdóttir, and O. A. Nielsen, "Improved methods to deduct trip legs and mode from travel surveys using wearable gps devices: A case study from the greater copenhagen area," Computers, Environment and Urban Systems, vol. 54, 2015, pp. 301 – 313, ISSN: 0198-9715.

[13] L. Montini, S. Prost, J. Schrammel, N. Rieser-Schüssler, and K. W. Axhausen, "Comparison of travel diaries generated from smartphone data and dedicated gps devices," Transportation Research Procedia, vol. 11, 2015, pp. 227 – 241, Transport Survey Methods: Embracing Behavioural and Technological Changes Selected contributions from the 10th International Conference on Transport Survey Methods 16-21 November 2014, Leura, Australia,ISSN: 2352-1465.

[14] F. Biljecki, H. Ledoux, and P. Van Oosterom, "Transportation mode-based segmentation and classification of movement trajectories," International Journal of Geographical Information Science, vol. 27, no. 2, 2013, pp. 385–407, Special Issue: Geoinformatics 2010, ISSN: 1362-3087.

[15] O. Uzuner, X. Zhang, and T. Sibanda, "Machine learning and rule-based approaches to assertion classification," Journal of the American Medical Informatics Association, vol. 16, no. 1, 2009, pp. 109–115.

[16] Department of Mobility and Public Works, "Flemish Travel Behavior Survey," 2015, URL: http://www.mobielvlaanderen.be/pdf/ovg51/samenvatting.pdf [accessed: 2018-11-04].

[17] A. P. Bradley, "The use of the area under the roc curve in the evaluation of machine learning algorithms," Pattern Recognition, vol. 30, no. 7, 1997, pp. 1145 – 1159, Special Issue: Geoinformatics 2010", ISSN: 0031-3203.

[18] Sebastian Raschka, Python Machine Learning. Packt Publishing Limited, 2015.

[19] World business council for sustainable development, "SMP2.0 Sustainable Mobility Indicators – 2nd Edition," URL: https://www.wbcsd.org/Projects/SiMPlify/Resources/SMP2.0-Sustainable-Mobility-Indicators-2nd-Edition [accessed: 2018-05-23].

[20] E. Steiger, T. Ellersiek, and A. Zipf, "Explorative public transport flow analysis from uncertain social media data," in Proceedings of the 3rd ACM SIGSPATIAL International Workshop on Crowdsourced and Volunteered Geographic Information, ser. GeoCrowd '14. New York, NY, USA: ACM, 2014, pp. 1–7.

[21] A. J. Lopez, I. Semanjski, S. Gautama, and D. Ochoa, "Assessment of Smartphone Positioning Data Quality in the Scope of Citizen Science Contributions," Mobile Information Systems, vol. 2017, jun 2017, pp. 1–11, ISSN: 1875905X.

Cyber-threats Analytics for Detection of GNSS Spoofing

Silvio Semanjski*, **
* Department of Communication, Information, Systems & Sensors
** Royal Military Academy
Brussels, Belgium
e-mail: silvio.semanjski@rma.ac.be

Ivana Semanjski*, **
* Department of Industrial Systems Engineering and Product Design, Ghent University,
Ghent, Belgium
** Industrial Systems Engineering (ISyE), Flanders Make
Ghent, Belgium
e-mail: ivana.semanjski@ugent.be

Wim De Wilde, **
** Septentrio N.V.
Leuven, Belgium
e-mail: wim.dewilde@septentrio.com

Alain Muls*, **
* Department of Communication, Information, Systems & Sensors
** Royal Military Academy
Brussels, Belgium
e-mail: alain.muls@rma.ac.be

Abstract—**Spoofing of the Global Navigation Satellite System (GNSS) open service (unencrypted) signal is of continuous interest to professionals and non-professional users. The main reason for this is the risk of unaware use of manipulated GNSS data, which becomes extremely relevant in all Safety-of-Life (SOL) Position-Navigation-Timing (PNT) applications, such as aircraft navigation or high precision time synchronization of traffic control systems. In this paper, we aim to develop an approach to detect spoofing of the GNSS signal based on the machine learning technique. The developed approach shows high potential in detecting the spoofed signal in the sequence of the non-spoofed GNSS signals by achieving the success rate of 96%.**

Keywords-Global Navigation Satellite System; Spoofing; Support Vector Machines; Safety-of-Life; Position-Navigation-Timing; GPS; GNSS; PNT; SVM; SOL

I. INTRODUCTION

Spoofing of the GNSS open service (unencrypted) signal is of continuous interest to both GNSS industry and users [1] due to risk of unaware use of manipulated GNSS data in Safety-of-Life PNT applications, such as aircraft navigation or high precision time synchronization of traffic control systems. With advances in digital signal processing and availability of the electronic components required to build transmit capable Software Defined Radio (SDR) type of spoofers, the threat of GNSS signal spoofing proliferates and requires effort to implement spoofing detection at the GNSS receiver level.

The GNSS measurements performed by the user's receiver contains a number of observables whose monitoring and cross-correlation can be used to detect the GNSS spoofing, latest at the stage of generating Position-Velocity-Time (PVT) solution within the receiver. One of the known spoofing techniques, the Time Synchronization Attack (TSA) [2] is based on the manipulation of GNSS receiver clock offset by exploiting clock drift (time derivative of the clock offset) estimates, affecting pseudorange measurements and consequentially PVT solution.

In this paper, we examine the potential to detect the GNSS signal spoofing by applying the machine learning approach, namely the Support Vector Machines (SVM) classification. Among several GNSS spoofing detection methods being discussed in details in [1], detection by observing time manipulation or discrepancies within the GNSS receiver proves to be a challenge [2], and its implementation requires subtle approach when compared to others (such as signal angle-of-arrival, strength, doppler shift as the relative speed between satellite/spoofer and receiver, signal-to-noise ratio, and signal polarization [3]). The approach to monitor the clock bias by employing SVM classification of multiple variables used in different processing stages within the GNSS receiver has been chosen due to dynamic characteristics of the target receivers (moving aircraft relative to the spoofer), and computational effectiveness of the algorithm expressed as a scalable runtime in regard to the number of input samples. The literature suggests that in the latter case, the SVM classification emerges as an concurrent choice [4].

The paper is composed as follows: Section 2 gives a detail insight into the data set and the method description. This is followed with the results and the discussion sections. Section 5 presents the conclusion remarks.

II. DATA AND METHOD

A. Dataset description

Spoofing dataset (with matched power attack) has been generated with a modified Spirent GNSS signal and constellation simulator connected to a Wave Field Synthesis (WFS) anechoic chamber at the Fraunhofer FORTE facility [5][6]. The six channels represent the "authentic" GNSS signal. In parallel, the six other channels have exactly the same parameters, including the simulated spoofing attack. The spoofer only gets enabled for three minutes in the test scenario, so dataset includes non-spoofed and spoofed epochs. In our spoofing scenario, same used in [3], the spoofing attack hijacked the Pulse-Per-Second (PPS) output of the receiver because of the programmed clock divergence. Spoofing attack generated was an intermediate timing attack with 5 ns/s rate of time pulling.

The GNSS open services in general, such as Global Positioning System (GPS), have their navigation message modulated together with Coarse/Acquisition (C/A) code onto a carrier at the L1 frequency. The navigation message together with C/A ranging code provides users with the necessary information to generate the PVT solution. The navigation message data includes: the ephemeris parameters, required to compute the satellite coordinates, the timing parameters and clock corrections, used to compute satellite clock offset, the service parameters with satellite health information, ionospheric parameters model required to compensate for ionospheric propagation delay, and the almanac, allowing the computation complete satellite constellation required to perform rough initial localisation of the user's receiver during signal acquisition phase.

GNSS receiver decodes the navigation messages and together with use of C/A ranging codes provide observables, of which the following parameters are used in our model (Table I.).

TABLE I. OBSERVABLES OUTPUT OF THE BASEBAND PROCESSING STAGE OF GNSS RECEIVER

Parameter	Unit	Description
Receiver clock drift	ppm	Receiver clock drift relative to system time (relative frequency error)
Receiver clock bias	msec	Receiver clock bias relative to system time
Code variance	cm^2	Estimated code tracking noise variance
Carrier variance	$mcycle^2$	Estimated carrier tracking noise variance
C/N_0	dB-Hz	Carrier-to-noise density ratio per channel
PR	m	Pseudorange user-to-satellite
L	cycles	Full carrier phase

Next to the variables present in Table I., we manually labelled the records that represent spoofed signal. Hence, we created an additional variable called *Class* that indicates weather the exact record belongs to the spoofed period or not. This variable will be used as the dependent categorical variable in our classification problem.

B. Support vector machines classification

Support Vector Machines (SVM) are supervised machine learning algorithms which can be used both for classification [7][8] or regression analysis [9][10]. In further description, we will focus on the SVM classification analysis as the GNSS spoofing problem, having the categorical dependent variable with two possible values (signal spoofed or not-spoofed), corresponds to the classification problem.

The SVM classification method relies on the concept of decision hyperplanes that define decision boundaries (separate between a set of objects having different class memberships). However, in practical applications, this task is not very simple and use of structures more complex than linear ones is needed to correctly classify the objects. For this purpose different mathematical functions, also called kernels, can be used in order to map objects in the n dimensional space [11][12]. Such mapped objects aim to have structures that are easier to separate, based on the class membership, than the original set of objects for which the mapping was not preformed. To do so, we firstly divide our dataset in two parts: the training (Z_1) and the test dataset (Z_2). This division is made based on the 75%-25% principle, randomly sorting the 75% of data into the training set and 25% into the test set. As we wanted to obtain scalable runtime in regard to the number of input samples we selected the C-SVM classification type for our problem. The literature suggests that in such cases the C-SVM is a better option over, for example, nu-SVM classification [4]. For the applied C-SVM type, the minimization error function is defined as:

$$\frac{1}{2}w^T w + C\sum_{i=1}^{N} \xi_i \quad (1)$$

subject to the constraints:

$$y_i(w^T\,\phi(x_i) + b) \geq 1 - \xi_i \quad (2)$$

$$\xi_i \geq 0 \quad (3)$$

where:

$i = 1, \ldots, N$,

w - the vector of coefficients;

C - the capacity constant;

b – constant;

ξ_i - parameters for handling non-separable data (inputs).

The index i labels the N training cases ($y \in \pm 1$ represents the class labels and x_i represents the independent variables). The ϕ stands for kernel function, which in our case is the Radial Basis Function (RBF) that transforms input to the feature space:

$$K(X_i, X_j) = \phi(X_i)\cdot\phi(X_j) = \exp\left(-\gamma\,|X_i - X_j|^2\right) \quad (4)$$

To map the multiclass problem into binary classification problem, we applied one-against-all approach. However, the values of capacity constants C (1) and γ (4) are important to keep the training error small and in order to generalize well [13]. Since it is not possible to know beforehand the best values of these constrains for a given problem, we applied the incremental grid-search on C, in range from 1 to 10, with the step equal to 1, and γ, in range from 0 to 0.5, with the step equal to 0.01. The values that achieved the best average 10-fold cross-validation accuracy were chosen for use on the test data. These values were 10 for C and 0.125 for γ.

For the v-fold cross-validation, the total number of cases was divided into v, where $v = 10$, sub samples $Z_1, Z_2, \ldots, Z_v$ of equal sizes ($N_1, N_2, \ldots, N_v$). The v-fold cross-validation estimate is the proportion of cases in the subsample Z that are misclassified by the classifier constructed from the subsample $Z - Z_v$. This estimate is calculated in the following way:

$$R\left(d^{(v)}\right) = \frac{1}{N_v}\sum_{(x_n, j_n)\in Z_v} X(d^{(v)}(x_n) \neq j_n) \quad (5)$$

where $d^{(v)}(x)$ is the classifier calculated from the sub sample $Z - Z_v$ and X is the indicator function for which is valid:

$X = 1$, if the statement $X\left(d^{(v)}\right) \neq j_n)$ is true

$X = 0$, if the statement $X\left(d^{(v)}\right) \neq j_n)$ is false.

The test sample estimate is the proportion of cases in the test dataset that are misclassified by the classifier constructed from the learning dataset. This estimate is computed in the following way:

$$R(d) = \frac{1}{N_2} \sum_{(x_n, j_n) \in Z_2} X(d(x_n) \neq j_n) \quad (6)$$

III. RESULTS

The overall success rate of the proposed approach was 96.4%, whereas the cross-validation error was slightly higher (96.8%). In total, 57 support vectors were used, of which 28 belonged among the "authentic" GNSS observations and 29 among the spoofed GNSS signal observations. In Table II. the overall summary of the obtained results is shown.

TABLE II. MODEL SUMMARY

	Value
Number of independents	8
SVM type	Classification type 1
Kernel type	Radial Basis Function
Number of SVs	57 (52 bounded)
Number of SVs (authentic GNSS signal)	28
Number of SVs (spoofed GNSS signal)	29
Cross -validation accuracy	96.765 %
Class accuracy (training dataset)	96.765 %
Class accuracy (test dataset)	95.359 %
Class accuracy (overall)	96.414 %

Considering the confusion matrix shown in TABLE III., none of the authentic GNSS signal records was confused to be the spoofed record. However, 3.6% of the records were misclassified as the authentic GNSS signal record, whereas they belonged among the spoofed signal records.

TABLE III. CONFUSION MATRIX

	Authentic GNSS signal	Spoofed GNSS signal
Authentic GNSS signal	88.34%	0.00%
Spoofed GNSS signal	3.64%	8.02%

The correlation matrix (Table IV.) shows the correlations among all the variables used in our model. Those marked with blue colour are significant at $p < 0.05$. One can see that this includes all the variables except the *Code variance*, for which the correlation with the *Class* indication is not statistically significant at $p < 0.05000$. The highest correlation is noted for the *Carrier variance*, indicating that 56.25% of the variations among the *Class* variable can explained by the *Carrier variance*. However, among the predictor variables, the highest correlation (0.99) is noted among the *Receiver clock bias* and *Receiver clock drift*.

Fig. 1 shows the *Receiver clock drift* per each second (on the *x* axis). One can clearly notice the indication of the spoofing period starting around 130 seconds into the test, lasting a bit less than 3 min (recording being started 50 seconds into the test). Fig. 2 shows the same period per each of the six channels (each channel corresponding to the satellite tracked). The initial jump in the *Carrier-to-Noise density ratio* clearly marks the beginning of the spoofing period, whereas the jump gets smoother after the initial jump in the value.

TABLE IV. CORRELATIONS TABLE

	Code variance [cm²]	Carrier variance [mcycle²]	C/N₀ [dB-Hz]	PR [m]	L [cycles]	Receiver clock bias [ms]	Receiver clock drift [ppm]	Class
Code variance [cm²]	1.000	0.322	-0.309	0.215	0.215	0.209	-0.066	0.049
Carrier variance [mcycle²]	0.322	1.000	0.278	0.406	0.406	0.405	0.359	0.750
C/N₀ [dB-Hz]	-0.309	0.278	1.000	-0.134	-0.134	-0.125	0.427	0.537
PR [m]	0.215	0.406	-0.134	1.000	1.000	0.999	0.259	0.376
L [cycles]	0.215	0.406	-0.134	1.000	1.000	0.999	0.259	0.376
Receiver clock bias [ms]	0.209	0.405	-0.125	0.999	0.999	1.000	0.257	0.375
Receiver clock drift [ppm]	-0.066	0.359	0.427	0.259	0.259	0.257	1.000	0.556
Class	0.049	0.750	0.537	0.376	0.376	0.375	0.556	1.000

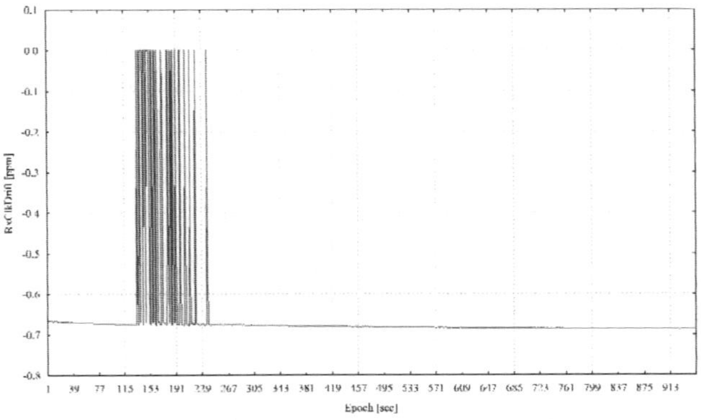

Figure 1. Receiver clock drift.

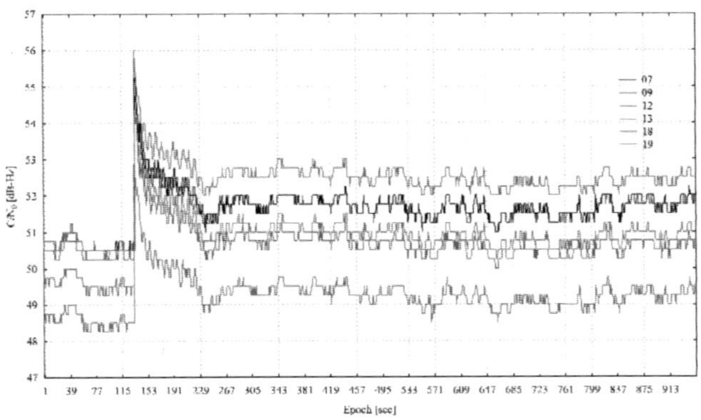

Figure 2. Carrier-to-Noise density ratio of the satellites used.

IV. Discussion

In our spoofing scenario, the spoofing attack hijacked the Pulse-Per-Second output of the receiver through the programmed clock divergence. Spoofing attack generated was an intermediate timing attack with 5 ns/s rate of time pulling. The results indicate that the proposed approach can be successfully used to detect GNSS spoofing that corresponds to the above-described scenario. Due to risk of unaware use of manipulated GNSS data, this is highly relevant for all GNSS applications. However, it becomes particularly relevant when it comes to Safety-of-Life PNT applications, such as aircraft navigation, or high precision time synchronization of traffic control systems. The former proves as a challenge due to GNSS receiver being a moving target, as opposed to the latter where a target is a fixed GNSS timing receiver.

The confusion matrix indicates that the proposed machine learning based approach was able to correctly detect weather the signal spoofed or the authentic one in 96.4% of the cases. However, the remaining 3.6% of the cases were confusions made between spoofed GNSS signal records that were misclassified as the authentic ones. Considering the Safety-of-Life applications, this is less preferred scenario (over relaxed one) compared to the possibility to misclassify authentic signal as the spoofed one (over causes one). Hence, there is still a room to improve the proposed approach.

The correlation matrix indicates the statistically relevant correlation among the variables selected for our model (significant at $p < 0.05$). One can also notice very high correlation among *Receiver clock bias*, *Pseudorange*, and *Phase cycle* variables. Such a high correlation indicates that sub selection of variables would be able to explain the variation between the indication of the spoofed and the authentic GNSS signal in an equally efficient manner. Hence, our future research will focus on simplification of the model in terms of the possibility to exclude some of the considered predictor variables and their replacement with potential predictors that could affect the confusion. Although the achieved success rate is quite high, for Safety-of-Life applications, we would aim look for a model, even with the similar success rate (if not possible to achieve the highest success rate), that would result in an over causes scenario, rather than the over relaxed one.

V. Conclusion and Future Work

Our research included synthetically generated GNNS signal over six channels (for six satellites) with simulation of the spoofing attack. By indicating the spoofing attack among the correct records (ones corresponding to the authentic signal), we have created a dataset that could be used for learning to recognise the spoofing attack in the machine learning approach. For the following, we have adopted the support vector machines-based approach. The achieved results show a high success rate in detecting whether the signal was spoofed or not (96.4%). However, the confusion matrix indicates that there is a space for the improvements in order to be able to use the suggested approach in the Safety-of-Life applications, such as aircraft navigation high precision time synchronization of traffic control systems. The correlation matrix also indicates that there is a possibility to improve the suggested approach, without increasing the complexity of the problem. This can be done by replacing the part of the predictor variables (those with the high correlation among them) with ones that could explain the part of the variation, among the spoofed or not-spoofed signal indication, which is not explained by the variables already present in the model.

Acknowledgment

The authors wish to thank Septentrio N.V. for supporting this work by providing datasets for the analyses.

References

[1] D. Schmidt, K. Radke, S. Camtepe, E. Foo, and M. Ren, "A Survey and Analysis of the GNSS Spoofing Threat and Countermeasures," ACM Comput. Surv., 2016.

[2] N. O. Tippenhauer, C. Pöpper, K. B. Rasmussen, and S. Capkun, "On the requirements for successful GPS spoofing attacks," in Proceedings of the 18th ACM conference on Computer and communications security - CCS '11, 2011.

[3] W. De Wilde et al., "Authentication by Polarization: A Powerful Anti-Spoofing Method," in Proceedings of the 31st International Technical Meeting of the Satellite Division of the Institute of Navigation (ION GNSS+ 2018), 2018, pp. 3643–3658.

[4] C.-C. Chang and C.-J. Lin, "Training v -Support Vector

Classifiers: Theory and Algorithms," Neural Comput., vol. 13, no. 9, pp. 2119–2147, 2001.

[5] A. Rügamer, G. Del Galdo, J. Mahr, G. Rohmer, G. Siegert, and M. Landmann, "Testing using Wave-Field Synthesis," in Proceedings of the 26th International Technical Meeting of The Satellite Division of the Institute of Navigation (ION GNSS+ 2013), 2013, pp. 1931–1943.

[6] C. Schirmer et al., "3D wave-field synthesis for testing of radio devices," in 8th European Conference on Antennas and Propagation, EuCAP 2014, 2014, pp. 3394–3398.

[7] S. Joo, C. Oh, E. Jeong, and G. Lee, "Categorizing bicycling environments using GPS-based public bicycle speed data," Transp. Res. Part C Emerg. Technol., vol. 56, pp. 239–250, Jul. 2015.

[8] I. Semanjski and S. Gautama, "Crowdsourcing mobility insights – Reflection of attitude based segments on high resolution mobility behaviour data," Transp. Res. Part C Emerg. Technol., vol. 71, 2016.

[9] E. I. Vlahogianni, "Optimization of traffic forecasting: Intelligent surrogate modeling," Transp. Res. Part C Emerg. Technol., vol. 55, pp. 14–23, Jun. 2015.

[10] J. Wang and Q. Shi, "Short-term traffic speed forecasting hybrid model based on Chaos – Wavelet Analysis-Support Vector Machine theory," Transp. Res. Part C, vol. 27, pp. 219–232, 2013.

[11] B. Schlkopf and A. J. Smola, Learning with Kernels: Support Vector Machines, Regularization, Optimization, and Beyond (Adaptive Computation and Machine Learning). Cambridge: The MIT Press, 2001.

[12] L. H. Hamel, Knowledge Discovery with Support Vector Machines. Hoboken: Wiley-Interscience, 2011.

[13] D. Anguita and L. Oneto, "In – sample Model Selection for Support Vector Machines," in The 2011 International Joint Conference on Neural Networks, 2011.

Comparing Route Deviation Bus Operation with Respect to Dial-a-Ride Service for a Low-Demand Residential Area

Antonio Pratelli, Marino Lupi, Alessandro Farina, Chiara Pratelli
D.I.C.I. Department of Civil and Industrial Engineering
College of Engineering, University of Pisa
56122 Pisa, Italy
e-mail: antonio.pratelli@ing.unipi.it, marino.lupi@unipi.it, alessandro.farina1@gmail.com, chiara.pratelli1@gmail.com

Abstract— **Flexible transit services, such as Route Deviation Bus, or RDB, match the features of fixed-haul traditional transit and demand-responsive service. They have been proven to be efficient on the grounds of both cost and performance in many low-density residential areas. This paper deals with a special form of advanced public transport operations, which is known by different names, such as route deviation line, point deviation bus line, corridor deviation line and checkpoint dial-a-ride. We present the results of a design analysis performed on a real network using a model proposed for the Route Deviation Bus problem, which is based on mixed integer linear programming. The study network is located in Campi Bisenzio, a small town in the surroundings of Florence (Italy). This urban area is characterized by a low level of the transit demand for the major part of the day. Two decades ago, the traditional line-haul system has been replaced with a mixed advance request and immediate request Dial-a-Ride system. In this paper, first, the RDB problem is briefly summarized. Second, the model is applied to the real case of Campi Bisenzio and the results drawn from the model application are shown in comparison with the existing on-demand service management as a mixed operations Dial-a-Ride system. We simulated the RDB service operating in the actual scenario and then we compared the two different operations modes, calculating their respective values in a set of performance indexes. In such a study case, the existing mixed Dial-a-Ride operations mode results are better than the switching to a route deviation bus service. However, this result seems to be highly influenced by the particular frame of the underlying street network. Nevertheless, we can view the obtained results as a meaningful trial performed on a real scale that highlights boundaries and better defines the application domain of the more frequently applied new RDB service operations for the low transit demand management. Finally, our results show that a route deviation strategy is more suitable to accommodate rejected requests, that is, those for which it is impossible to schedule the call, than any Dial-a-Ride strategy.**

Keywords - Flexible route design and planning; Route Deviation Bus operations; Dial-a-Ride transit systems; Integer programming.

I. INTRODUCTION

There are some transport systems that serve a low demand in time and/or in space. In such cases, the optimal service strategy must be suited in a way as to follow the demand.

Many types of transport systems operate under the so-called "demand responsive" manner. Among them, there is the route deviation system, also called Route Deviation Bus, or RDB, line. The RDB system consists of a number of tracks pertaining to the main route, and of other tracks pertaining to deviations. Passengers can be grouped in three different clusters: in the first cluster there are passengers boarding at main route stops that come before the deviate stop; the second cluster groups passengers alighting at main route stops that follow the deviate stop; the third cluster counts passengers at the deviate stop.

Such a classification leads directly to understanding that every objective function for the RDB problem must have at least two terms: the first one is the disutility that deviations impose, as an extra in-vehicle time, on passengers of the main route; the second one is the amount of benefit attained from those passengers that use deviated stops. The operating mode of RDB will be reviewed in short in the following section.

Major advantages of a route deviation service include:

- Increasing of the area served by a vehicle ;
- Better service productivity, through reducing empty vehicle trips;
- Improving system accessibility, by shortening walking distances.

However, this flexibility has an upper bound in terms of increase of the timetable adherence variance for base line, or main route, stops. Nevertheless, until now and as far as we know, the RDB problem has received little research contributions as mathematical model formulation when compared to the fixed line-haul problem. Studies of route deviation systems are reported in Bredendiek and Kratschmer [1], Filippi et al. [2], Daganzo [3], Pratelli and Schoen [4]. More recently, Qui and coworkers [5] identify as demi-flexible operation the policy group between flexible and fixed-route transit systems. Shen et al. [6] proposed a two-stage model to minimize the total cost of a flexible transit service operating as a demand responsive connector system with on-demand stations. The review made by Ronald and co-workers [7] investigates the application of an agent-based approach for simulating demand responsive transport systems. Lu et al. [8] presented a flexible feeder transit routing model suited for irregular-shaped networks. Lee and Savelsberg [9] investigated a flexible transport system known as a demand responsive connector, which transports commuters from residential addresses to transit hubs via a shuttle service, from where they continue their journey via a traditional timetabled service. Finally, Papanikolaou et al. [10] compiled a critical overview of the literature on the modeling issues related to flexible transit systems at strategic and operational levels.

Diana et al. [11] compared the performance in terms of the distance traveled of a conventional fixed-route transit system and of a demand responsive service. Different models were proposed to study the design of feeder transit services by comparing a demand-responsive service and a fixed-route policy [12].

The main task of this paper is to offer to transit planners an experimental contribution to make their choice between specific transit services for flex-route policy. Moreover, because many traditional fixed-haul transit systems in low-demand areas are switching to flex-route services, this paper intends to help towards the choice between alternative flex-route transit strategies suited for situations that have a low and sparse user demand.

The paper is organized as follows. In Section II, the RDB operations are described, while in Section III, the RDB problem is depicted in its mixed integer linear programming formulation [4]. In Section IV, an actual on-demand transit service scenario has been simulated as an RDB operating mode and then compared to the real mixed operations Dial-a-Ride system management. Section V ends the paper with a comment about the resulting comparison evidence based on the respective value set of performance indexes.

II. THE ROUTE DEVIATION BUS OPERATING MODE

The RDB, or demand-responsive service on set routes, is a transversal transit system that distributes and collects passengers in the crossed blocks supporting the main, or fixed, routes along radials and arterials.

RDB operation has been proposed and applied in order to enhance effectiveness of line-haul transit during off-peak periods, as well-suited service for small towns or as a component of a larger integrated transit system [13][14].

One of the main elements of such a system is the so-called equipped bus stop, or terminal, which accepts user subscriptions and makes the bus deviate from its main route (Figure 1).

Indeed, the terminal core is a control unit, which interfaces other local devices, such as "detour traffic lights", keys and displays. The user interface is a graphic screen, usually LCD display, plus few functional keys, which guide the user in his/her choice of menus. The calling terminal also informs users about the timetable and lines of the urban service, the expected time of arrival of the next bus and delays.

Periodically, each terminal consults the "detour traffic lights" and updates its forecast time-of-passage table with the new received data.

After having read the time of passage on the screen, the passenger may insert a coin or a smart-card to confirm his reservation. The terminal stores the subscriptions and sends a switching signal to the proper detour traffic light. There are two such detour traffic lights on the base route, one for each direction, close to the "detour point".

When a detour point is active, the control system sends a message to the on-coming vehicle, which informs the driver about the need of making a deviation. When the bus reaches the equipped bus stop, data are reset in the control system. This operation closes the cycle and detects whether or not the reserved service was actually given. The control system can record vehicle passages at detour points and at on-call terminals, so it can compute the actual mileage day by day.

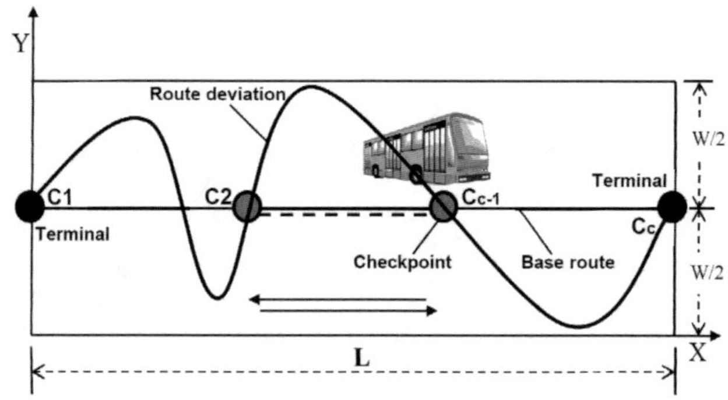

Figure 1. Route deviation bus policy.

III. THE RDB PROBLEM

Let us consider the problem faced by the bus route planner when designing a bus route with optional stopping, as described in the previous sections.

In this section, we shall deal with a simplified model and we will describe in brief a mathematical programming model, built in order to help the decision maker. We assume that a bus route has been designed regarding to the main stops served by the bus route. What remains to be decided is the location of the optional bus stops whose are served on a demand basis. A trade-off has to be found between the interest of passengers located at these extra bus stops, and the augmented travel time suffered both from passengers on the bus whose route is deviated, and from passengers waiting for the bus at regular stops downstream the deviation.

We assume, for simplicity, that the bus route has the characteristics of a "feeder" line (i.e., many-to-one), that is supposed to be true for all the stops, except for the last one where no passenger leaves the bus. This way, we do not need origin/destination matrices and we can base our model just on the (expected) passenger demand at each bus stop.

The bus route with regular and demand stops is formalized as a directed graph, with two types of nodes – those corresponding to regular stops, and those associated with optional demand stops – and three kinds of arcs: the arcs corresponding to the normal bus route, the arcs corresponding to deviations whose are actuated by passenger demand, and arcs associated to links whose passengers not served by a demand bus stop have to cover on foot. Figure 2 shows a simple deviation bus line layout with 7 normal stops, numbered from 1 to 7 and identifies the location of 3 possible optional stops: A, B and C.

The main decision concerns whether to activate or not the optional stops in A, B, C. If the route planner decides to serve, e.g., optional stop A, then a bus on the main route will deviate from node 2 to node A, and then to node 3 only if a demand in node A is detected. Otherwise, the bus route corresponds to the regular arc 1-2. On the other hand, if the route planner decides not to serve node A, then passengers potentially located at node A will have to walk from node A to the nearest fixed stop, which is here assumed to be node 2. The arc corresponding to pedestrian mode is the dashed one in Figure 2.

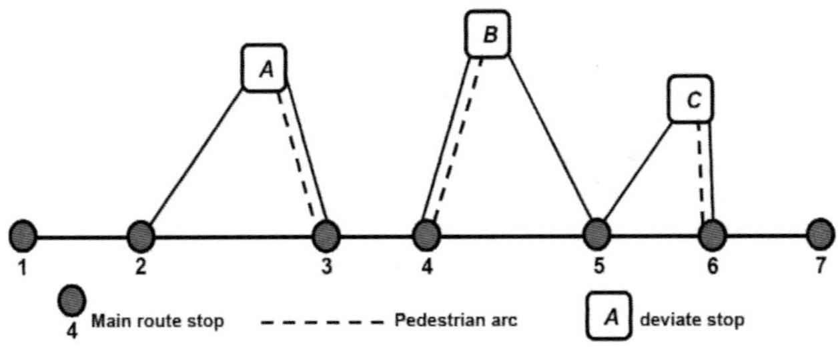

Figure 2. Basic graph layout of a route deviation bus line [4].

From the point of view of mathematical modeling, there are several issues arising from the problem above. The first issue has been already coped with and concerns origin/destination pairs. A second issue concerns cost computations. This model assumes that to each arc corresponds a unit cost proportional to the distance between the endpoints of the arc (an alternative could be to use an estimate of the travel time). The distance is augmented for the arcs corresponding to pedestrian flow, in order to give an estimate of their "perceived" distance. The travel time should be used; but in such a case, is also required to make a correction as time perceived in different ways, and depending on whether the passenger is walking or waiting for the bus. An aggregate measure of cost has been obtained by multiplying each unit cost by the flow, i.e., by the expected number of passengers on that arc.

IV. THE ROUTE DEVIATION BUS MODEL

In the optimal RDB design model based on a mixed integer linear programming problem, Pratelli and Schoen [4] consider the problem faced by the bus route planner when designing a bus route with optional stopping, as previously described. For sake of simplicity, the RDB model is herewith briefly resumed, and the interested reader is addressed to the original paper [4].

The service area is divided into segments by some regular stops along the base route, identified by 1, 2 … N (Figure 1). It is assumed that a bus route has already designed with its main stops. A trade-off has to be found between the interest of passengers located at these extra bus stops, and the augmented travel time suffered both from people on the bus whose route is deviated, and from passengers waiting for the bus at regular stops downstream the deviation. As said before, the bus route is like a "feeder" line, i.e., many-to-one, and in the last stop no passenger leaves the bus. Therefore, it does not need of any o/d matrix, and the RDB model is based just on *In(i)* and *Out(i),* number of users boarding and alighting the bus at stop, respectively. M is the bus capacity; Q is the maximum feasible deviation distance from the main route, on each side; $t(i,j)$ is the time associated to any single user boarded on the bus traveling on arc (i,j); $t^*(i,j)$ is the time on foot for a user walking from location i to j.

In each ride, the bus must visit all the regular stops. The total aggregated travel time T_0, obtained when the bus makes no deviations outside the base line, is given by (1):

$$T_0 = \sum_{i=1}^{n-1} t(i,i+1) f(i,i+1) \tag{1}$$

Demand is constant during the design period, even when it is associated to regular stops and deviate stops. The decision variables are binary-valued variables, defining both the decision or not of placing a deviated stop at some location, and the entities describing of flows along the different arcs. The decision variables are:

- $\delta(d_i)=1$ representing the decision to place a deviated stop at location d_i; $\delta(d_i)=0$, otherwise;
- $f(i,j)$ is the flow variable related to the amount of users on board of the bus travelling along arc (i,j);
- $f^*(i,j)$ is the flow variable of the number of users walking on foot from location i to regular bus stop j.

The RDB objective function to minimize has the following form:

$$\begin{aligned} \min Z = {} & K_b\left[\sum_{i=1}^{n-1}\left(t(i,i+1)f(i,i+1)+t(i,d_i)f(i,d_i)+t(d_i,i+1)f(d_i,i+1)\right)-T_0\right] \\ & +K_f\left[\sum_{i=1}^{n-1} t^*(d_i,i)f^*(d_i,i)\right] \\ & +K_w\left[\sum_{m=2}^{n}\sum_{i=1}^{m-1}\left(t_i(i,d_i)+t(d_i,i+1)-t(i,i+1)\right)I_n(m)p_{di}\delta(d_i)\right] \end{aligned} \tag{2}$$

Each one of the three terms in square brackets in the objective function (2) above, is to represent:

a) the total surplus travel time perceived by users boarded on the bus, which is defined as the total aggregated time elapsed on board during deviations;

b) the total travel time perceived by users who have to reach on foot a regular stop from the locations, which are not served by any deviate stop;

c) the augmented waiting time suffered by users at bus stops located downstream of the deviations caused by an upstream deviation: at bus stop m there are $In(m)$ users waiting.

Each term in (2) is multiplied by a time weight coefficient: K_b, K_f and K_w, which respectively consider the different time perceived by users when traveling in vehicle, walking and waiting [3]. A deviation at regular bus stop i can only occur if the decision is taken of serving the deviated bus stop, $\delta(d_i) = 1$, and either at least one passenger is waiting at d_i, or a passenger on the bus just before stop i asks to be alighted at the deviated stop.

Probability p_{di} that a route deviation will actually occur during a time slot Δt is given by $p_{di}=1 - \exp[(\alpha_{di} + \beta_{di}) \Delta t]$, given that both the process of passengers arriving at a deviated stop with rate α_{di}, and the process of requests to be alighted at deviated stops with rate β_{di}, form two independent Poisson' processes [4].

A set of constraints is defined to reproduce the relationships between the different flows and the decisions whether to activate or not deviated bus stops. The three constraints, $f(i,d_i) \leq M\delta(d_i)$, $f(di,i+1) \leq M\delta(d_i)$, $f^*(di,i) \leq M(1-\delta(d_i)$, impose the two logical conditions that a deviated arc have a positive flow only and only if the corresponding deviate stop is activated and, conversely, there is a positive flow of walking users only and only if the deviate stop is not activated. Flow conservation both at regular and deviate stop is represented by constraint $f(i-1,i) + f(d_i-1,i) + f^*(d_i,i)+In(i) = f(i,i+1) + f(i,d_i)+Out(i)$ and constraint $f(d_i,i)+ In(d_i) = f(d_i,i+1)+ f^*(d_i,i)+ Out(d_i)$. Randomness in bus route deviation is referred by $f(i,d_i) \geq p_{di}[f(i-1,i)+ f(d_i-1,i)+ f^*(d_i,i)+ In(i) - M(1-\delta(d_i)]$.

The latter, it is a logical constraint, and it is referred to randomness in bus route deviation. If $p_{di} > 0$ is the probability of at least one user waiting at deviated stop d_i, and the decision is taken to activate that deviated stop, then users entering node i will be divided into two streams: one on the deviated arc (i,d_i) and proportional to p_{di}; the other one on the fixed line arc $(i, i+1)$ and proportional to $(1- p_{di})$. A practical upper bound is imposed on max length, or max time, of any deviation. There is a last constraint, $g \leq \Sigma\delta(d_i) \leq G$, imposing that the total number of deviated stops to be activated must lie between a minimum number g and a maximum number G.

Finally, the RDB model results in a mixed integer linear programming problem, or MILP [15]. The above MILP has been implemented in the mathematical high level language AMPL [16] and the computational tests were run on a common PC using CPLEX solver.

V. Application Network and Framework

The town of Campi Bisenzio is located in the metropolitan area of Florence, central Tuscany (Italy). Campi Bisenzio (Figure 3) is a small town with a high density populated historic center, and some sparsely residential and industrial activities in its surroundings, along two opposite streamlines oriented to North and South, respectively. The rounded relevant land-use data are: 29 sqkm of municipal area; 35,000 inhabitants; average population density of 1,200 inhab/sqkm.

Therefore, transport demand is sparse and characterized by a high variability rate in time and space. There are several road links with quite different geometries. In such a condition, it is very difficult to serve transit demand by conventional line-haul operations, and flexible-route service looks the most proper choice. Since 1998 the previous three fixed line-haul transit service was replaced by a new Dial-a-Ride system conceived for mixed mode operations, named Personalbus. Today, the Personalbus service covers all the municipal area, even reaching zones that never were served by the previous fixed line-haul transit system. Personalbus is a demand-responsive door-to-door transit system, which operates in a Dial-a-Ride mixed mode, i.e., managing both advance requests and immediate requests.

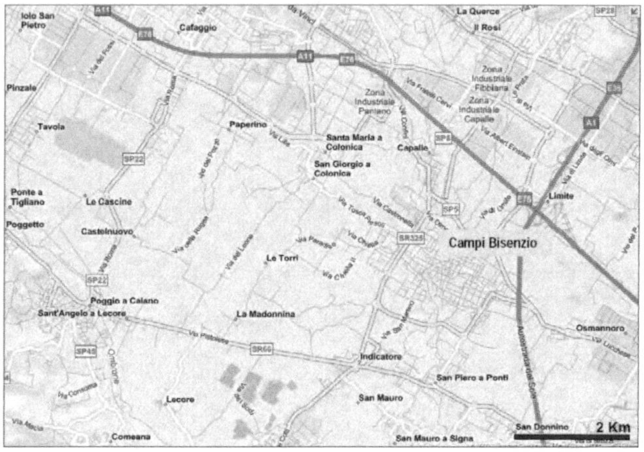

Figure 3. Map of the service area.

The core of Personalbus is the so-called Travel Dispatch Centre, or TDC, located at the ATAF headquarter, the main urban transit company of Florence. All the travel requests are collected, processed and managed by specific software, which solves for vehicle routes and dispatching for day-by-day basis on the stops as requested by patronage. The TDC is suited to manage:

- telephone travel requests, coming from user's house or directly from equipped stops; each travel request may be formulated into two ways. The first is in advance (e.g., the day before) or on systematic base (e.g., every Monday at 9:00 a.m.). The second is immediate, when the request is at least 15 minutes before travel starting;
- automatic travel request collecting and managing by its related insertion into the current optimal vehicle dispatching and scheduling plan;
- in-vehicle communication for driver instructions on the new vehicle route required by the accepted travel request(s).

Users call by phone the TDC and ask for booking their trip, specifying both desired departure and/or arrival time and location of stops for pick-up and drop-off. Then, TDC operator inputs data and runs the vehicle routing and scheduling software, giving to the user the corresponding answer to his/her trip request, in real time. At this point, a negotiation phase on the user's specified service times can eventually start between the TDC operator and the user. The first desired times can be corrected in order to meet both optimal system operations and tolerable user needs. Booking phase ends with definitive acceptance or refusal by the user of proposed trip solutions.

TDC's operators are able to manage the immediate requests negotiating with the user for the best pick-up time, which can span into a time window of ±20 minutes centered on the user preferred time. This avoids any flat refusal of the user by the transit company. At the most, it is the user who gives up his/her trip, but it happens very rarely.

Finally, it is useful to underline that time negotiation is possible because the Personalbus patronage, as usually happen in any demand-responsive system, have a "relaxed" travel time utility function. This last is quite different from a "tight-to-time" travel time utility function characterizing systematic users of conventional fixed-haul transit systems.

The success obtained by Personalbus is clearly showed in Figure 4, where is represented the patronage evolution in the first 5 years of starting up, from middle 1998 to 2002 [17].

Moreover, the value of the last year recorded patronage of the previous existing three fixed line-haul service is also depicted in Figure 4, and it is about many thousands less carried on by the flexible line one.

The monthly patronage ranges on 9,700 passengers carried on average, with peaks around 13,000 passengers per month (Figure 4). As said above, Personalbus Travel Dispatch Centre has to cope with both off-line and on-line requests, i.e., both advance requests and immediate requests. Table I shows a typical requests resume recorded in two weeks on Fall beginning.

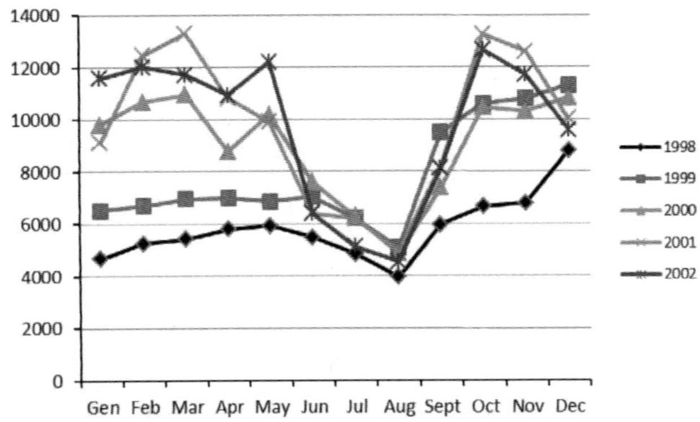

Figure 4. Personalbus monthly patronage from 1998 to 2002 [17].

From the values reported in Table I, it is fairly clear that the advance requests are almost prevalent in respect to the immediate requests. Due to this evidence, one can note that the service should be regular to some extent, instead fully demand-responsive. Moreover, data drawn from practice monitoring on user disposability to negotiate for immediate requests have revealed that shifts of plus or minus 20 to 30 minutes from the desired time are quite well accepted. This last fact gives force to the concept that demand-responsive system users have a perception of travel time fully different from line-haul system users, more and more linked to tight schedules.

These considerations have led to evaluate the hypothesis of a new transit system, operating in a mixed-mode between line-haul, for higher regular demand related to advance requests, and demand-responsive operations, for lower randomly demand related to occasional immediate requests. Roughly speaking, the new transit system to evaluate is the RDB bus system.

TABLE I. TWO TYPICAL TRIP REQUESTS WEEKS ARRIVED TO TDC.

	Total Requests	Total On-Line	% Advance	%Immediate
25 Sept	120	38	0.76	0.24
26 Sept	124	52	0.70	0.30
27 Sept	124	52	0.70	0.30
28 Sept	127	45	0.74	0.26
29 Sept	126	58	0.68	0.32
30 Sept	41	47	0.47	0.53
02 Oct	124	41	0.75	0.24
03 Oct	120	56	0.68	0.32
04 Oct	136	47	0.74	0.26
05 Oct	147	47	0.76	0.24
06 Oct	123	55	0.69	0.31
07 Oct	38	48	0.44	0.56

A. Comparison Indexes

Statistical data on costs are not available, therefore the comparison has been performed between the present DRT system service, i.e., Personalbus, and the proposed RDB system operations, through two comparison indexes, which are defined in respect to some relevant performance requirements:

$$\Delta W\% = \frac{T_{w,o} - T_{w,s}}{T_{w,o}} \times 100 \tag{3}$$

$$\Delta P\% = \frac{P_{att} - P_{RDB}}{P_{att}} \times 100 \tag{4}$$

Following Johnson et al. [18], the first index, $\Delta W\%$, represents the percentage variation of maximum waiting time at regular stops, and the symbols at the right member of expression (3) are: $T_{w,o}$ maximum observed waiting time of Personalbus; $T_{w,s}$ maximum waiting time resulting for the new RDB solution at hand.

The second comparison index, $\Delta P\%$, represented by expression (4), is the percentage difference between the actual satisfied demand, P_{att}, and the amount of demand, P_{RDB}, that the new RDB solution could satisfy.

B. Solving for the new RDB system network

Data recorded by Personalbus TDC have referred to compare the actual Dial-a-Ride mixed mode service operations to the new proposed RDB system operations. Basic data are related to each vehicle per day as bus mileage, daily effective service time, number of served requests, carried passengers per link, boarding and alighting passengers per stop.

The computational goals have been restricted to one representative operations period, which has selected in a test month with a satisfied patronage of 3,700 passengers. Real data are used to determine the frequency call at each stop.

The highest frequency call stops are used to build the main network "skeleton" leading to two fixed lines, namely Line 1 and Line 2, crossing the whole service area (Figure 5). Line 1 terminals are the industrial and commercial park of S.Angelo a Lecore (zone 8) and the railway station of Pratignone (zone 1). Line 2 terminals are the large interchange parking of motorways A1 and A11 (zone 3) and the residential zone of S.Donnino (zone 11) characterized by single-family detached housing. Each one of potential deviate stops has been placed as the centroid of a group of Personalbus stops not belonging to Line 1 nor Line 2 regular stops. These are stops characterized by low call frequencies, generally less than 0.15÷0.25. Therefore, the frequency call assigned to any potential deviate stop, i.e., deviation probability, was the weighted average frequency of the group, using number of calls of each stop as weight. This way, the result was in 13 deviate stops covering the whole area to serve.

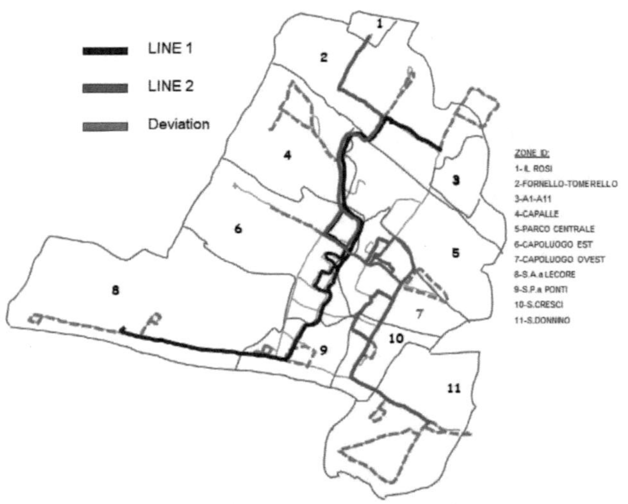

Figure 5. Layout of the new RDB network

Data related to Personalbus patronage was adapted to the new situation and an o/d matrix was obtained for the two RDB lines, respectively. Users having origin located on one line and their destination placed on the other line, were split assigning each of them to the closest stop common for both RDB lines.

At this point, a proper RDB problem was solved for each one of the two RDB lines, given both a minimum of 4 and a maximum of 7 deviate stops. The values for time weight coefficients in the objective function (2) were assumed in $K_b = 1.0$, $K_f = 2.5$ and $K_w = 2.2$. Definitive results showed the following issues:

- Line 1: Base line length is about 6.5 Km. Different combinations were analyzed, beginning with a number of 7 deviate stops to a number of 4 deviate stops. There are eight potential deviate stops on Northbound direction, and nine on Southbound direction. The RDB problem drops off the potential deviate stop located at the Pratiglione railway station, when solved for less than seven deviate stops. This is an obvious drawback highlighting the difference between theoretical and practical solutions.
- Line 2: Base line length is about 7.2 Km. As above, different combinations were analyzed including from 4 to 7 deviate stops. There are fourteen potential deviations in both directions. The theoretical solutions for less than 6 deviate stops not include the deviation associated to zone 4, where is located an important shopping center.

Both Line1 and Line 2 require a number of three vehicles dispatched on service for a period of 12 hours on a weekday (instead of six vehicles actually dispatched by Personalbus). Depending on the number of included deviate stops, there are different average vehicle headways, or frequencies, on regular stops for each of the two lines, respectively.

TABLE II. COMPUTED RDB SERVICE VALUES FOR THE TWO LINES.

Line 1	Route travel time	Lost demand (pax/m)	Headway (minutes)	Deviation utility ratio
Zero-Devs	1h 00' 26"	354	20	---
4 Devs	1h 43' 44"	193	35	0.72
5 Devs	2h 02' 54"	93	41	1.05
6 Devs	2h 12' 44"	53	45	1.20
7 Devs	2h 26' 29"	1	50	1.43
Line 2	**Route travel time**	**Lost demand** (pax/m)	**Headway** (minutes)	**Deviation utility ratio**
Zero-Devs	1h 14' 53"	354	25	---
4 Devs	1h 47' 44"	193	36	0.44
5 Devs	2h 09' 12"	93	43	0.72
6 Devs	2h 14' 56"	53	45	0.80
7 Devs	2h 37' 28"	1	53	1.09

Table II shows, in respect to different RDB solutions, the obtained values of average route travel time, monthly component of actual users not served by RDB, i.e., lost demand, and vehicle headway. In Table II are reported the values of no deviations situation, i.e., zero-devs, to reproduce the borderline case of line-haul operations.

In Figure 6 and 7, respectively, are depicted the same values of lost demand per month, and headway of Line 1 and Line 2 solution instances. It is trivial to notice that as the number of designed deviations increases, on one side the route travel times and headways also increase, and on the opposite side, the lost demand values obviously decrease.

Personalbus acts as a doorstep service and, therefore, an alternative RDB system operation needs the highest number of available deviate stops in order to keep the large part of the actual patronage. On the contrary, one must take into account of the transit company point of view, both in terms of efficiency and costs.

The high number of deviations implies both dispatching of many vehicles to maintain acceptable frequencies, and increasing in vehicle idle times, and lowering of user tolerability due to several deviations made upstream.

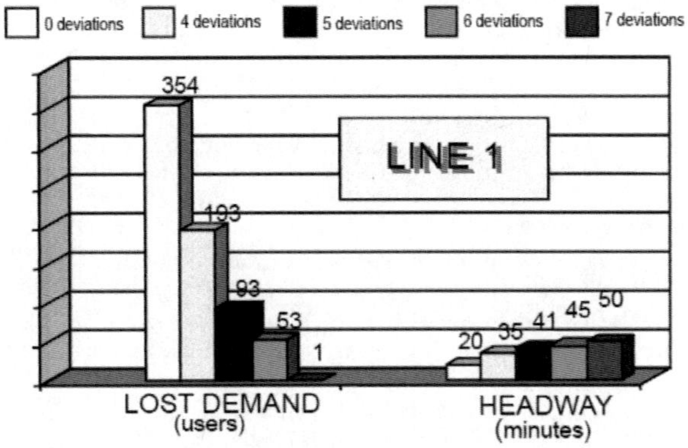

Figure 6. Lost demand and bus headways for Line 1 in the different instances of RDB operations.

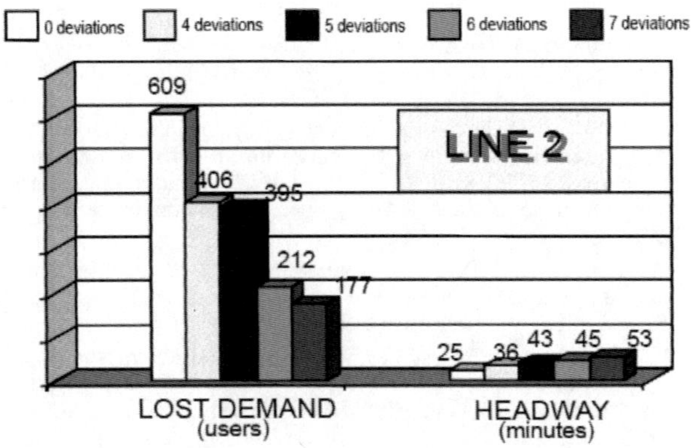

Figure 7. Lost demand and bus headways for Line 2 in the different instances of RDB operations.

The last column of Table II shows the values of deviation utility ratio, which has been used since some decades as rule-of-thumb in many flexible-route deviation system evaluations and programs, as said by Johnson and co-workers [18].

It is generally assumed that stable deviation route system operations are possible if the ratio remains under 1 when calculated as:

$$DUR = \frac{Deviation\ \ pick-up\ \ time}{Line-haul\ \ time} \qquad (5)$$

Line 1 have feasible deviation utility ratios only in case of 4 deviate stops. While Line 2 shows all the evaluated instances feasible, except the one with 7 deviations.

Table III resumes the performance indexes of all RDB solved instances from 4 to 7 deviated stops, which are compared to the Personalbus ones. The values shown for RDB solutions, in Table III, are averages of the corresponding values related to each one of the two lines under examination. Moreover, it is clear that lower values of waiting times are referred to an RDB service with few deviated stops, say 55% less for 4 devs or 31% less for 5 devs, than Personalbus. Such RDB solutions also imply the highest losses of satisfied demand with respect to the present service situation, i.e., over 16% or 13% when compared to Personalbus, respectively.

TABLE III. COMPARISON RESUME OF PERSONALBUS IN RESPECT TO DIFFERENT INSTANCES OF RDB.

TYPE	Freq. (bus/h)	Served demand (pax/m)	Max wait. time (minutes)	ΔW %	Lost demand (pax/m)	ΔP%
PERSON ALBUS	---	3710	25.00	0	0	0
RDB 4 devs	2.55	3111	11.25	- 55	599	- 16.1
RDB 5 devs	2.05	3222	17.25	- 31	488	- 13.1
RDB 6 devs	2.00	3445	18.75	- 25	265	- 7.1
RDB 7 devs	1.75	3532	22.50	- 10	178	- 4.8

VI. CONCLUSIONS AND FUTURE WORK

Future mobility is challenged to bundle up transport demands to handle an increasing mobility caused by spatial sprawl, economic growth and suitable working time [19]. Flexible route and demand-responsive transport systems offer an opportunity to overcome these challenges for future public mobility for the preservation of personal mobility, especially in sparsely populated rural and residential areas [20][21].

In this paper, the RDB model has outlined as a MILP problem and applied to a real case. Computational results are drawn in the test area of Campi Bisenzio, a large residential area located in the surroundings of Florence (Italy), for a new RDB system operating with two base lines and different instances of number of designed deviate stops. Numerical comparisons through performance indexes highlight that the actual demand-responsive transit system, called Personalbus and operating under Dial-a-Ride mixed mode service, is quite better than changing to any one of the considered RDB flexible route system alternatives.

Nevertheless, the main computational results are likely linked to the poor resemblance to a "corridor" shape of the study-case network. This is a further detailed confirmation of some general findings previously obtained by Daganzo using analytical models [3].

In addition, the fairly considerable length of deviations to base bus route is also often resulted not favorably to deviation route operations development, as enhanced by the computed values of deviation utility ratio, i.e., DUR in (5), related to many among the RDB design alternatives taken into account.

Finally, the presented study-case leads to meaningful experimental findings on planning and application domain of demand-responsive transit systems requiring for RDB service operations. This paper is intended to offer to transit planners a preliminary experimental evidence in the field of flex-route systems. Future studies can also cope with developments to incorporate ITS technologies, advanced math tools and innovative smartphone applications.

ACKNOWLEDGMENT

The authors are deeply indebted with prof. Fabio Schoen of the University of Florence for his fruitful help in the optimal RDB design model review, and its computational developing.

REFERENCES

[1] R. Bredendiek and W. Kratschmer, "The conception and development of an operation control system for flexible modes of operation," Proceedings of IFAC Control in Transportation Systems, Baden-Baden, pp. 97-103, 1983.

[2] F. Filippi and S. Gori, "Well-suited transit network design for low-demand areas," (in Italian) Trasporti & Trazione 5, pp. 215-225, 1994.

[3] C. F. Daganzo, "Checkpoint Dial-a-Ride systems," Transportation Research B, vol. 18B, pp. 315-327, 1984.

[4] A. Pratelli and F. Schoen, "A mathematical programming model for the bus deviation route problem," Journal of the Operational Research Society 5, vol. 52, pp. 494-502, 2001.

[5] F. Qiu, J. Shen, X. Zhang, and C. An, "Demi-flexible operating policies to promote the performance of public transit in low-demand areas," Transpn Res A, vol. 80, pp. 215-230, 2015.

[6] J. Shen, S. Yang, X. Gao, and F. Qiu, "Vehicle routing and scheduling of demand-responsive connector with on-demand stations," Advances in Mechanical Engineering, vol. 9, pp. 1-10, 2017.

[7] N. Ronald, R. Thomsonand, and S. Winter, "Simulating Demand-responsive Transportation: A Review of Agent-based Approaches," Transport Reviews, vol. 35, pp. 404-421, 2015.

[8] X. Lu, J. Yu, Yang X., S. Pan, and N. Zou, "Flexible feeder route design to enhance service accessibility in urban area," Journal of Advanced Transportation, vol. 50, pp. 507-521, 2016.

[9] A. Lee and M. Savelsberg, "An extended demand responsive connector," Euro J. Transp. Logist., vol. 6, pp. 25-50, 2017.

[10] A. Papanikolaou, S. Basbas, G. Mintis, and C. Taxilaris, "A methodological framework for assessing the success of Demand Responsive Transport (DRT) services," Transportation Research Procedia, vol. 24, pp. 393-400, 2017.

[11] M. Diana, L. Quadrifoglio, and C. Pronello. "A methodology for comparing distances traveled by performance-equivalent fixed-route and demand responsive transit services," Transportation Planning and Technology, vol. 32, pp. 377-399, 2009.

[12] F. Qiu, W. Li, and A. Haghani, "A methodology for choosing between fixed-route and flex-route policies for transit servicies", Journal of Advanced Transportation, vol. 49, pp. 496-509, 2015.

[13] M. Flusberg, "An innovative public transportation system for a small city: the Merrill, Wisconsin, case study," Transportation Research Record 606, TRB, pp. 54-59, 1976.

[14] A. Black, Urban Mass Transportation Planning, McGraw-Hill, Singapore, 1995.

[15] R. K. Ahuja, T. L. Magnanti, and J. B. Orlin, "Network Flows," Prentice-Hall, Englewood Cliffs, 1993.

[16] R. Fourer, D. M. Gay, and B. W. Kernighan, "AMPL a modeling programming language," II ed., Duxbury Thomson, 2003.

[17] ATAF Personalbus, http://www.ataf.net/it/azienda/progetti-innovativi/servizi-flessibili/ [retrieved: 10, 2018].

[18] C. Johnson, A. K. Sen, and J. Galloway, "On tolerable route deviations in van pooling," Transpn Res. 13A, pp. 45-48, 1979.

[19] A. König and J. Grippenkoven, "From public mobility on demand to autonomous public mobility on demand – Learning from dial-a-ride services in Germany," Logistik und Supply Chain Management, vol. 16, University of Bamberg Press, pp. 295-305, 2017.

[20] W. P. Chen and M. Nie, "Analysis of an idealized system of demand adaptive paired- line hybrid transit," Transportation Research B, vol. 102, pp. 38-54, 2017.

[21] E. Bruun and E. Marx,"OmniLink: Case study of successful flex route-capable intelligent transportation system implementation," Transportation Research Record No. 1971, pp. 91-98, 2006.

Big Data-driven Multimodal Traffic Management: Trends and Challenges

Ivana Semanjski[*, **], Sidharta Gautama[*, **]
* Department of Industrial Systems Engineering and Product Design, Ghent University,
Gent, Belgium
** Industrial Systems Engineering (ISyE), Flanders Make
Ghent, Belgium
e-mail:ivana.semanjski@ugent.be; sidharta.gautama@ugent.be

***Abstract*—Availability of big data on moving objects is strongly affecting the way we view and manage mobility. Mobility in urban areas is becoming more and more complex, posing the challenge of efficient multimodal traffic management. So far, existing solutions were mainly car oriented, failing to capture the full complexity of the mobility within the city. In this paper, we present the potential of big-data driven solution for multimodal mobility management that capitalizes on the existing data availability and is realized through the "guarded" data architecture.**

Keywords-big data; traffic management; platform architecture, autonomous vehicles; digital twin.

I. INTRODUCTION

Availability of big data on moving objects is strongly affecting the way we view mobility. More and more initiatives strive to enhance the traditional data gathering processes for transportation planning and mobility studies by integrating big data. As these data are more detailed than the traditionally collected ones with higher spatial and temporal resolution, new possibilities are also emerging. One of such domain is data driven mobility and traffic management. In this paper, we tackle the potential of the big driven traffic management, particularly focusing on urban areas. The main challenge here is the above mentioned data integration which is, in all spheres of mobility, still at quite early stage coupled with the multimodality, as the existing mobility management solutions are still mainly car oriented. To tackle this, we focus on identifying current trends and existing challenges on a way to fully data driven traffic management. Here, we identify six main challenges ranging from data, across mobility to the business related challenges and five major future trends in this domain. In our research, we focus only on land transport modes that are integrated into the urban traffic management ecosystem and propose a "guarded" data platform architecture that could facilitate the data-driven mobility management in urban areas.

The paper is organized as follows: in the Section 2, we give detailed state of the art literature review on big data and current status of the big data integration into mobility management domain. Following this, in Section 3 we tackle the traffic management and the existing challenges and trends. In Section 4, we present the "guarded" big data platform architecture as a potential solution for the existing challenges in the traffic management domain. In the final section, we give conclusion remarks and present the future work on the topic.

II. STATE OF THE ART

A. Big data definitions

Among first, and probably best known definitions of big data, is the 3Vs definition [1]. 3Vs defines big data as the increase of data volume (data scale becomes increasingly big), variety between the data (data comes as structured, semi-structured and unstructured data) and velocity of data generation (data collection-processing chain needs to be promptly and timely conducted to maximally utilize the potential value of big data). As a big data based analytics developed over time, one of the key elements distinguishing among, simply, a large dataset and the big data turned to be ability to extract intelligence and useful insight from the data itself. Following this idea, a 4Vs [2][3] definition was developed. In the 4Vs definition, original velocity is divided into velocity and value, with the intention to acknowledge the extraction of value from data as one of main big data characteristics. Hence, the 4Vs stand for volume (great volume), variety (various types of data), velocity (swift data generation), and value (huge information value with distributed with a very low density among data).

B. Big data in mobility studies

Traditionally, data on mobility are collected via travel surveys, interviews and diaries. These cyclic data collection processes are repeated every one, two, but more often, five or even ten years formatting time series of the noted travel behaviors. Based on the data collected in such a manner transportation planners and decision makers have a systematic overview of the mobility patterns and can follow the main trends observed in the travel behavior. However, numerous studies [4][5] have shown that data collected in this manner deviated systematically from the actual travel behavior. Today, more and more studies explore the potential of big data when it comes to replacing the traditional data collection methods for mobility studies [6]–[9]. The most frequently explored big datasets can be categorized as:

- Pure Global Navigation Satellite Systems (GNSS) data
- Mobile network data
- Mobile sensed data.

Pure GNSS data are collected via GNSS devices. The GNSS devices record the timestamp and positioning data of the moving object. Mainly these devices were installed in vehicles [10]. However, with the technology development, portable handheld GNSS devices were also used. The use of GNSS data for mobility studies mainly reflects in complementing the traditionally collected data on mobility behavior with more detailed activity detection [6][11]. However, existing studies highlight several challenges: discipline required to carry the portable device [12] and lack of the ability to have a full multimodal overview when the device is installed only in the vehicles [13][14].

Mobile network data are data collected by telecom operators as a byproduct of their daily activities. Most often, for mobility studies, these data include two elements. The first element corresponds to traces triggered by the serving network, so called network signalization data. The second one corresponds to traces triggered by the user interaction activity (e.g., call, SMS or data transfer activity), so called Call Detail Record (CDR). The geographical precision and time resolution of the CDR and network signalization data is somewhat lower than this is the case with the GNSS data. The reason for this lies in the fact that the network notes the base station (antenna) location, which covers the area where the user is located, and not the actual mobile phone device location. For this reason, the mobile network data seem to be a better candidate for longitudinal analysis of human mobility patterns [15]–[20].

Mobile sensed data are data collected from mobile phone sensors. This includes the above mentioned GNSS data as one of the possible sensors integrated into the mobile phone. However, the main characteristic of the mobile phone sensed data is the fusion of data sensed from multiple different sensors as accelerometer, microphone, gyroscope and others. One of the examples are positioning data that can be sourced from the GNSS sensor, Wi-Fi network location or mobile networks' base station location readings, or as the combination of any of the positioning sensors integrated into the mobile phone itself.

C. *Big data in traffic management*

When it comes to the use of big data in real-life applications, several topics seem to be of particular interest. The first one is the privacy related to the use of personal data and, when it comes to mobility, traces of the individuals' movements through the space [3][21]. The second one is the business related intelligences and value that one can gain from the big data oriented analytics [22]. The third one comes from the technical challenges that come with the big data integration as difficulties in regard to data capturing, data storage, data analysis and data visualization [23][24].

Concerning the integration of big data into the traffic management, literature shows that this area is still at quite early stage and that majority of papers in this domain are focused on car traffic and aspects as traffic flow prediction [25]. Here, methods mainly use so called shallow traffic prediction models and are still unsatisfying for many real-world applications. Several papers look at the deep learning methods, but still keep their focus on motorized transportation only [25]- [27]. Summary of these efforts can be found in comprehensive literature reviews that highlight advances and complexity in this domain [28][29].

In our paper, we focus on overcoming the limits of the existing solutions by considering the "guarded" data architecture that would be able to tackle the privacy issues through the guarded and data access control oriented solution. Furthermore, we focus on urban mobility from the end-users oriented point of view, considering not only car oriented traffic, but full spectrum of multimodal mobility that one can find in the cities of today.

III. TRAFFIC MANAGEMENT

Traffic management comprehends organization, arrangement, guidance and control of stationary and moving traffic [30]. The sub terms exist per different branches of transportation. Hence, the air traffic management is an aviation term encompassing all systems that assist aircraft to depart from an aerodrome, transit airspace, and land at a destination aerodrome. The sea traffic management defines a set of systems and procedures to guide and monitor sea traffic in a manner similar to air traffic management [31]. However, the mobility in urban areas has become so complex that the initial scope of the traffic management in urban areas, mainly focused on car transportation, has expanded to include a full spectrum of diverse transportation modes and numerus interactions between them. Hence, the traffic management in urban areas includes management of motorized vehicles, public transport, pedestrians, bicyclists and other flows and aims to provide safe, orderly and efficient movement of persons and goods, as well as efficient interaction between different transportation modes. For this reasons, the traffic management in urban areas is one of the most complex and challenging tasks when it comes to the traffic management.

A. *Big data integration challenges*

As mentioned above, current solutions for urban transportation management are mainly focused on motorized transportation, namely the cars. Systems monitor, record and/or guide car traffic flows by relying on sensing equipment installed on roads. Take-up of such system requires significant resources for city authorities. This investment is two-fold: (i) purchasing of the system that is vendor locked in and (ii) adjusting the, already existing equipment on roads, to the requirements of such vendor lock-in system. This often includes replacement of some costly elements as traffic lights and/or Variable Message Signs (VMS). It is a long-term commitment between the city authorities and the system provider that leaves the city with limited flexibility. On another hand, as cities strive to ensure higher quality of life in their area and well balanced transportation mode use that can ensure sustainability of the mobility system, such solutions only partially satisfies city needs as it mainly covers only one transportation mode. Hence, the challenges (*C*) towards a big data driven traffic management can be described as follows:

$$C = (MM, Open, B2B, P, DI, G)_{TM} \quad (1)$$

where:

MM – stands for the multimodality as a challenge of having a full spectrum of different transportation modes present in the cities under one umbrella.

Open – stand for the challenge of integrating different open datasets that might come from the city authorities or different crowdsourcing campaigns and hence, can be structured with clear data quality standards and responsibilities or semi-structured / unstructured with the "best effort" data quality responsibilities.

B2B – stands for business related challenges, as such system would require business-to-business cooperation among potential market competitors. Hence, clear IPR (Intellectual Property Rights), licensing, data access and processing conditions need to be integrated.

P– stands for data privacy challenge as big data often include handling of moving object (e.g., private mobile phones or cars data), camera feeds etc.

DI –stands for data integration challenge. This challenge is mainly related to the lack of uniform data standards across different transportation modes and/or geographic regions.

G – stands for data governance and traffic management governance among different regions, as big data driven traffic management relies also on traffic flows that approach cities from regions outside of the city authority governance (e.g., regional roads etc.). Hence, synchronization of the traffic management strategies is needed among different areas.

B. Trends

The existing trends in the big data driven traffic management include:

$$T = (T, S, MMI, AV, BS)_{TM} \quad (2)$$

where:

T – stands for transition of the traffic management strategies across different transportation modes. As it was the case in history that, for example, the aviation has taken over some lessons learned and best practices from maritime traffic navigation, telecommunications have taken over the data flow management from air navigation, it is becoming inevitable to translate and test different traffic management strategies across multimodal data. One of the potential polygons for this might be developing digital twins of urban areas.

S – stands for different infrastructure access strategies and levels of services that can be developed through such integrated overview of urban mobility. For example, city authorities can implement strategy to reward sustainable mobility behavior by granting the access to the city events, public transport tickets or high speed lines for private cars.

MMI – stand for integration of multimodal multisource data on mobility.

AV- as it is expected that autonomous driving will heavily rely on data, big data driven traffic management plays an important role in the transition towards fused traffic flows (combination of autonomous and traditional vehicles) and purely autonomous vehicles traffic flows.

BS- stands for braking the silos and allowing the cities to have a flexible solution without vendor lock-ins.

IV. BIG DATA DRIVEN TRAFFIC MANAGEMENT PLATFORM

It is not a rare case that cities have started collecting data on multimodal mobility by themselves and providing them as an open data [32]–[34]. However, there is only a limited level of adoption of such data sources in the traffic management market. For this reason, it this paper, we tackle the potential of integrating big data into a transportation management framework that could provide cities with the flexible and multimodal overview.

Figure 1 shows an example of the "guarded" big data platform architecture for transport and mobility management. The architecture includes several layers, namely:

- Raw data layer – an entry point to any raw (low lever, unprocessed) data on mobility that are being integrated into the architecture
- Data quality check layer – guards the input to the architecture by checking the quality of the raw data (e.g., is data structure and data collection frequency of adequate level). Such layer has the possibility to let the data further into the architecture structure (with the notion of the initial data quality) or to generate the report on the data quality so that the detected issues can be corrected.
- Standardized and normalized data layer – preforms data cleaning and standardization so that, regardless of the initial data source, at this layer all the data on the same topic (e.g., speed data) have the same format and can be processed further in a same manner.
- Data quality check layer (can be seen as a sub layer of the Standardized and normalized data layer) – layer where all the data transformation achieved in the previous layer are noted. For example, to get the speed data of the same format maybe one needed to reduce the temporal resolution of the initial dataset, hence has lower the quality of the initial data set.
- Processed insights layer – layer where insights of the higher level are created. For example, speed data were used to produce the travel time map.
- Access control layer – guards the access to the processed data and insights.
- User insights layer – layer where different users can have an access to the data. These user groups can be city operators, authorities, citizens' initiatives or private citizens. They can all have an access to the subset of data (or all) depending on their access rights (guarded by previous layer). One example of this can be police officer who has authorization to view the camera feed data, whereas city operator or private citizen does not has this authorization due to the privacy legislation. Another example can be the

presence of the license protected data, hence one can purchase the license and access the data or not.

Next to the bottom (data quality check) and top (access control) guarding layers, the architecture is guarded horizontally on both ends. This is because it is foreseen that data can enter the architecture at different levels. For example, one can provide the platform with the already normalized and standardized data, but the platform horizontally checks the input quality of this data and collects or provides quality feedback to the data provider. The same goes for each level of the architecture. On the other end, based on the licensing conditions, one can collect the data from the platform at each level. For example, the developers might be granted the access to the standardized data on mobility that they can use to produce different services. This is done through the horizontal access control layer.

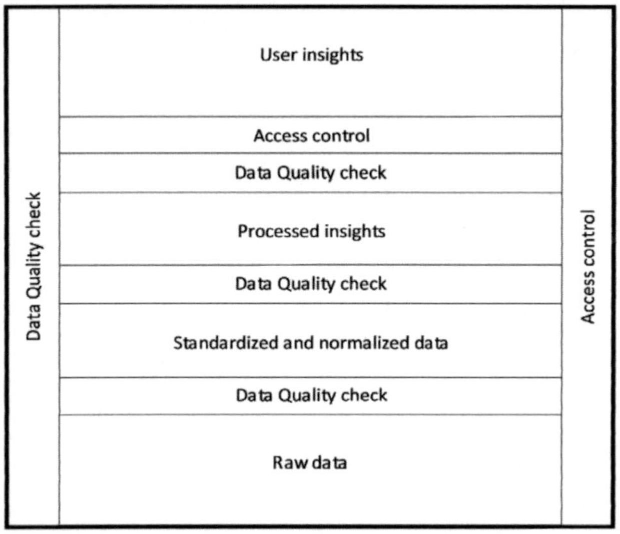

Figure 1. "Guarded" big data platform architecture

Figure 2 gives an example of the processing chain thought the "guarded" architecture. In this example, a public transportation company can integrate their data into the mobility platform that has the "guarded" architecture. These data can be integrated as one of the accepted standards for the architecture (e.g., European NetEx standard). Data can then be used by a local SME (Small Medium Enterprise) that develops a routing app. For commercial purposes, the use of the public transport data might be restricted by the license conditions. Hence, the SME gets the granted the access to the date if the license conditions are meet. The same dataset, might also be processed thought the architecture into the insights related to an public event organized by the city. Hence, the traffic management officer in charge of the event organization might have access to these data under different conditions and mighty view them in a different form. For example, these data can be an input to the alerting system that indicates if the crowdedness in affected area is above the certain threshold. In this context, the city event manager can request additional public transportation vehicle in the area or sent request to the police to regulate the smooth passing of the public transportation vehicles.

V. Conclusion And Future Work

With the current developments in the mobility and big data domains, it seems inevitable to move towards a data driven traffic management framework. Such a framework could allow cities and other mobility related authorities to capitalize on already existing data sources to improve mobility conditions in their areas. Furthermore, it is a reasonable step towards integration of strongly data driven, autonomous vehicles into the existing traffic flows, either as part of the mixed traffic flows or as purely AV flows. Although this is something that is not expected to happen in the near future, industry developments strongly point in this direction. Hence it is necessary to put cities in a position to think forward on how to integrate such developments and still efficiently manage overall multimodal mobility in their areas. In this paper, we have identified the main trends and challenges in this domain and suggested a "guarded" data platform solution that could meet these challenges. Furthermore, we recognized digital twins of urban areas as a forward thinking solution that could be used by urban authorities as a big data driven option for multimodal mobility management and a testing polygon for implementation of different strategies in real-life urban environment.

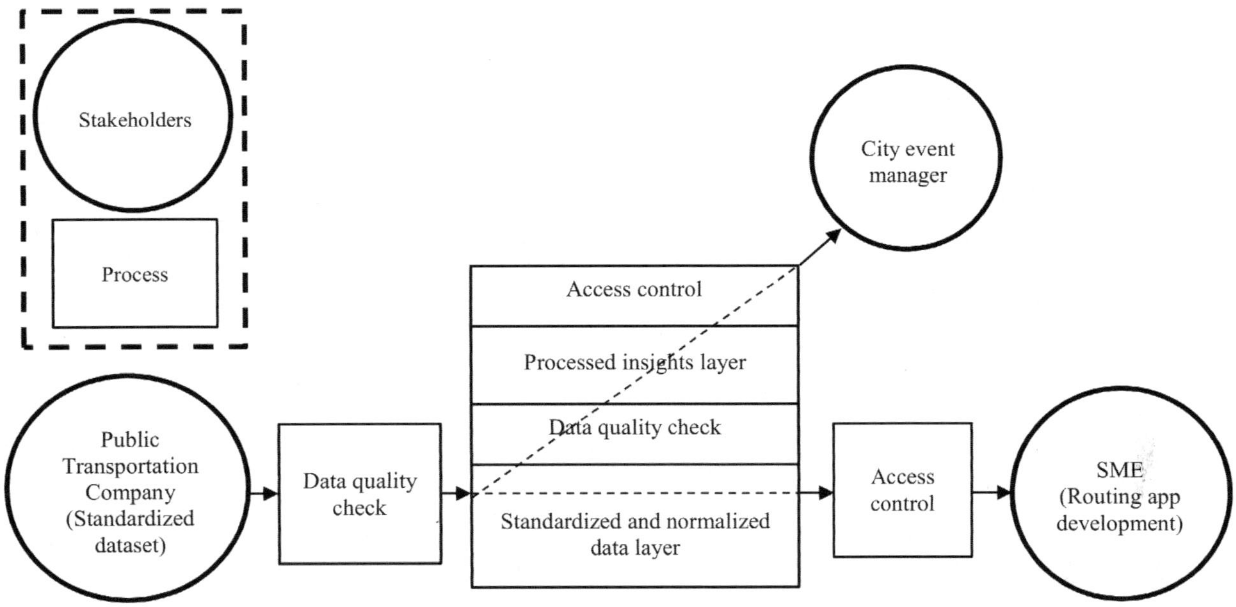

Figure 2. Process example

ACKNOWLEDGMENT

This research is funded by the EU Urban Innovation Actions (UIA) under the TMaaS (Traffic Management as a Service) project.

REFERENCES

[1] D. Laney, "3-d data management: controlling data volume, velocity and variety," 2001.

[2] B. J. Gantz and D. Reinsel, "Extracting Value from Chaos State of the Universe : An Executive Summary," IDC iView, no. June, pp. 1–12, 2011.

[3] M. Chen, S. Mao, and Y. Liu, "Big data: A survey," Mob. Networks Appl., vol. 19, no. 2, pp. 171–209, 2014.

[4] P. R. Stopher and S. P. Greaves, "Household travel surveys: Where are we going?," Transp. Res. Part A Policy Pract., vol. 41, no. 5, pp. 367–381, Jun. 2007.

[5] D. Ettema, H. Timmermans, and L. van Veghel, "Effects of Data Collection Methods in Travel and Activity Research," Eur. Inst. Retail. Serv. Stud. Eindhoven, Netherlands, vol. 2000, no. i, 1996.

[6] J. Wolf, M. Loechl, J. Myers, and C. Arce, "Trip Rate Analysis in {GPS}-Enhanced Personal Travel Surveys," Transp. Surv. Qual. Innov., vol. 2000, no. August 2001, pp. 483–498, 2003.

[7] S. Amin et al., "Mobile Century Using GPS Mobile Phones as Traffic Sensors : A Field Experiment," 15th World Congr. Intell. Transp. Syst., pp. 8–11, 2008.

[8] H. Gong, C. Chen, E. Bialostozky, and C. T. Lawson, "A GPS/GIS method for travel mode detection in New York City," Comput. Environ. Urban Syst., vol. 36, no. 2, pp. 131–139, Mar. 2012.

[9] I. Semanjski, S. Gautama, R. Ahas, and F. Witlox, "Spatial context mining approach for transport mode recognition from mobile sensed big data," Comput. Environ. Urban Syst., vol. 66, 2017.

[10] S. Turner, W. Eisele, R. Benz, and D. Holdener, Travel Time Data Collection Handbook. Arlington: Texas Transportation Institute, 1998.

[11] T. Feng and H. J. P. Timmermans, "Detecting activity type from gps traces using spatial and temporal information," Eur. J. Transp. Infrastruct. Res., vol. 15, no. 4, pp. 662–674, 2011.

[12] I. Semanjski and S. Gautama, "Sensing Human Activity for Smart Cities ' Mobility Management", Mobility Management, Rijeka, Croatia, InTech, 2016. .

[13] T. Feng and H. J. P. Timmermans, "Transportation mode recognition using GPS and accelerometer data," Transp. Res. Part C Emerg. Technol., vol. 37, pp. 118–130, Dec. 2013.

[14] J. Wolf, S. Bricka, T. Ashby, and C. Gorugantua, "Advances in the Application of GPS to Household Travel Surveys," Househ. Travel Surv., 2004.

[15] R. Ahas et al., "Feasibility Study on the Use of Mobile Positioning Data for Tourism Statistics - Consolidated Report," no. 30501, p. 46, 2014.

[16] F. Calabrese, M. Diao, G. Di Lorenzo, J. Ferreira, and C. Ratti, "Understanding individual mobility patterns from urban sensing data: A mobile phone trace example," Transp. Res. Part C Emerg. Technol., vol. 26, pp. 301–313, Jan. 2013.

[17] D. E. Seidl, P. Jankowski, and M.-H. Tsou, "Privacy and spatial pattern preservation in masked GPS trajectory data," Int. J. Geogr. Inf. Sci., vol. 30, no. 4, pp. 785–800, 2016.

[18] A. Vij and K. Shankari, "When is big data big enough? Implications of using GPS-based surveys for travel demand analysis," Transp. Res. Part C Emerg. Technol., vol. 56, pp. 446–462, Jul. 2015.

[19] O. Järv, R. Ahas, and F. Witlox, "Understanding monthly variability in human activity spaces: A twelve-month study using mobile phone call detail records," Transp. Res. Part C Emerg. Technol., vol. 38, pp. 122–135, Jan. 2014.

[20] A. Mishra, "Fundamentals of cellular network planning and optimisation-," Commun. Eng., p. 277, 2004.

[21] S. Sagiroglu and D. Sinanc, "Big Data : A Review," 2013 International Conference on Collaboration Technologies and Systems (CTS), IEEE, pp. 42–47, 2013.

[22] H. Chen, R. H. L. Chiang, and V. C. Storey, "Business Intelligence and Analytics: From Big Data to Big Impact," MIS Q., vol. 36, no. 4, pp. 1165–1188, 2012.

[23] C. L. Philip Chen and C. Y. Zhang, "Data-intensive applications, challenges, techniques and technologies: A survey on Big Data," Inf. Sci. (Ny)., vol. 275, pp. 314–347, 2014.

[24] A. Labrinidis, Y. Papakonstantinou, J. M. Patel, and R. Ramakrishnan, "Exploring the inherent technical challenges in realizing the potential of Big Data," Commun. ACM, vol. 57, no. 7, pp. 86–94, 2014.

[25] Y. Lv, Y. Duan, W. Kang, Z. Li, and F. Wang, "Traffic Flow Prediction With Big Data : A Deep Learning Approach," IEEE Trans. Intell. Transp. Syst., vol. PP, no. 99, pp. 1–9, 2014.

[26] L. Li, X. Su, Y. Wang, Y. Lin, Z. Li, and Y. Li, "Robust causal dependence mining in big data network and its application to traffic flow predictions," Transp. Res. Part C Emerg. Technol., vol. 58, pp. 292–307, Sep. 2015.

[27] A. Abadi, T. Rajabioun, and P. A. Ioannou, "Networks With Limited Traffic Data," Ieee Trans. Intell. Transp. Syst., vol. 16, no. 2, pp. 653–662, 2015.

[28] Brian L . Smith ! and Michael J . Demetsky, "Traffic flow forecasting : comparison of modeling approaches," Transportation (Amst)., vol. 123, no. 4, pp. 261–266, 1997.

[29] G. de Jong, A. Daly, M. Pieters, S. Miller, R. Plasmeijer, and F. Hofman, "Uncertainty in traffic forecasts: Literature review and new results for The Netherlands," Transportation (Amst)., vol. 34, no. 4, pp. 375–395, 2007.

[30] R. T. Underwood, Traffic management: an introduction. North Melbourne, Victoria, Australia: Hargreen Publishing Company, 1990.

[31] European Commission, "MONALISA project," 2018. [Online]. Available: http://www.sjofartsverket.se/en/MonaLisa/. [retrieved: September, 2018].

[32] Open Knowledge International, "Open Up Public Transport Data." [Online]. Available: http://opendatahandbook.org/solutions/en/Public-Transport-Data/. [retrieved: August, 2018].

[33] US City Open Data, "Datasets / Transit," US City Open Data Census, 2017. [Online]. Available: http://us-city.census.okfn.org/dataset/transit. [retrieved: September, 2018].

[34] European Union, "European Open Data in European cities," no.6, pp. 2016–2018., 2016.

International Academy, Research,
and Industry Association (IARIA)
412 Derby Way
Wilmington, DE 19810

CURRAN ASSOCIATES INC.
proceedings.com

ISBN 978-1-5108-9060-2

Twelfth International Conference on Emerging Security Information, Systems and Technologies (SECURWARE 2018)

Held at NetWare 2018

Venice, Italy
16 - 20 September 2018

IARIA